P9-CKX-284

from HOLLYWOOD with LOVE

from HOLLYWOOD *with* LOVE

THE RISE AND FALL (AND RISE AGAIN) OF THE ROMANTIC COMEDY

SCOTT MESLOW

DEY ST.
An Imprint of WILLIAM MORROW

DEY ST.

Illustrations by Alex Kittle.

FROM HOLLYWOOD WITH LOVE. Copyright © 2022 by Scott Meslow. All rights reserved. Printed in the United States of America. No part of this book may be used or reproduced in any manner whatsoever without written permission except in the case of brief quotations embodied in critical articles and reviews. For information, address HarperCollins Publishers, 195 Broadway, New York, NY 10007.

HarperCollins books may be purchased for educational, business, or sales promotional use. For information, please email the Special Markets Department at SPsales@harpercollins.com.

FIRST EDITION

Designed by Michelle Crowe
Heart illustration by Rebellion Works / Shutterstock, Inc.

Library of Congress Cataloging-in-Publication Data has been applied for.

ISBN 978-0-06-302629-2

22 23 24 25 26 LSC 10 9 8 7 6 5 4 3 2 1

To Jen—my real-life rom-com heroine

Contents

Author's Note

HOW EXACTLY DOES ONE DEFINE A "MODERN" ROMANTIC COMEDY? THE genre is too rich a subject for any book to be truly comprehensive—but in the pages ahead, I'll make my case for the specific movies and performers that have defined and expanded the boundaries of the genre over the past three decades. This book begins in 1989, when director Rob Reiner and writer Nora Ephron set an iconic (and highly influential) standard for what a modern romantic comedy could be with *When Harry Met Sally*. It "ends" more than thirty years later, in the early 2020s, as streaming services like Netflix and Hulu spurred a new gold rush—at the time of this writing, still ongoing—on the rom-com genre with full-blown franchises like *To All the Boys I've Loved Before*. My timeline may not encompass *every* rom-com you love, but it will offer one narrative of why this genre was so exciting in the 1990s and 2000s; why it collapsed in the mid-2010s; and why—fingers crossed!—it's looking just as exciting today.

In between, I'll track how the genre helped (or hindered) the careers of an entire generation of movie stars, including Julia Roberts, Sandra Bullock, Hugh Grant, Jennifer Lopez, Drew Barrymore, and Katherine Heigl; dig into the critical and commercial reactions to these movies, and what they say about our ever-shifting standards, attitudes, and fantasies about romantic love; and, finally, take you behind the scenes of the most influential and best-loved romantic comedies of the past thirty years, via the producers, directors, writers, stars, composers, set decorators, hairdressers, and anyone else who was integral in bringing these modern classics to life.

I selected the sixteen romantic comedies in this book (and their sequels, spin-offs, and spiritual successors) based on four major criteria:

Did they fit into the timeline? (Sorry, *Moonstruck*, you *just* missed the cutoff.)

How successful were they, both critically and commercially?

How influential were they, both at the time of their release and in terms of their legacy afterward?

Do they reveal something unique about the genre, or Hollywood, or the cultural moment in which they were made?

(It also didn't hurt if I really, really liked them.)

from **HOLLYWOOD** _with_ **LOVE**

Introduction

IF YOU'RE LOOKING FOR A FIRST-DATE QUESTION THAT WILL ACTUALLY tell you something about the person who may turn out to be the love of your life, here's an idea: What's your favorite romantic comedy?

If he picks something sappy, you'll know he's romantic. If she picks something raunchy, you'll know that she's funny. And if he sneers and says something like "I don't like chick flicks," you can sit back and relax, because, hey, now you know you don't need to go on a second date.

More than any other genre in film, rom-coms feel personal. They're movies people watch and rewatch—and rewatch, and rewatch, and rewatch—because, more often than not, they make you feel good. They give you something to laugh at, and they give you something to strive for. Rom-coms are, practically by definition, a hopeful genre: they tell you that you should be yourself (without apology or self-consciousness), hang on to your dreams (even when they don't make sense), and—above all—hold out for true love, because it always might be just around the corner.

But more than just personal, the rom-com is also universal, and one can't overstate the role the genre has played in shaping Hollywood, both creatively and financially, as we know it today. Rom-coms were key to launching the careers of an entire generation of A-list actors, from Julia Roberts to Tom Hanks to Hugh Grant to Sandra Bullock. They offered the few consistent opportunities for female writers, directors, and producers to make films in one of the only genres that was, more often than not, specifically aimed at women. And all the while, the movies themselves served as a gut-check on modern love, offering a revealing historical document on singledom, couplehood, and everything in between. (And *When Harry Met Sally* accomplishes all that in the scope of *one* movie.)

Over the rom-com boom of the 1990s and 2000s—before the film industry shifted toward a model that prioritized massive, franchise-generating blockbusters that cost hundreds of millions of dollars to produce—the rom-com showed that a different world was still possible: a world where the stars still had more to do than the stuntpeople, and where a chase through a crowded city street could end with your soul mate giving a teary-eyed speech instead of a punch from a supervillain.

It was all going so well, with romantic comedies connecting with audiences and adding up to hundreds of millions in box-office grosses for the studios that produced them . . . until the early 2010s, when a combination of bad choices, bad timing, and bad films converged, like the smarmy ex who shows up at *just* the wrong moment and ruins everything. But even in the bleakest time for the rom-com, a happy ending wasn't far off. Hollywood is an industry that moves in waves and trends—and at the time of this publication, the romantic comedy is looking as strong as it's ever been.

Before we dive into thirty years of rom-com history, it's important to define what a romantic comedy actually is (as mentioned in the Author's Note, these definitions are often fluid, but here goes nothing). Too often, a movie is called a romantic comedy just because it centers on a female protagonist. (See: the premature eulogy for the romantic comedy written by the *New York Times* critic A. O. Scott in 2008, which appreciatively cites *In Her Shoes* and *The Devil Wears Prada* as some of the genre's "better" specimens while failing to note that neither movie is actually a rom-com.) Just as often, a movie *isn't* called a rom-com when it should be. (See: the filmography of Paul Thomas Anderson, which contains *two* romantic comedies—*Punch-Drunk Love* and *Phantom Thread*—that are frequently and snobbishly mislabeled as dramas instead.)

These debates are best had with friends over a bottle of wine, so for the purposes of this book, I have kept my definition simple. A romantic comedy is a movie where (1) the central plot is focused on at least one romantic love story; and (2) the goal is to make you laugh *at least as much* as the goal is to make you cry.

If that sounds a little prescriptive, you can always look at individual cases and apply The Donald Petrie Test, named in honor of the director who suggested it to me: If you removed the love story from this movie, would you still have a movie? If the answer is no, it's a romantic comedy, like Petrie's own rom-com *How to Lose a Guy in 10 Days*—a movie I'll cover in detail within these very pages. If the answer is yes, it's a comedy with a romantic subplot, like Petrie's *Miss Congeniality*—a movie that falls *just* outside of the scope of this book.

So order your favorite meal—I hope you enjoy it as much as Sally did—pour a Bridget Jones–sized glass of wine, and let some romantic comedies into your heart. If you look for it, I've got a sneaky feeling you'll find that love actually is all around.

"It's just different. It's a whole different perspective."

—HARRY BURNS, *WHEN HARRY MET SALLY . . .*

CHAPTER 1

WHEN HARRY MET SALLY . . .

(And When Rob Met Nora and Changed the Course of Rom-Com History)

IF HISTORIANS HAD TO TRACE THE MODERN ROMANTIC COMEDY'S ORIGINS to a single time and place, they could hardly do better than the Russian Tea Room, on Fifty-Seventh Street in Manhattan, in the fall of 1984, when Nora Ephron and Rob Reiner sat down—as writers and directors have done for decades—for what would turn out to be one of the most remarkable lunches in Hollywood history.

Despite the chaperone-like presence of Reiner's producing partner Andrew Scheinman—who had befriended Reiner in 1974 after he kicked his keys down a grate at a tennis club, which Reiner recalls as so cute it was "almost like a romantic comedy meeting"—this was essentially the professional equivalent of a blind date. Ephron, the daughter of two Hollywood screenwriters, and a successful magazine writer herself, was coming off a prolific prior year; in addition to the publication of her first novel, *Heartburn*, which was widely (and correctly) understood as a thinly fictionalized version of her breakup and divorce from Watergate journalist Carl Bernstein, she had cowritten the Oscar-nominated script for the biographical drama *Silkwood*, making her first big splash as a Hollywood screenwriter. Rob Reiner, the son of TV comedy legend Carl Reiner, had shot to fame in the 1970s playing Michael "Meathead" Stivic on the groundbreaking sitcom *All in the Family*, but had announced himself as a promising talent behind the lens with his 1984 debut feature, *This Is Spinal Tap*.

Though Ephron and Reiner had never met, it was easy to see why they might be drawn to each other. Both Ephron and Reiner were the children of successful Hollywood writers. Both Ephron and Reiner were recently divorced from well-known public figures: Ephron from Bernstein, and Reiner from *Laverne & Shirley* star Penny Marshall. Both Ephron and Reiner had achieved further fame by telling stories that self-consciously blurred the lines between reality and fiction. Why shouldn't they sit down for a casual lunch and see if they might have anything they could work on together?

This meeting of the minds got off to a rocky start. "They told me an idea they had for a movie about a lawyer," Ephron later recalled. "It didn't interest me at all, and I couldn't imagine why they'd thought of me in connection with it."

Like any awkward date, Ephron had a choice to make: Should she smile and nod while counting the minutes until she could make a graceful exit? Or should she confess that she would never, ever work with these guys on this hypothetical lawyer movie? As was her habit, she decided to be honest and told them she wasn't interested. And with no pressing business left to talk about, Ephron decided to fill the remaining time by drawing on the skills that had made her a remarkably successful journalist with a particular knack for writing profiles of cultural icons like menswear legend Bill Blass or *Cosmo* editor Helen Gurley Brown: by asking deep, probing, sometimes intensely personal questions. The subject quickly turned to the personal lives of Scheinman, a perennial bachelor, and the recently divorced Reiner. Ephron wanted to know: What is it actually like to be a single man? By which she meant, of course, What are single men really thinking?

Ephron's unquenchable curiosity, her near-peerless ability to get to the heart of something, and her knack for repackaging those truths and sharing them with the widest possible audience was a skill set she had come by very honestly. Nora's mother, Phoebe—a successful screenwriter alongside husband Henry, with romantic comedies like 1944's *Bride By Mistake* and 1957's *Desk Set* under their belts—had drilled into her children the immortal philosophy that "everything is copy." She meant, more or less, that writers can and should use all of their life experiences—yes, *all* of them—as raw material for the stories they wanted to tell. Nora had taken this advice to heart. *Heartburn* was a "novel," but its damning narrative was so close to the reality of her divorce from Carl Bernstein that he fought for script approval over the film adaptation Ephron was writing.

And while that lunch ended without Ephron agreeing to collaborate on Reiner's idea for a lawyer movie, the conversation stirred something in all of them. A month later, the trio met again. Reiner had an idea: If the seemingly tiny but all-important differences between men and women were so stimulating to all three of them, why not write a movie about that?

Practically everything in *When Harry Met Sally*, which arrived in theaters five years later, sprang from Ephron's ability to draw and then use the raw, messy material from other people's lives. "She interviewed us like a journalist, got all these thoughts down, and that became the basis for Harry, and she became the basis for Sally," recalls Reiner. The movie chronicles twelve years of an ever-evolving relationship between Harry Burns, a charmingly cynical chatterbox, and Sally Albright, a bright romantic optimist. (Ephron had originally imagined Harry Albright, a neurotic Gentile, meeting Sally Burns, an upbeat Jewish woman. But when Reiner revealed he intended to cast his then-girlfriend Elizabeth McGovern as Sally, Ephron concluded that McGovern couldn't plausibly play a Jewish woman and swapped the characters' last names.) After an early scene in which Harry and Sally debate whether or not men and women can be friends without sex getting in the way, they end up becoming close friends. When they finally have sex, many years later, their friendship is briefly ruined before they make up and get married—so I guess we'll call that debate a draw.

Ephron, who called the writing sessions for *When Harry Met Sally* "as much fun as I've ever had," fondly recalled how she and Reiner "fought bitterly" about everything, with her taking Sally's side and Reiner taking Harry's side in their debates about what men and women don't understand about each other. Often, Ephron ended up working the substance of those debates directly into her script.

Ephron originally called the screenplay *Scenes from a Friendship*—an homage to Ingmar Bergman's *Scenes from a Marriage*, which also zooms in on a relationship between a man and a woman. (It's no coincidence that the most obvious precursor to *When Harry Met Sally* is Woody Allen's Best Picture–winning *Annie Hall*, which *New York Times* critic Vincent Canby said was "essentially Woody's *Scenes from a Marriage*.")

By the time *When Harry Met Sally* was in preproduction, both Ephron and Reiner were confident in the strength of the script and the alchemical purity of its balance between the male and

IT HAD TO BE HIM

For the music for *When Harry Met Sally*, Billy Crystal recommended Marc Shaiman, with whom he'd previously worked on *Saturday Night Live*. Reiner knew he wanted to score the movie with Great American Songbook standards, and Crystal was convinced that Shaiman was uniquely equipped to track down all the perfect deep cuts. "I, for some reason, do know every song ever written," says Shaiman. "I went and met with Rob, and I went with my Rodgers and Hart songbook, because I was so sure that 'I Could Write a Book' was the most perfect song for the movie. The last line of it is, *'Then the world discovers as my book ends how to make two lovers of friends.'*

"It was Rob's idea to use that song," says Shaiman. "I don't know whether I ever voiced it out loud to him—but I wondered if it was a good choice, because Diane Keaton sings that in *Annie Hall*, and there's no question about the fact that *When Harry Met Sally* is a descendant of Woody Allen movies. But when Rob has an idea, he sticks with it."

The soundtrack album for *When Harry Met Sally* was as much a hit as the movie itself, launching the career of an up-and-coming pianist named Harry Connick Jr. and sparking a national tour. But the album itself—which consists of Connick Jr.'s versions of classics like "Autumn in New York" and "Let's Call the Whole Thing Off"—was indeed a Hail Mary effort when several labels refused to release the rights to the original recordings of the songs by performers like Ella Fitzgerald. Since a deal had already been struck with Columbia to release the *When Harry Met Sally* soundtrack, Shaiman and Connick Jr. were given what Shaiman calls "a little bit of money" to go off and record new versions with an orchestra. The resulting album went double-platinum.

female perspectives. The challenge, they knew, would be finding the actors who could translate that balance to the big screen. Ephron, who once said that the movie itself has "no plot," was aware that finding the perfect Harry and Sally would be just as important as, if not *more* important than, the writing. "Rob always said it's the kind of movie that has a very high degree of difficulty in that it has no safety net," she said. "It entirely depends on your caring about those two people."

For Reiner, one obvious answer for Harry came very close to home. Since 1975—when he was cast to play Reiner's best friend on *All in the Family*—Billy Crystal had been Reiner's *actual* best friend. The years had only brought them closer. As Crystal recalls it, they were "inseparable" following Reiner's divorce from Penny Marshall, and he was in a unique position to understand just how much Harry was drawn from Reiner's own life. Still, Reiner was reluctant to cast Crystal in the lead—in part *because* he valued their relationship so much. "Rob's only concern was, 'Am I going to ruin a really good friendship by having a friend play Harry?'" says casting director Jane Jenkins.

Reiner embarked on a lengthy search for Harry that included conversations with possible stars like Richard Dreyfuss, Michael Keaton, and a hot up-and-comer named Tom Hanks—and all while Crystal quietly waited in the wings, hoping for a call from Reiner, who had carefully avoided the subject with his friends. "I knew from agents and managers that he had met with almost every male actor my age, except me," says Crystal. "I was not happy about that, but what could I do?" As Jenkins came to see it, it took all those false starts before Reiner had the perspective to see that Crystal was, indeed, the only actor who could play Harry exactly as Reiner saw him: a note-perfect cinematic riff on himself, as channeled through a friend who knew him better than anyone.

"Rob finally said, 'Why am I doing this? This is silly. Let's go to Billy,'" says Jenkins.

At the same time, Reiner's original plan to cast his girlfriend Elizabeth McGovern as Sally had fallen apart. When Reiner and McGovern broke up before *When Harry Met Sally* went into production—and Reiner concluded, apparently, that a man couldn't maintain a professional relationship, let alone a friendship, with an ex—casting director Jane Jenkins and her partner Janet Hirshenson were tasked with finding another actress who could play Sally. Though names like Debra Winger and Molly Ringwald were kicked around, the production zeroed in on its star actress very quickly. "Meg was literally the second actress that came in," recalls Jenkins. "She left the room, and Rob said, 'It's her part. Cancel everything else.'"

As it turns out, Reiner had been circling Meg Ryan to play the female lead in *something* for years. When Ryan was just eighteen, Jane Jenkins brought her in to read for the female lead in Reiner's 1985 rom-com *The Sure Thing*. "Rob said, 'She is actually *terrific*, this kid—but I don't think she's right,'" Jenkins recalls. "Two years later, we were doing *The Princess Bride*, and Meg came in. And Rob said, 'I love this girl—but she's not Buttercup. You know, if Bill Goldman had written that Buttercup should be the most adorable girl in the world, I would hire her right now. But I still think we could find the most beautiful girl in the world.'" As Reiner saw it, "the most adorable girl in the world" was exactly what he needed for Sally, whose quirks need to be so consistently endearing that by the climax of the movie, when Harry tells her that he loves that it takes her an hour and a half to order a sandwich, the audience nods along in agreement. Ryan, everyone agreed, was perfect. And in a Hollywood-worthy twist that had massive reverberations for the future of the entire rom-com genre, Ryan had to vacate her role in the dramedy *Steel Magnolias* to star in *When Harry Met Sally*. The role was recast with *Mystic Pizza* breakout Julia Roberts, who earned an Oscar nomination and a reputation as a rising star.

Finally, Reiner and Ephron—who was so present during production that Reiner referred to her, affectionately, as "another director"—had their Harry and Sally. Production began in August of 1988, and stretched through November (catching, among other things, that all-important autumn-in-New-York window). If Ephron approached *When Harry Met Sally* like a journalist, Reiner approached it like a socialite. As Reiner saw it, making a movie was like throwing a party, and it was the director's job to be a good host: "He had invited all these people to come to the party and it was up to him to make sure they had a good time," Ephron said.

Though Ephron is the only screenwriter credited on the movie, *When Harry Met Sally* had started as a conversation between Rob Reiner, Nora Ephron, and Andrew Scheinman; as production sped along, it was time to let other people shape the movie as well. Early into filming, Crystal sat down with Reiner for a gentle ultimatum. "The movie was so personal to him, I'd been starting to feel a little restricted," Crystal says. "I didn't want to play Rob; I wanted to be Harry. I told him he needed to move out of Harry so I could move in." *When Harry Met Sally* may have started life as a good-natured, battle-of-the-sexes-style debate between Ephron and Reiner. But once it became a movie, Crystal felt it was his job to play Harry as a genuine character, with his own tics and idiosyncrasies and arc, and not just as a Reiner surrogate. Reiner understood, and agreed to make room for Crystal to play Harry the way Crystal understood him—right down to the very Billy Crystal bursts of improv that led to scenes where he rambles about pecan pie in a goofy voice.

Meanwhile, in an effort to convincingly portray two characters whose connection endures in one form or another for twelve years, Crystal and Ryan did their best to form a genuine bond, which they hoped would translate on-screen: "After most of our shooting days, we spoke on the phone as Harry and Sally would, discussing what the day had been like and how we felt about the new one coming," says Crystal.

True to its title, *When Harry Met Sally* is laser-focused on the lead characters. "People would ask me: 'I don't understand. These are two professional people. And they never talk about their careers, or their work.' And I said, 'No, they talked about it all the time. I just wasn't rolling the camera,'" says Reiner. The only major subplot concerns Harry's best friend, Jess (Bruno Kirby), and Sally's best friend, Marie (Carrie Fisher), who fall in love in a parallel plot midway through the movie—but even they spend much of their time on-screen talking with or about Harry and Sally.

Instead of subplots and side characters, *When Harry Met Sally* has words. Lots of them. The movie is almost all dialogue; after a short introductory scene, the first fourteen pages of the script are just Harry and Sally having a freewheeling dialogue about love and sex and Day of the Week underpants, interrupted only by a waitress's shock at the complexity of Sally's pie order. Throughout the screenplay, Ephron's writing, always razor-sharp, proves a perfect blend with the softness and sweetness of romantic comedy tropes. Later in the movie, Harry's story about his wife, Helen, confessing she may never have loved him—the kind of wrenching anecdote that could easily have been the centerpiece of a breakup story like Ephron's own *Heartburn*—is drained of its venom by having Harry recount it at a baseball game, while periodically standing up to half-heartedly do his part in the wave.

Ephron wasn't *quite* right when she said *When Harry Met Sally* had no plot. The climax revisits the opening question of whether

WE'LL ALL HAVE WHAT SHE'S HAVING

For a movie that sprang from the intermingling of so many minds, it's fitting that *When Harry Met Sally*'s most iconic scene was also its most collaborative. The scene at Katz's Delicatessen in which Sally explains to Harry that women sometimes fake orgasms— and then proves it by delivering a showstopping fake orgasm on the spot—was proposed as a way the film could demonstrate "something that women know but men don't know," says Reiner (who was, by his own admission, shocked when Ephron told him and other women he polled confirmed it).

The scene was originally conceived as another round of verbal sparring, in which Sally would explain the fake orgasm without actually demonstrating it. It was Meg Ryan's idea that Sally should actually fake an orgasm on the spot. It was Billy Crystal who suggested the now-immortal capper of a line, "I'll have what she's having," which is delivered by a nearby patron shortly after Sally reaches her climax. And it was Rob Reiner's mother, Estelle, who was cast by her son to deliver the line, and who subsequently knocked the line out of the park.

Though she had gamely volunteered to do it, on the day the scene was supposed to be shot, Meg Ryan got cold feet. "That day was a very odd day for Meg, because she's going to have an orgasm, almost 100 times, in front of total strangers," says Crystal. "So she comes to my trailer at 7:30 and says, 'I can't do this, I don't want to do this.'"

Her reluctance was apparent to Reiner. After Ryan delivered a fairly muted performance in her first few takes, he came out from behind the camera and personally demonstrated the wild orgasm he had in mind—only recalling after the fact that his mother was sitting nearby the whole time. Still, his coaching must have helped; by the end of the day, Meg Ryan loosened up enough to deliver the lengthy, impassioned fake orgasm seen in the film.

In addition to Ryan's legitimately showstopping performance, the scene discussed women's sexual pleasure with a frankness rarely seen in mainstream cinema. Just as Ephron intended, men were shocked and women were delighted; as Rob Reiner later recalled, Princess Diana confessed at the London premiere that she would have laughed even harder at the scene if audience members hadn't been scrutinizing her reaction so closely. More than thirty years later, the sequence has turned out to have been great for business at Katz's Deli, which eventually put up a sign directing viewers to the booth where Harry and Sally sat. Katz's even hosted a fake orgasm contest in 2019. "You've got a whole restaurant of women faking orgasms," says Reiner.

"Well, there's a whole world of that, too," says Crystal.

men and women can be friends when Harry and Sally have sex and discover that it does, indeed, get in the way. Which raises the question: If they're not friends, what *are* they, and what does it mean?

The answer to that question was always in flux. *When Harry Met Sally*'s ending is rightly regarded as a rom-com classic, with Harry racing through the streets to reach Sally at a New Year's Eve party, delivering a speech about all the extremely specific things he loves about her and prompting her to tearfully reply, "I really hate you" (which means, of course, I love you).

But Ephron's first draft ended with Harry and Sally splitting up, which took Reiner's close association with Harry to its logical conclusion. At least in part because Reiner, nearing forty, had written off his own romantic prospects after a near-decade of singledom following his divorce from Penny Marshall, he felt that

When Harry Met Sally should end with a wistful shot of Harry and Sally bumping into each other on the street, with their intense friendship years behind them, and saying goodbye. "I just had them walking in opposite directions at the end," recalled Reiner. "And then I met the woman who became my wife during the making of the movie, and I changed the ending."

Yes: In a truly meta twist that only helps to solidify *When Harry Met Sally*'s claim as the most romantic rom-com of all time, Reiner met Michele Singer, his wife of thirty years, while shooting a scene for *When Harry Met Sally* at one of those iconic New York brownstones. He'd already been warned by cinematographer Barry Sonnenfeld that the love of his life was on the horizon. "I was bemoaning my lack-of-woman fate," Reiner says. "And he says to me, 'I know this girl. Her name is Michele Singer, and you're going to marry her.' And I said, 'What, are you nuts?'" When Singer later visited the set with Sonnenfeld's wife, Susan Ringo, Reiner was so instantly smitten he tagged along on their lunch date. Reiner and Singer were married before *When Harry Met Sally* even hit theaters.

This romantic optimism is threaded throughout *When Harry Met Sally*, which follows Harry's arc from a jaded anti-romantic who Sally once compares to the Angel of Death and ends with him rushing to tell Sally he loves her on New Year's Eve. If Harry became a happier, wiser, and more optimistic man over the course of *When Harry Met Sally*'s production, so did Reiner. Many years later, you can still hear it when Reiner reflects on the movie and its characters. "People ask me all the time whether Harry and Sally would still be together," says Reiner. "And I think they would."

When Harry Met Sally was a hit when it arrived in theaters in July of 1989—and while Reiner was far enough along in his Hollywood filmmaking that he already had a film adaptation of Stephen King's *Misery* lined up for 1990, new doors were opening for Ephron, who received ample and deserved credit for the movie's success. She had already taken a lesson from her experience as

WHEN ROB MADE OTHER ROM-COMS . . .

When Harry Met Sally makes an ideal centerpiece for an unacknowledged (and maybe unintentional) Rob Reiner trilogy of films about love at any age. *Flipped*, which came out in 2010, follows two twelve-year-olds navigating the awkward aftermath of first experiencing love at first sight. That, too, could have been a Reiner/Ephron collaboration; when Reiner came on to direct, he threw out a script by Nora and Delia Ephron in favor of one he wrote alongside longtime producing partner Andrew Scheinman. "We had nothing to do with his movie," says Delia Ephron. "It's not surprising the business of screenwriting happens in Los Angeles, the land of earthquakes, because the ground is never solid under you."

Meanwhile, 1999's *The Story of Us*—the closest we ever got to a thematic sequel to *When Harry Met Sally* from Reiner, albeit a pretty bleak one—casts Michelle Pfeiffer and Bruce Willis as a couple who embark on a trial separation to figure out if their fifteen-year marriage had any value in the first place.

Flipped was a minor critical flop and a major commercial flop; *The Story of Us* was a major critical flop and a minor commercial flop. But collectively, these three films reflect Rob Reiner's career-long interest in every form that romantic love can take—even if audiences ultimately preferred the happy note *When Harry Met Sally* goes out on.

a Hollywood screenwriter: If you want to make movies without compromise, you also need to direct them. "The director is constantly trying to screw the writer out of the things that mean the most," she said. "There is the pretense that there is a collaboration, but the truth is the director has all the power and you have none."

In 1992, Ephron made her directorial debut with *This Is My Life*, a Meg Wolitzer adaptation that Ephron also cowrote with her sister Delia. It was a job Ephron had talked herself into, and out of, for several years. "When I wrote *When Harry Met Sally . . .*, I knew that I could direct it," she said. "There was this little fly buzzing around my head: If Rob doesn't make this movie, maybe somebody would let me make it. Then I saw it and I thought, 'Well, thank God I didn't direct it, because Rob did a hundred times better job than I would ever have done on it.'" But 1990's *My*

WHEN HARRY MET "SEQUEL"

A 2011 short produced by Funny or Die casts Rob Reiner and Billy Crystal, spoofing themselves, as two has-beens so desperate to get a *When Harry Met Sally* sequel off the ground that they'll agree to any note they get from a studio executive. Literally, *any*.

The resulting "sequel," depicted as a fake trailer, casts Crystal as a widower mourning Sally's death as he moves into a retirement community. He's enchanted when he spies a fellow resident, played by Helen Mirren, making an extremely specific and elaborate dinner order. But when they tumble into bed together, *surprise*, she sprouts fangs and bites him in the neck, turning him into a vampire. *Grampires: When Sharon Bit Harry*, the title is revealed—only for the same half-interested studio executive to request a pivot to zombies instead.

Blue Heaven, directed by *Steel Magnolias'* Herbert Ross and based on another script by Ephron, taught her the reverse lesson: "It was completely destroyed by Herbert Ross. Destroyed. And I looked at it and thought, 'Well, I could have done just as terrible a job as he did,'" she said.

This Is My Life costarred Carrie Fisher, and was prominently advertised as hailing from "the writer of *When Harry Met Sally*...," but after a slow start, the movie never even got the chance to find its audience. "The studio was going to release it wide (across the country) if grosses were high enough, but they weren't," says Delia Ephron.

But it wasn't long before Ephron got the chance to take another crack at the romantic comedy—and this time, finally, for the director's chair. She was originally approached to rewrite a movie called *Sleepless in Seattle*, written on spec by a high school English teacher and tae kwon do studio owner named Jeff Arch. It was a solid script that, like most romantic comedies, could obviously benefit from Nora Ephron's witty, hyper-verbal touch.

Ephron's rewritten version of *Sleepless in Seattle* attracted the attention of several up-and-coming actresses, including Julia Roberts, who had just starred in 1990's *Pretty Woman* (who we'll be talking about much more in the chapters to come). Though producer Ray Stark saw *Sleepless in Seattle* as an opportunity to reteam Julia Roberts with *Pretty Woman* director Garry Marshall, Roberts wanted Ephron to direct, and by the time Roberts dropped out, saying simply that she "couldn't do it," Ephron was already solidly planted in the director's chair. Jeff Arch had written his script with Meg Ryan and Kevin Costner in mind, but Ephron had other ideas. She had visited the Hawaii set of John Patrick Shanley's *Joe vs. the Volcano*, and while the movie had ultimately underperformed, she left utterly convinced of the chemistry between stars Meg Ryan and Tom Hanks.

Ephron's personal philosophy of romantic comedy—built on a genuine, long-entrenched love of the genre and the lessons she'd learned from *When Harry Met Sally*—was actually fairly simple. "Romantic comedy, as a genre, is basically *The Taming of the Shrew* and *Pride and Prejudice*, both of which are about either character or class as obstacles to love," she said. The conflict in *Sleepless in Seattle*, as in *When Harry Met Sally*, was character. (For all her strengths as a rom-com writer, Ephron's characters all tended to be a lot like her—white and wealthy—so class was never really a serious obstacle.) But *Sleepless in Seattle* was built around an extremely unusual structural idea: a romantic comedy in which the would-be lovers don't even *meet* until the very end.

For a genre that pretty much always lives or dies on the sparks between its two leading actors, it was a risky concept. Ephron was convinced her stars had the individual chemistry to make

AN IMPROV TO REMEMBER

Rita Wilson had originally approached Nora Ephron about playing the role of Annie's friend and colleague Becky in *Sleepless in Seattle*—a role she assumed was intended for Carrie Fisher, and which eventually went to Rosie O'Donnell. Instead, Ephron asked Wilson if she'd be interested in playing Suzy, the sister of Sam, played by her real-life husband, Tom Hanks.

Wilson took the role and pulled off a rarity in a Nora Ephron movie, where the script is almost always exactly what you see on the big screen: an improv that actually made the final cut. It came in one of the film's most memorable comic scenes, as Suzy bursts into tears while describing the tragic, romantic climax of 1957's *An Affair to Remember*, to the amusement and bafflement of her brother and her husband (Victor Garber). "We did the scene *exactly* as written, and I don't even remember why I started crying. I did not intend to do that," says Wilson. "It said something in the script, like, 'She gets emotional' or something. Nora was thrilled.

"So when we finished the scene I asked her: 'Nora... Can I do one little improv at the end of this?' And I think, because she knew she got what she wanted, she said yes." Wilson decided to keep riffing on the ending of *An Affair to Remember* to see how the men would react. "I improvised that last part: 'He sees her and he looks at her and she looks at him and then they know, *they know!*' And that caused Tom and Victor Garber to look at each other like, *What the hell is going on here?* And that enabled *their* improv about *The Dirty Dozen.* That was not scripted—and Nora, thankfully, kept it in."

Wilson remains proud that she managed to spark a rare unscripted moment in an Ephron film. "There was one thing about Nora: You had to say dialogue exactly as she had written. Think of it as being a composer, and the composer has written very specific notes, and there's no room for improvisation in these notes because you're going to mess with the melody," says Wilson.

audiences root for them even if they weren't sharing the screen, but it's hard to overstate just how easily this could have gone off the rails. If *Sleepless in Seattle* didn't get the tone just right, audiences were going to turn on Meg Ryan, who abandons her sweet, allergy-riddled fiancé (Bill Pullman) for some guy she hears on the radio. Meanwhile, Hanks had significant concerns about his character, who he felt was too meek and docile in the original draft. "Tom Hanks had a lot of input," says Delia Ephron. "He was very demanding—we had to repeatedly juice up his scenes—and I learned from him about writing for stars: how stars need stuff, interesting stuff, how they have to drive the action."

The fact that it worked at all was a testament to the skill of Ephron and her collaborators, and to Ephron's own instinct and ability for how to push the rom-com forward into the 1990s. "Our dream was to make a movie about how movies screw up your brain about love, and then if we did a good job, we would become one of the movies that would screw up people's brains about love forever," said Ephron. Even then, Ephron had an eye on the movie's long-term legacy. "She said, 'I want this film to be a classic. I want it to play fifty years from now, and you'd still say 'What year was this movie made?'" recalls Rita Wilson.

At the time of this publication, *Sleepless in Seattle* hasn't yet hit its fifty-year anniversary, but then and now, its status as a timeless classic is probably secure. At $17 million, *Sleepless in Seattle* had the then-biggest opening weekend for any rom-com in history—bigger even than *When Harry Met Sally* (or, for that matter, *A League of Their Own* and *Pretty Woman*, which the studio had used as comparison points for its own hopeful projections). *When Harry Met Sally* had marked the arrival of the most important voice in modern romantic comedy, and *Sleepless in Seattle* proved that it wasn't a fluke.

And Hollywood was already paying attention. There's plenty of justifiable cynicism about how the movie industry works, but for reasons artistic or commercial (and ideally both), the studios really do prefer to make good movies, and it's certainly a bonus if it's not too expensive to do it. If a director as multifaceted as Rob Reiner, or a writer/director as singularly gifted as Nora Ephron, could—in the course of a single romantic comedy—please audiences, launch movie stars, and make a boatload of money all at the same time . . . well, what other writers, directors, and stars might be waiting in the wings? If there was any skepticism before, it was clear now: A new golden age for rom-coms had arrived.

THE EPHRON ROM-COM WE NEVER GOT TO SEE

A writer as prolific as Nora Ephron inevitably leaves a few tantalizing projects on the table. One of her longtime passion projects—a romantic drama based on the real-life love story between Pulitzer-winning Korean War correspondents Marguerite Higgins and Keyes Beech—never got off the ground despite years of earnest effort, and has since been mourned by Ephron diehards as a potential long-lost classic.

But there are other, lesser-known Ephron concepts that were never produced, including at least one romantic comedy that might have sat comfortably next to *Sleepless in Seattle* and *You've Got Mail*. Ephron's longtime assistant J.J. Sacha describes the long-lost Nora Ephron romantic comedy we could have (and should have) had, which was conceived under the working title *Red-Tail Love*, and based on a true story that lit up headlines in New York City shortly after the release of *You've Got Mail*.

"There was a famous mating pair of red-tailed hawks in the late '90s," says Sacha. "They became animal celebrities. They were on this famous building. An office on Fifth Avenue. And because of these hawks, birders—the people who watch birds—were coming out. It's, like, this *massive* deal. And so Nora and her sister Delia crafted this romantic comedy around these birders. Two birders who fall in love at the same time these hawks are doing this mating thing. The metaphor was very clever. But it was just one of those that never quite found its footing—maybe it didn't have the stars— and it just didn't get made." (If you want to imagine what the rom-com might have been, *Wall Street Journal* birdwatching columnist Marie Winn's 1998 book *Red-Tails in Love* covers the story in admirable detail.)

Meg Ryan

AMERICA'S SWEETHEART (UNTIL SHE WASN'T)

When Harry Met Sally may have propelled her into superstardom, but for the record: Meg Ryan never planned to be an actress. While studying journalism at New York University, she went out for a few commercial and soap opera auditions, hoping to make enough money to pay off some bills. But as Ryan would quickly learn, starring in a soap opera is one way to do a lot of acting very, very quickly. In just three years as Betsy Stewart on *As the World Turns*, Ryan gamely played out a sham wedding, a "who's the father?" pregnancy, and a secret affair.

Even then, audiences seemed to like Meg Ryan best when she was falling in love. On May 30, 1984, when her character Betsy finally married the dashing Steve Andropoulos—in a traditional Greek Orthodox ceremony, of course—a whopping 20 million viewers tuned in, making it the second-highest-rated soap opera episode in history. Shortly after, Betsy had a horrible car accident, went into a coma, and emerged from the bandages a few months later with a totally different face. This was the best solution the *As the World Turns* writers could find to explain why Betsy had a totally different face—because Meg Ryan had quit the series, believing that there might be some demand for her talents on the big screen.

She was right. Nora Ephron—who, having made four movies with Meg Ryan, was in a position to know—once said that Ryan was "as good as anyone who has ever acted in the movies and been funny." But while *When Harry Met Sally* kicked off a string of rom-coms that anointed Meg Ryan as "America's Sweetheart," or "The Girl Next Door," or whatever other cliché you want to append—a title that you could plausibly claim Ryan held through the entirety of the 1990s—she was always uneasy being pigeonholed that way. "It's an old-fashioned idea, so anachronistic," she says. "I understood it was a compliment about being lovable, and it felt nice, you know? But it also felt, after a time, like ideas were being projected onto me that had nothing to do with me. The girl next door to what?"

Unlike Julia Roberts in *Erin Brockovich* and Sandra Bullock in *The Blind Side*—roles that earned each actress an Oscar—Ryan never quite found a role in which mainstream audiences would accept her as something other than the dazzling, bright-eyed actress they first fell in love with in *When Harry Met Sally*.

But audiences' failure of imagination was always a disservice to Ryan, who was just as excellent in movies like Luis Mandoki's *When a Man Loves a Woman*, playing an alcoholic in a performance that recovering alcoholic Roger Ebert said he "couldn't find a false note in." Yet throughout the 1990s, she repeatedly turned up in romantic comedies, from the massive hits everyone remembers today (like *Sleepless in Seattle* and *You've Got Mail*) to the oddities that quickly vanished (like *I.Q.*, the movie in which Tim Robbins romances Meg Ryan with the help of his uncle Albert Einstein, or *French Kiss*, the movie that was titled *Paris Match* until Billy Crystal lawyered up over the possibility that audiences might confuse it with his own upcoming rom-com, *Forget Paris*).

If one had to pinpoint the moment that the cultural tide turned against Meg Ryan, one could start by grabbing a bunch of tabloids from the year 2000, when her on-set affair with *Proof of Life* costar Russell Crowe served as the perfect counterpoint for gossip columnists who were especially into dramatic irony. It didn't matter that Ryan revealed that her marriage to Dennis Quaid had become unhealthy long before she met Crowe, or that Quaid himself had been unfaithful—it just mattered that America's Sweetheart was stepping out on her husband. "Meg was expected to adhere to this standard that others aren't," said a friend of Ryan's at the time. "Her marriage wasn't supposed to fail. So when it did, it was almost as if she failed everybody."

By 2003, when Ryan branched out from audiences' expectations by starring in Jane Campion's psychosexual thriller *In the Cut*, it became painfully clear that many audiences and critics would prefer that she had stayed in the box they'd built around her. The backlash came to a head in Ryan's famously awkward 2003 interview with talk-show host Michael Parkinson, who judgmentally peppered her with questions and later described her as a "rude and stupid" guest who "deserved what she got." Following the incident, the press wasn't much kinder. "Ryan gave the British public an unscripted glimpse into the life of the pampered A-lister ungraciously submitting to the publicity process and looking with uncomprehending distaste, as if through a thick glass screen, at the non-American media and public she was forced to court," wrote *The Guardian* in one of many typical breakdowns of the incident that played out in the British press for months.

Watching this interview today, as people are starting to reckon with the genuine destruction caused by the tabloid scrutiny of several generations of young female stars, reveals something very different from the hazy cultural memory of it. When Ryan describes her original ambition to go into journalism, it's Parkinson who needles her for being "wary" of journalists. And when Ryan nervously challenges the premise of his question, he fires back, explaining what he presumes to be her own feelings to her: "Yes, you *are* wary of journalists. You're wary of me. You don't like being interviewed. You can see it in the way you sit. The way you *are*."

Of course, Ryan had her reasons for being wary of journalists—particularly those who browbeat her in a public forum where there were no easy exits. After her subsequent movie *Against the Ropes* flopped with audiences and critics, Ryan retreated from the big screen for a few years.

"I think the feeling with Hollywood was mutual. I felt done when they felt done, probably," she says.

Even now, many years after the Russell Crowe affair and the string of flops have been largely forgotten. Apart from a long-in-the-works remake of *The Women*—which finally came out in 2008, without her intended co-star Julia Roberts—Ryan didn't appear in much, and what she *did* appear in wasn't particularly well-received. "I get offers to do things now, but they're not things I want to do," she says.

But in the absence of marquee romantic comedies, Meg Ryan found the opportunity to pursue her own passions. In 2015, Ryan reunited with Tom Hanks for her directorial debut, a period war drama titled *Ithaca*. It was a family affair for Ryan, who also cast her son Jack and enlisted her then-partner, singer-songwriter John Mellencamp, to write the score.

While Ryan hasn't appeared in a film since, there are at least hopeful signs that she's interested in returning to the rom-com genre with the wisdom she's accrued since her days as, she now says wryly, a "scarlet woman." She would have narrated *How I Met Your Dad*, a Greta Gerwig–starring spin-off of *How I Met Your Mother*, if CBS hadn't decided to pass on the series in 2014. In 2020, she provided the voice of narrator "Meg Ryan" in *Cut and Run*, a self-described "light-hearted dark comedy" about organ thieves. In 2019, Ryan revealed that she was developing a romantic comedy at the production company Working Title, which she also hopes to direct. "I don't think that because things are tragic they're deeper," she says. "Think about Nora Ephron. Her observation about romantic comedies is that they were commenting on their time in an intelligent way, but with the intention to delight."

Either way, Ryan is perfectly content to have left her days as America's Sweetheart behind. "There's this idea that being out of the spotlight is somehow dissatisfying," she says. "It's not. It's actually pretty enriching and great."

"I want the fairy tale."

—VIVIAN WARD, *PRETTY WOMAN*

CHAPTER 2

PRETTY WOMAN

(And the Making of America's Greatest Rom-Com Heroine)

EVEN FOR AN INDUSTRY IN WHICH PROJECTS LIVE OR DIE ON BOTH SEREN-dipity and timing, it's a miracle that *Pretty Woman* exists at all. A romantic comedy about a sex worker and a ruthless billionaire would seem destined, in theory, to alienate everyone: too bleak for women, too off-putting for men, too adult for children. It is surely the only movie released under the Disney banner, ever, in which the love story leads to a blow job long before it leads to a kiss.

Before *Pretty Woman* was an inescapable cultural juggernaut (and before it was called *Pretty Woman*) it was *Three Thousand*, a script written on spec by an aspiring screenwriter named J. F. Lawton. After dropping out of film school, Lawton had taken a job cutting trailers for Cannon Films, a production house best known for B action franchises like *Death Wish* and *American Ninja*. Sensing an opportunity to break in, Lawton turned his screenwriting efforts toward the kinds of genres Cannon specialized in: martial arts, goofy sci-fi thrillers, and even a "wacky firemen comedy." Everything he wrote was deliberately, shamelessly commercial . . . and despite his best efforts, nothing he wrote got produced.

So, having initially zigged toward the kind of movies that had seemed likeliest to land him a stable screenwriting career, Lawton decided to zag in the other direction with a spec screenplay titled *Red Sneakers*. "I wrote a slightly autobiographical story about a young troubled guy who meets a one-legged lesbian stand-up comic who's also a drug addict and an alcoholic," says Lawton. How much of that was *slightly* autobiographical? "In real life, she wasn't one-legged."

Though never produced, Lawton's seemingly uncommercial spec script attracted the attention of red-hot stars like Madonna and Cher, and earned him a round of meetings that culminated in a new professional relationship with manager Gary W. Goldstein. Encouraged, Lawton decided to write another script based on what he saw when he left his apartment and walked around Hollywood Boulevard, passing rows of sex workers and dingy porno theaters within the same blocks of the tourist-attracting glitz and glamour of the Hollywood Walk of Fame.

The script begins by introducing Vivian, a woman in her early twenties who has been working as a prostitute since she was sixteen. "She has done everything and will do anything," says Lawton's script. "Humiliation is for the shy. Fear is for the innocent."

In addition to Lawton's conversations with actual sex workers at a twenty-four-hour diner near his apartment, *Three Thousand* was directly influenced by two films that were roughly as far from romantic comedy as you could get. The script's blend of moralism and social satire—as well as its corporate raider subplot—is inspired, in part, by Oliver Stone's *Wall Street*, which came out the same year Lawton wrote his script, and Hal Ashby's 1973 *The Last Detail*, a dramedy whose production was infamously delayed over concerns that the script had too much profanity. (The final cut ultimately contained sixty-five "fucks"—a record at the time.)

The resulting screenplay is a dark, often heartbreaking drama that falls somewhere between a dark drama and a twisted psychological thriller. *Three Thousand* contains a mere forty-six "fucks," but by any other measure, it's even darker than the movies that inspired it. The story climaxes with Edward literally dragging the crying Vivian out of his car and dumping her back onto Hollywood Boulevard. After stubbornly and proudly rejecting his envelope full of cash, she crawls into the gutter and picks it up after Edward drives away. The script ends, with caustic situational irony, as Vivian—seeing the world through "utterly blank and empty eyes"—takes her wide-eyed, drug-addicted roommate Kit, a fellow sex worker, on a long-promised trip to Disneyland.

In 1988, Lawton workshopped his *Three Thousand* screenplay at a Screenwriters and Directors lab at the Sundance Institute, with Pamela Gidley playing the role of Vivian and Peter Gallagher playing Edward. The actors played roughly half a dozen scenes from the script over the course of about two weeks, with a group of Hollywood up-and-comers and already-made-its watching and weighing in with creative input. "Alan Alda and I had some great conversations about the script and what I was trying to do with it," says Lawton. "He was like, 'You know, this ending's a little dark.'"

The Sundance workshop—which at the time was viewed, often correctly, as both a platform and an incubator for the young talent who would soon explode in Hollywood—pushed interest in *Three Thousand* to a staggering new level. "I suddenly became the flavor of the week," says Lawton. "I mean, *everybody* was reading it. And a lot of people were like, 'This is a great writing sample . . . but we can't make this movie.'"

The exception was Vestron Pictures, a somewhat eccentric offshoot of a Connecticut-based home video chain, which specialized in *exactly* this kind of movie. Just a few years earlier, Vestron had scored a massive box-office hit with *Dirty Dancing*, another romantic dramedy centered on an intimate young love affair, which had more than a few tonal similarities to *Three Thousand*. Though the studio hadn't released anything nearly that successful in years, *Three Thousand* was obviously in their wheelhouse, with a relatively small budget to match. "We were talking about, like a million and a half, or maybe two million—a little art film," says

THE VIVIANS THAT WEREN'T (OTHER ACTRESSES/ACTORS)

Though she'd been attached when the movie was still Vestron's *Three Thousand*, Julia Roberts is far from the only up-and-coming star who was up for the lead role. Actresses who read for the role of Vivian included Michelle Pfeiffer, Kim Basinger, Sharon Stone, Madonna, Bridget Fonda, Emma Thompson, Winona Ryder, Patricia Arquette, Drew Barrymore, Daryl Hannah, Jennifer Jason Leigh, and Molly Ringwald before Roberts was finally, formally cast.

Several of those actresses have since reflected on why they weren't right for the movie. "It's a story about a prostitute who becomes a lady by being kept by a rich and powerful man. I think that film is degrading for the whole of womankind," says Daryl Hannah. Jennifer Jason Leigh describes her meeting with Garry Marshall: "He said: 'She's only been doing this a few weeks, so it's still a lot of fun for her.' Yeah, it's a lot of fun getting into a car with a 68-year-old and giving him a blowjob. Really exciting."

The right actor for the role of Edward was just as tricky to pin down. After Sean Connery and Al Pacino both declined, a long list of actors—John Travolta, Harrison Ford, Albert Brooks, Mickey Rourke, and Sylvester Stallone—passed as well before Richard Gere finally, reluctantly signed on.

Lawton. Gary Goldstein, who had also signed on as a producer, insisted that he had the perfect star for the movie: Julia Roberts, then a relatively unknown up-and-comer who had just broken out in Donald Petrie's slice-of-life dramedy *Mystic Pizza*.

And then—after a string of pricy flops that left them hopelessly overleveraged, and unable to complete even the film deals they'd already agreed upon—Vestron filed for Chapter 11 bankruptcy, killing *Three Thousand*'s prospects overnight. The film's intended star was relieved, because she wasn't at all convinced she was capable of channeling the darkness *Three Thousand* would require. "I had no business being in a movie like that," says Roberts. "This small movie company folded over the weekend, and by Monday, I didn't have a job."

And that's where this chapter would end if not for the first in what would turn out to be a series of extremely unlikely fairy-tale endings for the movie. Arnon Milchan—an Israeli intelligence operative who eventually pivoted into the movie business—saw the closure of Veltron as a possible fire sale, and he sent a representative to comb through the company's scripts in case anything good could be bought for cheap. When the representative called and suggested that a love story between a hooker and a businessman had potential, Milchan said he'd pay as much as $3,000 for it. He eventually acquired the rights for $2,500—a full $500 less than the price Edward offers Vivian to spend the week with him in the film, and an astonishingly low sum for even a screenplay written on spec by a relatively unknown writer.

Milchan took the script around town, lauding its commercial potential. His salesmanship paid off when he successfully sparked a bidding war over *Three Thousand* between Universal and Disney. In the end, Disney won—to the shock of pretty much everybody involved with *Three Thousand*, including Julia Roberts. "I thought, 'Went to Disney? Are they going to animate it?'" she says. It turns out that the studio was just as skeptical of Roberts, though producer Steve Reuther convinced them Roberts might

GETTING STAGE FRIGHT

One apparent barrier to Roberts's casting in *Pretty Woman* was her firm refusal to do any nudity. As Roberts later explained: "I'm really against nudity in movies. When you act with your clothes on, it's a performance. When you act with your clothes off, it's a documentary. I don't do documentaries." It's a position she was challenged on by legendary agent Sue Mengers, who had mentored Roberts's own agent, Elaine Goldsmith. "Honey, it's about a hooker," Goldsmith recalls Mengers saying. "We're not talking beaver here." When Roberts blushed and fretted about what she'd say to her mother, Mengers replied, "Tell her you're in a Disney movie. She won't know the difference. Honey, if I had your body, I'd be shopping nude down the aisles at Gelson's."

In the end, Roberts booked the role while sticking to her no-nudity clause, though the film's numerous sex scenes still caused her plenty of stress. When filming the bathtub scene, Garry Marshall says, he told her he "put goldfish in the tub so she forgot [she was nude] and started looking for them." He also pulled a prank when Roberts dipped under the bubbles, sending everyone away so she would discover she was alone on set when she reemerged.

Though Roberts was warned early on that her no-nudity stance would cost her opportunities, the astonishing success of *Pretty Woman* meant she was never really challenged on it again. "That movie was like an avalanche for her," said William Morris agent Joan Hyler at the time. "After the film took off, she got every script in the business. There was Julia Roberts . . . and everyone else."

have enough potential star power that they brokered a meeting with the movie's new director, Garry Marshall, who the studio felt had injected some much-needed comedy into the legendarily tear-jerking movie *Beaches* (and turned some theoretically uncommercial material into a sizable hit in the process). "Garry said to me that half the people at Disney were concerned that you couldn't dress me up—that I could have on jeans and look sort of dirty or whatever but you couldn't dress me up—and the other half were saying the opposite," says Roberts. At Disney, Roberts was forced to win the role of Vivian all over again. After performing a number of readings for the studio, she rode out a three-week contractual period until Disney finally picked up her option on the last possible day.

But if Disney didn't seem like the most logical home for this grim, tragic story about a doomed love affair between a billionaire and a sex worker, it was only because the studio hadn't yet had time to turn it into a Disney movie. The trick relied on something Disney had been doing, to unprecedented success, from the very beginning: making audiences show up for a fairy tale.

This was, of course, something rom-coms had been doing for ages. No matter how unpleasant some of their twists can be, Shakespeare's romantic comedies end in happy couples getting married. For decades, Hollywood made romantic comedies in which any obstacle was brushed away in the course of true love. "Nobody's perfect!" says a cheery Osgood Fielding III at the end of *Some Like It Hot*—a perfect summation of the principle that allows romantic comedies to gloss over any impediment. This cheerful insistence on a happily-ever-after is part of what links romantic comedies and fairy tales in the first place.

This is the point at which it would be very easy to smooth over the details of how *Three Thousand* became *Pretty Woman* and describe this as an all-too-familiar cautionary tale: Young up-and-coming screenwriter writes a brilliant drama, only to have Disney swoop in and slap on what is, quite literally, a fairy-tale ending.

But Lawton—as screenwriter, as originator, as unsuspecting guru—is adamant that the story is more complicated than that. "Over the years, it's been exaggerated how dark the original was, and how different it was," says Lawton. "I wasn't intending to write a romantic comedy. And I didn't. But I'm good with Disney. I appreciate what they did. I'm not going to sugarcoat everything, but Disney had a model. And it was a smart model: They made modestly budgeted movies, and they promoted the *hell* out of them."

"What bothered me about the script was that it didn't make me care about either of the characters," director Garry Marshall says. "Neither of them generated much sympathy and I rooted for no one." His solution for the problems he had with the script included dramatically lightening the movie's characters, story, and overall tone, which meant it was J. F. Lawton's turn to get on board with whatever *Three Thousand* was becoming—which, as an ambitious screenwriter, he happily did. "It's clearly not going to be this art film. It's going to be something else," Lawton recalls thinking. And so Lawton, whose career had finally taken off when he veered away from conventional commercialism, found himself working to transform his dark drama into what was swiftly becoming one of Hollywood's most commercial genres.

To facilitate the genre shift he wanted for *Three Thousand*, Disney chairman Jeffrey Katzenberg had a short but firm list of things that needed to be changed. Instead of being a drug addict hardened by years of sex work, Vivian would be in her very first week on the streets of Hollywood Boulevard, having turned to sex work to pay for college. There would also be scenes that emphasized Vivan's unusual cleanliness, including an elaborate ode to dental floss on the night Edward picks her up. ("I had all those strawberry seeds, and you shouldn't neglect your gums," she tells him.)

Over the course of two fairly aggressive rewrites, Lawton was personally responsible for tweaking some of the darker bits from

NOT THE FAIRY TALE

Pretty Woman "is not pro or con sex work," insists J. F. Lawton, though it has been interpreted either way, and sometimes both ways simultaneously. Lawton and Garry Marshall insisted that, even within the scope of a romantic comedy, they tried to make the movie as accurate as possible to the actual experience of sex work without taking a side. When one studio executive expressed skepticism about the idea that a billionaire would hire a sex worker off the street and bring her back to his hotel, Marshall's response was simple: "Are you crazy?" Marshall also personally insisted on including the opening conversation between Vivian and Kit, in which they discuss the murder of a fellow sex worker, to illustrate the unique dangers of sex work. And when Disney balked at the idea that Vivian would typically make just $100 per hour, Julia Roberts visited a free clinic frequented by actual sex workers, who confirmed that the number was accurate.

At the same time, one major element of the *Three Thousand* script was dropped: Vivian's addiction to cocaine. In *Three Thousand*, Edward initially offers Vivian $2,000 for the week; she insists on another $1,000 before she'll agree to his stipulation that she avoid using any drugs while they're together. (At one point, she even sneaks away from Edward and takes a hotel limousine back to her apartment to get high, only to discover that Kit has already used all the cocaine in her absence.) In *Pretty Woman*, Vivian is sober; she tells Edward that she "stopped doing drugs at thirteen."

his original draft, including the removal of a subplot that revealed Edward was cheating on a girlfriend in New York. His rewrite also changes the street-hardened Vivian of *Three Thousand* into a woman "too pretty and healthy to have been on the street for long" (though not, as Katzenberg had suggested, in her very first week on the job).

He also worked to change Kit, Vivian's best friend and a fellow sex worker, from a meek and tragic figure hopelessly strung out on drugs to the more spunky, spirited version that appears in *Pretty Woman*.

The process of lightening up *Three Thousand* led, inevitably, to discussion of an ending that wouldn't conclude with Vivian heartbroken on a bus to Disneyland. Everyone agreed that Lawton's original ending was much too grim for the crowd-pleaser *Three Thousand* was becoming. But J. F. Lawton, Garry Marshall, and the studio executives were all in agreement about one thing: Vivian and Edward could not, and should not, end up together at the end of the movie.

But couldn't there be some kind of sign that Vivian was headed toward a brighter future? One proposed ending gave Vivian a new career as a day-care worker. Another saw Barnard Thompson (Héctor Elizondo), the stuffy but kindhearted manager at the Regent Beverly, offering Vivian a permanent job under his wing at the hotel. Yet another saw Vivian begin a promising new romance with David, the polo-playing grandson of the businessman whom Edward verbally spars with over the course of the movie.

None of those ideas fully satisfied anyone, least of all Lawton, who felt that a story about such a complex relationship couldn't just end with Vivian and Edward shaking hands and walking away. For better or worse, *Three Thousand* was the story of a passionate, tempestuous love affair, and a businesslike conclusion to their arrangement just sold out everything that had come before it. It was Lawton, the original crafter of that grim ending, who laid out the options. "I finally said to Garry, 'Look: He either has to break her heart or he has to fall in love with her,'" says Lawton. "It's not going to work any other way."

So: Which was it? Was Garry Marshall directing the modern tragedy J. F. Lawton had originally imagined? Or was this movie really going to be a modern-day fairy tale, with a handsome prince arriving to save our heroine from a life of poverty and loneliness? Marshall—who acknowledges that he hails from "the school of happy endings"—knew which one felt right to him, and that's the one he chose.

It's one thing to hope for a happy ending; it's another to earn it. Lawton's solution to reconciling the lopsided power dynamic at the core of Vivian and Edward's relationship was adding a scene that makes it very clear that Vivian has chosen to leave Edward. Losing Vivian makes Edward realize how much he needs her, and so he chases her down, attempting to restart their relationship as a partnership between two equals instead of a rich man paying a poor woman to do whatever he wants. "In my version, they met on the street, and she says, 'What the hell do *you* want?' But you know they're going to get together," says Lawton.

To Lawton's surprise, Disney's initial reaction was that his rewrites had lightened up the movie *too* much. Imagine that. Eventually, Garry Marshall called Lawton in for a meeting to personally deliver the news: "They're going to fire you."

Though extremely common in Hollywood, past and present, this firing happened at a pivotal time for *Pretty Woman*, so early in its transformation that it didn't even have that title yet. Of the many writers Disney brought in to pitch revisions, it was Stephen Metcalfe, a veteran of the theater, who had the clearest vision: *Pygmalion*, George Bernard Shaw's play—which centers on Henry Higgins, a cultured phonetics professor who makes it his project to transform an uncouth flower girl named Eliza Doolittle into a refined society woman—happened to line up almost perfectly with the basic idea of *Three Thousand*. All that was left was to graft

THAT'S HOLLYWOOD FOR YOU

Given his pivotal role in turning *Three Thousand* into a romantic comedy, why wasn't Stephen Metcalfe credited on the final film? The answer comes down to a decision by the Writers Guild of America's arbitration committee, which has a formal process for who gets credit for what when multiple writers are involved in a project. Metcalfe—not understanding, at the time, that the WGA typically expects writers to submit extensive, specific documentation of their work on a script—dashed off a quick response in between other screenwriting projects. "My written statement to the arbitration committee was something along the lines of, 'I think the work I did on the script speaks for itself,'" says Metcalfe. "I was an idiot."

In the end, J. F. Lawton was the only writer who was formally credited on the film. But while Metcalfe hasn't benefited from the movie's extensive royalties—and laments that he didn't have the opportunity to work on the stage musical, which arrived on Broadway in August of 2018, and which Metcalfe says he had a strong vision for—it wasn't all bad for him. "Because my contribution to *Pretty Woman* was common knowledge in Hollywood, the phone didn't stop ringing for many, many years," he says.

the time-tested structure of Shaw's play onto Vivian and Edward's love story.

Disney liked the approach, and Metcalfe was formally hired to turn *Three Thousand* into a romantic comedy. The softening is obvious from the very beginning of his rewrite. In Metcalfe's script, Vivian's caked-on makeup gives her "a hard, older look that doesn't quite succeed" in covering up how "innocently beautiful" she'd look without it. As Vivian heads out to Hollywood Boulevard, she glances in the mirror, "not really liking what she sees." The script is much, much closer to the *Pretty Woman* that made it to the big screen. It begins not with Vivian on the street, but with Edward at a fancy party; it ends not with Edward tossing her back onto Hollywood Boulevard, but emerging from a limo to whisk her away.

While Metcalfe started his rewrite, the studio was targeting Sean Connery to play Edward. "First impression? They were taking the idea of Henry Higgins way too seriously," says Metcalfe. Connery eventually passed, feeling he was too old for the role. Even Sting—yes, *that* Sting—was briefly and fruitlessly discussed. But while Edward was proving maddeningly difficult to cast, there was one big-name actor who was seriously considering the role: Al Pacino.

Hopeful that they'd found their leading man at last, Stephen Metcalfe, Garry Marshall, and Julia Roberts rushed off to New York City to do a full read of the script with Pacino. The actor made an immediate impression—though not in a way that anyone, including Pacino himself, felt like the movie needed. "Al Pacino, dressed in black from head to toe, shirt open to his navel, was . . . Al Pacino," says Metcalfe. "Intense. Feral. Mercurial. Genius and wack job, hubris and insecurity, in equal measure."

The script reading was not a resounding success either. Pacino, true to form, barked out his lines in his inimitable, spittle-flecked way. His chemistry with Roberts was "questionable at best," says Metcalfe. Still, a star is a star, so Metcalfe sat down to rewrite his script with Pacino in mind. The draft was nearly finished when Pacino called—having decided, sensibly, that the role wasn't right for him after all. Around that time, Metcalfe left for another project, leaving the remaining creative team to solve the movie's lingering problems.

At least two other screenwriters took their own cracks at the script, including one who added a series of sadomasochistic sex scenes that were lopped out of the story almost as soon as they were added. Due to the Writers Guild of America's *omertà*-like code that governs which screenwriters get credit for what, it's still hard to puzzle out exactly which screenwriters are responsible for what ended up in the final cut. Garry Marshall once credited screenwriter Barbara Benedek, best known for cowriting 1983's *The Big Chill*, for rewriting the script to make Lawton's despicable Edward into "a Donald Trump–style executive with a vulnerable side."

Along the way, Marshall and Roberts went back to New York to plead their case to Richard Gere, who was mainly known for dramas and, even after a string of underperforming movies, was indifferent about the role. "I still hadn't decided," says Gere. But Marshall felt he had a secret weapon in Julia Roberts, so he dropped her off at Gere's apartment in order to make the pitch. "You couldn't meet this girl and not fall in love with her," says Gere. "We got Garry on the phone. She was sitting across from my desk and she starts writing on a piece of paper. She shoves it toward me, and it says, 'Please do this movie.' It was like, *How can you say no?*"

But despite the rewrite designed to make Edward a little more complex, no one was confused about which of the movie's leads was the star. Gere had shot to fame a decade earlier—playing a sex worker, no less—in Paul Schrader's *American Gigolo*. Now he was playing the straight man to Roberts in her first headlining role. The adjustment wasn't easy. "Usually in my films, *I'm* the wild, exotic flower. I'm the crazy one that's all over the place," says Gere. "And in this one, Julia is the wild, exotic flower. And she's all over the place. Very early on in rehearsals, it became clear. In fact, Garry said: 'Look, this is the way it's going to work. One of you moves, one of you stays still.' So within the stillness, I had to find a way of playing this guy." Even then, he was never fully satisfied with the role he'd agreed to play. Richard Gere "complained every day on the movie," says Roberts.

If Gere wasn't happy with the character he was playing, it's hard to imagine what he would have made of the character in Lawton's original script, which Gere says he never even read. In Lawton's script, Edward is essentially a sociopath. He alludes to having started his business career with a heaping pile of family money—though he boasts of doubling it in just eight years—and takes obvious glee in tormenting the older businessman whose company he has come to Los Angeles to acquire. *Pretty Woman* gives Edward a tragic backstory designed to justify his cold exterior: a difficult relationship with his own cruel father. When he decides to help the older businessman save his company instead of acquiring it, the man replies that he's proud of Edward, and we're meant to understand that this long-awaited approval from a father figure is what Edward has needed all along.

According to J. F. Lawton, this elaborate reimagining of Edward's character arc also came from a very real and painful place for Garry Marshall himself. "I think I can say this," says Lawton. "Garry's father was a monster. [He] never appreciated Garry. And Garry did everything he could for his father. He tried to the very end. As I understand it—Barbara, Garry's wife, said this—at the end, no one would speak to his father except Garry. And he was desperate for his father's approval. And so, part of Edward's transformation came from genuine issues that Garry had with his father."

But by all accounts, the most important decisions that redefined the movie—the ones that would soon set another template for what a rom-com would look like in the '90s—were largely unplanned and improvised. Jason Alexander, who plays Edward's

BIG MISTAKE. HUGE!

As an unproven screenwriter struggling to make it in a difficult industry, J. F. Lawton found himself relating much more to the Hollywood Boulevard side of his story than the Beverly Hills side. To make sure he properly depicted how the other half lived, Lawton put on his nicest suit and took a bus to Rodeo Drive. When he entered a men's dress shirt store, a clerk asked if he needed any help; when Lawton said he was just browsing, the clerk replied, "We have nothing here for you. You're in the wrong place."

Mortified, Lawton left the store—and promptly wrote the experience into *Three Thousand*, with Vivian as his surrogate. In his version of the script, Vivian gets revenge by returning to the store the next day in a fancy outfit, where the rude saleswomen don't even recognize her, and flipping them off before leaving again. It was Julia Roberts herself who ad-libbed the now-iconic line, *"Big mistake. Big. Huge,"* on her way out the door.

piggish friend Stuckey, recalled that Marshall shot each scene a minimum of three ways: one that leaned into the drama, one that leaned into the comedy, and one in which the actors were encouraged to do whatever felt right, which often led to extensive ad-libbing and improvisation. "I got a panicked phone call from one of the producers, Steve Reuther, who was like, 'Oh, it's out of control. Nobody knows what's going on,'" says Lawton. At meeting after meeting, Hollywood executives would start by expressing sympathy for Lawton, telling him how much they'd loved his *Three Thousand* script and how sorry they were that everyone in town was talking about how disastrous Disney's production had become.

But when the dailies started to arrive, the undeniable chemistry between Julia Roberts and Richard Gere made whatever production drama that had existed feel secondary. For a movie so often remembered for its big set pieces—the shopping trip on Rodeo Drive, the polo match, the San Francisco opera—it's amazing how much of *Pretty Woman* is just Vivian and Edward sitting around in Edward's hotel room, enjoying each other's company.

By the time production was in full swing, Marshall says he had fully fleshed out his vision of *Pretty Woman* as a fairy tale: Edward was Prince Charming, Vivian was Rapunzel waiting in his penthouse to be rescued, and the hotel's kindly desk clerk was the fairy godmother, right down to the elegant gown he secures for her. In case this parallel wasn't blatant enough, Marshall personally wrote a lengthy speech for Vivian in which she described a childhood fantasy about being a princess. "Suddenly this knight on a white horse, with these colors flying, would come charging up and draw his sword, and I would wave. And he would climb up the tower and rescue me," she says as she realizes she wants more from a relationship than the money and comfort Edward could provide. At another point, Kit compares Vivian to "Cinde-fuckin'-rella," which is a legitimately impressive example of *Pretty Woman* distilling its blend of fairy-tale fantasy and an extremely adult situation into a single made-up word.

It's not until the ending that *Pretty Woman* fully commits to choosing one side over the other. On the way to the airport, Edward directs his driver back to Hollywood Boulevard, stops for flowers, pulls up while the car is blaring *La Traviata*, and suppresses his fear of heights long enough to climb the fire escape. It is a very literal answer to Vivian's fantasy about being rescued by a knight who climbs a tower, though Vivian recognizes that Edward is getting his own fairy-tale ending: When he asks what happens to the guy who climbs up and rescues her, she replies, "She rescues him right back."

But while all those fairy-tale motifs might make it sound like Marshall had finally hit upon a coherent vision for what *Pretty Woman* should be, that's also not *quite* right. Throughout the entire production, no one, including Marshall, was exactly sure what genre *Pretty Woman* belonged to until it left the editing bay. When asked about the moment at which it became obvious that *Pretty Woman* had become a romantic comedy, Lawton shrugs: "When it was finished. And I think, even then, they weren't sure." Sneaking into a test screening in Sherman Oaks to gauge the audience's reaction for herself, Roberts recalls that she "had no idea what we were actually going to see when we got there," only to discover that the movie had emerged from the editing bay as a crowd-pleasing romantic comedy. "Almost until the film was released—at least up to the test screenings—they were still calling it a drama," says Lawton. "It wasn't until they started showing it to audiences that all of a sudden Disney said, 'It's the comedy hit of the year!'"

THAT'S WHY THE LADY IS A . . . PRETTY WOMAN

Throughout production, the movie's title was a sticking point. Lawton's *Three Thousand*—a reference to the amount of money Edward pays Vivian to stay with him for a full week—was deemed unacceptable by Disney, who fretted that it would be misunderstood as a sci-fi movie set in the future. (It's for that reason that Lawton is adamant, even today, that his spec script spelled out the title—*Three Thousand*—instead of *3000*, as is commonly misreported.)

Garry Marshall rejected several of Disney's proposed alternate titles, including *Hollywood Off the Boulevard* and *Scarlet Woman*. He *did*, however, like the studio's suggestion that they could just borrow the title of a popular song and use it in the movie. There were three contenders: Frank Sinatra's "The Lady Is a Tramp," Tom Jones's "She's a Lady," and Roy Orbison's "Oh, Pretty Woman." Marshall finally settled on "Oh, Pretty Woman," which editor Priscilla Nedd laid over the montage of Vivian's shopping spree, and the movie finally had a title. The deal turned out fine for Roy Orbison too. The *Pretty Woman* soundtrack—which also featured Roxette's hit power ballad "It Must Have Been Love"—eventually went triple-platinum, reintroducing his decades-old hit to a new generation of moviegoers.

As it turns out, this confused, inefficient, eventually serendipitous development and production process is what ended up giving *Pretty Woman* its unique texture. No one would mistake the final cut of *Pretty Woman* for a documentary, or an even remotely realistic depiction of life as a sex worker or a corporate raider, as Lawton had originally intended with *Three Thousand*. But the inherent darkness also remains, lurking within the story and occasionally coming to the surface. It's there in the movie's opening scenes, when Vivian and Kit walk past a crime scene in which a sex worker was murdered, and in the climax of the movie, when the sexually menacing Stuckey attempts to rape Vivian when they're alone in the hotel room. (This dark sequence—which would never appear in a mainstream rom-com today—was indeed changed for the 2018 stage musical adaptation, where Vivian fights Stuckey off herself instead of being rescued by Edward.)

Garry Marshall may not have filmed *Three Thousand* as Lawton originally wrote it, but it's still easy to imagine a darker version of *Pretty Woman* based on the movie that *did* get released. But by choosing to end the movie with Edward's unapologetically cheesy grand gesture, and the unlikely couple locked into a blissful embrace, *Pretty Woman* was also unwittingly setting the template for what the modern rom-com would look like, which would veer away from realism in favor of fantasy. In the years that followed, many other rom-coms—which you'll read about in the chapters to come—veered happily toward wish fulfillment too, creating a set of expectations for future rom-com filmmakers to deconstruct in movies like *The Break-Up* and *(500) Days of Summer*. Presented with two life paths she could go down, Vivian says she wants the fairy tale; as it turns out, that's what audiences wanted too. "That movie *was* a fairy tale," says Roberts. "We did everything but put a glass slipper on."

Among its many ripple effects, the fairy-tale ending had consequences for those who wanted to see a *Pretty Woman* sequel. While it's not *impossible*, it's not easy to find a good love story that would take place after happily-ever-after. Garry Marshall once described

GETTING THE BAND BACK TOGETHER

Though rumors of a *Pretty Woman 2* occasionally swirled in the years that followed, the movie never even made it into preproduction. But 1998 brought the next best thing: *Runaway Bride*, a romantic comedy that reteamed Roberts and Gere with Marshall in the director's chair.

The script for *Runaway Bride*, by the screenwriting team Sara Parriott and Josann McGibbon, had been kicking around Hollywood for nearly a decade, with writers like Elaine May and Audrey Wells contributing extensive rewrites. Along the way, a whole parade of stars joined, and then abandoned, the project. One version was set to star Geena Davis and Harrison Ford; another would've starred Téa Leoni and Ben Affleck. "We could get actors to the altar, but then they'd suddenly start having second thoughts and disappear on us," joked producer Scott Kroopf at the time.

In the end, the *Runaway Bride* script found its way to Richard Gere, who committed on the condition that the studio could also secure Julia Roberts. The two stars successfully lobbied Garry Marshall to direct, making *Runaway Bride* a full-blown reunion for the trio, with Héctor Elizondo also taking a supporting role.

Reviews were mixed when *Runaway Bride* hit theaters in July of 1999, but the movie was a smash hit, grossing more than $300 million worldwide. Despite the runaway success of *Runaway Bride*, and the massive paydays Roberts and Gere received for starring in it, they never costarred in a romantic comedy, or any other movie, again. Roberts did collaborate twice more with Marshall, on the holiday anthology films *Valentine's Day* (2010) and *Mother's Day* (2016), before Marshall's death at age eighty-one. Héctor Elizondo, who plays Barney Thompson in *Pretty Woman*, appeared in both films as well.

a series of inane-sounding rejected pitches for *Pretty Woman 2*: Edward buying a sports team and Vivian screwing up their rookie season, or the wealthy couple, for reasons that are truly incomprehensible, deciding to rob a bank together. "There were a lot of strange premises, but we didn't find anything we liked," said Marshall. For his part, J. F. Lawton recalls one encounter with a *Pretty Woman* fan he met in Alabama. "She said, 'What about the sequel? When is there going to be a sequel?' And I was like, 'Well . . . what would *happen* in a sequel?' And she said, 'I just want to see them be nice to each other.'"

Even if a *Pretty Woman 2* never really made sense, you can understand why everyone, including filmgoers, the studio, and the people who made it, were always tempted by the idea. It's not easy to harness lightning in a bottle, and it's more or less impossible to make it strike twice. *Pretty Woman* is practically the definition of a happy accident, requiring a ludicrous number of lucky breaks, spread out across pretty much everyone involved in making it, to exist at all. "If I had written *Pretty Woman*, Hollywood never would have made it," says Lawton. "A story with a hooker who doesn't get punished? Who doesn't die? Who doesn't apologize? A straight-out *romantic comedy* about a hooker? Hollywood wouldn't have made it. It just slipped through the cracks."

Sandra Bullock

MISS CONGENIALITY

Circa 1992, any bad-movie aficionado with a knack for spotting talent might have paused their VHS copy of *Love Potion No. 9* to say, "Wait—*who* is that?" There, in the middle of a rom-com based on an old novelty song about a potion that makes people horny, was a then-unknown actress named Sandra Bullock, whose talents were much sharper than the dialogue she was delivering.

In *Love Potion No. 9*, Bullock plays Diane Farrow, a nerdy scientist who becomes irresistible to men after she (somewhat confusingly) drinks Love Potion No. 8. "You know . . . all my life, I've felt ugly and now I have the world's most desirable man telling me that I am beautiful," says Diane. "I have the Prince of England at home pining for me. I mean, this is like a dream come true. I could be a princess."

Love Potion No. 9 is hardly an overlooked classic, but it does set the template for the rom-com and rom-com-adjacent roles on which Bullock would build her career. The movie required an actress who could convincingly play both a socially awkward klutz and a supermodel-glamorous leading lady in the span of about ninety minutes. It may have taken some wildly unconvincing prosthetic buckteeth, but Bullock pulled it off as well as anyone could reasonably have expected.

True breakout success came a few years later in 1994's *Speed*, where she starred opposite Keanu Reeves. But the first real proof that Sandra Bullock could open a movie on her own—and her first essential entry into the rom-com canon—came a year later, in Jon Turteltaub's *While You Were Sleeping*.

Like so many breakout performances, it required a series of seriously lucky breaks, and the utter disinterest of better-known stars, before Bullock won the lead role. The original script for *While You Were Sleeping* was conceived as a riff on *Sleeping Beauty*, and accordingly, it centered on a man who falls in love with a comatose woman. But when a development person at Meg Ryan's production company turned the script down—asking writers Daniel G. Sullivan and Fredric Lebow why an actress of Ryan's stature would sign on to star in a rom-com where she spends the whole movie unconscious in a hospital—they decided to rewrite the script with the genders flipped, in a dual effort to decrease the fundamental creep factor of the premise and attract a major actress to star.

That second goal didn't pan out. The lead role in *While You Were Sleeping* was turned down by Meg Ryan, Julia Roberts, Nicole Kidman, and Demi Moore. Though Sandra Bullock had just scored a hit with *Speed*, she wasn't yet a household name, and she certainly wasn't a superstar. Executive producer Arthur Sarkissian claims he eventually came to see that as an asset: "I couldn't see any of those superstars being a person working in a toll booth. You just wouldn't believe that," he says.

Like so many rom-coms, *While You Were Sleeping* asks the audience to buy into a fundamentally insane contrivance: In this case, that a comedy of errors would result in a woman pretending to be the fiancée of a comatose man she's been crushing on from afar (and then, of course, end up falling in love with his not-comatose brother). In many cases, the difference between a good rom-com and a bad rom-com is whether or not the filmmakers can find the right actors to invest those contrivances with warmth and depth and humanity. As CTA fare collector Lucy Moderatz, Bullock manages to anchor the movie by feeling like a real person. In her hands, Lucy's loneliness and desire for connection justifies every crazy twist of the plot, and makes her feel like a plausible, lovable human.

The success of *While You Were Sleeping* made Sandra Bullock a star—an inevitability, but not something Bullock was ever entirely comfortable with. "You realize after something like *While You Were Sleeping* that in the near future you'll no longer encounter people who don't have a preconceived idea of who you are," she says. It also earned Bullock a splashy *Entertainment Weekly* spread declaring that she might be "the next Julia Roberts." (This concept must have been a hit with readers, because the magazine ran identical headlines for Reese Witherspoon in 2002, Jennifer Garner in 2004, and Amy Adams in 2007.) The question of a "rivalry" between Sandra Bullock and Julia Roberts has always been a complicated one, egged on by years of gossip columns that cynically pitted women against each other. "The press started this whole rivalry between us," says Roberts. Bullock joked, "I think Julia and I should do a film where we make fun of this whole thing."

But whether or not there were any hard feelings, there's no question that Bullock and Roberts were often up for the same roles—a difficulty in any competitive industry, and certainly in Hollywood, where talented actresses frequently end up relegated to supporting roles in stories centered on men. By anchoring movies that made a bunch of money, both Bullock and Roberts had passed an all-important test, but they still needed to chase down the relatively few starring roles that existed for women each year. The same year she joked about making a movie with Julia Roberts, Bullock landed the lead role in the historical drama *In Love and War* by accepting a smaller salary than Roberts's own $12 million asking price. That same year, TriStar picked up the spec script for *My Best Friend's Wedding* as a vehicle for Julia Roberts—beating out a competing offer from Warner Bros., who saw it as a vehicle for Sandra Bullock.

Though *While You Were Sleeping* solidified her status as an A-lister, Bullock has always been ambivalent about being pegged as a rom-com star, and about the genre in general. One of her biggest hits, 2000's

Miss Congeniality, is one of those movies that's often mischaracterized as a romantic comedy when it's actually a comedy with a romantic sub-plot. (As *Miss Congeniality* director Donald Petrie himself notes, the movie would still have a solid story to tell—an undercover FBI agent investigates a bomb threat at a beauty pageant—if you lopped out Bullock's romance with Benjamin Bratt entirely.) "Usually comedy is only available to us ladies in the romantic comedy. That's why I hate romantic comedies," she said in 2010, just a year after starring in the smash-hit rom-com *The Proposal*. "I want to make comedic-comedies—let's get back to being funny!"

True to her word, Bullock hasn't appeared in a romantic comedy since. Instead, she starred opposite Melissa McCarthy in the comedic-comedy *The Heat*—a movie that stood out, in part, because neither of its main characters had a romantic subplot (over the objections of some studio executives who heard the pitch). "It's not a rom-com," promised director Paul Feig. "I think this ended up being a very, very sweet love story," says Bullock. "I mean, every movie is a love story—but this one just happens to be amongst friends."

Bullock's hesitation about being pigeonholed as a rom-com heroine has ultimately served her career well. It's what makes it possible for Bullock to jump from an effects-heavy sci-fi blockbuster like *Gravity* to a caper like *Ocean's Eight* to a horror-thriller like *Bird Box* in the span of just a few years, with audiences faithfully following her to any genre in which she sets up shop. And it's what gives Bullock both the versatility and the clout to read a bunch of scripts, decide she doesn't like *any* of the available roles for women, and convince a studio to reconfigure a script with a male protagonist with her in mind, as she did with 2015's *Our Brand Is Crisis*.

That last lesson may be a by-product of 2009, which on paper looks like the apex of Bullock's career, and in practice must have reminded her just how unpredictable and precarious Hollywood can be. That year, Bullock scored her highest gross in fifteen years in *The Proposal* and won a Best Actress Oscar for her role in the inspirational sports drama *The Blind Side*. But as talented as Sandra Bullock undeniably is, those successes came incredibly close to never happening: Before Bullock got a chance to say yes, Julia Roberts passed on both of those roles too.

"A toast before we go into battle: True love.
In whatever shape or form it may come."

—GARETH, *FOUR WEDDINGS AND A FUNERAL*

CHAPTER 3

FOUR WEDDINGS AND A FUNERAL

(And the Kind of Rom-Com That Can Win an Oscar)

BY SHEER COINCIDENCE, IT WAS FEBRUARY 14, 1995, WHEN ACADEMY president Arthur Hiller and actress Angela Bassett announced the nominees for the 67th annual Oscars ceremony. But if Valentine's Day might have seemed from the outside like a particularly good omen for a romantic comedy that had, by this point, become a full-blown cultural phenomenon, the creative team behind *Four Weddings and a Funeral* were skeptical that the Academy would pay any attention to their little-movie-that-could. What were the odds that Oscar voters who had awarded Best Picture to Steven Spielberg's *Schindler's List* just one year earlier would deem this cheery rom-com a serious contender for the top prize? "I didn't believe that a comedy would *ever* be granted the same kind of gravitas," says *Four Weddings* director Mike Newell.

The movie's Best Picture nomination—opposite *The Shawshank Redemption*, *Pulp Fiction*, *Quiz Show*, and *Forrest Gump*, which eventually won—was a coup for a genre that rarely receives serious consideration for Best Picture. Which raises the question: Why *was Four Weddings and a Funeral* the rom-com that was taken seriously?

The story starts, like a sizable chunk of the British romantic comedies to come, with Richard Curtis. You don't have to be a romantic to make a romantic comedy, but it certainly helps—and Richard Curtis, the writer of *Four Weddings and a Funeral*, was always a romantic. He reflects fondly on the first time he fell in love, when he was eight years old—first with *The Sound of Music* star Julie Andrews, and then with the Dutch actress and model Sylvia Kristel, who starred in a series of French soft-core pornos called *Emmanuelle*.

Childhood crushes aside, Curtis's career-long fascination with love stories can be traced to Carolyn Colquhoun, whom he dated when they were both studying at Oxford University in the 1970s. Though Curtis can be (and frequently is) as ironic and self-deprecating as one of his poncy protagonists in films like *Four Weddings and a Funeral* or *Notting Hill*, the way he describes this breakup sounds more like a superhero origin story. "She broke my heart spectacularly, as a result of which I wrote about unbroken hearts for ten years," says Curtis. "I owe her my movie career."

His entire second year at the university had been tied up in the relationship; his entire third year was tied up in recovering from the end of it. "I did a lot of work in the end, simply so I could hide from my heartbreak," he says. "Maybe if I hadn't gone out with that particular girl then I would have been happier but, on the other hand, I don't think I would have written all the films that I then wrote to, as it were, put life right."

Following graduation, Curtis had quickly achieved success as a TV writer, working alongside his classmate and friend Rowan Atkinson on series like the BBC historical sitcom *Blackadder* and the wacky ITV physical comedy *Mr. Bean*. He had even written a romantic comedy called *The Tall Guy*, which cast Jeff Goldblum as the straight man in a comedy duo, a movie loosely based on

MR. BEAN STEALS A SCENE

As the lovably tongue-tied Father Gerald, who makes a mess of an entire wedding ceremony—he somehow manages to say both "Holy Goat" for "Holy Ghost" *and* "Holy Spigot" for "Holy Spirit" in the same brief service—Rowan Atkinson practically runs away with the movie. But despite Richard Curtis's extensive personal and professional relationship with Atkinson, Mike Newell wasn't convinced that Atkinson was right for the part. "He was known as an outrageous comic actor—and that worried me, because he was far and away the best known of all the actors, and this was a modest cast," says Newell. "There were a couple of people who I thought would be marvelous for it, but they said no. And because those certain people had said no, it was plain mad not to cast Rowan. Why would you not cast a great comic actor if you had the chance? I just bit my tongue and shut up. And I was very glad I did."

his own experiences working alongside Atkinson. It's a little odd to hear star Jeff Goldblum delivering Curtis's dialogue—if any modern screenwriter's words are designed to be spoken in a British dialect, it's Curtis's—but it was a first step into a career as a rom-com filmmaker.

Then again, Curtis himself didn't know he was a rom-com filmmaker, not yet. He was just writing what interested him, which happened to be stories about men bumbling their way into true love, just as he was. "When I wrote *Four Weddings* I didn't know what a 'rom-com' was," Curtis says (though the term first turned up in the *Oxford English Dictionary* in 1971). "I thought I was writing an idiosyncratic, autobiographical film about a group of friends, with a bit of love in it."

Like *The Tall Man*, this new comedy was inspired by Curtis's real life: a single man attending wedding after wedding as his various friends and acquaintances tied the knot, wondering if it would ever be his turn at the altar. At one point, Curtis actually sat down and counted how many weddings he'd attended, and while he's been inconsistent on the exact number when asked over the years, it was clearly dozens and dozens. One, however, sticks out for him: "It was inspired by a real incident when I met a very attractive girl at a wedding and failed to follow up on it," says Curtis. For *Four Weddings*, Curtis came up with a surrogate: Charles, who develops an instant crush on Carrie, an American woman he meets at a wedding and spends the night with, and whose heart he eventually wins for good.

So far, so normal—especially for a British romantic comedy, a genre that has used weddings as a backdrop since the days of Shakespeare. But Curtis decided that he'd build his plot around an unusual structural principle: an entire movie set almost *only* at weddings. If his couple only met at weddings, he reasoned, audiences wouldn't be missing any of the good bits. "What I'd always found frustrating in films is that you often saw a really interesting scene between two lovers, then it cuts to two weeks later and you don't know what they've been doing. So I tried to construct something where you see pretty well every minute they spent together," he says. So if one wedding would be a good place to meet the woman of your dreams, why not four of them? And just to break up the monotony—maybe one more sequence set somewhere else?

Curtis had conceived of the movie as *Four Weddings and a Honeymoon*. The climax would have been closer to farce, with Charles following the newly married Carrie on her honeymoon with another man in a hopeful, last-ditch effort to win her heart anyway. It was Helen Fielding—the future *Bridget Jones's Diary* author, and a longtime friend and confidante of Curtis (more about her on page 159)—who suggested that the movie needed a funeral to break up all that celebrating, and to add a different, darker color to the movie's palette. She "told me it was time I grew up and got some profundity in my work," says Curtis. It was an unconventional but novel way to ensure that Curtis's celebration of life and love also acknowledged the uncomfortable, inevitable truth about where those paths will someday lead— and a genuine rarity for the rom-com genre in general, which, like Curtis, tended to reflexively focus on the lighter side of the circle of life.

Throughout the process of writing *Four Weddings and a Funeral,* Curtis admits he "shamelessly nicked incidents" from the weddings he attended. Conservative MP Bernard Jenkin, who dated (and eventually married) Anne Strutt, a woman Curtis had also pursued in college, has claimed that Curtis stood "watching with a notebook" throughout his wedding.

Curtis tasked his partner, the cultural commenter and script editor Emma Freud, with reading every draft of *Four Weddings and a Funeral* and telling him what didn't work. He says he "lived in terror" of her frequent note "C.D.B.," which stood for "could do better"—a succinct but maddeningly vague way of communicating that a scene could be sharper or faster or funnier or more heartbreaking if Curtis could only dig deep enough into his brain to improve his own work. Even worse was "N.B.G.," for "no bloody good," which signaled anything Freud deemed an outright disaster. It took seventeen grueling drafts before *Four Weddings and a Funeral* was in good enough shape to start showing it to people— but based on the ecstatic reception it later received, the toil was worth it.

One of the first people who read *Four Weddings and a Funeral* was Duncan Kenworthy, who had come up in the industry as Jim Henson's assistant on the puppet fantasy movie *The Dark Crystal*, and eventually went on to produce an Arabic version of *Sesame Street*. At the time Curtis finished the *Four Weddings* script, Kenworthy had risen up the ranks to become managing director of the Henson Company in the U.K.—and while his schedule was so full that he originally had no intention of producing *Four Weddings*, he greatly admired the script and offered to help Curtis find the right director for the material.

And then—in a serendipitous, almost rom-com-like twist of fate—the right director presented himself. Fresh off directing the Irish magical realist drama *Into the West*, Mike Newell was looking for his next project. When Newell stopped by his agent's office, his agent wasn't around, so he decided to look through the stack of scripts on his secretary's desk—"Generally being nosy," he admits. Newell noticed that one of the scripts was unusually weathered, as if it had already been read many times. The secretary noticed his interest. "You should read that one, it's *very* funny," she advised. From the first page, Newell was interested. "Once you've started, you simply can't stop," he recalls, drawn in by the patter of the dialogue and the structural conceit of the screenplay. When he learned that *Four Weddings* didn't yet have a director attached, he personally angled for the job.

By then, Duncan Kenworthy was similarly stuck on the material. Deciding that he couldn't stand to pass on a project he believed in, he took a leave of absence from the Henson Company to produce *Four Weddings* himself. Curtis, Kenworthy, and Newell formed a creative triumvirate, hashing out key decisions (and not infrequently arguing about them—see the sidebar on casting) in their efforts to get the best possible version of the movie onto screens.

Fortunately, they had plenty of time on their hands in preproduction—because for all their enthusiasm, the budget required to convincingly stage four weddings and one funeral was proving maddeningly difficult to drum up. Kenworthy spent 1992 trying, and failing, to come up with enough money to get *Four Weddings* into production. Nobody bit. And with no reason to rush through preproduction, the triumvirate embarked on one of the most unusually extended casting calls in rom-com history. "We auditioned for over a year," says Kenworthy. "Not intentionally, but because we couldn't get the film off the ground. The money wasn't there, the interest wasn't there."

"We interviewed and auditioned everybody. Every promising young actor in London. *Enormous* numbers of people," says Newell. Curtis's witty script had been polished so many times that every character in the sprawling ensemble got at least a good line or two; unlike other film genres (but like any good rom-com), *Four Weddings* presented a good opportunity for a talented actor to make a strong impression by making audiences laugh and/or swoon.

Eventually, the script found its way to a young actor named Hugh Grant—who might have rolled his eyes at this description, since he didn't really think of himself as a young actor at all. "I was drifting, like most people do when they come out of university," says Grant. "I thought acting would last about a year." This wasn't just false modesty. Grant was so inexperienced on his first professional film shoot that after his first take, he walked off the set, unaware that the director would need him to shoot multiple takes of the same scene. Apart from a role in the acclaimed

Merchant-Ivory film *Maurice*, after which Grant cheerfully says he "managed to sell out," his movies tended toward the broad and cheesy. (If that sounds harsh, it's an appraisal shared by Grant, who lampooned many of his early films as "Europuddings," in which bad non-English scripts were translated and cast with English actors because they would then be easier to sell to audiences in the United States.)

By the late 1980s, what had started as a post-collegiate lark for Grant hadn't exactly blossomed into an illustrious acting career—but it was at least an excuse for some fun, shooting costume dramas with titles like *Rowing with the Wind* and *The Bengali Night* all over the world. "I shamefully used to take these films because they were offering lots of money and ten weeks in Spain with pretty girls, but they'd be the most dreadful films with very bad wigs, bad costumes, and bad accents," says Grant.

Like so many other young, handsome British actors of the era, Grant was brought in to read for Charles, the lead role in the film. Having grown accustomed to starring in "highly paid, terrible miniseries" that were shot in foreign countries, Grant was surprised to be sent a screenplay he actually liked, from his home country no less: "I remember calling my agent and saying, 'I think there's been a mistake, because you sent me a good script,'" he says.

By Grant's own account, the audition was disastrous. "It was in the Jim Henson studio for some reason and in front of the writer, director, producer and 50 full-size Muppets, which was unsettling," he says. "I read the speech I had made at *my* brother's wedding, which I thought would charm them but I think it slightly sickened them."

As it turns out, Grant was mostly right. He had needed to charm all three members of the triumvirate, but his floppy-haired, self-deprecating charm had only worked on one of them. Mike Newell was convinced that Hugh Grant was perfect for the role of Charles, the posh, stammering, charmingly self-deprecating hero who anchors much of the film. "It was clear to me—and I don't think it was as clear to Richard—that Hugh could really speak the dialogue," says Newell.

Richard Curtis wasn't convinced. Despite Newell's impassioned case for Grant, Curtis stubbornly stuck to his vision for

RICHARD CURTIS CAN ADMIT WHEN HE'S WRONG

Today, no one is quicker than Richard Curtis to acknowledge how wrong he was about Hugh Grant, who became his muse and starred in the next four rom-coms Curtis worked on. "I suggest that—after you have let an idea stew, written the film you wanted without the compromises of a commission, let it be brutally edited by someone you love, and then re-written it 15 times—you cast Hugh Grant as the lead. It doesn't matter who the character is—if she's a middle-aged cop on the verge of retiring, Hugh will be perfect. If he's an Eskimo schoolboy, Hugh is exactly what you are looking for," says Curtis. "Whatever your script is like, no matter how much stewing and rewriting—if the punters don't want to sleep with the star, you may never be asked to write another one."

(Grant would later test Curtis's hypothesis by playing a plantation owner, a Korean restaurateur, *and* a tattooed cannibal warlord in 2012's *Cloud Atlas*, but people don't really talk about that one.)

the character. "The absolutely key thing for that film when I was writing it was that the person who was playing the lead would not be good-looking," he says. "That was the absolute starting thesis of the film." Grant puts it even more bluntly: "The guy, as written, was meant to be like Richard Curtis himself, who wears glasses and is not necessarily the guy who would get the girl."

And besides, Curtis had his eye on a different actor to star: Alan Rickman. "An absurdity," says Newell. "A fine, fine actor, Rickman—but it wouldn't have been any good at all."

The argument that ensued about casting Charles was "not comfortable," Newell allows, though he had already made up his mind not to back down about Hugh Grant, no matter what. So, when the perennially underfinanced film was delayed due to even more money troubles, and Grant took another role, Newell insisted on waiting until Grant was available again. "I just dug my heels in and said, 'You're mad if you try to recast him. He's the only one who's got the trick,'" Newell says. The production did their best to dress Grant down, with what Grant says were meant to be "the worst imaginable clothes" and "the world's worst haircut" (though both became trendy after *Four Weddings* was actually released and everybody saw how suave Grant looked in them).

There's no getting around the subject of money and class, which is baked into the *Four Weddings* screenplay. The characters are unmistakably upper-crust; the flat shared by Charles and his roommate Scarlett is a mess, but you never get the sense that they have any trouble paying for it, though we never find out what Charles does for a living (if, indeed, he has a job and not just family money he can coast on). At one point, Charles's friend Tom says his family is the seventh-richest in England. "I suppose it was because Richard came from that world that these people all led charmed, gilded lives," says Newell. "They were posh folk, and you said to yourself, 'Well, I can see that this might be enticing to other posh folk . . . but what about the rest of us?'" To mitigate the problem, the *Four Weddings* creative team obsessed over the casting of Charles's friends, weeding out any actors who even faintly felt like "snobby, gilded youth—which it could so easily have become," says Newell. They settled on an eclectic mix of young talents that included John Hannah, James Fleet, and Kristin Scott Thomas, whose freshness and lack of familiarity to the audience increased the impression that this was an actual group of close-knit friends.

Fortunately, for the role of Carrie—the enigmatic American woman who beguiles Charles at wedding after wedding—the triumvirate had already found an ideal star: Jeanne Tripplehorn, who was poised for stardom following breakout performances in *Basic Instinct* and *The Firm*. And with Grant, Tripplehorn, and the rest of the ensemble in place, the production had finally drummed up the money required to begin filming. At $5.5 million, *Four Weddings* wasn't exactly costing blockbuster money—though the always-in-flux budget was still slashed by a further $1.2 million shortly before production began, causing Kenworthy to scramble to figure out how the movie could work with even tighter financing. "The only way you can prove that you were right and they were wrong is to make a lousy movie," says Kenworthy. "And when you make a good movie they say: 'You see? You didn't need the extra money.'" A budgetary crunch is a unique problem for a movie that unfolded at five different social events, which each required large venues and a large crowd of extras. Squeezed for money and time, the production did what they could to skate by. The film's Scottish wedding was shot just fifteen miles outside of London. "It was nothing like Scotland, but there were a dozen people in kilts," says

Newell. The illusion was somewhat improved when cinematographer Michael Coulter made time to get an establishing shot of the countryside while he was on a personal vacation.

Unfortunately, a budgetary crunch wasn't the only unexpected problem that plagued the run-up to the *Four Weddings* shoot. Just weeks before production was slated to start, Jeanne Tripplehorn's mother died unexpectedly, and she dropped out, forcing the triumvirate to scramble for a new lead actress in just two weeks. Fresh off her Oscar win for *My Cousin Vinny*, Marisa Tomei was offered the role; she declined. In the end, an agent called from Los Angeles with a much-needed life raft: Andie MacDowell was in London promoting *Groundhog Day* when she read the script, which she called "one of the best I've ever come across." As soon as the production found out she was available, she was cast. "God, we were grateful to get her," says Newell. "She's heaven. This marvelous, sunny, kind of girl-next-door character. There couldn't be very much wrong with the man to whom *she* had given her heart." MacDowell later revealed that her performance was inspired by no less a cinema giant than Katharine Hepburn, who also specialized in playing romantic leads with such charm and vitality that a man might spend the rest of his life (or at least the rest of a film) trying to win her heart: "This is the kind of role she would have played 40 years earlier," she said.

The unusual structure of *Four Weddings* provided the greatest challenge for MacDowell, whose Carrie is always a bit of a cipher. Because Charles (and the audience) only see her at weddings, much of Carrie's arc unfolds off-screen. Though Carrie gets engaged, married, and divorced over the course of the movie, we're not privy to most key events in her life, with Charles (and the audience) scrambling to catch up with what we've missed each

"EXCESSIVE THRUSTING"

Studio executives fretted about the movie's decidedly R-rated sexual content and language, worried that morality concerns would keep *Four Weddings and a Funeral* out of the lucrative rebroadcast market on American television. Among the things requested for removal from the original script: "blowjobs," "excessive thrusting," "screaming orgasms," and the phrase "enormous erection" (especially when mentioned in conjunction with a priest).

The movie's title was also a subject of enormous debate. "A fax came through from America saying there was a feeling that boys didn't like weddings and no one like funerals," says Curtis. "The title suggested a film that everyone in the world would want to miss." A partial list of the many, many proposed alternate titles includes *Still Single After All These Years*, *Girls in Big White Dresses*, *Salmon and Champagne*, *Skulking Around*, *Going to the Chapel*, *A Tale of Rings and Other Things*, and—rather cynically—*Four Weddings, Some Sex, and a Funeral*. In the end, the production was split between the original title and *The Best Man*; when someone suggested that the movie might be confused with a 1964 drama that was *also* titled *The Best Man*, *Four Weddings and a Funeral* won.

It was the right choice. Since the movie's release, the title has become so iconic that I could fill an entire chapter of this book with just the TV shows that have riffed on it, from *Melrose Place* ("Four Affairs and a Pregnancy") to *The Simpsons* ("Four Beheadings and a Funeral") to *Sex and the City* ("Four Women and a Funeral") to *Fresh Off the Boat* ("Four Funerals and a Wedding").

time. Some of this is intentional—Carrie's mysteriousness is part of what Charles (and the audience) is meant to find so alluring—but Curtis concedes that the character was also probably a little underwritten. "Mike said that, before you hand in a script, you have to read it 30 times as each character. I don't know how fully I did it with the Andie part," says Curtis. "I didn't think very hard about where she'd been or what she'd done."

Though *Four Weddings* opens with a madcap dash to a wedding that's also a clear attempt to break the world record for how many times you can say "fuck" in the first five minutes of a rom-com (the number, for the record, is twelve), the movie's tone is surprisingly slippery to pin down. In between comic set pieces, like an incredibly awkward wedding hookup or a stammering priest, *Four Weddings* sometimes plays more like a verbose, low-budget drama. Hugh Grant, in particular, was concerned that Mike Newell's direction was draining this romantic comedy of its, well, comedy. "He seemed to be giving direction against what I thought were the natural beats of the comedy," Grant says. "He was making a film with texture, grounding it, playing the truths rather than the gags." But in the middle of a rushed and underfinanced shoot, Newell's decision had exactly the effect he intended: Amid all the antics, Charles and his friends felt like plausible people occupying a plausible emotional world. "Mike was obsessed with keeping it real," says Curtis. "Every character, no matter how small, has a story, not just three funny lines." Characters that could have been little more than vehicles for jokes or exposition end up with their own mini-arcs. Charles's younger brother, who is deaf, makes a promising love connection with a woman who develops a crush on him at one wedding and learns some sign language by the next one. Scarlett, Charles's lovably eccentric roommate, finds love with her own strapping American.

And—in what's probably the most bittersweet and best-acted scene in the movie—Charles's friend Fiona finally confesses she's in love with him, knowing all along that he doesn't feel the same way about her.

Four Weddings maintains its tonal juggling act through the first three weddings, and by then, the audience is right where Curtis and Newell had wanted them. "If you think of all of the great romantic comedies, it's the mix of romance and sadness that opens those sort of receptors through laughing," says Kenworthy. "And then you make them cry."

No one should be surprised by the funeral—it's right there in the title—but it's still a shock when, at the reception for Carrie's wedding, Charles's gregarious friend Gareth suddenly dies of a heart attack. "I've always had the theory that things are really funnier if there's proper pain somewhere," says Grant. Delivering the eulogy at the funeral that follows, Gareth's partner Matthew delivers a showstopping, lump-in-everyone's-throat performance of W. H. Auden's 1936 poem "Funeral Blues," which culminates with the lines, "The stars are not wanted now; put out every one, pack up the moon and dismantle the sun, pour away the ocean and sweep up the wood; for nothing now can ever come to any good." This scene proved to be so popular that, shortly after *Four Weddings and a Funeral* was released, Faber and Faber rushed out a paperback collection of Auden poems titled *Tell Me the Truth About Love*. They put Hugh Grant's face on the cover, and it sold 275,000 copies.

Resolving to finally get his life in order after the funeral—we're left to assume, since most of this happens off-screen—Charles hastily decides to resume dating, and soon proposes marriage to, his ex-girlfriend Henrietta (whom his friends have saddled with the unfortunate nickname "Duckface"). On his wedding day, Carrie reveals that she and her husband have separated, sending Charles into a tailspin. On the last-minute advice of his younger brother—and while he's literally standing at the altar in the chapel—Charles suddenly spurns Henrietta, earning a well-deserved punch in the face as he breaks up the wedding. (In a movie that's unusually generous to its supporting cast—and

LOOK AT THESE PHOTOGRAPHS

In a true Mega—Happy Ending, *Four Weddings and a Funeral* closes with a series of still photographs revealing the fates of all the characters. Charles and Carrie have a baby; Scarlett marries her hunky American; "Duckface" marries a man who could hardly treat her worse than Charles did; Matthew finds love with a new man (played by producer Duncan Kenworthy); and Fiona marries none other than Prince Charles, who was legally separated from Princess Diana at the time.

The production never asked permission to feature Charles's image, and the Royal Family never said anything about it. But when Curtis and Newell reassembled the *Four Weddings and a Funeral* cast for the Red Nose Day special, inspiration struck: Maybe, for the sake of charity, Prince Charles would actually agree to appear as Kristin Scott Thomas's husband in the special?

Duncan Kenworthy reached out to Prince Charles's private secretary, who asked for a week to consider. When he called back, the secretary regretfully declined. "It was sweet of you to ask, but he's not available on the day that you want him, though he's very friendly towards the whole thing," he said. "By the way: Did you ask for permission at the time?"

despite a tacked-on credits shot revealing that she got her own happy ending—the movie's utter lack of interest in or sympathy for Henrietta is the one sour note.) While he recovers, feeling both guilty and sorry for himself, Carrie shows up to validate his choice. They kiss in the rain, true love wins the day, and

LET THE RAIN FALL DOWN

The most enduring legacy of the climactic rain sequence is Andie MacDowell's much-mocked line, "Is it still raining? I hadn't noticed." The line has repeatedly been voted one of the worst movie lines of all time by British filmgoers, and there are some *Four Weddings and a Funeral* screenings in which audience members mockingly shout the line in unison at the screen, *Rocky Horror Picture Show* style.

In the years since the release of *Four Weddings and a Funeral*, MacDowell has defended this line on romantic grounds: "The character was so in love, she wasn't thinking about the fricking rain." (It also, intentionally or not, aligns *Four Weddings* with such rom-com greats as 1952's *The Quiet Man* and 1961's *Breakfast at Tiffany's*, which also feature passionate rain kisses despite rain-kissing being, uh, not that comfortable in practice.) And while the line is undeniably awkwardly delivered, the more plausible reading is that Carrie is making a joke. The whole movie has been full of quippy Brits. Why shouldn't the American get one in?

Whatever explanation you prefer, the line has taken on a life of its own. Curtis has acknowledged it's "the worst line in the film." Mike Newell now laughs about it. "Every beautiful thing has got to have a flaw," he says.

everyone—yes, *everyone*—gets a happy ending by the time the credits are over.

The end of *Four Weddings* is a full-on retreat from the realism of Mike Newell's vision, veering hard into deliberately sappy rom-com territory. But whether you love or hate seeing Hugh Grant and Andie MacDowell kissing in the rain (I see you, Team Fiona), it's hard to argue with the results. Everyone involved in the production of *Four Weddings and a Funeral* knew they were making a movie they could be proud of. No one knew they were making something that would strike such a chord that it would eventually gross $245 million worldwide, or a little more than *fifty-five times* what it cost to produce.

BRINGING HOME SOME HARDWARE

Four Weddings and a Funeral may not have taken home the Oscar for Best Picture, but it did win the prize for Best Foreign Film at the César Awards, the highest film honors in France, topping movies like Quentin Tarantino's *Pulp Fiction* and Steven Spielberg's *Schindler's List*.

It's a memory Mike Newell recalls with some sheepishness. "That night, we said to [the team running the César Awards], 'Look, it's too late now. We promise not to tell anybody. But if we haven't won, could you let us know? Because we'd dearly love a drink. And what we *can't* do is to get plastered and then go on and have to behave like good boys.' And they said, 'What are you talking about? Mr. Spielberg is in the audience.' And our inference was, *If he's here all the way from California, of* course *you haven't won here. Of* course *he has*."

"So we all got . . . very slightly plastered. I was certainly not entirely sober. And then, God help us, they called our name. And we had to go up on the stage, up these rickety stairs. I caught the toe of my shoe on the top and very nearly went sprawling. And there, sitting in the middle of the fourth row, was Spielberg. And I tried to make signs at him that said, 'Look, I'm awfully sorry. Your movie is so much better than our movie. Oh, I'm so sorry.'"

It's no knock on *Four Weddings* to say that its uncanny success, while owing to the quality of the movie, was also the result of a clever and groundbreaking release strategy. The first and biggest decision was to release *Four Weddings and a Funeral* in the United States before the United Kingdom, counting on a wave of positive buzz from overseas to drown out any British dissenters arguing that this low-budget rom-com was better suited for the BBC than the big screen. After a world premiere screening at the Sundance Film Festival earned rave reviews, the general release was moved up to March 9, 1994. Distributor Russell Schwartz credited some of the movie's success to timing: "After a winter when snow blanketed the East Coast, it's the first spring movie with pretty people in pretty clothes."

The U.S. marketing campaign for *Four Weddings and a Funeral* cost $10 million—literally twice as much as it cost to make the movie—and it didn't kick into high gear until the second weekend in release, in an effort to maximize the word-of-mouth from people who had seen it on the first. By August of 1994, this low-budget British rom-com with a virtually unknown lead actor had grossed $52 million in the United States alone. But the cleverest move of all was to pitch *Four Weddings and a Funeral* to an untapped but potentially lucrative group of filmgoers: those who swore up and down that they weren't interested in a genre with as much mainstream appeal as rom-coms. "It's what the *Seinfeld* crowd, who usually feel they have nothing to see, want to go to the movies for," said screenwriter Terry Curtis Fox in a postmortem published by *Entertainment Weekly*. Maybe it was the writing—or maybe it was just the copious cursing and/or the British accents—but the general cultural perception was that *Four Weddings* was a comedy for the urbane and culturally savvy, and audiences responded accordingly.

And soon enough, so did the Academy. As Mike Newell says, no one involved with *Four Weddings and a Funeral* thought the movie had any chance at an Oscar nomination, and no one thought it had a serious chance at winning Best Picture—though Curtis and Kenworthy admit to having hope "for a nanosecond" when presenter Al Pacino opened the envelope and said "For—" before finishing the title *Forrest Gump*.

But the nomination alone was an early sign that this era would set strict boundaries around the rare romantic comedies that were deemed good enough to "transcend" their genre trappings and earn a Best Picture nomination at the Academy Awards. The list of Best Picture nominees that came after—*As Good as It Gets, Shakespeare in Love, Lost in Translation, Sideways, Midnight in Paris, The Artist, Silver Linings Playbook,* and *Phantom Thread*—have, more or less, followed in the footsteps of *Four Weddings and a Funeral*. Each movie cross-pollinates the romantic comedy with enough drama that it can plausibly be defended as "serious," and each movie centers both the perspective and the emotional journey of a white and male protagonist, rewarding him with a wistful romance and a life lesson learned by the time the credits roll.

It's no coincidence that this narrow slice of rom-coms found success with the Academy. A 2012 investigation by the *Los Angeles Times* revealed that the Academy was 77 percent male and 94 percent white, resulting in a measurable and persistent bias toward movies about white men—and while the Academy responded by making a concentrated push to increase diversity, the numbers had only shifted to 69 percent male and 84 percent white by 2020. Whether conscious or not, this long-standing bias reflected

MORE WEDDINGS

Though *Four Weddings and a Funeral* never got a formal sequel, two distinct follow-ups arrived in 2019. The first, "One Red Nose Day and a Wedding," is a brief short, written by Richard Curtis to raise money for his charity Comic Relief and directed by Mike Newell, which reunites the surviving cast of *Four Weddings and a Funeral*. The short film is set at the wedding of Charles and Carrie's daughter Miranda (Lily James) to Fiona's daughter Faith (Alicia Vikander), and is packed with winks and nods to the original movie, including a teasing shot at the "Is it raining?" line by Andie MacDowell and Hugh Grant.

The second, a Hulu miniseries co-created by Mindy Kaling that's also titled *Four Weddings and a Funeral*, is a looser riff on the original. Despite having Richard Curtis as an executive producer, a small supporting role for Andie MacDowell, and—credit where credit is due—four weddings and one funeral spread out across its ten-episode run, the series bears virtually no resemblance to the original movie, telling a story about a group of American expats living and loving in London, with Nathalie Emmanuel and Nikesh Patel leading the cast.

the types of love stories the Academy deemed worthy of serious consideration—and, by extension, the type of love stories the studios would make at all. It raises a question Hollywood still hasn't seriously reckoned with: Do critics and voters like the *best* stories, or the ones that most comfortingly reflect their own lives?

Hugh Grant

THE HARDEST-WORKING CAD IN HOLLYWOOD

Four Weddings and a Funeral director Mike Newell has a favorite anecdote that perfectly sums up Hugh Grant's approach to acting. They were filming the movie's climactic rain sequence, when Carrie shows up on Charles's doorstep to proclaim her love for him, when Newell realized there was a big problem on the horizon: The fake rain was going to drown out all the dialogue.

In a normal film, that wouldn't be a problem. Actors go into sound booths to rerecord muddy dialogue so it can be dubbed into movies all the time. But Charles's unique way of speaking created a unique challenge for Grant. "Hugh had developed this character trait, which was a hesitation," Newell says. "There was a little half-stutter at the back of a great deal of what he said, so Hugh's delivery was full of little stops and starts."

As Grant delivered his lines, drowned out by the pounding rain, Newell fretted over how he would later dub over his own performance, hitting every single one of Charles's nervous stutters and tics. "I thought, *This is going to take us weeks of unrelenting labor. And it won't be any good when we've finished it, because* nobody *could reproduce what Hugh did*," says Newell. In the end, he worried for nothing. Grant arrived at the recording booth and redelivered the entire speech flawlessly. "He did it in two takes. He had rehearsed, and rehearsed, and rehearsed, and got every tiny, little hesitation and stutter worked out in advance. What he had to do was, simply, to reproduce it."

There's a paradox underlying many of the great rom-com performances, which must drive many actors mad: It takes an incredible, focused amount of talent and work to play a character who seems loose and relaxed and authentic. This work—though not terribly different from the Method approach popularized by actors like Robert De Niro and Daniel Day-Lewis—is often underestimated by critics who shrug that a handsome, charming British man like Hugh Grant is essentially playing himself.

Hugh Grant typically hides the amount of work he puts into his performances under a thick layer of irony. ("I spent all day yesterday on a rooftop in Brooklyn, kissing Sandra Bullock," complained Grant, with tongue firmly in cheek, while filming *Two Weeks Notice* in 2002.) But occasionally—and with a heavy dose of self-deprecation that nods at how ridiculous he thinks the whole "acting" business is—he will reveal just how seriously he takes his job as an actor. "I do a ridiculous amount of homework and granular analysis of every moment in the film," says Grant. "I build up these vast biographies of the character. Hiding behind the mask of someone else seems to loosen me up and make me better."

In *Four Weddings and a Funeral*, he may have done his job too well. Shortly thereafter, Grant was immediately typecast as the character he'd played in the film: a floppy-haired, twinkly-eyed dreamer whose intimidatingly quick wit was softened by a stammering, guileless awkwardness. It mattered to no one that this character was worlds away from the actual Hugh Grant—a much cagier and more self-assured figure—and was clearly an avatar for writer Richard Curtis, who had lucked into an ideal leading man to serve as his on-screen surrogate. "He became Richard Curtis and Richard Curtis became him. Richard had invented this world called Curtisland, and they went to live there. He took Hugh with him," says Mike Newell.

The result was a trio of movies—*Four Weddings and a Funeral, Notting Hill*, and *Love Actually*—that solidified the "Hugh Grant" type in the minds

of audiences around the world. "What Richard wrote was—whether intentional or not—a short franchise. Three movies in which Hugh's character doesn't really change," says Newell. But after nearly a decade as
the King of Curtisland, Grant had had his fill of being conflated with the
man himself. "That always made me grind my teeth a bit," says Grant.
"Because that character in the Richard Curtis films was a bit repetitious.
But it wasn't me. It's really kind of Richard."

Still, Grant appreciates the extended shelf life enjoyed by the romantic comedies he made with Curtis, as well as similar rom-com hits like *Two
Weeks Notice*, *Bridget Jones's Diary*, *About a Boy*, and *Music and Lyrics*,
which have largely defined his career. "I never thought, *I want to do lots
of romantic comedies*. I never had any particular interest in that genre,"
says Grant. "I'm amazed at how well they have stood the test of time in
terms of people still wanting to see them. They're scattered all over cable
channels and streamers, so they must provide some service." Still, Grant
seems broadly relieved that—due to both age and the acting choices he's
consciously made over the past decade or so—his days as a rom-com
leading man seem to be behind him. "I think it's just that I got old and ugly
and I'm not appropriate for romantic comedy films anymore, which has
been a great blessing," he says.

But anyone attempting to analyze the great performances of Hugh
Grant's career would be doing an incomplete job if they didn't also ex-
amine the moment that nearly derailed his career in its infancy. Grant's
near-instant rise to superstardom had also been abetted by his very, very
public relationship with then-girlfriend Elizabeth Hurley, who became
such a fascination for the British tabloids that the Versace dress she wore
to the *Four Weddings and a Funeral* premiere now has its own Wikipedia
page. And then, in June 1995, while in Los Angeles promoting his big Hollywood debut, *Nine Months*, Hugh Grant was arrested after being caught
by police in his car with a sex worker who called herself Divine Brown.

It was one thing for audiences to accept a Hollywood version of this
story starring Julia Roberts and Richard Gere. It was another thing en-

tirely to learn that the hot actor of the moment had cheated on his famous girlfriend by paying $60 for a blow job in his BMW. Hurley, who issued no statement immediately following Grant's arrest, later revealed she "felt like she had been shot" when she heard the news.

It is not hard to imagine how—just a year after *Four Weddings and a Funeral* made Hugh Grant a superstar—his entire acting career could have drowned in a sea of embarrassing tabloid headlines. "America's celluloid ghetto was positively glowing with *schadenfreude*," wrote *The Guardian* in one typical postmortem shortly after Grant was arrested. And his awkward mug shot, which was widely disseminated—a half-unbuttoned striped brown shirt, hunched shoulders, a grim "Oh God, my life is ruined" look in his eyes—did not do wonders for his image as a popular sex symbol.

In the end, what saved Grant's career was how well he embodied a stammering, contrite, lovably awkward Brit while delivering his apology on *The Tonight Show with Jay Leno* just a couple of weeks later. "Let me start with question number one: What the hell were you thinking?" asked Leno. And out of respect for the amount of work Hugh Grant puts into every performance, I will attempt to transcribe his subsequent apology on *The Tonight Show* with as much accuracy as possible:

"Yeah. Yeah. What it says, um. It's not easy, um. You know, the thing is, um—people give me tons of, um, ideas on this one. I keep reading new, you know, psychological theories, and stuff like that. You know, that I was under pressure, or I was tired, or I was lonely, or I fell down the stairs when I was a child, or whatever. But I, um—you know, I think that would be . . . bollocks, really, to hide behind that, something like that. You know, I think you know in life, pretty much, what's a good thing to do and what's a bad thing. And, um, I did a bad thing, and there you have it."

Grant finished and reached for his coffee mug. The audience roared. Leno followed up with a winky quip about how everyone in Hollywood was *shocked* to learn that there were prostitutes on the Sunset Strip. Everyone laughed. Grant eventually got off with a fine and probation. *Nine Months* made $138 million at the box office.

It was, in short, a master class in crisis management—what *The Independent* later described as "the greatest PR save of all time." But personally, I can't watch that *Tonight Show* clip without counting every stammer and "um," or noting that "bollocks" is an awfully smart word choice for a man who would surely benefit from reminding audiences—even subconsciously—of the foul-mouthed British man they loved in a very British romantic comedy released just one year earlier. There are benefits to knowing where your strengths lie, and Hugh Grant has always been unusually savvy about knowing what side of himself to project to the world.

"Every woman needs a man. And you ain't no exception."

—SAVANNAH'S MOTHER, *WAITING TO EXHALE*

CHAPTER 4

WAITING TO EXHALE

(And the Audience Hollywood Has Always Neglected)

NOTHING ABOUT TERRY McMILLAN'S PATH TO SUCCESS AS A NOVELIST was easy. She wrote her first book, *Mama*, at night while working a day job as a typist at a law firm. When she was informed that her publisher wouldn't be providing any resources for marketing, publicity, or a book tour, McMillan personally sent out thousands of letters, many specifically aimed at Black audiences, offering to show up and read from the novel for anyone who was interested. Enough people who received those letters liked the book and took McMillan up on the offer, earning her a loyal following in precisely the demographics commonly neglected by the publishing industry.

Two years later, her second novel, *Disappearing Acts*, had sold briskly to readers (though she'd been forced to fend off a $4.75 million lawsuit from her ex-boyfriend, Leonard Welch, who argued that a character was largely modeled on him—a self-own of the highest order). And even if the literary establishment tended to overlook her success, McMillan, who once said she'd happily keep writing if only five thousand people read her books, had made it: "Long before mainstream booksellers had heard of Terry McMillan, black bookstores were filling record orders of her books," reported *The New York Times*.

In 1991, McMillan, at forty, was successful, confident, beautiful, and eager to meet a man who, as she would go on to write,
could "take her breath away." She looked at her friends and saw
that, after years of personal and professional growth, they were in
much the same place. But as McMillan and her peers compared
notes about what *wasn't* working in their lives, they realized they
kept returning to the same question: Where had all the good men
gone?

"All my friends were going through something with their boy-
friends, or lack thereof," she says. "We were having a tough time.
And I just said, 'This is such bullshit. Love shouldn't be this hard.'
Most of my friends were smart, educated, attractive. We were
pretty hot. It *shouldn't* be this hard. Because we all want the same
thing. Just to be loved, and to have a good time, and feel good, and
live happily ever after. And I said, '*Men* are stupid. *They* make it so
fucking hard.'"

As she was fond of doing, McMillan channeled her observations and experiences into her writing. And if her previous two
novels had earned her a devoted group of readers, her third would
make her a literary superstar.

Long before *Sex and the City* and its Cosmo-swilling quar-
tet of single women, *Waiting to Exhale* was offering up four close
friends—Savannah, Bernadine, Robin, and Gloria—navigating
sex in the city of Phoenix, Arizona. "I told the truth about what
Black women feel when they fall in love," says McMillan. "And
we hadn't seen that. I really wanted it known—not knowing
how many people would ultimately read the book—that Black
women love the same way as any other woman. We have sex. We
fall in love. We are sensual. We are all the stuff that every other
woman is."

I COULDN'T HELP BUT WONDER . . .

The 1998 premiere of HBO's *Sex and the City*—which also chronicles the lives of four close friends with unusual sexual frankness, but with white women instead of Black women—was an unstoppable cultural juggernaut. It was also judged by a subset of vocal *Waiting to Exhale* fans to have borrowed heavily from McMillan's novel, though neither *Sex and the City* writer Candace Bushnell nor series creator Darren Star ever acknowledged the influence. "I mean, that was pretty obvious to a lot of us," says McMillan. "To this day, I think they robbed us. There were a lot of people who were pissed off about that show. But I wasn't. I really wasn't. My audience seemed to be more upset about it than I was. I had sort of gotten past *Waiting to Exhale*, and it took a long time for people to let me do that. Back then my attitude—without sounding racist—was that white people would get away with a lot of stuff Black people can't. And to some extent, that's still true."

Waiting to Exhale reached its intended audience in numbers so staggering that even the publishing industry couldn't ignore it or explain it away. Upon its publication on May 28, 1992, the book sat on the *New York Times* bestseller list for thirty-seven weeks; the paperback rights sold for $2.64 million. "I've had 1,500 people show up for a reading for *Waiting to Exhale*," said McMillan at the time. "1,200 in Chicago, 1,000 people waiting in line in Washington. I think I've signed more than 10,000 books, and the people who come are 90 percent Black. In some cities 98 percent."

Hollywood is a cautious business; if you're going to cut against the grain—which, in this case, meant making a movie not primarily aimed at white audiences—it helps if you have proof that there's a market for your project. The runaway success of *Waiting to Exhale* was that rare opportunity: a major studio movie based on a book by a Black female novelist, with a narrative centered on four Black women. McMillan, who had studied film at Columbia University but dropped out after a year—"I was even on the screenwriting track," she says—was intrigued by the possibility of turning her novel celebrating Black women into a film that might be enjoyed by Black women, who had been all but ignored by the Hollywood studios. "As an African-American writer, I didn't know a lot of writers whose books were being turned into films, so I didn't have what you would call a real frame of reference," says McMillan. "You read about this stuff or saw it on *Entertainment Tonight*. But I always loved movies, and I was just flattered that they wanted to *make* it into a movie."

Help, and flattery, came in the form of Ronald Bass, who was personally recommended to McMillan by her close friend, the novelist Amy Tan. Bass, a screenwriter who had earned a Best Original Screenplay Oscar for *Rain Man* in 1988, had subsequently worked with Tan on the 1993 film adaptation of her novel *The Joy Luck Club*. Tan had been impressed by his ability to channel her novel into something Hollywood-friendly while retaining its core as a Chinese-American narrative, despite being white himself. It certainly didn't hurt that Bass could help her navigate Hollywood, where he had a reputation as a prolific screenwriter with a knack for churning out hits. In fact, some rival screenwriters suspected he was a little *too* prolific. Bass's deeply unconventional screenwriting process relied heavily on a team of assistants dubbed "the Ronettes"—all young women looking to break into screenwriting—who would assemble at Bass's Brentwood home to embark on marathon research and brainstorming sessions designed to hone his screenplays into unmistakable hits. Some writers grumbled that Bass was getting credit for putting his name on work that was actually being done by the Ronettes; Bass insisted that the work was all his own, and a 2000 *New Yorker* investigation eventually landed on Bass's side, with the concession that his scripts were sometimes improved by plot points and dialogue suggested by his helpers.

For the process of adapting *Waiting to Exhale*, Bass and McMillan developed a method for writing the screenplay. "She was living in northern California near the East Bay side of Oakland, in a beautiful house with a poured concrete floor, and I was living in Brentwood. We were going back and forth over the phone a lot," says Bass. "Writing with an author is a wonderful thing—*if* you can get along. It's really their story. And if you're going to adapt it, you're going to change an awful lot, and you want that to be with someone that you respect."

Sensitive to both McMillan and the novel's many fans, Bass committed to one guiding principle in the adaptation process: While he could make suggestions, Terry McMillan *always* got to decide if they'd end up in the final script. "I'm my best critic when I'm writing," says McMillan. "I know when I'm bullshitting, and I know when I'm putting words in a character's mouth that they would never say. Ron would come up with things and I would say, 'Ron, that doesn't make any sense.' Or, 'My character would *never* do that.'" Bass was quick to agree. "If at any time Terry said, 'No, they wouldn't say that or do it like that,' that was it. There were never any arguments. She was always the final authority." Bass also dismissed concerns that a white, male screenwriter might not be the right person to adapt a story uniquely centered on Black women. "Every film is about disappearing the distance between the audience and the character on the screen," he says. "This was a movie about four women who were professionals, who were successful, who had problems that *everybody* watching that film could relate to. They weren't clichés and stereotypes of what a Black woman was allowed to be."

For such a character-focused story, *Waiting to Exhale* needed a director who truly understood how to work with actors, and the production eventually settled on an unlikely but inspired choice: Forest Whitaker. Though he had little experience behind the camera, the actor had spent the 1980s working with some of the most respected directors in Hollywood, including Martin Scorsese, Oliver Stone, and Clint Eastwood, and had just begun

A STAR ISN'T BORN

Forest Whitaker originally planned to have Terry McMillan appear in a brief cameo in *Waiting to Exhale*—a request that she originally agreed to fulfill, though somewhat reluctantly. After a long series of fruitless takes, she decided to bow out. "It's a scene in the movie where this chick—who's, like, some kind of hippie, is playing a guitar, sitting by a water fountain," says McMillan. "It was in Arizona, and it was hot as hell. Forest says, 'Terry, walk across.' And I'll tell you: I think, by the fifteenth time I walked across, back and forth, back and forth, I said, 'You know what? I'm going to push her in that pool in a minute, okay? I'm so sick of that guitar I'm going to push her in that pool. Forest, I'm sorry. I'm done. I don't want to be in this movie.' And I wasn't. I was so fucking tired of walking back and forth. I didn't even have to say anything. They just wanted me to do the walk. And I was like, 'No. Uh-uh. No.'"

to forge his own directing career. Two years before *Waiting to Exhale*, Whitaker had directed the HBO film *Strapped*, a gritty thriller starring Bokeem Woodbine. It was not the most obvious audition for *Waiting to Exhale*, but McMillan was convinced he was the right person for the job. "Forest is a gentle soul," says McMillan. "He knew how to see. He had a certain kind of tenderness, and an understanding of how people act. I think it was from him being an actor."

The movie's unique blend of tones required actresses who were versatile enough to be both as funny and as dramatic as the script would require. McMillan's novel had centered on four distinct and multifaceted Black women, and she was determined that the film adaptation would do justice to the same. "You didn't see Black women being sexy and hot and silly and funny," says McMillan. "In a lot of films where you saw Black women, we were also kind of depressed, and begging somebody to just touch us. I'm like, 'Are you kidding? Are you kidding me? Uh-uh. No. We are *sexy*.'"

The production quickly zeroed in on two stars who had exactly what they needed. In 1992, Whitney Houston made her acting debut opposite Kevin Costner in the phenomenally successful romantic drama *The Bodyguard*, which was written by Lawrence Kasdan and directed by Mick Jackson. The movie's success despite a critical drubbing demonstrated why casting a popular singer can be such a wise move; the soundtrack, which includes Houston's iconic cover of Dolly Parton's "I Will Always Love You," was (and remains) the bestselling movie soundtrack of all time.

At the same time, the production approached Angela Bassett, who had earned an Oscar nomination for playing Tina Turner in 1994's *What's Love Got to Do with It*. Forest Whitaker says he "always wanted" Angela Bassett for Bernadine, out of appreciation

BABYFACE BRINGS IT

Both separate and inseparable from the success of *Waiting to Exhale* was the soundtrack, arranged by super-producer Kenneth "Babyface" Edmonds, who was personally recruited and talked into the job by Forest Whitaker. The sixteen-song album, which consists solely of female artists, lined up classic singers like Aretha Franklin and Patti LaBelle alongside of-the-moment artists like Mary J. Blige, TLC, and Brandy. Whitney Houston herself both opens and closes the album with the singles "Exhale (Shoop Shoop)" and "Count On Me."

The *Waiting to Exhale* soundtrack earned eleven Grammy nominations and went platinum seven times in just the first year of its release. The lead-off single, "Exhale (Shoop Shoop)," was particularly remarkable because the "shoop shoop" in the hook was originally intended as a placeholder until something better came along. "Every time I tried to write any kind of lyric to it, it felt like it was getting in the way," says Babyface. "So, ultimately, because I couldn't think of any words, I was just kind of 'shoop shooping' and then the shoops started to make sense to me." The song was Houston's last number-one hit before her death in 2012.

for the way she "never plays stereotypes." When both Houston and Bassett agreed to join the ensemble—as Savannah and Bernadine, respectively—*Waiting to Exhale* had its stars.

But Savannah and Bernadine are only half of the story, and finding Robin and Gloria turned out to be a longer casting hunt. Lela Rochon had played small roles in movies like Eddie Murphy's *Harlem Nights* and Reginald Hudlin's *Boomerang*. The latter movie, which also starred Eddie Murphy, had been a successful rom-com in its own right, though its success was largely attributed to Murphy's white-hot streak as a comedic leading man: "We thought this movie would start a chain of films like this and it didn't," reflected Hudlin years later. Rochon, who appeared in *Boomerang* as a woman seduced and eventually abandoned by Murphy, was frustrated that even a role in a hit didn't seem to be opening new doors in Hollywood. By 1994 she had resolved to quit acting if she couldn't land a decent part within a year, when she heard that a *Waiting to Exhale* adaptation was in the works. Inspired by what felt like an actual character she could play, Rochon called in favors to line up a conversation with Terry McMillan and wrote Forest Whitaker a personal letter begging for an audition, which led to her being cast as Robin.

Loretta Devine, who had starred in the original cast of *Dreamgirls* on Broadway in 1981, had never quite broken through into film, with only minor supporting roles to her name. She auditioned for the role of Gloria, thinking she wouldn't get the part; when she was told by someone who didn't know her personally that a "woman from New York" had booked the role, she assumed she was officially out of the running, not realizing that the woman from New York was her.

With the script and cast in order, filming for *Waiting to Exhale* began in February 1995—a relatively tight schedule, since the movie would be released in December of that same year. Houston recalled a "hard and long" shoot, with some days that began at 6 A.M. and stretched until after sundown. And while the four lead actresses worked to develop a genuine bond—even spending a night at Houston's house while her aunt served a lavish dinner, and drinking champagne until early in the morning—the structure of *Waiting to Exhale* required them to shoot most of their scenes apart, as various men drift in and out of their lives. Savannah flirts with other men while hoping her lover (Dennis Haysbert) will leave his wife. Bernadine rages at being betrayed

THE BACHELORS

Though *Waiting to Exhale*'s narrative is focused largely on the four central women, the supporting cast is stacked with talented male actors, including Mykelti Williamson, Dennis Haysbert, Giancarlo Esposito, and Wesley Snipes, who had emerged as one of the most bankable Black actors of the 1990s after *New Jack City*, *White Men Can't Jump*, and *Demolition Man*. Snipes, who appears uncredited, says he was actively pursuing films like *Waiting to Exhale* after his string of hit blockbusters: "I decided I wanted to really act again," he says. "I had just made some adjustments in my managerial camp that afforded me the opportunity to be more open to do small roles in good films."

Playing a character who mistreated one of the *Waiting to Exhale* women could have unintentional, lifelong consequences; Michael Beach, who played Bernadine's cheating husband, says, "I was often verbally attacked and a couple of times smacked on the shoulder or the back of the head by strangers in public."

There was also some friendly competition among the actors to make the *best* impression on the lead actresses, with Gregory Hines ultimately proving himself the winner. "He brought me flowers my first day, and none of the other guys did that, so all of the women were jealous. I loved that," says Loretta Devine.

by her cheating husband (Michael Beach), whom she supported in his career by abandoning her own. Gloria navigates a difficult relationship with her teenage son (Donald Faison) while pursuing a promising romance with her new neighbor (Gregory Hines). And Robin cycles through a series of losers, fantasizing about her on-again/off-again lover Russell (Leon Robinson) while she tries to figure out what she actually wants out of life.

One of the movie's centerpiece scenes comes early, when Robin brings a colleague named Michael (Wendell Pierce) back to her apartment. Michael is a dork, and Robin isn't particularly attracted to him, but he knows how to scuba dive, owns his own boat, and regularly takes trips to the mountains, and who knows what a man might turn out to be if you give him a chance? So, Robin slips into some lingerie and gets into bed with Michael, resigning herself to some brief, unsatisfying sex. As Michael uselessly thrusts away on top of her, we're treated to Robin's interior monologue: *Does he think he just did something here?*

Like so much of *Waiting to Exhale*, this sequence was consciously designed to poke holes in a lazy Hollywood trope: In this case, the assumption that all men are good in bed. "Not once have you ever seen a woman jump up from 007 and say, 'That wasn't all I thought it was going to be.' They're always dynamic lovers. That is a bunch of bull," says Terry McMillan.

Taken on its own, this could be a funny throwaway scene designed to push the plot forward—an encounter with a goofy loser that's disappointing enough to shove Robin back to the unreliable-but-hot Russell. But something interesting happens in Robin's not-particularly-blissful postcoital state. Michael, who has until this point come across as entirely self-centered, senses that Robin wasn't entirely into his haphazard thrusting and realizes he's curious about what she actually wants. And when asked to articulate her needs out loud (and thus breaking from the internal monologue to the exterior), Robin is forced to articulate them for herself too. The answer, to what seems to be her own surprise, is upper-middle-class domestic life: a few kids, a little vacation house in Scottsdale, and the financial security to eat out at a restaurant two or three times a week. "I want to be *happy*," she says. "You don't want much. I could give you that and a whole lot more," Michael promises in reply.

It's a suggestion of straightforward domestic happiness that comes up infrequently in the rom-com genre, which was built on grand gestures and meet-cutes. But the earnestness of Robin's fantasy is, in practice, much closer to the kind of solid, unassuming foundation on which many actual marriages are built. Despite the awkwardness of their hookup, you start to imagine—as Robin clearly imagines—that this might actually evolve into the relationship that will bring her the happiness she's been looking for.

It doesn't work out; while Michael's honeyed promises turn out to be exactly the kind of seduction she needed in the first place, she firmly rejects him when he embarrasses her during a workplace meeting, and he swiftly exits the movie altogether. But the implicit question hangs over the scenes where Savannah admits to herself that she just wants a warm body in bed with her for the night, or when Gloria makes a desperate pass at an ex who is clearly not interested, or when Bernadine meets a grieving soon-to-be-widower and ends up holding him and falling asleep at the end of a sexless night: What, if anything, can these women expect from the men in their lives?

The answer, more often than not, is not much. Early in *Waiting to Exhale*, Angela Bassett gets to play out one of cinema's great hell-hath-no-fury scenes, as Bernadine delivers a lengthy, profane soliloquy while she dumps her cheating husband's clothes into his BMW, lights a cigarette, and sets the whole thing on fire. In a different kind of rom-com—the kind in which every road leads to love—her husband might realize the error of his ways and come up with a grand gesture to win her back. In this one, Bernadine's prize is her hefty divorce settlement. After trying out a few different guys over the course of the movie and finding them all lacking, Robin discovers she's pregnant and decides she'll raise her unborn baby on her own. Stuck in a dead-end relationship with a married man, Savannah openly preaches the value of a good one-night stand: "I don't need to be in love with him to do it. Hell, my body needs this." Only Gloria gets a relatively conventional rom-com arc, after a meet-cute with her sweet-hearted new neighbor leads to a healthy relationship that helps her learn to let her son live his own life. But even if each woman's path to happiness doesn't turn out to be a committed, long-term partnership, their endings feel right, and even happy, just the same.

Waiting to Exhale opened on December 22, 1995, in the Christmas frame that is typically regarded as one of the year's most lucrative for films. Its competition included the big-budget pirate blockbuster *Cutthroat Island*, the comedy sequel *Grumpier Old Men*, and the family-oriented *Tom and Huck*, as well as successful holdovers like *Jumanji* and *Toy Story*. When the dust settled, *Waiting to*

WAITING TO CRACK UP

As 20th Century Fox prepared to release *Waiting to Exhale*, the team behind the movie would sneak into test screenings to see for themselves how it was playing with audiences. The problem, as McMillan recalls, is that no matter how discreet they tried to be, Whitney Houston would inevitably blow their cover. "Let me tell you, Whitney was *loud*," says McMillan. "When she laughed, everybody realized she was in the audience. Sometimes she would actually say her lines, and you couldn't miss her voice. It got to the point where we had to say, '*Please*, Whitney.' And she's like, 'Oh, you guys. You don't know how to have fun.' So I would have to pop her. And then we would *both* be cracking up."

Exhale was the week's highest-grossing movie by a huge margin, opening with $14.1 million and topping out at $81 million worldwide.

The passion for the movie exceeded those numbers, it seems. The release was celebrated as an event, with groups of women getting together for "*Exhale* parties" built around heading to the theater to see the movie. Fox 2000 president Elizabeth Gabler recalled crowds of women that would, quite literally, refuse to exit the theater after the movie was over. "We couldn't get them to leave. All these young women in their twenties and thirties wanted to stay and talk about what they'd just seen," she says.

Though most were too sheepish and image-conscious to say it on the record, the smash success of *Waiting to Exhale* caught many studio executives (largely male, almost always white) off-guard. "Hollywood is dominated by well-intentioned white liberals who share a mistrust that the black middle class will show up," admitted one anonymous studio executive at the time. "The industry was taken aback by the 'I'm black and I'm proud' response to this movie."

But if Hollywood was surprised, the creative team behind *Waiting to Exhale*—who had waited for a movie like this for most of their lives, and finally just made it themselves—was not. "Those sisters who loved the movie gave *Exhale* parties," says Loretta Devine. "They rented out theaters in small towns. They grab me on the street. But when I go to see casting people out in L.A. it's like they never saw the film—like they can't face the fact that the story of four black girls did well." Terry McMillan agreed: "That $14.1 million was Black money," she says. "It was also a show of respect for me, the book, us. That's what that was about. And, they couldn't have made a larger statement. You guys need to pay attention."

Just as she'd done with her novels, Terry McMillan had delivered a story that had reached an underserved audience that was

THE DEBATES CONTINUE

The critic bell hooks excoriated *Waiting to Exhale* in her 1996 essay collection *Reel to Real: Race, Sex and Class at the Movies*. She argued that the film adaptation excised some of the key scenes in McMillan's original novel, like Bernadine using some of her divorce settlement to write checks to groups like the Urban League and the NAACP, for a simplified narrative that channels the "racist, sexist stereotype of black women being hard, angry, and just plain greedy." Most of all, she objected to the way she felt *Waiting to Exhale*—a movie based on a novel by a Black woman, directed by a Black man, and starring four Black women—was consequently judged within the greater culture to be exempt from criticism by Black and non-Black viewers and critics alike, as if the movie's mere existence was enough. "Had everyone involved in the production of this movie been white and male, its blatantly racist and sexist standpoints would not have gone unchallenged," she concludes.

McMillan, for her part, is frustrated by the idea that her specific characters were interpreted as stand-ins for Black men, Black women, or Black people as a whole. "Intelligent people know you don't write a book or film and say that this is how all people behave, that all Black men are poor lovers, or that all Black men love white women, all Black women burn up their husbands' stuff after they say they're leaving them. It's not true. Smart people should know this," says McMillan. "Not just myself, but other African-American writers—we're not trying to represent the entire Black race. We are trying to tell a story about the characters who inhabit the pages of our book. That's it."

both obsessive and hungry for more. Once again, the people in power failed to recognize the opportunity, let alone capitalize on it. While McMillan's subsequent novel *How Stella Got Her Groove Back* made it to the big screen in 1998—with McMillan and Bass co-screenwriting again and Angela Bassett in the lead—the success of *Waiting to Exhale* sparked only a minor trend of Hollywood studios seeking out material by and about Black people. *Waiting to Exhale*'s success, while undeniable, was not widely regarded by studio executives as a repeatable phenomenon, though filmmakers like *The Best Man*'s Malcolm D. Lee and *Brown Sugar*'s Rick Famuyiwa both mentioned it in the run-up to the releases of their own films. If the upper echelons of the Hollywood studios had been more diverse—or, at the very least, wise enough to recognize that they were leaving lots of money, as well as great stories, on the table—things might have been different. But even the movies that came after *Waiting to Exhale*, like Theodore Witcher's 1997 romantic dramedy *Love Jones*, were held to a different standard of success. When *Love Jones* grossed $12.7 million on a $10 million budget, Witcher says, his Hollywood opportunities instantly dried up. "White people get more bites of the apple. That's just true," he says. "You can fail three, four times and still have a career. But if you're Black, you really can only fail once."

Maybe the most enduring and poignant image of *Waiting to Exhale* comes at the very end of the movie, moments before the credits roll. Savannah, Bernadine, Robin, and Gloria have been through a lot, both separately and together, and they decide to ring in the New Year together as well. As Whitney Houston and CeCe Winans's "Count On Me" plays over the soundtrack, the women celebrate surviving another year together with a beach bonfire and a champagne toast, with fireworks exploding in the sky behind them. It's an unconventional ending for a romantic comedy, without a single romantic partnership on-screen—but a powerful image of love just the same.

That toast on the beach was the end of the story until 2010, when McMillan published a sequel novel titled *Getting to Happy*, which begins with a lengthy author's note. "For those of you who may have seen the movie that was based on my novel *Waiting to Exhale*, please be aware that it was indeed a movie," she writes. "As one of the screenwriters, I acknowledge that we strayed from the book, took many liberties and ended it the way a film should leave you: hopeful and somewhat pleased. Well, sorry to say that after those women left that campfire on New Year's Eve 1990, way out in the middle of nowhere surrounded by nothing but each other and a pitch-black desert in Phoenix, they found out that apparently exhaling is a relative state that is difficult to sustain."

Just a week after *Getting to Happy* was published, Fox purchased the rights and started developing a sequel that would have

GETTING TO TV

Getting to Happy was derailed by Houston's tragic death, but at the time of this publication, it looks like *Waiting to Exhale* might finally get its long-awaited sequel as a TV series on ABC. Sisters Attica and Tembi Locke are writing the new adaptation, with Anthony Hemingway slated to direct and Lee Daniels attached to produce. The series is described as focusing on "the next generation of our women through the lens of the tangled friendships and complicated lives of their daughters." "It deals primarily with the children," McMillan confirms. "And I'm sure that the three actresses who we still have will have *some* kind of roles."

continued the story of *Waiting to Exhale*, reuniting the film's cast, with Forest Whitaker returning to the director's chair. Those plans were derailed by the unexpected death of Whitney Houston in February of 2012. Though Elizabeth Gabler suggested that the movie would only be delayed—and even tentatively floated Oprah Winfrey as an actress who might be interested in taking over the role of Savannah—the *Getting to Happy* adaptation quietly disappeared altogether. For now, that story ends where audiences left it in 1995: with four women looking forward to the future on a beach, breaking out in great peals of joy and laughter not because of any of the men they'd met, but because of each other.

Bill Pullman, Patrick Dempsey, et al.

THE OTHER GUYS

In 2005, a little-seen rom-com called *The Baxter* put the spotlight on a rom-com archetype who, dating all the way back to Ralph Bellamy in 1940's *His Girl Friday*, has always stood just *outside* the spotlight: the Other Guy.

The official website for *The Baxter* has the most comprehensive description of the Other Guy that I've ever seen. "In every romantic comedy, there's always that scene at the end where the leading man barges through the chapel doors just as the leading lady is about to marry the Wrong Guy," it says. "The guy left at the altar. The wrong guy. That guy is called the Baxter. The Baxter is the kind of guy you 'settle' for because you can't be with the one you really love."

If you're nodding your head, it's because you've seen some version of this character in a sizable chunk of the rom-coms ever released. *The

Baxter, and "the Baxter," are probably named in honor of C.C. Baxter, the sad-sack hero played by Jack Lemmon in Billy Wilder's legendary 1960 rom-com *The Apartment* (though C.C. Baxter *does*, in the end, get the girl in that one).

The laziest way to make the audience feel okay about the Other Guy getting steamrolled by the romantic lead is by throwing in a scene that makes him irredeemably awful—like *The Wedding Singer*, in which it's revealed that Matthew Glave routinely cheats on Drew Barrymore, or *Wedding Crashers*, in which it's revealed that Bradley Cooper routinely cheats on Rachel McAdams. But even when audiences can be nearly certain that the actual star-crossed soul mates will end up together by the end of the movie, the best rom-coms at least attempt to make the Other Guy a compelling alternative, if not a true love, in his own right.

To that end, the best Other Guy of the '90s is Bill Pullman, playing Walter, in *Sleepless in Seattle*. Though Annie (Meg Ryan) doesn't even meet Sam (Tom Hanks) until the end of the movie, poor Walter is clearly doomed from the moment he appears on-screen. Though Annie says they're "madly in love," she doesn't even really seem to like him. She frowns at his cute little improvised song about dim sum, grimaces at him when he's not awake, and—though she says his name approximately eight hundred times throughout the movie—even the sound of it clearly irritates her.

Walter's big character trait is that he's horribly allergic to nuts, strawberries, whole wheat, and more or less everything else. His other big character trait is that he is an incredibly decent human being. Annie spends the entire movie obsessing over a guy she heard on the radio, and while she is not very good at hiding it, her obsession is facilitated by her best friend (Rosie O'Donnell), who also happens to be Walter's mutual colleague. But if Walter is suspicious about his extremely sketchy fiancée and her "reporting trip" to Seattle, he gives no sign of it. In a movie with the word "sleepless" in the title, he is the one character we know for a fact sleeps soundly every night. And when he finds Annie in the closet, essentially cheating on him with the radio she's holding, he makes a pretty funny *Clue* reference instead of getting mean about it.

Playing the guy who is doomed to get dumped for Tom Hanks was, perhaps unsurprisingly, not Bill Pullman's first choice. "Those were rough times," says Pullman. "But, you know, there were just a lot of stories at the time where the second male lead got the shaft. And I wasn't in a position, box-office-wise, to take the first male lead."

You could fill up a bingo card with the similarly lovable Other Guys that would come in the years that followed: Justin Chambers in *The Wedding Planner*, Keanu Reeves in *Something's Gotta Give*, Jordan Fisher in *To All the Boys: P.S. I Still Love You*. But there's one other that deserves extra attention: Patrick Dempsey, playing Andrew Hennings, in 2002's *Sweet Home Alabama*.

If *Sleepless in Seattle*'s Walter was a dork with endearing qualities, Andrew Hennings is—apart from his overbearing and omnipresent mother—a romantic figure so over-the-top dashing it beggars belief. He is a likely candidate to be President of the United States. He arranges an after-hours proposal at Tiffany's so Melanie (Reese Witherspoon) can choose any ring she likes. He is played by Patrick Dempsey, which means he is exactly as handsome as Patrick Dempsey. When Melanie inevitably dumps him at the altar to be with the man she actually loves, Andrew literally smiles. "So this is what this feels like," he says, proudly standing up to his mother, before gently kissing Melanie on the hand and exiting the movie. (Don't worry, the credits reveal he ended up marrying a Vanderbilt.)

What's striking about Patrick Dempsey's first round of Other Guy-dom is the moment in his career when it happened. Three years after *Sweet Home Alabama*, he debuted as Dr. Derek "McDreamy" Shepherd on ABC's *Grey's Anatomy*, catapulting him past the "second male lead who gets the shaft" territory lamented by Bill Pullman.

And what did Dempsey do with his reinvigorated star power? Booked a role in which he was the first male lead who got to win out over the other guy. *Made of Honor*, which came out in 2008 and is essentially a gender-flipped riff on *My Best Friend's Wedding*, casts Dempsey as a suave bachelor who realizes he's in love with his best friend (Michelle Monaghan) just as she gets engaged to an Other Guy.

The Other Guy, in this case, is played by fellow *Grey's Anatomy* star Kevin McKidd—and unlike *My Best Friend's Wedding*, the true love story turns out to be between Monaghan and Dempsey, who interrupts the wedding and successfully convinces Monaghan that they're soul mates. (In return, McKidd's character got to punch Dempsey in the face, but true redemption came eight years later when Dempsey returned to the Other Guy role in *Bridget Jones's Baby*—because come on, no one is going to get between Bridget Jones and Mark Darcy.)

What's conspicuous about these movies is how cleanly and swiftly the Other Guy is dispatched once the plot no longer needs him. Maybe he's a jerk, maybe he's a saint, maybe he gets a little tacked-on happy ending during the credits—but he was always more an obstacle than a character, so the movies aren't actually interested in what it must feel like to see someone you love find a happily-ever-after with someone who isn't you.

And that brings us back to *Sleepless in Seattle*. *Sleepless in Seattle* does not actually show the moment when Annie confesses to Walter and his heart presumably breaks into a million pieces, but by the time the movie cuts back, he is being shockingly kind about the whole thing. "Look, Annie, I love you. But let's leave that out of this," he says. "I don't want to be someone that you're settling for. I don't want to be someone that *anyone* settles for. Marriage is hard enough without bringing such low expectations into it, isn't it?" Annie gives the ring back and asks if he's okay, but precisely twenty-seven seconds later, she tells Walter she has to run off to the Empire State Building, where the windows have been illuminated with a giant red heart, so she can be with the *actual* man of her dreams.

Sleepless in Seattle immediately cuts to the streets of Manhattan, and the rest of the movie is Annie and Sam's (unforgettably dreamy) meeting on top of the Empire State Building. But the next time you watch the ending of *Sleepless in Seattle*, spare a thought for Walter, finishing that bottle of Dom Perignon alone on Valentine's Day as he stares at that big heart on that big skyscraper.

(And don't feel *too* bad for the guy, because he got together with Sandra Bullock in *While You Were Sleeping* like two years later.)

"I'm the bad guy."

—JULIANNE POTTER, *MY BEST FRIEND'S WEDDING*

CHAPTER 5

MY BEST FRIEND'S WEDDING

(And the Deconstruction of America's Greatest Rom-Com Heroine)

FROM ITS FIRST SCENE, 1997'S *MY BEST FRIEND'S WEDDING* PRIMES THE audience for the kind of rom-com they've seen before: the kind of movie in which a plucky, lovable heroine overcomes every obstacle in her path to live happily ever after with the man she loves. Julianne (Julia Roberts)—who has the very rom-com job of newspaper food critic—tells her editor and friend George (Rupert Everett) the story of her brief, aborted love affair with Michael. In Julianne's telling, Michael was a short-lived college fling who was madly in love with her. Though she broke Michael's heart, she says, she meant so much to him that he insisted on remaining best friends anyway. In the years since, the friends have supported each other through everything: "losing jobs, losing parents, losing lovers." At one point, she says, Michael drunkenly suggested a pact: If neither of them were married by the time they were twenty-eight, they'd settle down together. Julianne is just a few weeks away from her twenty-eighth birthday. How old is Michael now? George wants to know. She smiles. "Twenty-eight."

So Julianne is shocked and disappointed when Michael calls her not to make good on their old pact, but to tell Julianne she needs to come to Chicago, because he's getting married to someone else and needs her by his side. "I've never felt this way about anybody, and she's all wrong for me," he says, as Julianne—in full-on klutzy rom-com heroine mode—literally tumbles to the ground at the news.

If you paused the movie right there, the rom-com lovers in the audience might assume they could fill in the rest of the movie in their heads. Julianne heads to Chicago to meet Michael's fiancée, who turns out to be shallow or mean or some other version of awful. As Julianne silently, nobly pines for Michael from afar, the old college spark between them is rekindled. After a series of hijinks, and at least one big speech, Michael realizes he's marrying the wrong woman, dumps his horrible fiancée at the altar, and delivers his vows to Julianne, the Best Woman, instead. After all . . . what kind of rom-com would it be if Julia Roberts didn't get the guy?

My Best Friend's Wedding came at a crossroads in Julia Roberts's life and career. It had been six years since she broke out in *Pretty Woman*. Her attempts to define herself beyond the rom-com genre, with performances in movies like the historical biopic *Michael Collins* and the gothic horror drama *Mary Reilly*, had resulted in dismissive (and sometimes straight-up hostile) reviews. At the same time, riskier genre riffs like the rom-com/crime thriller *I Love Trouble* and the sudsy romantic dramedy *Something to Talk About* had been indifferently received by both critics and audiences. And Roberts's love life had become daily tabloid fodder, shifting fans' attention away from her performances and toward the drama of her personal life. Following her 1991 split from Kiefer Sutherland just three days before their wedding, and her 1995 divorce from

JULIA'S LESS-LOVED LOVE STORIES

In the years between *Pretty Woman* and *My Best Friend's Wedding*, Julia Roberts did star in a few romantic comedies, including Charles Shyer's *I Love Trouble*, a movie that only comes up today in the context of how much Roberts and Nick Nolte hated each other. (Roberts called him "completely disgusting"; in a separate interview, he sniped back, "She's not a nice person. Everyone knows that.") Soon after came Lasse Hallström's *Something to Talk About*, playing a woman whose life is turned upside down when she learns Dennis Quaid is cheating on her, and Woody Allen's *Everyone Says I Love You*, an odd little musical in which Allen cast her as his love interest.

But the most head-turning project from this era was the one Roberts *didn't* end up making. In 1993, she was slated to star in a romantic comedy called *Shakespeare in Love*, which was so close to shooting that sets and costumes were already being created. But when Roberts's intended costar, Daniel Day-Lewis, decided to pass on the project (amid rumors they were dating), she exited as well. It wasn't until five years later that *Shakespeare in Love* finally arrived on the big screen, with Gwyneth Paltrow and Joseph Fiennes in the lead roles. Paltrow took home an Oscar for Best Actress, and *Shakespeare in Love* won Best Picture—the first rom-com since *Annie Hall* to do so. "Julia Roberts was going to do it for a long time, and then that version fell apart," reflected Paltrow on the movie's twentieth anniversary. "It ended up in Miramax, and I was the first person they offered it to." (That is, for the record, Paltrow's version of the story; for years, rumors have swirled in Hollywood that she swiped the role from former friend Winona Ryder after discovering the script at Ryder's house, though Paltrow told Howard Stern in 2015 she would "swear on a Bible" that the story was false.)

country singer Lyle Lovett—which came less than two years after their wedding—the paparazzi had recognized that *any* Roberts gossip, no matter how pointless, was guaranteed to sell issues. Which is how, by the late 1990s, America ended up with tabloids breathlessly chronicling her every move, no matter how banal. (One representative example from the era helpfully revealed that Roberts had purchased three bracelets bearing the words "hot," "fat," and "crazy" on a shopping trip in lower Manhattan.)

It was clear that something needed to change—and from a purely mercenary perspective, Roberts's smartest move was a tactical retreat to the genre that made her a superstar in the first place. And so no one was particularly surprised when TriStar Pictures announced Roberts's next starring role in *My Best Friend's Wedding*, playing a restaurant critic who schemes to win the heart of her best friend (Dermot Mulroney) away from his new fiancée (Cameron Diaz) before his wedding day.

The title, the premise, and the star of *My Best Friend's Wedding* seemed to herald a modern throwback to the classic screwball comedy, in which witty dialogue, farcical situations, and the machinations of a strong-willed woman typically lead to a happily-ever-after with the male lead. But as the narrative unfolds, *My Best Friend's Wedding* gradually reveals itself as something more like a challenge to audiences: How much *do* you like Julia Roberts, anyway?

My Best Friend's Wedding was written on spec by Ronald Bass, who had spent the years since the release of *Waiting to Exhale* as the creator of several TV shows, including a series based on his film *Dangerous Minds*. For his return to film—and with a script he had no idea if anyone would actually buy—Bass sat down and mapped out, in his mind, exactly what he was trying to accomplish with *My Best Friend's Wedding* in advance. "I had two main goals going into it," he says. "One: Julia didn't get the guy. Two: The best-looking, smartest, most loyal, most compassionate, most caring person in the movie was gay."

THE G.B.F.

Ron Bass wanted to write a movie in which the best and most admirable character was a gay man, and by any metric, he succeeded with *My Best Friend's Wedding*. When the dailies arrived after Hogan shot a scene with Roberts and Everett in a taxicab, Sony executives personally called to express their enthusiasm for the chemistry between the two characters. According to director P. J. Hogan, the only consistent thing about the test screenings was that Rupert Everett scored very, very high.

Following the success of the movie, Everett's character also proved influential. While *My Best Friend's Wedding* didn't create the trope of a rom-com heroine having a gay best friend—*The Advocate* cites Charles Grodin's character in 1984's *The Woman in Red*—it's certainly one of the earliest and most prominent examples. "I don't know why *Will & Grace* don't give us royalties. Since then, *everybody's* best friend is a fabulous gay guy," says Bass. By 2013, the trope had become so prevalent that a teen comedy was simply titled *G.B.F.*, with the assumption that audiences would understand what the acronym meant.

Rupert Everett himself has complicated feelings about the rom-com trope he helped to inspire, and the way that *My Best Friend's Wedding* ultimately left him typecast in a different direction. "It was a great opportunity, but the difficult thing was I wasn't going to be able to graduate to another kind of role. I think that's a role that you can only be exciting in a couple of times, otherwise it becomes, *Oh, that again*. You can't just flog an idea to death like that," says Everett.

The character Bass is describing is Julianne's editor and friend George—who is indeed the best-looking, smartest, most loyal, most compassionate, and most caring person in the film, as well as a gay man. Though the Gay Best Friend is a rom-com stereotype of its own today, with its own problems worth unpacking— George, likable as he is, is essentially just a device in Julianne's story, with no real arc of his own—it was still relatively rare to see *any* gay character in a major studio film in 1997 (though *Four Weddings and a Funeral* had planted an important flag with Gareth and Matthew a few years earlier). "I don't want to say 'some of my best friends are gay,' but a lot of my friends *are*," says Bass. "And I have never seen any of them depicted on screen. Gay people were always depicted as very effeminate, or very comedic, or their sexuality became so frightening to people."

Once the script for *My Best Friend's Wedding* was completed, Bass sent it to his agent, who informed a network of producers that a new Ron Bass spec would be going up for auction. Bass had planned in advance not to formally start shopping the script around until he returned from a trip in Hong Kong, but somehow—he swears he still doesn't know how—the script leaked on his way to the airport. Bass estimates that about fifty people received the script; in the end, there were two offers. The first came from TriStar, which successfully bought the movie as a Julia Roberts vehicle, with Jerry Zucker—the *Airplane!* director who had more recently established his Hollywood romance bona fides with *Ghost* and *First Knight*—then attached to direct. The other, ultimately unsuccessful offer had come from Warner Bros., who thought *My Best Friend's Wedding* would be an ideal fit for Sandra Bullock. The actresses were once again up for the same role—as they would be both before and after this— and this time, Roberts booked it. But Bass thinks either version would have worked. "It would have been fabulous. And completely different," he says.

With a hot script and Roberts already lined up to star, the next challenge was finding the right director for the material after Zucker bowed out (though he stayed on as a producer). Enter P. J. Hogan, an Australian director who had broken out in 1994 with *Muriel's Wedding*, a passion project he'd spent five years drumming up financing to make, which became an unexpected hit when it was picked up for distribution by Miramax, a distributor on a hot streak in the '90s after handling indie hits like *Pulp Fiction* and *Clerks*. Hollywood, sniffing money and talent in the water after *Muriel's Wedding*, came calling—though it wasn't quite clear where Hogan would go next after *Muriel's Wedding*, an offbeat dramedy that pointedly climaxes with its wedding-obsessed protagonist asking for a divorce.

My Best Friend's Wedding didn't just need the right star—it needed a filmmaker who understood how to make audiences care about a character whose flaws were *actual* flaws, and not just the cute "flaws" screenwriters designed to make a glamorous actor seem more down-to-earth and approachable. Hogan was the right director for the job. "The main note [while developing and producing] *Muriel's Wedding* was, 'The main character's not sympathetic. We hate her,'" says Hogan. "And I was like, 'Well . . . *I* love her.'" Julia Roberts had been a fan of *Muriel's Wedding*, and she was convinced Hogan, who had made audiences across the world care for Muriel Heslop, had the sensibility to walk the very specific tightrope *My Best Friend's Wedding* would require.

When Hogan sat down to read the script, he discovered, to his surprise, that *My Best Friend's Wedding* was a closer cousin to *Muriel's Wedding* than he had expected. "What really surprised me was that it wasn't really very romantic," he says. "In fact, my experience of reading the screenplay was, 'Wow, *I'm* not sure I like her very much.' And usually in romantic comedies, everything the main character does in order to win love and to find happiness is totally justified. Even if it's kind of awful. What Meg Ryan does to Bill Pullman in *Sleepless in Seattle* is kind of awful. And as I was reading it, I was thinking, *God, it's got that damn romantic comedy problem. She's kind of awful.* And I got to the end, and she *didn't* get the guy. And I thought, *Oh, my God, that's the point. This takes the form and smashes it on the floor.* Most romantic comedies are about how all's fair in love and war, which is something I have never really believed in. And this was a screenplay about how all is *not* fair in love and war. It was a romantic comedy that wasn't very romantic."

Hogan knew what *My Best Friend's Wedding* could be, but the question was: Did Julia Roberts have the same vision? In theory, the director is in charge on a movie set—but when a studio is building an entire movie around an A-lister, that star has tremendous power over the production, and Roberts's deal allowed for a significant amount of creative oversight. Hogan agreed to meet with Roberts so he could figure out whether she saw *My Best Friend's Wedding* the same way he did: as a trenchant deconstruction of the same genre on which Roberts had quite literally built her own superstardom. "I thought, *Julia has to make a death-defying leap*," Hogan says. "She has to bring the audience along with her, with the character, and somehow still have them not hating her by the end." He had been a fan of Roberts from afar, but meeting her—much like Garry Marshall, Richard Gere, and seemingly everyone else who came into her orbit—left him awed at her sheer charisma in person. "I thought, immediately, *This will work. I'll go with this actress anywhere*," Hogan says. At the same time, she not only shared his vision for a rom-com as subversive as he wanted to make—she took it further than he'd planned. "Julia was absolutely committed to Julianne's dark side—which no one, I think, had allowed her to do in her previous [romantic comedies]," says Hogan. "She was so committed to the dark side that I was a little bit worried."

The next step was finding the right actor to play Michael, the best friend who is so incredible that he can send someone as radiant as Julia Roberts off the deep end. Actors in contention included Matthew McConaughey, Edward Burns, and Matthew Perry, whose career had exploded after the 1994 premiere of *Friends*, and who briefly dated Julia Roberts around that time. (As for why Perry didn't land the role: "I think it may have just been I didn't want them to break up while shooting," says Hogan.)

But if not for one truly disastrous table read, *My Best Friend's Wedding* could have been a very different movie, because Hogan had an actor he thought would be *perfect* for Michael in the back of his mind all along. "My first choice was actually Russell Crowe," says Hogan, whose wife, the writer/director Jocelyn Moorhouse, had worked with Crowe on 1991's *Proof.* "Russell was, I thought, probably the most amazing actor I had ever encountered. I kind of knew Russell was going to be a really big star."

There was just one big hurdle ahead: getting Julia Roberts to sign off on Crowe. Hogan was worried. "Julia had casting approval. No one was getting in this movie if Julia didn't approve," says Hogan.

Still, Hogan was convinced Crowe was the actor for the job, so he invited him to a table read opposite Roberts and hoped sparks would fly. "I don't know what went wrong," says Hogan. "It was one of the worst table reads I've ever experienced. Russell was seated opposite Julia. He gripped that script, and he stared at that script, and he didn't look at her *once*. He read every line in a monotone. At one point, Julia was literally leaning over the table, staring, like, *inches* from Russell's face, trying to make eye contact. And he wouldn't look at her. At the end of the reading, Russell came up to me and said, 'I thought that went pretty well.' And then I *knew*: Russell was not going to be in *My Best Friend's Wedding*."

Meanwhile, the creative team behind *My Best Friend's Wedding* was in a similarly far-ranging hunt for an actress to play Kimmy, Michael's fiancée. "Kimmy was a really important part, because you're up against Julia Roberts, who the audience expects to get the guy at the end," says Hogan. "If Julia's character wipes the floor with Kimmy, the film isn't going to work. Julia is a movie star, and movie stars don't usually share the screen with other movie stars. But whoever plays Kimmy has to be a movie star as well."

Still, Julia Roberts was concerned that an actress who was *too* charismatic—and who Michael ultimately chooses over Julianne—might steal the movie from her altogether. Many, many young actresses auditioned, including Drew Barrymore, Calista Flockhart, and Reese Witherspoon. In the end, Hogan settled on model-turned-actress Cameron Diaz, who had broken out in *The Mask* a few years earlier but was still one year away from the Farrelly Brothers' *There's Something About Mary* (see chapter 6), which would propel her to superstardom. "There was something about Cameron's sunniness that implied strength," Hogan says. Julia Roberts disagreed, preferring Drew Barrymore for Kimmy—and with casting approval, she could have booted Diaz out of consideration altogether. Hogan recalls "a lot of negotiation" that ended in a modest compromise: Diaz could stay if Hogan would cast Dermot Mulroney, whom Roberts "adored," as Michael.

With the core love triangle in place, there was one last major role to fill: George, the "best-looking, smartest, most loyal, most compassionate, most caring" character in Bass's original draft. In

the final cut, George—who, despite the movie's title, is *clearly* Julianne's actual best friend—practically runs away with the entire
movie, delivering the biggest laughs and anchoring the gorgeous,
bittersweet ending. But during casting, Hogan and Bass were still
working on the rewrite; the original draft, in which George plays
a smaller role, attracted virtually no attention from the actors they
had originally targeted. "No name actor wanted that part," says
Hogan. "If memory serves, Julia wanted Benicio del Toro. A brilliant actor, but . . . not known for his comedy."

Then again, neither was Rupert Everett, a journeyman British
actor who had mainly appeared in historical dramas like *Dance
with a Stranger* and *The Madness of King George*. "Basically, Rupert
played cads who got killed in the end," says Hogan. "So when Rupert's agent said, 'This part is for Rupert Everett,' I said, 'Well . . .
I don't think so.' And the agent was really, really ballsy about it
and said, 'No, I know Rupert. Rupert *is* this part.'" Hogan agreed
to a meeting with Everett and walked away convinced that the
droll, breezy, and witty actor might actually be what *My Best
Friend's Wedding* needed (though it still took a few screen tests before Everett formally won the role). Bass and Hogan's rewrite of
the original spec script—which was already intended to beef up
George's role in the story—was done with Everett's voice in mind.
The character's nationality was even changed from American to
British to accommodate him.

The new, larger role for George was just one of several ideas
Hogan had suggested to punch up the original script. There was
just one problem: Bass had a clause in his contract at the time that
said no one could rewrite his scripts. "P. J. sat in my living room
and he said, 'How are we going to get around this, that I can't
rewrite you?'" says Bass. "And I said, 'We're going to ignore it.
You and I *both* have to be satisfied with everything that happens.'"

FRIENDS AND FRENEMIES

In a classic case of art, however briefly, imitating life, Julia Roberts and Rupert Everett became inseparable friends during the filming of *My Best Friend's Wedding*. From the first day of shooting, Everett says, "it was clear that Julia and I had a strange on-screen chemistry. Just as in real life you click with someone for no apparent reason, similarly on screen sometimes a vivid relationship effortlessly materializes."

There are perks to hanging out with a star as big as Roberts. Everett recalls a charmed experience that included trips in a limo, with cocktails waiting, to the Sony jet, which would take them to New York City for the weekend. "A star never really had to touch the ground," he says.

Everett also had a front-row seat to Roberts's uneasy relationship with Cameron Diaz, whom he calls "the antithesis of Julia," and who Roberts clearly viewed as actual competition in Hollywood's upper echelons of actresses. Everett recalls Roberts asking, "Why can't Cameron relax around me?" though he believed it was Julia who couldn't relax around Cameron. "If the girls didn't hit it off, so what?" says Everett. "The scenes between them were charged with the dangerous energy money can't buy, when art flirts with life."

The first rewrite session did not go entirely smoothly, due in large part to the presence of the Ronettes—Bass's all-female group of young screenwriting consultants. "I had been warned about The Ronettes, but I thought it was sort of an urban myth," says Hogan. "But I arrived to work with Ron, and there was Ron in the middle of a big circle that reminded me of like a group therapy session. And they were all young women. And he would have an idea, and The Ronettes would pitch where the story could go now, or what could happen here. With *My Best Friend's Wedding*, I think that was a really great way to work for Ron, because he was certainly not lacking for the female perspective on that screenplay."

But what worked for Ron Bass didn't work for P. J. Hogan, who arrived to that first meeting wholly unprepared for the audience that would be picking apart his every idea. "I sat down, and all The Ronettes took out their notepads, and Ron said, 'Shall we discuss the script and your ideas to improve it?'" says Hogan. "And I froze. It was like being auditioned. And I just said, 'Ron, I can't work this way, I'm sorry. I'm sorry to everybody in the room, but I really can't do this. Would you mind, Ron, if The Ronettes left and I just worked with you?' And Ron was a little upset with me. He thought it was very disrespectful to The Ronettes. Which, I suppose, it was."

Bass and Hogan's screenwriting partnership faced another test early when Hogan came in with a concept for a seafood restaurant sing-along to "I Say a Little Prayer," a Burt Bacharach and Hal David composition that was originally performed by Dionne Warwick. George—now pretending to be Julianne's fiancé—tells an elaborate lie about their courtship that crescendos in the entire restaurant joining in, including servers wearing little red lobster claws on their hands. It is by far the most cartoonish scene in the movie, and Bass—whose script was in the slightly heightened mode of any good rom-com, but otherwise essentially realistic— was baffled by the decision to inject something so wacky into the movie. "I said, 'You realize, don't you, this is a six-minute scene where they're just fucking singing a song?'" says Bass. "He said, 'Yeah. I wish it was ten.'"

As ridiculous as the scene seemed on its face, Hogan also had a battle-tested defense for it. *Muriel's Wedding* had relied heavily on the music of ABBA to illuminate the inner life of its awkward main character, and Hogan had seen firsthand how much it helped audiences slip into her world. As Hogan saw it, *My Best Friend's Wedding* wouldn't just be a romantic comedy. It would be a stealth *musical*—albeit one where the musical numbers would be parceled out sparingly enough that audiences wouldn't even consciously notice it. That's the reason why *My Best Friend's Wedding* opens with a dreamy, candy-colored rendition of "Wishin' and Hopin'"; or why a key emotional scene at Kimmy and Michael's wedding is scored with three goofballs harmonizing "Annie's Song" after sucking from a helium tank; and why the first part of the movie pivots around Kimmy's endearingly awful performance of "I Just Don't Know What to Do with Myself" at a karaoke bar.

Hogan and Roberts ended up dueling over the climax to that all-important karaoke scene, in what turned out to be a microcosm of the tonal tug-of-war at the heart of *My Best Friend's Wedding*. In the scene, Julianne has set Kimmy up to embarrass herself, secretly knowing that she can't carry a tune. She hopes that Michael will be mortified and repulsed at his fiancée's awkwardness. But the plan backfires when Kimmy refuses to be shamed, gamely sticking it out and belting out the final verses to an appreciative crowd while Michael looks on adoringly.

On the day the scene was shot, the big question was how *Julianne* would react to Kimmy's performance, and Hogan and Roberts found themselves at odds. Hogan wanted Julianne to admit that she'd lost the round and clap along with the rest of the crowd. Roberts felt that, even in defeat, Julianne wouldn't give Kimmy an inch. "She did not want to do it," Hogan says. "She said, 'No. There's no way. I lost. I'm not clapping for her. I hate her.' And I said, 'Julia, please, just give me one take where you clap. We've got to have some sort of light here.' And Julia begrudgingly did it, but said, 'I'm only doing it once.' And of course she and I knew that would be the take I'd use." Sure enough, that's the take that made the movie.

Debates like this popped up throughout the production of *My Best Friend's Wedding*, with the tone of the entire movie itself hanging in the balance. While *My Best Friend's Wedding* generally plays it fairly light—particularly in the extended interlude where George arrives in Chicago and pretends to be Julianne's fiancé—there are also moments of great discomfort that can be blamed squarely on Julianne. In most romantic comedies, these transgressions are forgiven, or at least swept under the rug, as necessary evils on the path to true love. It may be horrible when Charles spurns Henrietta at the altar in *Four Weddings and a Funeral*, but the film (and the audience) forgives him just minutes later, when Carrie shows up at his door and justifies the heartbreak that led to that point. *My Best Friend's Wedding* has Julianne do similarly awful things to blameless people, but without the comforting assurances that it'll all be worth it when Michael realizes they should have been together all along. When Julianne goads Kimmy into offering Michael a job opportunity Julianne knows he'll hate, or ghostwrites an email designed to create a rift between Michael and Kimmy's father, *My Best Friend's Wedding* is dancing right on the edge of making its heroine completely irredeemable.

The uneasy questions that were laced into the movie—just how bad *is* Julianne? and what consequences should she face for it?—sparked feverish debate about the movie's ending from the very beginning. No one on the creative team behind *My Best Friend's Wedding* believed that Julianne should successfully win Michael's heart away from Kimmy; that was, after all, why Bass had written this story in the first place. But if not Michael, couldn't Julianne meet *somebody*? The studio was concerned. "They didn't say she should get the guy, but there was very friendly pressure for her to get *a* guy," says Hogan. "And, you know, the argument wasn't completely illogical. She's at a wedding. People meet people at weddings."

The original ending for *My Best Friend's Wedding* finds Julianne sitting alone at Michael and Kimmy's wedding, sadder and wiser as she lets the man she loves slip away. She goes outside to call George. Suddenly, a devastatingly handsome single man, played by John Corbett, approaches. "Hi, I'm Andy Connelly. We haven't met," he says. And while Julianne (quite reasonably) responds that she's on a phone call and he's being rude, she decides to go dance with him after some prodding from George, delivering the only bad advice he's given in the entire movie. "If I was there, you wouldn't miss one dance," George sighs. "But I'm not."

As Julianne twirls with Andy Connelly on the dance floor, giggling joyfully, the implication is unmistakable: Julianne is being rewarded, via the scales of cosmic justice themselves, for giving up on her scheme at literally the last possible moment. Test audiences—who are often dismissed, fairly or not, for pushing movies into safer and blander directions—absolutely despised this mealy-mouthed compromise of an ending. Bass witnessed it firsthand at an early test screening in Arizona. "The air in the room just disappeared," says Bass. "The whole point of the movie was that she would survive not getting the guy. They hated that *so much*. That's exactly what they didn't want." Hogan was similarly horrified. "I had been really worried that the audience would turn on the character—and in that first preview, the audience *did* turn on the character," he says. "In a big way. They wanted to tear the film off the screen." Sony Pictures executive John Calley stalked up to Bass and delivered an ultimatum: "Fix this. You've got until tomorrow at 2 o'clock."

Rattled, both Bass and Hogan left the screening and tried to figure out what, if anything, could save *My Best Friend's Wedding* without compromising everything they liked about it in the first place. Hogan was flummoxed, and comments from a focus group held immediately after the screening didn't offer much useful criticism. One woman suggested that Julianne deserved to be alone forever. A man said that if either of his two daughters acted like Julianne had acted, he'd kick them out of his house.

In the middle of this panic it was Jerry Zucker—the producer once intended for the director's chair—who had the answer: While the test scores were daunting, *My Best Friend's Wedding* was actually a lot closer to the movie it needed to be than it might seem. From his seat, he observed that the audience had actually enjoyed most of the movie. It was only near the end—when Kimmy had instantly forgiven Julianne for her many transgressions, and when Julianne had subsequently been rewarded with a charming stranger on the dance floor—that they turned on *My Best Friend's Wedding* altogether.

This romantic comedy, which had been so carefully engineered to interrogate its heroine, had ultimately gone too easy on her. A precise series of reshoots were conceived and shot to fix that problem. First came the climactic confrontation between Julianne and Kimmy at Comiskey Park, which was tweaked so Kimmy would explicitly call out Julianne's awful behavior instead of forgiving her right away. "You kissed him! At my parents' house! On my wedding day!" she yells. And when Julianne tries to reply, she cuts her off: "Shut up. Now: I love this man, and there is no way I'm gonna give him up to some two-faced, big-haired food critic."

The second, most essential fix came down to the ending, which had a very particular needle to thread. No one wanted to watch a Julia Roberts rom-com with Julia Roberts sitting alone and miserable at the end. But a deus ex machina with John Corbett's smiling face hadn't worked either. Wasn't there some way *My Best Friend's Wedding* could land between those two poles? How about in the form of the movie's best-loved character, who was otherwise tragically absent from its closing scenes?

My Best Friend's Wedding's actual ending is as sublime as that of any romantic comedy of the era. As Julianne sits alone at the wedding, her cell phone rings. It's George, of course, checking in on his friend one last time. "I can just picture you there, sitting alone at your table in your lavender gown," he says. "Did I tell you my gown was lavender?" she replies.

As "I Say a Little Prayer" plays over the soundtrack, George delivers his big speech, teasing Julianne about a mystery man before he's revealed to have shown up in person to sweep her off to the dance floor. "Although you quite correctly sense that he is gay—like most devastatingly handsome single men of his age are—you think, *What the hell. Life goes on*," he says. "Maybe there won't be marriage. Maybe there won't be sex. But by God, there'll be dancing."

To Ron Bass, this late-in-the-game rewrite had the added bonus of bringing *My Best Friend's Wedding* closer to the kind of movie he had wanted to make all along. "The point of the movie is that the person you love the most in your life doesn't have to be the person you're sleeping with," says Bass. "It might be your child. It might be your parent. It might be your colleague at work. It might be your best social friend. It's the person who you love. And it's not a crime to say that *that* love was the most important thing to her."

My Best Friend's Wedding opened on June 20, 1997. It was a date that was widely regarded around Hollywood as a sign that the studio had no faith in the movie, because it was opposite what was sure to be one of the biggest blockbusters of the summer:

HERE COMES THE GROOM

Like so many hit romantic comedies of the era, the success and longevity of *My Best Friend's Wedding* has led to numerous efforts to continue the story. In 2015, Ron Bass cowrote a sequel pilot for ABC, which would have kicked off a TV show centered on Julianne and George—now roommates as well as colleagues—in the run-up to George's wedding. The network ultimately passed, but Bass still has plenty of ideas for a sequel movie: "It could still be George's wedding. Or Michael and Kimmy's marriage could be falling apart all these years later, and Jules puts it back together. Or it could be a really difficult romance for *Jules*, that seems to be with the wrong guy."

Batman & Robin, which featured George Clooney's first (and last) performance as the Caped Crusader. "Everybody told us we were fucked," says Hogan. Even Roberts's agent suggested she should spend the summer promoting her other movie, the action-thriller *Conspiracy Theory*, which wasn't due to hit theaters until August.

Though *Batman & Robin* premiered on top that first weekend, as everyone had predicted, it collapsed after some brutal word-of-mouth reviews by its second. Meanwhile, *My Best Friend's Wedding* endured, drawing audiences throughout the entire summer. By the time *Conspiracy Theory* hit theaters that August, *My Best Friend's Wedding* had already grossed well over $100 million, becoming Roberts's biggest hit at the U.S. box office since *Pretty Woman*.

While Roberts never made a rom-com quite as unconventional again, she had proved that there was an appetite for romantic comedies that challenged a series of tropes that were, by 1997, already beginning to feel a little entrenched. There are few more reliable premises for a romantic comedy than a love triangle, but Roberts had harnessed her own star power, and her status as a rom-com heroine, to make one in which the resolution could be genuinely surprising to the audience. "I felt like Julia never got her due from *My Best Friend's Wedding*," says Hogan. "You know, that's the great thing about Julia. She wanted to mess with her image. She *really* wanted to. She just believed that somebody in love is capable of doing terrible things. And if somebody said, 'You're messing with the cash cow here' . . . Julia never cared about that." If you could make a rom-com where Julia Roberts doesn't get the man of her dreams and end up with a blockbuster-sized hit . . . well, what other kinds of romantic comedies might audiences be interested in seeing?

DESTINATION WEDDINGS

For a movie that is so firmly rooted in Chicago, *My Best Friend's Wedding* has proven surprisingly easy to adapt for other languages and cultures. *My Best Friend's Wedding* fans who want to see the story filtered through a non-Hollywood lens can check out 2016's *Wo zui hao peng you de hun li*, a Chinese-language remake set in London, or 2019's *La Boda de Mi Mejor Amigo*, a Spanish-language remake set in Mexico City.

The team behind the original movie doesn't have any actual creative involvement in the remakes, but they're not complaining: "We keep getting these little pieces of paper, Jerry Zucker and I, for $100,000 each," says Ron Bass.

Judy Greer

THE BEST BEST FRIEND

At a roundtable interview in 2017, Kathryn Hahn casually tossed off a movie pitch that's so good it's silly she didn't get a green light on the spot. "Judy Greer and I both had been playing best friends at the same time, always neck and neck for the same best-friend parts," said Hahn. "My husband was like, 'You guys should do, like, a *Rosencrantz and Guildenstern*–type movie where it's the best friends, and every so often you see Kate Hudson running around.'"

Hahn—whose roster of rom-coms (take a deep breath) includes *How to Lose a Guy in 10 Days*, *Win a Date with Tad Hamilton!*, *A Lot Like Love*, *The Holiday*, and *How Do You Know*—is no slouch in the genre. But she had also chosen her hypothetical costar well. The Best Friend is a vital but perennially underappreciated aspect of the romantic comedy: occasionally wise, typically quirky, and always supportive of the protagonist who needs someone to lean on as they navigate the course of true love. Who else but Carrie Fisher would be there to answer the phone, no questions asked, in the middle of the night? Who else but Rupert Everett would pose as your boyfriend *and* lead a restaurant in a sing-along version of "I Say a Little Prayer"? Who else but Kathryn Hahn would pose as a couples counselor just to help Kate Hudson mess with Matthew McConaughey?

But as far as I'm concerned, one thing is undisputable: There is a *best*

best friend, and her name is Judy Greer. No modern actress has played the best friend as many times, with as much variety and verve, as Greer, whose own list of rom-coms includes (take an even deeper breath) *Kissing a Fool*, *What Women Want*, *The Wedding Planner*, *27 Dresses*, *Love & Other Drugs*, *Playing for Keeps*, and the beloved, rom-com-adjacent *13 Going on 30*.

How do you end up specializing in being not-the-lead in twenty-five years' worth of romantic comedies? It starts with the type of roles targeted by young actors hungry to get started: whatever they can get. "I was going in for leading roles, but I would just audition for literally anything that they would let me come in for. I did not give a shit," Greer says. After making her film debut in *Kissing a Fool*, Greer quickly found a niche in rom-coms. She auditioned for every female role in *What Women Want* (except for the lead played by Helen Hunt) before she was finally cast as Erin, the shy office worker who protagonist Nick Marshall discovers is contemplating suicide. (For the record, Greer had been hoping to land the part of Nick's old fling Lola, who was ultimately played by Marisa Tomei.)

What Women Want was also the movie where Greer learned the perils that can come with a supporting role in a big Hollywood rom-com. Director Nancy Meyers "would do as many takes as it took to get it looking exactly perfect," recalls Greer. "I was like, *You guys know I'm not a stuntperson, right?* I'm rolling down the stairs every single time we do this scene, and every time I trip on the stairs and fall, it hurts. But I'm young, and it's early in my career, and I'm just so scared to speak up."

Greer filmed *What Women Want* at the same time as she filmed her role in *The Wedding Planner*. Penny, Greer's character in *The Wedding Planner*, was originally scripted as a "plump, middle-aged British woman," but Greer happened to be the first person who auditioned, and eventually landed the role. "They said, you know, 'We couldn't find anyone better than you—and trust me, we looked. We kept trying,'" she says. "They just got stuck with me." When both *What Women Want* and *The Wedding Plan-*

ner turned out to be hits, Greer's career in rom-coms started to look like a self-fulfilling prophecy. "There's just some that just fucking *hit*, man, and I was in a couple of them," she says.

And if she wasn't going to be the lead, there was always demand for a funny supporting actress to play the best friend or assistant or rival. "You sort of wish to be the princess, but—but if you can't be, then you can be the lady-in-waiting," she says. "I just personally never thought of myself as the fairy princess, so I always loved the best friend. The best friend has more fun and more freedom. Why wouldn't you want that? Why wouldn't you choose that? But, you know, I guess there's a lot of girls out there who want to be the princess."

Given her experience, it's no surprise that Greer is both extremely lucid and extremely specific about the unique requirements of being a supporting actor in a rom-com. "I've always felt like one of the sad roles of the supporting characters is exposition," she says. "When you're playing them a lot, you get really good at it. And then also, sometimes, you get really resentful. Why do I have to be the one to say, you know, *'But you just turned 30!'* or *'But you just repainted your bedroom!'* or *'But your brother lives in Denver!'* I don't have to tell *my* friends things they already know. Why do I have to say that? That feels like lazy writing to me." As Greer sees it, it's her job to make this kind of banal dialogue sound as interesting as possible; her bag of tricks, she confides, includes delivering a line with a mouthful of food.

There's also the extremely thankless job of being the avatar for product placement—an easy way to squeeze some extra profit out of a movie that is often judged to be beneath the lead actors. In that case, it falls to a supporting actor to fulfill the obligation—a task that fell to Greer in Brandon Camp's 2009 romance *Love Happens*. "In one scene, I had to walk into the flower shop holding a can of Sierra Mist," she says. "And I was like, 'Why? I don't want to carry this can of Sierra Mist.' And they were like, 'You have to. They're giving us money for the movie.' And I'm looking over at Jennifer Aniston like, 'Why do *I* have to? Why can't she do it?' And they said, 'Because she has the deal with Smart Water, and she can't carry anything in her hands but Smart Water.' And I'm like, 'Well . . . how much are we getting? No one else in the movie has to carry this can of Sierra Mist!' I already have to say all the most boring lines ever, and make them sound interesting and real and organic. And now I also have to carry a can of Sierra Mist."

In 2014, a tragicomic Funny or Die short poked fun at underwritten best-friend characters by casting Greer as a woman who has nothing to do whenever she's not coaching her best friend to sprint to an airport after the man of her dreams. That same year, she wrote an essay collection titled *I Don't Know What You Know Me From: My Life as a Co-Star*, in which she cheerfully celebrated the oddity of a career as a supporting actress. Her career, and her public sense of irony about it, also earned Greer a loyal fandom of cinephiles who love her performances but think she deserves more; the online clothing and accessories store SuperYaki.com, which describes itself as "a shop for people who watch very good movies," sells a bestselling shirt that reads JUDY GREER SHOULD'VE BEEN THE LEAD in large yellow block letters.

And while Greer genuinely and effusively appreciates the vocal support from fans, a closer examination of her recent roles reveals that the campaign has done its job: These days, more often than not, Judy Greer *is* the lead. In the past decade, her roles have included Cornelia, an ape in *War for the Planet of the Apes*, and Karen, the daughter of *Halloween* protagonist Laurie Strode in the rebooted trilogy.

You will note that none of those roles are in romantic comedies. "People are like, 'You're always the best friend!'" she says. "And I'm like . . . well, technically I haven't played anyone's best friend in about fifteen years. I guess women in their forties don't have best friends anymore. We don't need friends. We're very tired."

But whether or not Greer ever returns to the rom-com genre—seriously, who will green-light that Kathryn Hahn team-up already?—

she has both appreciation and affection for the genre that made her the platonic ideal of a best friend for a generation of rom-com fans. "When I moved to Los Angeles, my fantasy was to be the star of romantic comedies," says Greer. "But I got to be *in* romantic comedies, and that's pretty fucking awesome."

"Is that . . . is that hair gel?"

—MARY JENSEN, *THERE'S SOMETHING ABOUT MARY*

CHAPTER 6

THERE'S SOMETHING ABOUT MARY

(And the Birth of the Raunch-Com)

IT WAS A SUNNY DAY IN MIAMI IN THE WINTER OF 1997, AND PETER AND Bobby Farrelly had a problem. The brothers, co-directing their latest project, *There's Something About Mary*, were in the middle of a production that was already being eyed with a lot of skepticism by executives at 20th Century Fox. On this particular day, they had planned to shoot a scene in which Mary, played by Cameron Diaz, would unwittingly spike her hair with an errant blast of semen from her date (Ben Stiller), which she mistook for hair gel. Diaz had doubts about the scene from the moment she had read the script, and the Farrellys, sympathetic to her concerns, had already vowed it would be cut from the film if she didn't like how it turned out.

Now the big day had arrived, and the star had cold feet. "That's, like, a potential career-ender," Peter Farrelly recalls her worrying. "Every time you're walking down the street: '*Hey, there's cum-head!*'"

As everyone on location at Miami's Cardozo Hotel waited for her big entrance, Diaz was in her trailer with her hairstylist, Anne Morgan, who had been tasked with giving Diaz this singular hairdo. Neither woman was enthusiastic about it. After some hemming and hawing, Morgan made an executive decision. "It's not cool. It's too much," she told Diaz. "We've gotta tell Peter and Bobby."

Morgan left the trailer to negotiate the terms, and after a little back-and-forth, a deal was struck. First, they'd shoot it Peter and Bobby's way: a massive, vertical spike of hair sticking straight up from Diaz's forehead, described in the script as an "ACE VENTURA–STYLE WAVE" and so rock-hard it looked like you could cut a diamond with it. Then they'd try it Diaz and Morgan's way: a much, much smaller bump designed to preserve whatever minimal sense of realism *There's Something About Mary* might have (not much), as well as a larger chunk of Diaz's dignity.

And the moment Diaz emerged from the trailer with the massive, surfer-wave spike the Farrellys had imagined—and the entire

OVERTHINKING IT

Ben Stiller also had a problem with the semen-in-the-hair scene. But unlike both the studio and Diaz, his concerns weren't about whether the scene was too scatological; they were about whether it was logical at all. "My big thing with that scene was that I argued with the Farrelly brothers all during the shot, asking 'How he could not feel it on his ear?'" says Stiller. "I was lobbying them to have a back story that the character had somehow, like, lost sensitivity in his ear, like he had gotten hit as a kid or something. They finally told me it doesn't matter, and I should quit thinking about it." Some jokes just don't need to be explained.

crew immediately broke into hysterics—it was obvious to everyone, including Diaz and Morgan, which version would ultimately win out. "The less you did it, the more you get that, *ewww*," says Bobby Farrelly. "But the further you go, the funnier it was."

It was a lesson that would govern *There's Something About Mary*'s more-is-more approach to gross-out humor, which the Farrellys had pioneered with their first feature, 1994's *Dumb and Dumber*. Though *Dumb and Dumber* is technically about two men who fall in love with the same woman, you could hardly call it a romantic comedy; the woman is married to another man and totally disinterested in both of her suitors, who are the idiots of the title. For *There's Something About Mary*, the goal was different: marrying the zany, anything-for-a-gag approach of *Dumb and Dumber* with a love story that the Farrellys wanted the audience to care about.

It helped that they were building this very raunchy movie on the bones of a relatively conventional rom-com script. The first version of *There's Something About Mary* can be traced all the way back to 1988—a full decade before the movie actually hit theaters—when screenwriters John J. Strauss and Ed Decter spent their spare time kicking around ideas for movies. One night, as they tried to come up with something that would be "universally relatable," they started talking about high school, and inspiration struck. "This was, of course, before Facebook," says Strauss. "And we lit on this notion: God, what about that high school unrequited love? That high school crush that you always had, but nothing ever came of it? Where is that person now? Probably everybody has some version of that."

Strauss and Decter imagined Ted, a man who was so fixated on his high school crush that he would go to extremes to hire a private investigator to track her down. What if the investigator uncovered enough information about her that Ted could remake himself, *Pygmalion* style, into the man of her dreams? And if that high school crush really *was* so great . . . what if the detective fell for her too? And as pure as his feelings might be, how would the investigator even begin to explain—let alone justify—the bizarre truth about how he came into her life in the first place?

If you read that plot summary and thought Ted sounded like a creep, so did Strauss and Decter. In a complete 180 from the movie that eventually hit theaters—in which Ted, the geeky hero played by Ben Stiller, squares off against the sleazy and pig-headed detective played by Matt Dillon—the initial draft of *There's Something About Mary* cast Ted as the villain, and the private investigator as a basically decent guy in an incredibly awkward position. "We thought, *The guy paying to spy on her is the worst guy in the world to end up with her*," says Decter. "And the detective is defending her. In a way, he's saving Mary from the creepy guy looking for her."

The movie was a classic love triangle, with a dash of manic screwball energy, written in the midst of a boom market for adult-skewing rom-coms like *Moonstruck*, *Bull Durham*, and *Broadcast News*. As such, Strauss and Decter happily embraced the conventions of the genre. "Our script was a very traditional romantic comedy," says Strauss. "There were some broader moments, and certainly some mystery. But we really prided ourselves on keeping it grounded, and making the characters and situations relatable and believable." When the script was finished, it sparked a small bidding war, and was eventually purchased by Touchstone—the same Disney label that released *Pretty Woman*—which promptly sent *There's Something About Mary* off to languish in development hell.

This is not an unusual experience in Hollywood, where promising scripts are acquired, ignored, and quietly snuffed out without a single frame being shot. But this extended trip into development hell was frustrating to both Decter and Strauss, who thought *There's*

Something About Mary's commercial prospects had only grown rosier in the intervening years. Under a new Writers Guild rule that offered writers the chance to lobby for the rights to their old material if it went unproduced for five years or more, Strauss and Decter successfully reclaimed the rights to *There's Something About Mary*.

At the same time, Peter and Bobby Farrelly had released their quirky bowling comedy *Kingpin*, starring Randy Quaid, Woody Harrelson, and Bill Murray. It had been a modest hit, though nowhere nearly as big as *Dumb and Dumber*, and they weren't sure what they wanted to make next. The brothers, who had read and admired an early draft of *There's Something About Mary*, bumped into Dexter and Strauss at a film screening hosted by a mutual friend. When the Farrellys asked what had happened to *There's Something About Mary*, the screenwriters revealed that they had recovered the rights from Touchstone exactly one day earlier, and the Farrellys replied, "Well . . . what if *we* wanted to make it?" Within two weeks, they had sold the movie to Fox.

With the movie set up at Fox, the Farrellys sat down for a hefty rewrite that would use the core structure of the love triangle as a jumping-off point for the movie *they* wanted to make: a genuinely romantic comedy that would also pack in as many raunchy gags as they thought they could get away with. And with two PG-13 movies that had already required some cagey negotiations with the MPAA under their belts, they were ready to see what kind of movie they could make without any constraints. "We decided, upfront, to go R," says Peter Farrelly. "And then, since we were already R, we went to the outer edge of R."

Enter, among other things, the semen-in-the-hair gag. It had been a long time coming, though it had been a fight to get it into something—*anything*—from the very beginning. Peter Farrelly had originally come up with the idea years earlier, when he and

Bobby were pitching ideas for *Seinfeld*. Though the sitcom would soon become legendary for airing an episode about a masturbation contest without ever actually using the word "masturbation," Farrelly's semen gag was still just a little too edgy for NBC primetime in 1992. But the idea had lingered in his brain for a full half-decade, just waiting for the right opportunity to resurface, until he saw an opportunity to insert it into *There's Something About Mary*.

Could they get away with it? Peter did the hard math required of any director trying to juggle their own artistic goals with the rigid standards imposed by the MPAA, trying to game out whether a joke that crude would tip *There's Something About Mary* into NC-17 territory—an unacceptable kiss of death for a studio comedy. "If it's for titillation, it's NC-17. If it's for laughs, it's R," he decided. In went the semen gag, sandwiched neatly between scenes of a penis caught in a zipper and a deranged shoe fetishist.

As ridiculous as this type of calculation sounds, it was essentially a thesis statement for *There's Something About Mary*: thinking hard about where the line might be, and choosing the moments to cross it with what felt, to the Farrellys, like surgical precision. But when they delivered their rewritten script to the studio, executives were horrified by most of the movie they'd bought, and by the "hair gel" scene in particular. "20th Century Fox said, 'What's this?' I said, 'It's hysterical.' And they said, 'No. It's fucking *pornography*,'" says Peter Farrelly.

So began a months-long battle over a strand of semen. The Farrellys promised the studio they would shoot the scene so it could easily be cut from the movie if it didn't get laughs. The studio refused to let them shoot it at all. The debate eventually went all the way up the chain to Bill Mechanic, then the CEO of Fox, says Peter Farrelly. "Finally, I said, 'How many movies are you guys going to make this year?' He said, 'Twenty-two.' I said, 'Well, why don't you just make twenty-one and let *us* make one?' And I just kind of stared at him. And Bill smiled, and said, 'Fuck it. Let him do it.'"

According to the Farrellys, this battle was worth fighting because the raunchiest gags were exactly what would set *There's Something About Mary* apart from the rom-coms of the era. "One of the problems with the romantic comedy is that the formula is generally understood by the public," says Bobby Farrelly. "Boy meets girl, boy loses girl, boy tries to win girl back. The trick is to be different and do these things in ways that are fresh—but still accomplish that thing where the audience walks away happy."

But if *There's Something About Mary* is a gross-out comedy on the exterior, it remains a rom-com under the hood. The key to the movie's love story—and the storytelling choice that allows the audience to get behind a guy who is so stubbornly fixated on a girl from high school that he hires a P.I. to track her down—is that Ted isn't dissuaded when the detective tries to get rid of him by falsely describing Mary as an overweight mail-order bride with four children by three fathers. After thinking it over, Ted says he still wants to reunite with her anyway. "That's when every woman in the world says, 'Okay, he deserves her,'" says Peter Farrelly. "He's not chasing Cameron Diaz. He's chasing a person with a soul. He doesn't care how she looks." And he doesn't know how she looks. Not yet.

But as much as the Farrellys wanted audiences to feel invested in the love story between Ted and Mary, they also struggled to tell the story in a way that felt as propulsive and daring as the hard-R jokes they were peppering throughout the script. During their rewrite, they hit a rut around the halfway point of the movie when they realized that, if they continued along the natural course it felt like the screenplay was taking, the rest of the story would unfold as the predictable rom-com Bobby had feared. After chewing on the problem for a while, Peter was inspired by a chance viewing of Wes Anderson's *Bottle Rocket,* which was remarkable in 1996 for its unconventional, zigzagging plot. It made him wonder if *There's Something About Mary* could be a romantic comedy where the love story *didn't* go where audiences were expecting. "Ted doesn't *have* to get Mary," he told Bobby. "Why are we stuck on that? We're stuck on it because that's what always happens. But what if he doesn't? What if something completely different happens?"

This is the reason there is absolutely no way to deliver a straightforward plot summary of *There's Something About Mary.* The heart of the movie is the love triangle between Mary, Ted, and the P.I. Pat Healy, but the rest of the movie is a series of eccentric side characters and wild gags as Mary accrues an ever-increasing number of

ARE YOU READY FOR SOME FOOTBALL?

Even the small-but-pivotal role of the famed NFL quarterback fighting for Mary's heart had been altered by the film's boundary-pushing humor. The Farrellys' first choice, Drew Bledsoe of the New England Patriots, apologetically dropped out after the very '90s mistake of leaping into a mosh pit at an Everclear show, saying he couldn't withstand any more bad press after the incident was reported. Their second choice, Steve Young of the San Francisco 49ers (and a member of the Church of Jesus Christ of Latter-Day Saints), thought hard about it but ultimately passed. "That's the funniest script I've ever read," the Farrellys recall him saying. "But I cannot do it— because if I do it, it's R-rated, and I know all the Mormon kids will be sneaking in and I wouldn't feel good about that." For his part, Brett Favre says no one told him he was third choice for the role: "If I'd known that, I would have never done it." Welcome to acting, Brett.

desperate suitors. (The suitors, for the record, include Ted, Detective Pat Healy, an American pizza deliveryman pretending to be a British architect with a spinal injury, Mary's creepy high school ex-boyfriend Woogie, and then–Green Bay Packers quarterback Brett Favre.) Aiming to surprise audiences, the Farrellys resolved to write without a clear resolution in mind, giving each of them a fair shot to win her heart by the time the credits rolled. "We didn't know ourselves that she was going to end up with Ted," says Peter Farrelly. "That's the way we write. Some people work out a plot, and they'll put it all on index cards, all the way through the story. We don't do that. We let the story unfold as we're writing it, and we let the universe do its thing and point us in the right direction. And also . . . we're not that smart."

This extremely zen approach to screenwriting also led to the film's climactic twist, where it's revealed that Ted's best friend, Dom, is also Mary's much-hyped but never seen ex-boyfriend Woogie, who had manipulated everyone just so he could reconnect with Mary. Though it's hard to imagine the movie without this climactic twist, it was never a part of the original plan. The Farrellys originally invented "Woogie" as a generic, hypothetical stand-in for the kind of guy someone like Ted thought he could never compete with: handsome, charming, and athletic. It wasn't until the Farrellys reached the end of their script—and discovered they'd planted Woogie, like Chekhov's gun, in the first act without firing him in the third—that they realized no one would expect Woogie had grown up to become Chris Elliott. And they knew it would work because they hadn't expected it either.

With a narrative that is always threatening to fly off the rails, the Farrellys needed a core trio of actors who could ground the material. The role of Ted, the film's dorky-but-endearing hero, came down to three young comedic actors who quickly proved to be emblematic of the Farrellys' knack for harnessing young talent: Ben Stiller, Owen Wilson, and Jon Stewart. "I thank God we didn't pick Jon Stewart," says Peter Farrelly. "We very easily could have. But he went on to do bigger things, more important things, at a time we needed his voice."

In the end, the Farrellys couldn't decide between Owen Wilson, who they'd admired so much in *Bottle Rocket*, and Ben Stiller, who had forged a promisingly eccentric, ahead-of-its-time comedy career throughout the early 1990s in the sketch series *The Ben Stiller Show* and the Gen-X touchstone *Reality Bites*, which he also directed. Liking both actors (and the dorky-but-lovable vibe they were bringing) equally, the Farrellys deferred to the preference of 20th Century Fox executive Tom Rothman on the condition that they could cast Matt Dillon—who the studio feared was "too indie and too dark" for the comedy—as the sleazy detective Pat Healy. Rothman chose Stiller.

There's Something About Mary caught Ben Stiller at a strange point in his career. Though he had come to prominence as a comedic actor (and, as the son of comedians Anne Meara and Jerry Stiller, was essentially comedy royalty), his career was also littered with projects that were perceived as failures, from the acclaimed but low-rated *The Ben Stiller Show* to the underperforming dark comedy *The Cable Guy*, which he directed after *The Ben Stiller Show* was cancelled. Though he preferred directing to acting—and had shown a more sober side of himself as both a director and actor in *Reality Bites*—he spent the immediate aftermath of *The Cable Guy* in a kind of acting frenzy, starring in no fewer than four movies released in 1998. His career could have gone any number of ways, but *There's Something About Mary* finally took this hard-to-pin-down young creative and stuck him to the wall. The earnest, awkward, why-does-bad-stuff-always-happen-to-me persona Ben Stiller solidified here would show up again later in massive hits like the *Meet the Parents*, *Madagascar*, and *Night at the Museum* trilogies.

But as much as the movie rests on Stiller's shoulders, no role was more important than Mary, who needed to be so singularly wonderful that audiences wouldn't wonder why every man in the movie instantly falls head-over-heels in love with her. As Peter Farrelly recalls, only one actress besides Cameron Diaz was seriously considered for the role: Courteney Cox, then white-hot at the height of *Friends'* popularity. "We shot *There's Something About Mary* from December to March," says Farrelly. "I told Courteney I was sending her the script, and I heard back, 'She can't do it. She's got scheduling issues. She's doing *Friends*, and that's right in the middle of their shooting.' So we went to Cameron." Years later, Farrelly ran into Cox, who told him she was furious that he'd never sent her the script for *There's Something About Mary* like he'd promised. As far as Farrelly can guess, someone on her management team passed on the movie without saying a word to her about it.

THE REAL MARY

There's a rumor that has dogged the creative team behind *There's Something About Mary* for years: Similar to a real-life Warren, was there a real Mary who inspired the script? Strauss and Decter both insist that the character was completely fictional. "It wasn't based on any person—although, weirdly, some people have claimed that it was based on them," says Decter. "More than one Mary who's an old acquaintance of ours has claimed, erroneously, that the movie was about them," says Strauss. "But I honestly believe we just pulled it out of thin air."

Nevertheless, the Farrellys were thrilled to get Cameron Diaz—fresh off her supporting performance in *My Best Friend's Wedding*—and their delight only grew once she arrived on set in Florida. Diaz was "just exactly what you would expect her to be: fun, happy, witty, charming, smart, energetic," says Peter Farrelly. She was also dating Matt Dillon, which Farrelly swears he didn't know when both actors were cast. "That was one of those bizarre things," he says. "That was just a complete coincidence, but a nice coincidence."

With the core cast in place, the Farrellys worked on filling out the many supporting roles scattered throughout the movie—which, like almost everything in *There's Something About Mary*, turned into a minor battle. Concerned that the movie had no big stars, the studio lobbied for a name actor for the role of Mary's developmentally disabled brother, Warren; Chris Farley and Robin Williams were two of the names that were tossed around. But the Farrellys had a hard time imagining a big star in the role because they were drawing from their actual lives. Warren was based on a man named Warren Tashjian, who lived near the Farrelly Brothers when they were growing up in Providence, Rhode Island, and who actually makes a small cameo in the movie. Warren's scenes are played for laughs, but the Farrellys also took him seriously. At the same time, the role was an incredibly risky one for an actor to take on, knowing that there was a very real chance they'd be criticized for mocking the developmentally disabled.

W. Earl Brown, who had played a small but memorable role in 1996's breakout horror hit *Scream*, first heard about *There's Something About Mary* when a fellow actor at his gym mentioned the role. He decided to go in with a plan that happened to dovetail with the Farrellys' intentions: Play it as honestly as he could. "I knew the only way to make it work was to make it believable," says Brown. "Because if the audience thinks you're making fun of this character yourself, it ain't going to be funny, and they're going to fucking hate you." The Farrellys loved the approach, and Brown booked the role, taking it so seriously that Peter Farrelly describes his performance as Method. "I didn't get to know him that well because all I knew was his character," says Farrelly. "He didn't break it."

WARREN'S SECRET ORIGIN STORY

In the script, Mary's brother, Warren, attacks anyone who touches his omnipresent earmuffs. This reaction is never explained—but as Brown saw it, his job was to figure out why Warren was so sensitive about his ears. "I hate pretentious actors, and this sounds pretentious," says Brown. "But when Warren was a little kid, a bee was buzzing around his ear. And a well-meaning stranger tried to shoo the bug away, and the bee stung him. So he associates anybody touching his ears with that extreme pain."

The production of *There's Something About Mary* continued in this fashion, with the Farrellys working overtime to find people who understood their unusual approach to the material. The movie primes audiences for its heightened, almost cartoonish universe from the very beginning with a performance by Modern Lovers front man Jonathan Richman, a singer who serves as the movie's de facto narrator. In a device the Farrellys admit they borrowed from Elliot Silverstein's 1965 western-comedy *Cat Ballou*—which pulls the same trick with Nat King Cole and Stubby Kaye—Richman and drummer Tommy Larkins periodically pop up to play catchy ballads that directly comment on the plot. Before the audience meets Ted or Mary, there's Richman and Larkins in a tree, delivering a wistful musical tribute to Mary.

This, too, was a gamble that might not have paid off. When the Farrellys approached Richman with the idea, they warned him there was "an 80 percent chance" the musical interludes wouldn't even make the final cut of the movie. The trade-off was that the studio would be paying for Richman and Larkins to go to Miami for the ten-week shoot, which meant the worst-case scenario for the duo was a pretty decent vacation in Florida.

By the time the Farrellys wrapped production, they were content that they'd made the movie they wanted; they just weren't sure if anyone else would like it. The first, all-important test screening, which was held in the spring of 1998 on the Fox studio lot, was

STRUMMING ALONG

After reading the script, Jonathan Richman "made up the theme song 'There's Something About Mary' within the hour," he says. He called Peter Farrelly and sang it to him over the phone, and Farrelly immediately signed off without requesting any changes. The trickier part was filming the opening—an elaborate crane shot in which Richman and Larkins perform the song in a tree about ten feet off the ground, which required Richman to convincingly lip-sync the whole thing in a single take. Richman, confident it would be simple, refused the help of a stunt coordinator—only to find that he was hopelessly dizzy once he was actually in the tree. A pulley system was hastily assembled, and Richman managed to pull it off in one take, though the Farrellys gleefully taunted him as "Evel Knievel" from below.

a mini-reunion of the crew that had shepherded different forms of *There's Something About Mary*, from Ed Decter and John Strauss to the Farrellys to key cast members like Lin Shaye, who plays Mary's neighbor Magda. "We go to this little screening room and the movie starts," says Strauss. "And everybody is screaming with laughter. Including us. It was just the most spectacular two hours I think I can ever remember, other than maybe my children being born. Whatever god you choose to believe in, here it is—in the form of, you know, sperm in Cameron Diaz's hair." Lin Shaye arrived late to the screening and was startled by the rumble she felt entering the theater. "I thought there was an earthquake. The theater was shaking with laughter, and I saw people fall out of their seats. There was this one big guy that leaned forward, and an usher had to come and pick him up."

Of course, making an uproarious comedy was one challenge; selling it to audiences was another. And the competition that summer was looking unusually fierce. "I remember Peter called me and said, 'Oh, my God, Matt Stone and Trey Parker are releasing a movie called *BASEketball*. The *South Park* guys are going to kill us," says Decter. The studio's uncertainty about *There's Something About Mary* is still evident in the trailer, which nervously reminds audiences that Magda's "dead dog" Puffy is not an actual dog that was killed, downplays potentially controversial elements like Mary's brother, Warren, and squeezes in no fewer than two shots of Cameron Diaz in her underwear.

There's Something About Mary opened in the middle of July at number four, behind a slew of summer blockbusters including *The Mask of Zorro*, *Armageddon*, and *Lethal Weapon 4*. The $13.7 million opening wasn't awful, but it wasn't a blockbuster success either; by any reasonable estimate, the movie would probably end up making a little more money than it had cost to produce.

A DOG-EAT-CHEEK WORLD

No catalogue of the gross-out moments in *There's Something About Mary* would be complete without Mary's neighbor Magda and her dog, Puffy. In one scene, Magda lets Puffy lick her mouth for what feels like roughly 10 million seconds of screen time—an unforgettable moment that was not in the script. "There was something in the makeup that the dog got obsessed with, and he started licking," recalls actress Lin Shaye. "I remember thinking, as an actor, *Just carry on.* The crew and Cameron were crying, they were laughing so hard—and they were trying *not* to laugh, because they would have ruined the take. By the end, Puffy had literally licked an entire hole in the latex on the left side of my face—which was fortunately not on the camera side. I remember Pete running out after, and he said, 'That's cinema gold. That scene will go down in history.'" In a movie that was engineered to push boundaries, even the Farrellys couldn't have planned it.

But something nearly unprecedented happened over the rest of the summer, through the fall, and even into the early weeks of 1999: As the presumed blockbusters dropped off the charts, *There's Something About Mary* endured. The word-of-mouth appeal of the movie turned out to be so unstoppable that its highest-grossing weekend at the box office was the first weekend of September— nearly two full months after it had originally arrived in theaters. By the time its run was over, *There's Something About Mary* had grossed $176 million domestically and $193 million at the international box office, making it the biggest comedy of the year, and just barely topping the $170 million earned by *Pretty Woman* to become the top rom-com of the decade. It was a particularly impressive feat given the movie's unapologetically hard-R rating, which limited its audience over fellow 1998 rom-coms like Nora Ephron's *You've Got Mail* and Frank Coraci's *The Wedding Singer*.

The studio that had been so reluctant to approve basically any of the things that turned *There's Something About Mary* into a breakout hit was suddenly desperate to get a sequel into production. Strauss recalls half-heartedly tossing out a concept for one that would have focused on Ted figuring out how to fend off rival suitors who recognized that Mary was out of his league. W. Earl Brown pitched a separate sequel about Ted and Mary's wedding, which would be invaded by a group of women who were angry that Mary had it all, with a beefy subplot about Warren competing as a weightlifter in the Special Olympics. Several years after the movie's release, the Farrellys were nudged to consider making *There's Something Else About Mary*, though no one could come up with a good idea for what the "something else" was going to be.

In the absence of a slam-dunk idea, the likely salaries for Stiller and Diaz—whose individual star power had risen dramatically on the back of the movie's success—also became prohibitively expensive, and both actors took this financial glory as an opportunity to stretch themselves creatively. In the years that followed, Diaz took on dramatic roles in Spike Jonze's *Being John Malkovich*, Oliver Stone's *Any Given Sunday*, and Martin Scorsese's *Gangs of New York*. Though she made several more rom-coms—including 2002's *The Sweetest Thing*, which took a shot at delivering *There's Something About Mary*–style raunch from a female perspective—she ultimately retired from acting in 2014 to focus on her family and her natural wine brand. "I just decided that I wanted different things out of my life," says Diaz. "I had gone so hard for so long, working, making films, and it's such a grind. And I didn't make any space for my personal life."

Though *There's Something About Mary* launched his career as one of the most bankable comic actors in Hollywood, Stiller has always seemed uneasy about how much the movie defined his career. "Honestly, when it started I was just stepping into a Farrelly brothers movie," he says. "That thing that I suddenly became known for . . . man-child. . . . humiliations . . . broad physical comedy was never my goal. It never excited me." He returned to the rom-com genre over the years, in movies like 2000's *Keeping the Faith* (opposite Jenna Elfman and Edward Norton), 2004's *Along Came Polly* (opposite Jennifer Aniston), and 2007's *The Heartbreak Kid*, a kind of anti-rom-com that reteamed him with the Farrellys. But at heart it's clear that, even after all these years, Stiller still prefers directing to acting. In 2018, he helmed the dramatic Showtime miniseries *Escape at Dannemora*, in which he never appeared in front of the camera, and he couldn't have seemed happier about it.

Though they're proud of all the gross-out gags that made it into the final cut of *There's Something About Mary*, the Farrelly Brothers are a little disappointed that so much of the cultural legacy of the movie is wrapped up in the edgy jokes and not the twisted story they concocted. "I was very, very proud of that script, and not just for the gross-out, all of it," says Peter Farrelly, who is currently working on a stage musical adaptation of *There's Something About Mary*, with the goal of reaching Broadway by the summer of 2022. "If you had those jokes in a different story, believe me, nobody would be talking about it. Those jokes only worked because you loved those characters."

Any which way you look at it, *There's Something About Mary* expanded Hollywood's understanding about what a rom-com could look like—and the audience that might line up to watch it. The following year saw the release of Paul Weitz's *American Pie*, which courted a similar audience by smuggling a couple of relatively earnest teen love stories into a movie sold on an awkward teenage boy humping a warm pie. Soon enough, Judd Apatow—who had worked with Ben Stiller on *The Ben Stiller Show*, and later said that the extensive improv in his own movies was inspired by how Stiller worked—would pick up the gauntlet the Farrelly Brothers had thrown down and remake Hollywood comedy in his image. The culture had taken the lesson from *There's Something About Mary*'s success, though the movie itself still feels like an anomaly that slipped through the cracks and found a sizable audience waiting for it. "Would *There's Something About Mary* get made today? Who knows?" says W. Earl Brown. "Hell, it wasn't supposed to get made *then*."

GOING OUT WITH A BANG

Jonathan Richman also plays a key role in the movie's big, final joke, when a stray bullet hits him mid-song and sends him into the harbor. Like so much of *There's Something About Mary*, this shocking gag came in a moment of inspiration: the actual ending called for *Ted* to die. But Richman happened to be visiting the set with his daughter, and the Farrellys suddenly decided it would be funnier if the seemingly omniscient narrator—who has apparently existed on a different plane of reality the whole time, for no apparent reason—was shot and killed instead while he performed a reprise of the song that opened the movie. Peter Farrelly asked Richman how quickly he could get into costume, and Richman replied, "As soon as wardrobe brings it." After a few takes—each of which required a fresh suit coat, since the squib would leave a bloody hole in the jacket—the Farrellys captured the gag. "Me dying was so much better than the original idea," says Richman. "I was so glad I was there that day, so they didn't use the other stupid ending."

Adam Sandler

THE UNLIKELY LEADING MAN

There is nothing about Adam Sandler's early career that screams rom-com heartthrob. As a breakout *Saturday Night Live* cast member in the early 1990s, he was best known for playing characters like Cajun Man and Opera Man, who drew laughs from Sandler's usual comedy playbook: weird songs, obnoxiously high-pitched voices, and a tendency to shift from a mumbling, high-pitched baritone into a hoarse yell. His first hit movie, 1995's *Billy Madison*, technically has a romantic subplot, in which the man-child at the center of the film falls in love with his teacher after he's forced to repeat elementary school. (Would you believe that, against all odds and reason itself, she falls for him back?)

Virtually the same arc played out in the following year's *Happy Gilmore*, with the third-grade teacher being swapped out for a PR pro who is eventually won over by Sandler's singular (aggressive) charms. But just when it seemed like Sandler might spend the rest of his career wooing blond comic actresses in movies named after the character he played, something interesting happened with his next big hit: 1998's *The Wedding Singer*, which costarred Drew Barrymore, who would go on to describe Sandler as her "cinematic soulmate."

On paper, nothing about *The Wedding Singer* should have been different. A sad-sack wedding singer could hardly have been a more obvi-ous fit for Sandler's very broad wheelhouse. And the movie was written by Sandler's *SNL* buddy Tim Herlihy, who was also behind *Billy Madison* and *Happy Gilmore*. (Someday, film scholars will crack the mystery of why Herlihy didn't just call the script *Robbie Hart*, after the character Sandler plays in *The Wedding Singer*, to complete his trilogy of movies named after the wacky man-child played by Sandler, but alas.)

The Wedding Singer was different, though. Previous Sandler films were slapstick comedies with tacked-on romantic subplots. *The Wedding Singer* was a romantic comedy with some tacked-on slapstick. Audi-ences who showed up for the rapping grandma they saw in the trailer—whose performance of "Rapper's Delight" does, indeed, make the final cut—discovered that they'd been led into a surprisingly sweet romantic comedy.

The climax of *The Wedding Singer* features a few of the normal tropes Sandler fans have come to expect: a ludicrously despicable rival to be bat-ted away, an appearance by Steve Buscemi, a gratuitous celebrity cameo (this time by Billy Idol), and so on. But it also features Sandler singing a song—*without* affecting a weird voice—that demonstrates a surprisingly earnest idea of the long-term impact of romantic love. In an original song called "Grow Old With You," Robbie Hart tells Julia about what he'll do de-cades *after* they've first fallen in love: give her medicine when she's sick, give her his coat when she's cold, carry her when her arthritis is too painful to deal with alone. It's a goofy, nakedly sentimental moment. It's also one of the few times that a rom-com of the era openly acknowledges that com-mitting to be with someone means being prepared for much more than the moment when a typical rom-com would happily let the credits roll.

A few years after *The Wedding Singer*, Paul Thomas Anderson cast Sandler as the lead in *Punch-Drunk Love*, a subversive romantic comedy that accumulates much of its power by riffing on the types of charac-ters Sandler normally plays. *Punch-Drunk Love*'s Barry Egan is another

Sandler man-child—but the film situates him in the real world and takes him deadly seriously. Paul Thomas Anderson–serious. And ultimately, the answer to the character's problems turns out to be the same: acknowledging his personal failings and falling in love. "I have a love in my life. It makes me stronger than anything you can imagine," he says.

Like the great rom-com stars of any era, Sandler has scored his biggest hits by repeatedly teaming up with the same actress for a whole string of movies that trade on the innate chemistry between them (and the audience's recognition of that chemistry). *50 First Dates*—Sandler's first post–*Wedding Singer* collaboration with Drew Barrymore—happened because Barrymore sent him a script she thought they should do together. Here, the tension between Adam Sandler the dude-bro icon and Adam Sandler the rom-com star became explicit; the script was originally titled *50 First Kisses*, which was changed when the marketing team reported that the word "kiss" was turning men away.

But a hypothetical backlash from his core fan base hasn't stopped Sandler from returning to the rom-com genre over and over again, in movies like *Spanglish* (opposite Paz Vega) and *Just Go With It* (opposite Jennifer Aniston) and *Blended* (opposite Drew Barrymore, again) and *Murder Mystery* (opposite Jennifer Aniston . . . again). Though Sandler has been credibly accused of making movies set on tropical beaches or cruise ships just so he can get paid to hang out with his friends, audiences don't seem to mind. When his movies get bad reviews—and they usually do—they still make truckloads of money anyway. There's a reason Netflix continues to double down on its very expensive deal with Sandler's production company Happy Madison, which ensures a steady stream of Sandler and Sandler-adjacent films for subscribers to binge every year.

Through it all, Sandler has maintained his quiet but public embrace of the rom-com genre, and of romantic love in general. On 2019's live *100% Fresher* tour, which doubled as a career retrospective for Sandler, he closed out shows with a new version of "Grow Old With You," rewritten to pay tribute to his real-life wife, Jackie. "When I'm on a diet you take away my potatoes, say 'fuck all those guys' after reading *Rotten Tomatoes*, I hope they all die miserable deaths as I grow old with you," he sings. And if wishing agony on your life partner's haters isn't yet widely understood as a part of what true love looks like in the modern era, Sandler is just ahead of the curve.

"I like you. Very much. Just as you are."

—MARK DARCY, *BRIDGET JONES'S DIARY*

CHAPTER 7

BRIDGET JONES'S DIARY

(And the Highs and Lows of Being a Modern Singleton)

IT WAS AN UNASSUMING SUNDAY IN FEBRUARY OF 1995 WHEN READERS of the British daily newspaper *The Independent* were introduced to a promising new writer: Bridget Jones. The self-deprecating, self-obsessed writer kicked off her first column by evaluating her recent consumption of alcohol ("excellent") and calories ("poor"). "Oh why hasn't Daniel rung?" she wondered on the page about her rakish colleague-turned-suitor. "Hideous, wasted weekend glaring psychopathically at the phone and eating things."

Before she blossomed into one of the most celebrated rom-com heroines of this (or any) era, Bridget Jones was conceived as a piece of serialized satirical fiction—a pastiche of modern singlehood, written by a modern singleton named Helen Fielding. Later—when Bridget had grown exponentially more famous than anyone, especially her creator, had ever expected—Fielding explained Bridget Jones's mercenary origins. "I was trying to write an earnest and frankly unreadable novel about cultural divides in the Caribbean, and was rather short of cash," she says. "I assumed no one would read it, and it would be dropped after six weeks for being too silly."

Before Bridget Jones, Fielding had had an eclectic career in media: producing documentaries, writing columns for a variety of newspapers, and offering off-the-cuff feedback to her Oxford classmate and close friend Richard Curtis (including the all-important suggestion that his idea for a film called *Four Weddings and a Honeymoon* should instead be *Four Weddings and a Funeral*). Her first novel, *Cause Celeb*, published in 1994, centers on Rosie Richardson, a literary publicist not entirely unlike both Helen Fielding and Bridget Jones, and satirizes the self-absorbed uber-rich who ham-fistedly attempt to "help" African refugees with methods that do much more to burnish their own public images and egos. Fielding's writing can be described as breezy and bemused, but the satire of *Cause Celeb* is tinged with genuine, righteous outrage. It was a tough novel to describe, let alone sell; while reviews were mostly solid, sales figures stalled, and the book wasn't published outside of the United Kingdom.

Stuck on that second novel that just wasn't coming into focus (the sophomore slump, as it's often called by writers), Fielding wrote for newspapers to pay the bills. But if *Cause Celeb* hadn't been a massive seller, it had at least caught the attention of *The Independent*'s Geraldine Bedell and her husband, features editor Charles Leadbeater. By his own admission, his tenure up to that point had not been particularly successful. Hungry for a hit—"Almost by accident and out of desperation," he says—Leadbeater started kicking around an idea for a column that might appeal to young professional women, who he deemed an underserved audience by most print newspapers. He was inspired by what he overheard from the women who worked at *The Independent*. "They would come in to work in the morning, and one minute they would be talking about Gordon Brown, and the next about their makeup," says Leadbetter. "And I thought it would be a good idea to have a fictional column to reflect that kind of thinking, which doesn't compartmentalize things." When he mentioned the idea to Bedell, she recalled *Cause Celeb* and suggested that Helen Fielding might have exactly the voice he was looking for.

Leadbeater arranged a meeting with Fielding and proposed his idea. She was intrigued—even throwing out the name "Bridget Jones," off the cuff, as the kind of modern British everywoman who the column would be about and for. She was certain she did not want to use her own name. "I really wanted to be taken seriously—and indeed, still do," says Fielding. "I thought if they knew what I was writing about . . . why it takes three hours between getting up and leaving the house, or diets, or 'has he rung or hasn't he rung?' . . . I just felt they would look down on me."

SEX AND THE CITIES

Shortly before the publication of Helen Fielding's Bridget Jones columns in *The Independent*, American writer Candace Bushnell found similar success with a column for the *New York Observer* called Sex and the City, which riffed on the dating lives of herself and her friends. Bushnell's columns were eventually collected in a bestselling book, which was loosely adapted into the hit HBO series *Sex and the City* in 1998.

Though it's fairly easy to draw parallels between *Bridget Jones's Diary* and *Sex and the City*—drinking, swapping mortifying stories with friends, reflecting obsessively on one's sex life—the books are most interesting when read for their differences. The glamorous New York City lifestyle depicted by Bushnell is leagues away from Bridget's more humble life as a mid-level media employee.

The Bridget Jones columns quickly found their target audience. By chronicling the extremely specific daily concerns of one extremely specific professional woman—work, romance, family, diet, and anything else that might pop up in her daily life—Fielding's columns had tapped into something that spoke to many women across the country. "A couple of people wondered whether we could sustain it for very long," says Leadbeater. "And some—like my dad—simply did not get it. But very quickly we got this fantastic reaction from women. And then everyone got it, the letters came flooding in, and it just went on from there."

In the early days of Bridget Jones, no one besides certain staffers at *The Independent* knew Fielding was writing the columns—including close friends like Tracey MacLeod, who was the inspiration for Bridget's friend Jude, and Sharon Maguire, on whom Bridget's friend Shazzer was based. But as Bridget Jones grew more popular, and Fielding trawled her personal life and her friends' lives for new material, the column's true authorship became harder and harder to mask. Eventually, Maguire asked Fielding who was writing the column, and Fielding came clean. "Her face was very red and flushed," Maguire recalls. "Then, of course, we read it and realized all of our lives were being mined. It was very much based on her life at that time, and our lives. And I didn't mind, strangely enough, that my bad, inappropriate dates—and all of our sexual proclivities—were being mined for general humor, week-to-week. Helen also used to do a wonderful thing where she would enact revenge on people in the column. If we went somewhere and she didn't like what had happened, or she didn't like the way somebody was treated, she would then enact revenge in the column later that week. That was always very satisfying, to see certain people satirized and belittled in the column."

The Bridget Jones columns were masterful in their ability to filter real-world events through Bridget's incisive worldview. Fielding would get up at 5 A.M. on Tuesdays to make her tight deadline, and would sometimes need to process a major piece of news, figure out how Bridget would feel about it, and flip around a column about it before her deadline arrived. Princess Diana died on August 31, 1997. Two days later, readers of *The Independent* could pick up a copy for the catharsis of seeing Bridget grappling with the loss in real time.

> 10.10AM: *Am going to put on telly and they will say it has been a mistake and she is back then we will see her coming out of the Harbour Club with all the photographers asking her what it was like.*

> 13.30PM: *Keep having to look at newspaper headline again to make self believe it.*

But if half of Bridget's appeal was how it felt like she walked around the same London as her readers in real time, the other half came in her tumultuous (and wholly invented) romantic life. The very first sentence of the very first column introduces Daniel Cleaver, Bridget's devil-may-care boss who is swooningly described as "successful, clever, witty, and good-looking." After a very brief pregnancy scare and an unceremonious dumping—which plays out over almost a year's worth of columns—Bridget attends a New Year's Eve party and is introduced to a handsome, wealthy divorcé named Mark Darcy. "While there were no obvious superficial no-no signs—cable sweater, hankies in trouser pockets, red face or braces, black polo-neck sweater, pipe or white socks—he had an extremely irritating snooty expression suggesting he just could not be arsed," wrote Bridget in that week's diary entry.

It does not take an English literature scholar to recognize this scene as a riff on Jane Austen's 1813 novel *Pride and Prejudice*, in which the (prejudiced) protagonist Elizabeth Bennet encounters a (prideful) man named Darcy at a party she never really wanted to attend. Fielding, who had loved *Pride and Prejudice* from her

BRIDGET CRITICS

The decades since the publication of *Bridget Jones's Diary* have seen several feminist reappraisals. Some have been positive, citing the popularity of the book as a victory for the concerns of women that were, until recently, rarely depicted in literature. Others have been critical, arguing that Bridget's daily concerns are a regressive and toxic depiction of modern womanhood. In a 2013 column for *The Guardian* titled "Why I hate Bridget Jones," columnist Suzanne Moore blasted the character as the "epitome of post-feminism: vapid, consumerist and self-obsessed." In one line in *Bridget Jones's Diary* frequently quoted by detractors, Bridget muses, "There is nothing so unattractive to a man as a strident feminist."

Fielding, who calls the "strident feminist" line one of her favorite bits from the first book, says she wrote it with irony but understands if it doesn't resonate for all readers. "My feeling was, and is, if women aren't allowed to laugh at themselves, they haven't got very far on the equality front, have they?" she says. Though it was more or less the conceit of the original column, Fielding also feels that Bridget was unfairly held up as a universal stand-in for all women, especially when compared to some of the most celebrated himbos in British literature: "Nobody worries about what Bertie Wooster is saying about masculinity," she says, referencing the foppish P. G. Wodehouse character who bumbles through life getting into jam after jam.

childhood, had decided to drop her heroine into a modernized version of it. "My female role models were Elizabeth Bennet and Maria from *The Sound of Music*," says Fielding. "And Mr. Darcy and Captain von Trapp were both these locked-up men that needed that *joie de vivre* and informality, and the women needed this slightly more sensible person to keep them from going completely off the rails."

These traditional, arguably retrograde models for what constitutes an ideal male-female relationship—on which the Bridget-and-Mark relationship is explicitly based—are a part of why some feminist critics have been frustrated by Bridget Jones's "defeatist view of womanhood." In *Bridget Jones's Diary*, Bridget is symbolically rescued from lonely singledom by Mark; in the sequel, she is literally rescued from a prison by him. Fielding, for her part, says her deliberate riff on these romantic archetypes was written "unselfconsciously" because she "wasn't thinking about how it would be received."

Bridget Jones arrived in the midst of a broader vogue for these kinds of relationships in popular culture. Serendipitously, the publication of the Bridget Jones columns dovetailed with a general renaissance in *Pride and Prejudice* fandom due to the BBC's 1995 miniseries adaptation of *Pride and Prejudice*, which starred Jennifer Ehle as Elizabeth Bennet and Colin Firth as Fitzwilliam Darcy. "The whole nation was gripped," says Fielding. "Streets were quiet. It was like lockdown. Everyone was in love with Mark Darcy, and everyone was in love with Colin Firth." Fielding wrote her Mark Darcy not just as a modernized Fitzwilliam; she wrote him as a modernized riff on Colin Firth's specific riff on Fitzwilliam Darcy.

By 1996, Bridget Jones had grown popular enough that Fielding adapted the columns for a novel. The narrative, which had been haphazard by design in the newspaper columns, grew cleaner and more propulsive: a love triangle, more or less explicitly modeled on *Pride and Prejudice*, between Bridget, her boss Daniel, and the stoic human rights attorney Mark Darcy. By the end of the novel, Bridget and Mark are happily coupled off, and while she's still counting off her cigarettes smoked, alcohol drunk, and lottery tickets purchased, she's not beating herself up anymore. "An *excellent* year's progress," the diary concludes.

The columns had always been popular, but few modern novels have had as seismic an impact on the literary world as *Bridget Jones's Diary* did when it was published in 1996. The book was an instant hit, sitting on the bestseller charts for dozens of weeks and spawning a mad dash for similarly pitched novels like Lauren Weisberger's *The Devil Wears Prada*, Emily Giffin's *Something Borrowed*, and Sophie Kinsella's *Confessions of a Shopaholic*, which were collectively (and often derisively) referred to as "chick lit." Much like the columns, *Bridget Jones's Diary* had reached an audience of readers that the publishing world had often neglected. "It touched a nerve about the female state of loneliness and confusion in the '90s," says Fielding's pal Sharon Maguire. "If we're not conforming to the conventions of marriage, and having babies in our 30s, where *do* you look for a meaning to life? It dealt with the fear of loneliness. Whatever choices feminism has given us all—whether you've got empowerment, economic independence, all of those things—the fear of loneliness is still a valid fear."

And when any book, of any time period, is that successful, the film industry starts calling. For a brief window of time, Fielding was developing Bridget Jones as a possible BBC sitcom. It was producer Debra Hayward, who had worked with Richard Curtis when she was head of development at Working Title, who suggested the material might work better as a film.

Working Title could hardly have been a more obvious fit for the material. The studio behind *Four Weddings and a Funeral* and Hugh Grant and Julia Roberts's subsequent hit *Notting Hill* was uniquely suited to take a British romantic comedy and give it global appeal. As it turned out, the first major creative hire had been living in Bridget Jones's world all along. Though she had only directed documentaries and commercials, Fielding was convinced that her friend Sharon Maguire was the right person to shepherd *Bridget Jones* to the big screen. While the studio was skeptical of Maguire, Fielding convinced Working Title to take a meeting with her. "They decided to take a chance with me, I guess, because they thought that at that time they wanted to make something kind of indie and guerrilla-style," says Maguire. "They were going to spend, at the most, two million on it, and they were going to cast it at that level. Basically, I was just told, 'Don't fuck it up.' I thought, 'Well, all right, I'll try not to then.'"

But Maguire's indie, guerrilla-style *Bridget Jones* was always at odds with her ideal actor to play Daniel Cleaver: Hugh Grant. Grant was reluctant to line up yet another Working Title romantic comedy, but Maguire was persistent. "I'd ring him regularly," says Maguire. "He nicknamed me Stalker Maguire."

Whatever his doubts about the project, the odds increased of getting Hugh Grant excited once Richard Curtis joined the project to work with his old friend Helen Fielding as a co-screenwriter. "I kept saying, it's not working. Just get Richard Curtis to come in and help rewrite it. Eventually they did, and as soon as Richard came on board, I signed on the dotted line," says Grant. Hot off the success of *Notting Hill*, Curtis's presence as co-screenwriter was enough to attract the attention of Grant, who seemed to relish being Curtis's muse. With Grant attached, the budget of *Bridget Jones's Diary* ballooned to match. "I don't think it would have been a meaningfully *different* movie [without Grant], but there was just no spotlight and no expectations," says producer Debra Hayward. "We got Hugh Grant, and all of a sudden it sort of exploded into something bigger."

Sharon Maguire had landed her dream Daniel Cleaver. Now it was time for Helen Fielding to line up her dream Mark Darcy. Though Fielding speaks openly about the oddity of seeing actors who don't quite resemble the characters she had in her head, there had always been one man who could play Mark. "The only movie star I cast in my head was Mr. Darcy—or Colin Firth, as he is often called," says Fielding.

By this point, Bridget Jones had enough star power that Firth couldn't possibly be unaware of his barely disguised literary alter ego. "Helen had been saying publicly I'd be her choice for Darcy," says Colin Firth. "We came across each other at a party. She asked if I minded her saying that. I said not at all. A friend told me later she'd taken that to mean I was keeping myself free for the next five years."

Was this comparison too weird? Too meta? Too self-indulgent? Too likely to get him hopelessly typecast as stuffy, handsome dudes named Darcy? In the end, Firth brushed all those concerns away and took the role. "I did briefly wonder if it was a good idea or not," says Firth. "In the end my sense of humour encouraged me to do it. I think it's more amusing if it's me, and it's more amusing for me as well."

But if the production had secured the perfect Daniel Cleaver and Mark Darcy, finding the perfect Bridget was going to be a Herculean challenge—in part because the appeal of Bridget Jones was that she needed to feel like someone you knew. "Nearly everybody who worked on the film had a different idea of who Bridget is," says Maguire. "And nearly everybody who has read the book knows Bridget. Either it's themselves or it's their friend."

It's not easy to find a British or Australian actress in Bridget Jones's age range who wasn't at least *considered* for the lead role; Toni Collette, Helena Bonham Carter, Cate Blanchett, Emily Watson, and Rachel Weisz were all floated as possibilities. *The Washington*

BRIDGET BEFORE RENÉE

Long before Renée Zellweger was cast, a curly-haired brunette named Susannah Lewis was the face of Bridget Jones. Lewis was working as secretary to the managing editor of *The Independent* when Charles Leadbeater asked her if she'd pose as Bridget for the author photo that ran alongside Helen Fielding's column (as you might have thought, it wasn't Fielding herself). After she agreed, Lewis and freelance photographer Nick Turpin went to a champagne bar down the street, where Lewis—in true Bridget fashion—ordered a glass of wine and lit a cigarette. Turpin took a photo in profile, with a curl of dark hair hanging over her face, and readers were treated to a hazy picture of what Bridget "looked like."

Though Lewis had been told the photo was close enough to a silhouette that she'd never actually be recognized, the success of the Bridget Jones columns made her a minor celebrity. "It was a standing joke that Helen Fielding was watching my every move," she says, amused by her fictional doppelgänger. "I began to wonder if I was modelling myself on Bridget, or she was modelling herself on me." Her image was also used for the first cover of *Bridget Jones's Diary*, though she claims that the publisher, Picador, paid her just 500 pounds for the privilege.

Post—which called the casting hunt the most closely watched since "Who will play Scarlett O'Hara?"—said Kate Winslet was the name most frequently suggested by Bridget Jones fans, though Gwyneth Paltrow and Minnie Driver were mentioned as well.

A name that did *not* tend to come up was Renée Zellweger. Zellweger, who had broken out a few years earlier in Cameron Crowe's romantic comedy *Jerry Maguire*, was not on anyone's shortlist for the role. She recalls her agent revealing that he had suggested her for *Bridget Jones's Diary* to Working Title executive Eric Fellner. "Eric said: 'That's the dumbest idea I've ever heard and don't ever come to me with any more of your stupid ideas,'" Zellweger says.

But the net was being cast widely enough that Zellweger eventually came in for a reading. "I figured that when she walked in the room, we'd know. She did walk in the room, and we did know. And we went, 'Oh fuck, she's a Texan,'" says Maguire.

The story of *Bridget Jones's Diary* would not be complete without a brief survey of the blisteringly negative response in the British tabloids when Renée Zellweger was cast. By the time the film was in production, Bridget Jones had been widely accepted as a stand-in for the average, modern British woman. Now a slender American movie star was being flown in to do the job. Tabloids railed against the casting as "clunking, Hollywood idiocy," and pulled a quote from Helen Fielding out of context to gin up a false controversy claiming that the author was outraged by the casting. (In reality, Fielding was just joking around, complaining that she herself hadn't been considered to be seduced on-screen by Colin Firth and Hugh Grant.) "I felt really bad for [Zellweger]. It must have been awful for her," says Fielding.

The creative team behind *Bridget Jones's Diary* stood behind Zellweger's casting, but privately, at least several of them had

THE BRIDGET DIET

In the first novel, Fielding writes that Bridget's of roughly average height for a woman and tends to fluctuate between 125 and 130 pounds. The character's obsession with losing a few pounds, however, meant that the creative team ultimately decided that Zellweger should gain some weight for the role. "To be self-deprecating but have no reason to be self-deprecating—I would think that would be annoying to watch for two hours," Zellweger told *Vanity Fair* at the time. "You'd go, 'Stop talking about her chubby thighs!' It would be ridiculous, and even unlikable, as a character."

With just a few weeks before filming began, the process of rapid weight gain turned out to be less pleasant than Zellweger had hoped. "I was repulsed walking down the Easter-candy aisle at the market the other day. I can't think of eating another chocolate bar or pizza, butter, or dessert. It all sounds disgusting to me now because I have to eat so much of it," she said. Zellweger eventually gained seventeen pounds, and though she felt the process was right for the character, she was frustrated by how much scrutiny that part of her process drew. "Bridget is a perfectly normal weight, and I've never understood why it matters so much. No male actor would get such scrutiny if he did the same thing for a role," she says.

similar concerns. "I can't pretend that I didn't slightly raise an eyebrow myself when her name was brought up," says Hugh Grant. "I'll confess now: I *was* a bit worried. But we're able to laugh about it now," says Maguire.

The constant blizzard of skepticism around Zellweger's casting was both premature and unwarranted, but it was also a reminder to the movie's creators that the stakes were perilously high. In addition to extensive sessions with voice coach Barbara Berkery, who had helped Gwyneth Paltrow perfect the accent that helped to win her an Oscar for *Shakespeare in Love*, Zellweger went undercover in the publicity department at the U.K. publishing house Picador, which had published *Bridget Jones's Diary* in the first place. Working under the name Bridget Cavendish (in a nod to producer Jonathan Cavendish, who was said to be her brother), Zellweger went mostly unnoticed as she sat through meetings, answered phones, called newspapers to pitch Picador books, and clipped tabloid articles complaining about an American being cast to play Bridget Jones (which she wrote "rubbish" on)—all while practicing her best version of Bridget's slightly posh accent on her coworkers. "She wasn't what I had anticipated—scrubbed, unaffected and dressed in neat, casual clothes, she fitted in straight away," says Camilla Elworthy, the head of publicity who was Zellweger's "boss" for her three-week stint. Elworthy was the only one who knew "Bridget" was Zellweger, and only one colleague openly noted her uncanny resemblance to an American movie star. "I had to take just one person into my confidence: a colleague in the press office whom I overheard saying on more than one occasion: 'Don't you think Bridget looks just like the girl from *Jerry Maguire?*'" says Elworthy. "I quietly explained that there was a very good reason for that and hissed at her to shut up."

If the run-up to the production of *Bridget Jones's Diary* was laden with anxiety, shooting itself was as smooth as it gets. *Pride and Prejudice* might be the single sturdiest backbone a romantic comedy could be built around, and Helen Fielding's modernized, transmogrified riff on it worked just as well on the big screen. The biggest problem was a surplus of material; Maguire's first cut of *Bridget Jones's Diary* came in at three and a half hours.

And then there was the ending. Everyone agreed that the book's ending, which shifts the focus to Bridget's mother as she becomes invested in a crooked time-share, wouldn't work for the film adaptation, which was more narrowly focused on the love triangle between Bridget, Mark, and Daniel. But what *would* serve as the right capper in the fight for Bridget's heart? "Richard had some ideas that I just was like, 'No,'" recalls Fielding. "Like, somebody singing a pop song out of the window. Richard loves that, and I *don't* like that, because I don't see any part of the *Bridget* universe in which someone would sing a pop song outside the window. *She* wouldn't like it."

This reluctance was in direct contrast to film history itself, in which film audiences had lustily embraced Curtis's supremely schmaltzy vision of Hugh Grant and Andie MacDowell kissing in the rain. But if a serenade wasn't the answer, in the end, Curtis's

RIVAL SUITORS

A running theme on the *Bridget Jones* press tour was the friendly rivalry that developed between Colin Firth and Hugh Grant, who never missed an opportunity to poke fun at each other. Though the tabloids have occasionally tried to spin their relationship into an actual rivalry, just for the record: They were just goofing around. "I remember, at the premiere of *Bridget Jones's Diary* in New York, I felt someone behind me kick my seat. I turned around, and it was Hugh," says Sharon Maguire. "He went, 'Colin's really good in this, isn't he?' I said, 'Yes. Of course. He's really good.' And he went, 'I hadn't expected him to be this good. He's brilliant, really.'"

heightened, rom-com-friendly sensibilities led to the solution. "It was Richard who suggested, 'Why don't these two middle-class men have a fight? How long is it since we've seen a good old fight on a movie like in the Westerns?'" says Maguire.

The climactic fight between Daniel Cleaver and Mark Darcy was scripted as a relatively straightforward brawl, full of right hooks and haymakers, until Grant objected that neither Daniel nor Mark would have any idea what they were doing in a fight. In rehearsals, the group cancelled a planned meeting with a stuntman and collaborated on developing a fight that was comical in its ineffectuality, full of hair-pulling, heavy breathing, and awkward détentes. Colin Firth, who calls it "one of the most organic things ever committed to film," was delighted: "The last time these two characters fought was probably when they were 7 years old in the school playground." It was Fielding's idea to heighten the ridiculousness of the scene by scoring it with The Weather Girls' "It's Raining Men."

It's not the fight, however, but the short, relatively sweet aftermath that solidifies Mark Darcy as a rom-com hero for the ages. Mark, who reads a passage from one of Bridget's old diary entries about how awful he is, leaves her apartment. But when Bridget chases him down, afraid she's lost him for good, she realizes he's just gone down the street to buy her a new diary: "To make a fresh start," he promises.

It was an ideal rom-com ending: Two lovable people who had overcome a series of trials, with each other and with themselves, and discovered at the end that they belonged together. It was not dissimilar in tone and content from the crowd-pleasing endings of *When Harry Met Sally*, or *Four Wedding and a Funeral*, or *There's Something About Mary*. And it made audiences swoon.

But the ending *was* in contrast to a trend that was rapidly over-taking the entertainment industry at the same time. In the same year *Bridget Jones's Diary* was released—to a robust gross of $281 million worldwide on a $25 million budget—Hollywood was awed by the massive box-office earnings of *The Lord of the Rings: The Fellowship of the Ring* and *Harry Potter and the Sorcerer's Stone*, which each got within spitting distance of grossing $1 billion worldwide. And with multiple sequels for each of those franchises forthcoming, it was increasingly obvious that the safest way to replicate a hit was to make a movie just like it.

This formula is in direct opposition to the conventional arc of a satisfying romantic comedy, which begins with a couple apart and ends with a couple together. Though the massive success of movies like *Pretty Woman* and *There's Something About Mary* had encouraged writers, directors, studios, and stars to fish around for sequel ideas, there's a reason none of those ideas had panned out: By any non-mercenary reading, those stories were over.

INTERPRETING THE MASTERS

Helen Fielding wasn't the only writer who used Jane Austen as a framework for her modern rom-com—Amy Heckerling's teen rom-com *Clueless* was loosely based on Austen's 1815 novel *Emma*, reimagined in Beverly Hills. After *Clueless*, a number of movies aimed at teens also riffed on the classics, including 1999's *10 Things I Hate About You* (Shakespeare's *The Taming of the Shrew*), 2006's *She's the Man* (Shakespeare's *Twelfth Night*), and 2010's *Easy A* (Hawthorne's *The Scarlet Letter*). High school book reports would never be the same.

But audiences of the era made it clear: They wanted to see more of the characters they already loved, and Helen Fielding was happy to oblige. She even had a sturdy structural model for the sequel: Jane Austen's *Persuasion*, which follows a young woman who ends her engagement to a man who is clearly her true love.

Even if the idea made sense in theory—and even worked, to admittedly diminishing returns, in Fielding's second novel, *Bridget Jones: The Edge of Reason*—it didn't translate to the film adaptation that came a few years later. The truly awful film version of *Bridget Jones: The Edge of Reason*—which unconvincingly splits up Bridget and Mark—teases yet another possible dalliance with Daniel Cleaver, and ultimately brings Bridget and Mark back together again, making the whole movie an elaborate exercise in pointlessness. Sharon Maguire did not return to direct, citing a busy schedule (including a "modern *Pride and Prejudice*," written by Pulitzer-winning playwright Wendy Wasserstein, that ultimately fell apart). Though credited as a screenwriter, Fielding largely stepped away from direct creative involvement in the production. "By that time, I'd had enough of the whole business. Having had a success, I could sort of see a [film] sequel was going to be hell," she says. Though *The Edge of Reason* follows the broad beats of Fielding's novel, Debra Hayward has similar regrets. "When we decided, in the second movie, to take it to Thailand . . . you take what is essential and domestic and small about the character, and you blow it up, mistakenly thinking a sequel should be bigger . . . I mean, it was a mistake."

Bridget Jones's Diary would hardly be the first successful movie to have a regrettable, disappointing sequel, and while *The Edge of Reason* still made plenty at the box office, there was no obvious creative reason to make yet another sequel. The story could easily have ended here—and for twelve years, it did. But something interesting happened more than a decade later, as time caught up to both Bridget Jones and the team of collaborators who made her such an iconic rom-com heroine in the first place. *Bridget Jones's Baby*, which hit theaters in 2016, also marked the return of Sharon Maguire.

There were two major events that shaped *Bridget Jones's Baby* before a single scene had been shot. The first was the decision to spin the story off in a different direction from Helen Fielding's 2013 novel *Bridget Jones: Mad About the Boy*. That book had sparked international headlines, and enraged plenty of vocal diehard *Bridget Jones* fans, when it was revealed that the novel reintroduced Bridget, now fifty-one, as a widowed single mother following the death of Mark Darcy, complete with a hot young boyfriend. It was Fielding's way of making sure the third *Bridget Jones* novel didn't turn her into the kind of "smug married" Bridget had railed against from the beginning. "I'd already established that she was with Darcy, and there's no way he would leave her, because he's the quintessential gentleman. He wouldn't leave her with children. So, he had to die. It's a shame, but he had to die," she says.

What Fielding *wasn't* prepared for was how the news of Mark Darcy's death, which was revealed in an excerpt of *Mad About the Boy* published in the *Sunday Times*, would immediately beget a national period of mourning. "It was on the news. It was the second lead after the Syrian crisis," says Fielding. "It was really weird. People shouted at me in the street for killing him." Suddenly, a narrative that had frequently been dismissed as comfort food was doing something that made people uncomfortable: depicting a rom-com heroine who got her happy ending, then had it ripped away from her, with unexpected decades as a singleton mother stretching ahead of her.

This was, somewhat understandably, not deemed the most fertile of ground for a third film in the *Bridget Jones* franchise, which had earned a loyal audience by letting fans leave the theater happy that Bridget and Mark had come together again. It was also no small risk to dump Mark Darcy, a widely beloved character played by the widely beloved actor Colin Firth, who had won an Oscar for *The King's Speech* in the intervening years.

I CAN SEE DANIEL WAVING GOODBYE

The road to *Bridget Jones's Baby* was a bumpy one, and nowhere is that more obvious than the years-long, ultimately unsuccessful attempt to get Hugh Grant to return for it.

In 2012, Working Title co-chairman Tim Bevan insisted that reports of Hugh Grant exiting the still-untitled third *Bridget Jones* movie were untrue. Grant's publicist responded by issuing a terse statement: "Hugh is keen that *Bridget Jones 3* happens, but Renée, Colin and he all have some issue with the present script. They are hoping to help work them out."

Whatever problems all three original stars had with the script, two of them managed to sort them out by the time production began. Grant did not, apparently mainly due to his dislike for where the script took Daniel Cleaver. "They did have a script, and it was all ready to go into production, but I always said, 'I don't think it *is* ready,' and we had long battles," said Grant in 2014. "And I'm definitely not in. I'm out. But I think they are going to make one anyway, without me." Still, he ultimately seemed to take the whole thing in stride: When asked if he'd seen *Bridget Jones's Baby* in 2016, he confirmed that he had, and added, "There's some very funny stuff in it."

The team at Working Title had a tough decision to make. "Do we do *that* or do we, you know, give the audiences more of what they love?" says Debra Hayward. "And what we thought is that it jumped too far ahead in the future. *Mad About the Boy* would have been brilliant, but it felt like it was a massive jump from the second film. We felt we couldn't miss out on that moment where she becomes a mum." So it came that *Bridget Jones's Baby*, covering Bridget's pregnancy and childbirth, was conceived—with Helen Fielding's novel covering the same time period in Bridget's life releasing, unusually, more than a month after the movie had already arrived in theaters.

The other major event that shaped *Bridget Jones's Baby* was the departure of Hugh Grant, which meant the elimination of Darcy's primary rival for Bridget's heart. This wasn't the plan; early drafts of *Bridget Jones's Baby*, which featured Cleaver prominently, were heavily rewritten to accommodate a new love interest named Jack Qwant (Patrick Dempsey). Qwant, a tech billionaire, hooks up with Bridget at a music festival. She also hooks up with Darcy, her estranged ex, shortly after they both attend the funeral for Daniel Cleaver, who has apparently died in a plane cash. (Don't worry: A stinger at the end of the movie reveals that Cleaver has miraculously been found alive, so fans can hold out hope for *Bridget Jones 4*.) When Bridget winds up pregnant and decides to carry her pregnancy to term, the question becomes: Which of these men is the baby's father? And, more to the point: Which of these men does Bridget *want* to be the father?

If this all sounds incredibly contrived . . . well, it is. And yet, while the bare plot of *Bridget Jones's Baby* is silly, it gains considerable power simply by putting a woman in her mid-forties, with the experiences Bridget has had, at the center of a rom-com story.

Much of this is due to Zellweger herself. Following a feverish, ubiquitous spate of acting that included everything from the historical football rom-com *Leatherheads* to the underappreciated western *Appaloosa* to the inexplicable "What if a bee filed a lawsuit?" movie called *Bee Movie*, Zellweger took a self-imposed hiatus from Hollywood in 2010. Amid widespread, often cruel speculation about her disappearance from the big screen, she wrote an essay for *Vanity Fair* in which she revealed the reason for her break. "I took on a schedule that is not realistically sustainable and didn't allow for taking care of myself. Rather than stopping to recalibrate, I kept running until I was depleted and made bad choices about how to conceal the exhaustion," Zellweger wrote.

She broke that hiatus for *Bridget Jones's Baby*, and it is no coincidence why she is so convincing in that role, which puts the character through a rom-com version of the star's real-life arc. "There is the inevitability of your body changing and you growing older," says Zellweger. "I want to work in a way where I can portray women who are relatable throughout my life."

These parallels were not lost on Firth, who returned to the role of Mark Darcy for the third time in fifteen years, bringing with him a revised and mature perspective. "What's interesting—and it didn't quite fully occur to me until now—is that what adds resonance is that the audience have aged, inevitably, with us," says Firth. He was also in a position to appreciate what Zellweger was bringing to the role. "I've played Mr. Darcy enough times. I enjoy playing Mr. Darcy, but I'm not hungry to play Mark Darcy again. It's not an ambition. But it *is* something of an ambition to see Renée inhabit that role again because I think it's one of the best characters ever created." This raises the obvious question: Will Bridget Jones turn up on the big screen again?

Bridget Jones's Baby ends with Bridget and Mark walking down the aisle, ready to raise their son together, which feels like a fairly effective grace note for this story to go out on. Then again: The previous two *Bridget Jones* movies also ended with Bridget and Mark happily coupled, and that didn't stop the sequels from breaking them up yet again.

Renée Zellweger—who earned her first Best Actress nomination at the Oscars for *Bridget Jones's Diary*, and finally won one eighteen years later, for playing Judy Garland in 2020's *Judy*—has no obvious need to revisit the character another time. But if she does, *Bridget Jones: Mad About the Boy* provides one intriguing, if audience-displeasing, template: What would Bridget be like as a single mother dating a younger man? Fans might rebel, but it might be worth it to see a rom-com that regarded a single mother in her fifties as the *beginning* of a funny, romantic love story, instead of someone not even worthy of depicting on-screen.

The real lesson of Bridget's decades-long history is that the character is both compelling and resilient enough to stand up to any hypothetical scenario—a valuable commodity in an entertainment industry that increasingly prefers to double down over making a new bet. When pressed, Helen Fielding admits that she's even kicked around a fourth *Bridget Jones* movie that could slip neatly into the modern era, with Mark Darcy or Daniel Cleaver or Jack Qwant or *no one* by her side. "I kind of started a script," says Fielding. "But obviously, with the [Coronavirus], there's a lot of questions. I mean, you *could* have the virus in *Bridget*. I found, when I wrote the columns, that you can do anything. It's difficult. But you can."

Drew Barrymore

THE SELF-MADE SUPERSTAR

For decades, Drew Barrymore's mother, Jaid, has told a story about her daughter's first acting gig. It was a dog food commercial, and Barrymore landed the part when she was all of eleven months old. Though Barrymore hails from a storied acting legacy—stretching all the way back to her great-grandfather Maurice Barrymore on one side and her great-great-great-great-grandparents Thomas and Louisa Lane on the other—she earned her commercial the old-fashioned way: by winning the role at an audition, over hundreds of other would-be child stars who were being ushered into show business by their parents.

Drew Barrymore's first acting job was an unusually early path to the kind of actual stardom she eventually attained. When you "audition" a baby, you're not exactly looking for acting talent; you're looking for a baby that will naturally do what the project needs with a minimal amount of time and hassle. And since this was a dog food commercial, the audition came down to one question: How well does the baby interact with a dog?

When the puppy was brought into the room at her audition, Barrymore laughed. That was good. When the puppy came close to her, she stuck out her hand and nuzzled its fur. That was very good. And then—shocking everyone in the room—the puppy bit her on the nose. That was very bad. "There was something like 25 people there, and they were all shocked, probably thinking, 'Oh my God, lawsuit,'" recalled Jaid Barrymore, quoted in Drew's own cowritten memoir. "Then Drew suddenly threw her head back and started laughing, and everyone was charmed out of their mind. They all broke into applause, and Drew just looked around and beamed. She just drank it up."

This, uh, "charming" anecdote is pretty typical of the first half of Drew Barrymore's life and career, in which adults encouraged her Hollywood career while consciously ignoring the dangerous and unpleasant things that might be happening to her as a result. Six years later, when the seven-year-old Barrymore was catapulted into superstardom via 1982's *E.T. the Extra-Terrestrial*, this dynamic became exponentially more true, and exponentially more destructive to Barrymore's health. "From the time I became famous in *E.T.*, my life got really weird," says Barrymore. "One day I was a little girl, and the next day I was being mobbed by people who wanted me to sign my autograph, or pose for pictures, or who just wanted to touch me. I was this seven-year-old who was expected to be going on a mature 29."

In the subsequent years, the adolescent Barrymore's life played out in the tabloids. In her very candid 1991 memoir *Little Girl Lost*, which was published when she was fourteen years old, Barrymore describes a lifestyle of near-constant partying—facilitated by her spotlight-hungry mother, and either ignored or encouraged by the other older people around her—which resulted in her addictions to alcohol and cocaine. When Barrymore entered treatment at age thirteen, a tabloid reporter staked out various rehab centers until he spotted her mother visiting one and wrote a story about it. After eighteen months, she came out of rehab and swiftly secured legal emancipation via a court order—a recommendation from her doctors at the clinic, who had concluded she would be better on her own than in the unhealthy parental situation she had left behind.

Barrymore came out of rehab ready to go back to work and discovered that her career in Hollywood was over. Her tabloid reputation meant that casting directors had lost interest. "To have such a big career at such a young age, then nothing for years—people going, 'You're an unemploy-able disaster'—that's a tough trip to have by the time you're 14," says Barrymore. "To have access to so many things, then to nothing."

She eventually fought her way back into Hollywood, in roles which tended to riff on her reputation: the 1992 erotic thriller *Poison Ivy*, in which she plays a troubled young woman who seduces her best friend's dad, or the 1993 thriller *Doppelganger*, in which she plays a troubled young woman with a dark dual identity, or the 1995 romantic drama *Mad Love*, in which she plays a troubled young woman who runs off with her boyfriend and ends up committed to a psychiatric hospital.

Barrymore's extended cameo in 1996's *Scream*, which ends when her character is killed about twelve minutes into the movie, is generally cited as her big Hollywood comeback—but to hear Barrymore tell it, her true transition into the adult acting career she actually wanted came about a year later, when she cold-called Adam Sandler to suggest that they should make a rom-com together.

At the time, Sandler was a *Saturday Night Live* breakout with two hit comedies under his belt, but both of them had been squarely in line with Sandler's brand of screw-up-your-face-and-yell-really-loud comedy. No one saw him as a romantic lead—except Barrymore, who was convinced they could be what she saw as a "modern, weird, Hepburn-Tracy old Hol-lywood couple," with a career-spanning series of rom-coms to match. "I knew it in my bones," says Barrymore. "I was drawn to his light. I wanted to make love stories, but I wanted them to have a certain energy that was about true love and chemistry and timelessness, and I was convinced of us doing something together."

Barrymore and Sandler's first meeting, at a coffee shop, was not particularly promising. "We looked like the worst blind date you've ever seen," says Barrymore. "I showed up in purple hair and a leopard coat, and he was in his classic cargo pants." Still, she made her case: "I shook his hand with fervor, thanked him for meeting me, and began to plead my case to him. I told him that, for whatever reason, I knew that we were supposed to become a team."

Barrymore's earnestness eventually led to 1998's *The Wedding Singer*, which—at Barrymore's own urging—received an uncredited rewrite by Carrie Fisher designed to make Barrymore's character less of a love interest and more of a co-lead. "I don't even know if we set out to do a romantic comedy, but it just kind of got romantic," says writer Tim Herlihy. The movie showed another side of both Barrymore and Sandler—more on his side of the story on page 154—and outgrossed rom-com icon Nora Ephron's own *You've Got Mail* at the box office that year. The chemistry between Barrymore and Sandler had the extra benefit of appealing to fans of both, increasing the take from demographics who might not normally turn up for a rom-com. And just as she'd predicted, Barrymore would repeatedly re-team with Sandler in the years to come, in 2004's *50 First Dates* and 2014's *Blended*. "Every 10 years, we get to fall in love again," she said while promoting *Blended* in 2014.

But the most significant development in Barrymore's career as a rom-com icon came in 1999, when Flower Films, the production company she cofounded, released its first movie: *Never Been Kissed*. The movie stars Barrymore as Josie Geller, a twenty-five-year-old copy editor who agrees to go undercover at a high school to report on what teens are really doing. The experience gives her an opportunity to revisit and rewrite her own awkward adolescence with the experience of adulthood, which culminates with Josie giving a big climactic speech at prom: "There is a *big* world out there," she says. "Bigger than prom, bigger than high school. And it won't matter if you were the prom queen, or the quarterback of the football team, or the biggest nerd in school. Find out who you are, and try not to be afraid of it."

On the movie's twentieth anniversary in 2019, Barrymore explained why, exactly, *Never Been Kissed* was the first movie she produced through Flower Films: "All we wanted to do was make something that felt like the way so many of us feel growing up. It's raw and ridiculous, beautiful and helps you decide what is important and what isn't," she wrote. It was, explicitly, an opportunity to look back on a difficult adolescence with the wisdom of experience, rewrite the story, and move on to a happier adulthood—an idea to which Barrymore could relate in a very personal way.

Throughout the 2000s, Flower Films produced or co-produced a series of romantic comedies, each starring Barrymore: 2004's *50 First Dates* (opposite Sandler), 2005's *Fever Pitch* (opposite Jimmy Fallon), 2007's *Music and Lyrics* (opposite Hugh Grant), and 2009's *He's Just Not That Into You* (opposite an absurdly overqualified ensemble cast that included Scarlett Johansson, Jennifer Aniston, Jennifer Connelly, Ben Affleck, and Bradley Cooper). Later, both Flower Films and Barrymore threw their creative muscle behind a singularly strange and compelling TV rom-com riff: Netflix's *Santa Clarita Diet*, which believed so much in the love story between its protagonists Sheila (Barrymore) and Joel (Timothy Olyphant) that Sheila—after becoming a zombie—spent a decent chunk of the series trying to convince her husband to accept his own bite so they could enjoy eternal life as zombies together. When asked, she'll mount a passionate defense of rom-coms: "That's why people read *Pride and Prejudice* again and again. We need that stuff. It's healthy to have that sense of yummy hope. It can't all be, 'This is the harsh reality.' What's going to get us out of bed in the morning?"

Following the cancellation of *Santa Clarita Diet*—and the largely overlooked release of another rom-com, *The Stand In*, which was derailed by the COVID-19 pandemic—Barrymore has diverted her innate on-camera charisma into a syndicated talk show called *The Drew Barrymore Show*, which frequently delves into her Hollywood past in ways that embrace the lighter side while skimming over the dark. (One representative clip captured her delight when a poll revealed that Hawaii, where it takes place, and for some reason Minnesota, had named *50 First Dates* its favorite rom-com to revisit on Valentine's Day.) In 2015, she released a new memoir called *Wildflower*—her first book since the harrowing *Little Girl Lost*—

which promises, and delivers, a series of stories "told from the place of happiness she's achieved today."

It's the same attitude that animates her evident pride in *Never Been Kissed*, which feels, more than twenty years later, like the clearest distillation of every part of her life into a single film. "You try so hard to do something important and meaningful. But when you strike the universal chord of goofiness, it's far more important," says Barrymore, reflecting on *Never Been Kissed*. "And, goddamn it, we all beat the fuck up on ourselves, going, 'We'd better do something important and meaningful in this world, and make an impact and a difference and change something'—and in the end, it's like, 'Did you make anyone feel like they weren't alone?' That might be the coolest thing you ever do with your life."

"Nice Greek girls are supposed to do three things in life: marry Greek boys, make Greek babies, and feed everyone until the day we die."

—TOULA PORTOKALOS, *MY BIG FAT GREEK WEDDING*

CHAPTER 8

MY BIG FAT GREEK WEDDING

(And the Biggest Movie No One in Hollywood Understood, and Still Might Not)

RITA WILSON AND TOM HANKS WERE BAFFLED. THEY HAD SPENT MONTHS working every Hollywood contact in their Rolodexes in their efforts to produce a promising script called *My Big Fat Greek Wedding*. The writer, Nia Vardalos, was an unknown—but if you were looking for a couple of Hollywood superstars to shepherd your rom-com, you couldn't do much better than Wilson and Hanks, who had played no small part in *defining* the genre over the preceding decade. Yet whenever it finally seemed like their pitch had found an executive who might understand the project, the executive would ask a version of the same question: Which big-name Hollywood actress do you see starring in it?

If there was anything *My Big Fat Greek Wedding didn't* need, it was a new lead actress. As far as Wilson, Hanks, and logic itself were concerned, the production already had its star: Nia Vardalos, who had written the story, based on her own life, and had changed the material into a play. She had then put it on as a one-woman show with basically no budget but a seemingly endless well of passion. Anyone who didn't understand that Nia Vardalos *was My Big Fat Greek Wedding* didn't understand *My Big Fat Greek Wedding* at all. "I just kept thinking, *Would you be saying this to Jerry Seinfeld? Would you be saying this to Ray Romano?*" says Rita Wilson. "Would you be saying this to *men* who were also comedians and writers? It just seemed very unfair. And because Tom and I are both actors, we were like, 'We've seen this woman. We know what she can do. She's going to be able to do this.'"

The sheer existence of *My Big Fat Greek Wedding* came down to three elements that factor, in some degree, into basically anything that gets made in Hollywood: tenacity, timing, and luck. The tenacity occurred within Nia Vardalos herself, who by 1997 had been auditioning for years without ever finding a role that felt like it was written for her. Sure, she'd booked commercials, and a few brief guest spots on sitcoms like *The Drew Carey Show* and *Boy Meets World*, which were at least enough to cover rent in Los Angeles for the month. But the roles she really wanted—roles that were tailored toward the skill set of a funny, cheery Greek woman—weren't just hard to come by, they didn't exist. Eventually, Vardalos's agent decided she had seen enough. She called Vardalos in for a meeting and bluntly laid out the problem as she saw it: "You're not pretty enough to be a leading lady and not fat enough to be a character actress."

The agent's proposed solution was—to use a polite word—unconventional. "We're going to change the spelling of the last part of your name from 'os' to 'ez' and send you out as a Hispanic," she said. And when Vardalos replied that she was Greek, not Hispanic, and was not willing to pretend she belonged to another culture, her agent shrugged. "Well, there are no Greek parts, so I can't get you work."

This was just the latest and most galling version of a problem that had dogged Vardalos for her entire acting career. Though she had originally studied classical theater in Toronto, she had been frustrated by the rigidity of her program. "I enjoyed performing Shakespeare, but how many roles were there for a robust and curly-haired loudmouth?" she says. "I spent many nights trying to straighten my hair, trying to lose weight, trying to fit in, so that I could look like the 'classic' classical actor."

Vardalos eventually found a warmer reception at the famed improv studio Second City, though even that hadn't come easily. She took a gig working the front desk and left the phone off the hook when the shows began so she could sneak into the theater to watch. When a cast member fell ill, she volunteered herself as someone who already knew the written material for the show. The next day, she was hired for the cast. After four years in Toronto, she joined the Chicago company.

Vardalos spent her time at Second City honing her skills as a comic performer, and proving to herself that there were plenty of ways to use her talents that would actually resonate with audiences. The looseness and unpredictability of improv meant she was going out on stage every night without a safety net, and audiences were responding to her style of comedy. But moving to Los Angeles with hopes of working in film or television had resulted in a series of dead ends. The problem, Vardalos decided, wasn't her; it was Hollywood. "The solution was to write my own role," she says. "And it honestly was the only way forward."

With a mix of frustration and inspiration, Vardalos sat down to write something drawn from her own life—something sharp and witty she was confident *only* she could write. She started by making a list of her own personal anecdotes, narrowing it down to the stories she remembered telling at parties that had made people laugh hardest. She settled on a screenplay idea that conveniently came with its own natural structure: her recent wedding to a man who had converted to the Greek Orthodox Church when they got married, and the general chaos that resulted from introducing a non-Greek newcomer to her large, lovable, and smothering Greek family.

The first draft of the screenplay for *My Big Fat Greek Wedding* took just three weeks to write—a detail that later attracted plenty of attention in the press, who marveled at the apparent ease of her success to Vardalos's bemused irritation. "I wrote the first draft in three weeks—but I wrote *fifty* drafts," she says. Though she'd never written a screenplay before (and had to borrow a friend's computer to do it), and she knew that Hollywood didn't have anything that looked or sounded like this script, she was confident that audiences would show up if she could just get it made. In her wildest dreams, she thought, *If the script was produced, I might even get the chance to play a bridesmaid.*

The trick would be getting *My Big Fat Greek Wedding*, in any form, in front of as many eyes as possible. But without the support of a Hollywood studio—or a manager who was even interested in reading the script—Vardalos resolved that she'd need to do it herself. Inspired by performers like *Saturday Night Live* alum Julia Sweeney, Vardalos reconceived her *My Big Fat Greek Wedding* screenplay as a one-woman stage show, and—after a few workshops held at the HBO workspace—used her savings to book a ninety-nine-seat theater where she could perform it. The tiny *Los Angeles Times* ad for the play included a phone number for the "box office," which was actually Vardalos's personal number. When people called to buy tickets, she'd answer the phone, affecting a different voice to imply a support staff for the show that quite literally didn't exist. With no advertising budget, Vardalos went to her Greek Orthodox church and handed out flyers at the post-service coffee hour, hoping at least that the show might become a word-of-mouth hit among Los Angeles's tight-knit Greek community.

The gambit worked better than she'd hoped; before long, she was selling out the small theater, playing her one-woman show to laughter from Greek and non-Greek audience members alike, who would spread the word—and, not infrequently, return for encore performances with new friends in tow. At just $10 a ticket, Vardalos never made money on the show, but money wasn't the goal—it was the chance to deliver her material to a receptive audience, and figure out, in real time, what *My Big Fat Greek Wedding* could be. "I was trying out material from the screenplay, five shows a week, and learning what worked and what didn't. It was the ultimate development process," says Vardalos. Basing the show around a wedding provided a structure on which Vardalos could channel any number of characters and hang a versatile array of jokes, which—owing in no small part to her improv days—she felt comfortable swapping in and out in real time. One night, when Vardalos was talking to her mother on the way to the theater, her mother quipped, "The man is the head, but the woman is the neck, and she can turn the head anywhere she wants." Vardalos slipped the line into the show on that same night, and was delighted to find that it brought the house down. In it went, permanently.

Vardalos spent months staging the play in a rotating series of ninety-nine-seat Los Angeles theaters like The Hudson and The Acme and The Globe—and finding a hungry audience everywhere she went. She also found the occasional interest of producers, who were interested in buying *My Big Fat Greek Wedding* if she would sign away *all* creative control. One studio affiliated with Disney called her in for a meeting and suggested Marisa Tomei could star in the film version. "I said, 'She's great, but she's Italian—and this is a Greek story,'" says Vardalos. Another producer offered her $50,000 for the script on the condition that a "real" writer could be hired to shift the perspective from a Greek family to a Hispanic family. Vardalos had created her own material; now she had to decide if she was willing to sell it to someone who didn't share her vision. She ultimately passed. "I was probably making about $14,000 a year," says Vardalos. "That was *so* much money, and I said 'no' in the weakest, shakiest voice imaginable."

It is no coincidence that the person who finally understood what *My Big Fat Greek Wedding* could be was a woman with her own deep ties to the Greek community. Rita Wilson—born Margarita Ibrahimoff—was born and raised in California, but her parents, Dorothea Tzigkou and Hassan Halilov Ibrahimoff, were immigrants who remained attached to their Greek roots and raised her in the Greek Orthodox Church.

Wilson, a devoted Broadway aficionado, had decided that she needed to seek out and attend more plays in her hometown. Though Los Angeles isn't really known as a theater town, she figured that a town full of actors must have *something* worth seeing, even if she had to dig deeper to find it. "The *Los Angeles Times* had a very, very small theater section which came out on Thursdays," says Wilson. "And there was a quarter of a page that would run ads—the size of a postage stamp. They were small because they were inexpensive. There it was, in this little square, the title: 'My Big Fat Greek Wedding.' And I knew right away, a Greek girl had written *this*. Greeks can recognize other Greeks like inner sonar homing devices."

Wilson turned up to see *My Big Fat Greek Wedding* with a minientourage of her sister, mother, and nieces. From the moment the show began, it was clear that Vardalos's very personal story had finally found a Hollywood power player who understood it on a molecular level. "Her laugh is so infectious," says Vardalos. "I'm sure she added five minutes to the show because she would start to laugh, and then the audience would laugh, and it would just keep going."

It is no accident that it took a Greek person, and a woman no less, to appreciate what Vardalos was doing without finding ways to rejigger it for what they presumed would be wider appeal. "I thought, *Oh my God, this is my life. This is just like how I grew up,*" says Wilson. She asked the "box-office attendant" if she could meet Vardalos after the show, not realizing that she was talking to Vardalos's husband, Ian (who, of course, knew *exactly* who she was). The theater was small enough that Vardalos couldn't even invite Wilson backstage, so they met in the lobby. "Her very first words to me were, 'I love you,'" says Vardalos. "And then she said, 'This should be a movie.' And I said, 'I have written the screenplay.'"

Vardalos handed Wilson a copy of the screenplay right there and then, hoping for the best. What she didn't know was that Tom Hanks and his friend and producing partner Gary Goetzman, who he'd met while working on 1993's *Philadelphia*, had just formed a production company. They called it Playtone, after the record company in their previous collaboration (and Hanks's directorial debut) *That Thing You Do!*, and they were looking for material to produce. Wilson was convinced that Hanks—who she describes as "the Ian in her life," and who also converted to the Greek Orthodox Church when they got married—would find just as much as she saw in *My Big Fat Greek Wedding.* "The phone rang the very next day with somebody calling to buy tickets for Tom," says Vardalos.

The appearance of two-time Oscar winner Tom Hanks seeing a $10 show at a ninety-nine-seat theater in Hollywood sent the audience into a tizzy. "I kept hearing 'Tom Hanks is here' and then, in a Greek accent, 'Tom Hanks,' 'Tom Hanks,'" recalls Vardalos.

For his part, Hanks tried to be as unobtrusive as possible, agreeing to take pictures and sign autographs for anyone who asked—as long as they waited until the show was over.

Moments before the show began, Vardalos stood in the wings of the theater, aware that one of the biggest actors in Hollywood was about to see her performance. *Oh, God, how am I going to do this? How do I have the nerve to walk out?*, she recalls thinking. Deciding, in the end, that her two options were being proud of herself or being mad at herself—and knowing that, in that immortal piece of show business wisdom, the show needed to go on either way—Vardalos swallowed her nerves and stepped onto the stage.

The week after he saw the show, Hanks sent her a letter— typed on one of the many typewriters from his now-legendary collection—expressing his admiration for the show. Shortly after that he called Vardalos, revealed he and Goetzman were starting Playtone and that, with Rita Wilson, they'd like to produce *My Big Fat Greek Wedding* as the company's first film. It was a type of conversation she'd had before, though never with a celebrity as big as Tom Hanks. But by then she had learned, a hundred times over, that it was her job to fight for the movie she wanted. "I would like to play the bride," she told Hanks.

He said yes. As far as Hanks was concerned, *My Big Fat Greek Wedding* had its star (though, as mentioned, other studio executives would take more convincing). But while Vardalos had a successful solo play—and would indeed go on to star as Toula, the Greek bride at the center of this fictionalized take on her own wedding—the film would require dozens of actors to surround her. The casting call for *My Big Fat Greek Wedding* was very specific: "Please submit actors who can play believable Greeks and actors who have comic timing. Please submit both name and non-name actors for the leads."

ART MEETING LIFE

Even as production on *My Big Fat Greek Wedding* heated up,
Vardalos and her family kept it a secret from almost everyone
they knew. "Nobody knew except for my immediate family," says
Vardalos. "It's hard to explain. There are several expressions for it
in Greek, but it means, 'Stay small.' We're loud, and we're in your
face, but we don't brag. So we all were in a pinky swear that nobody
knew that I was even in development with Tom Hanks. Even in a
room with Tom Hanks."

Vardalos did, however, get to bring her actual family to the set
for the movie's big climax. "My family showed up for the wedding
scene," she says. "My dad was walking around, and somebody said
to him, 'You sure seem happy.' And he said, 'Yes, because I don't
have to pay for this wedding.'"

"I felt that I had been marginalized because of my looks, so I
also felt a responsibility to my community," says Vardalos. "So I
requested that we search for Greek actors, but that we not be racist
about it. Look for Greek. Try to cast Greek. Don't be racist and
only cast Greek. Cast the best person for the role."

The extensive search turned up a number of actors who had
frequently been overlooked in Hollywood. Louis Mandylor, an
Australian actor of Greek descent who had been sidelined in small
supporting roles throughout the 1990s, was cast as Toula's brother
Nick at his first and only audition. Gia Carides, an Australian
actress with a Greek father who Vardalos had admired in Baz
Luhrmann's *Strictly Ballroom*, was cast as Toula's cousin Nikki the
same way. Michael Constantine—an American actor of Greek
descent who won an Emmy in 1970 for the TV series *Room 222*,

and spent the subsequent decades grinding it out as a guest star on shows like *The Love Boat* and *Remington Steele*—showed up to his audition wearing a fisherman's vest. "I remember thinking, *Boy, this man is authentic*," says Vardalos. "And then I looked down at his head shot, and he was wearing a fisherman's vest." He, too, was cast immediately.

The role that was hardest to cast was the one that *couldn't* be a Greek actor: Ian Miller, the fictionalized version of Vardalos's husband, Ian Gomez. (Gomez, an actor himself, was cast in the supporting role of Ian's best friend, Mike.) Everyone involved in the production saw that the character of Ian was a unique opportunity to bring a higher-profile actor into the *My Big Fat Greek Wedding* fold, and many, many actors were mentioned for the part. Owen Wilson was discussed. So was his brother Luke. Even Robert Downey Jr.—then just beginning to resuscitate his acting career after a very public struggle with addiction—was considered for the role. But after six months, Vardalos still hadn't found anyone who she felt could live up to John Corbett, an actor Vardalos had always admired, who had been the first name on her list from the very beginning.

There was just one problem: John Corbett was unavailable. Everyone assured Vardalos that they were committed to finding another actor who felt right for Ian—but even after a two-week production delay, the start of the *My Big Fat Greek Wedding* shoot was looming, and it was becoming clear that a compromise would need to be made.

In fact, the struggle to find the right actor to play Ian was the subject of a scheduled meeting between Nia Vardalos and Gary Goetzman at Toronto's Sutton Place Hotel. As they were discussing the problem—and yes, Vardalos is aware that this sounds exactly as implausible as a meet-cute in a romantic comedy—John Corbett walked into the bar. He was in Toronto filming another

KISS ME, CORBETT

On the day she was scheduled to film her first kissing scene with John Corbett—her first on-screen kiss ever—Nia Vardalos was so nervous that she approached him outside the makeup trailer and asked if they could kiss right then, away from the camera, so she'd feel less shy doing it in front of the cast and crew. He obliged, and the trick worked: "By the time we were on the set, filming it four hours later, it was fine, it was easy, I wasn't embarrassed," says Vardalos.

What they *didn't* know was that someone had caught them in the act and been too mortified to say anything. "We found out years later that the hair artist on the movie had come out of the makeup trailer at that moment, seen us kissing, and went, 'Oh, they're having an affair,'" says Vardalos.

rom-com, *Serendipity*, in which he'd play the luckless beau who had to compete with John Cusack for Kate Beckinsale's heart. (He lost.) As Vardalos and Goetzman approached Corbett to introduce themselves, they overheard him talking to the bartender about a script he'd just read and admired called *My Big Fat Greek Wedding*. Stunned, Vardalos and Goetzman interrupted and offered Corbett the role on the spot, in a handshake deal, if he could fit their new production dates into his schedule. He accepted.

Meanwhile, it was Tom Hanks who personally reached out to Joel Zwick—a prolific TV director who helmed the pilot of Hanks's own sitcom *Bosom Buddies*—to see if he'd be interested in directing *My Big Fat Greek Wedding*. Though Zwick had directed only one film, a little-seen 1989 flop called *Second Sight*, Hanks was convinced his work on big, family-driven ensemble comedies like

Full House and *Family Matters* made him the right person for the job. "He said, 'Y'know, this is just the kind of thing that you've been doing for years, in terms of understanding what makes people tick, what makes them funny, what makes it all work,'" says Zwick. It also didn't hurt that Zwick had a particular appreciation for the specificity of Vardalos's focus on the Greek community. "I was conceptualizing it as a valentine to immigrant America," he says.

The core of *My Big Fat Greek Wedding* is the love story between Toula and Ian, the sweet-hearted high school English teacher who

BIG FAT REJECTED CHANGES

In addition to multiple producers' efforts to buy *My Big Fat Greek Wedding* and turn it into a movie that wasn't about Greek people, Vardalos was repeatedly given suggestions for dramatic twists that could amp up the movie's drama, which she invariably discarded. Complaining that *My Big Fat Greek Wedding* had no villain, one development executive suggested that Toula should have a Greek suitor who she seriously considered over Ian. Another suggested that *Ian* should be the problem. "I remember wincing when a development executive advised me, 'Ian needs to cheat on Toula and win her back before the wedding.' But I try to avoid the formulaic pitfalls that send messages to men and women that we're at war," says Vardalos.

Another frequent note was that Toula's ancient grandmother should die right before the wedding, throwing everyone into grief and chaos. "And I would always say, 'When you go to a movie, it's like you're holding your arms out to your mother and saying, "Tell me a bedtime story."' When the audience has their arms outstretched, you don't take that opportunity to punch them in the solar plexus," says Vardalos.

sweeps her off her feet. The arc of their romance is as clean as it gets: They meet at her family's Greek diner, flirt at the travel agency where she ends up working, fall in love, and get married in the big fat Greek wedding promised by the title. But a simple plot summary belies the fact that nothing about *My Big Fat Greek Wedding* is typical. Vardalos was thirty-nine years old when the movie arrived in theaters—an age when many well-known actresses find that their opportunities in Hollywood are starting to dwindle. Unlike many rom-coms, which goose the drama by threatening a second-act breakup, *My Big Fat Greek Wedding* never even *hints* that Ian or Toula might be having any second thoughts about spending the rest of their lives together. And though Toula's meddling family causes a variety of smaller problems, they all remain stubbornly lovable. Ian's parents are stuffy and awkward but essentially kindhearted. The movie, by design, simply lacks a villain, or even a rival romantic suitor, like Bill Pullman in *Sleepless in Seattle*, Hugh Grant in *Bridget Jones's Diary*, or, uh, John Corbett in *Serendipity*.

The great trick behind *My Big Fat Greek Wedding* is that its incredible specificity makes it universal. If your father wasn't obsessed with the roots of words, or spraying Windex everywhere, like the father in the movie, he did *something* that was unaccountably strange and embarrassing that made you shake your head and laugh. "I stayed for the focus group and listened to what people were saying," says Wilson. "And it was 'They happen to be Italian or Spanish or Chinese or Jewish or Polish—but this is *my* family.'"

Like so many romantic comedies, *My Big Fat Greek Wedding* wasn't understood by many traditional gatekeepers in Hollywood, who simply couldn't imagine an audience for it. In Hollywood—and certainly in the romantic comedy—the studios almost entirely defaulted to what they saw as "normal," which was almost invariably upper-middle-class whiteness. (This is how you end up with an entire genre of movies in which everyone seems to work in journalism or architecture or architectural journalism.) Even when the movie scored well with test audiences, none of the Hollywood executives they courted were convinced that it had any real chance at success. "Our distributor at the time was Lionsgate, and when they came to the test screening, they didn't even stay for the focus group," says Wilson. "I was like, *How could they leave before the focus group?* I mean . . . Did they not see that this audience is in tears as they're watching this movie? So they left. They had no faith in the movie."

Undaunted, Playtone shopped the final cut of *My Big Fat Greek Wedding* to distributors where Hanks and Wilson had previously done business. "What they were seeing was the *exact* movie that came out. It's not like we made cuts or we made edits or anything," says Wilson. Still, every studio turned them down. By falling into the sweet spot between an indie movie and a Hollywood release, *My Big Fat Greek Wedding* found itself shunned on both sides. "The festival circuit was like, 'This is too commercial.' And the studios were like, 'We don't know what to do with a movie that's an indie. We don't know how to market this,'" says Wilson. Executives were also skeptical of Vardalos, fretting that the movie had no chance of reaching an audience without a big-name star in the lead. "We were basically a pariah," says Joel Zwick.

The movie was eventually distributed by IFC Films, which had released its first film just a couple of years earlier, though production company Gold Circle Films had to agree to cover all marketing costs. On April 19, 2002, *My Big Fat Greek Wedding* was released in 108 theaters, opposite the *Mummy* spin-off *The Scorpion King* and the Sandra Bullock thriller *Murder by Numbers*. Reviews were typically warm, with critics frequently singling out how natural and grounded *My Big Fat Greek Wedding* felt in an era of rom-coms that were increasingly untethered from reality: "Five minutes into the film, I relaxed, knowing it was set in the real world, and not in the Hollywood alternative universe where Julia Roberts can't get a date," wrote Roger Ebert, giving the movie three stars.

For indie movies like *My Big Fat Greek Wedding*, a release is a marathon, not a sprint; the movie didn't even go into wide release until August of 2002. As *My Big Fat Greek Wedding* was gradually released in more theaters throughout the spring and summer, Vardalos and Corbett embarked on a grueling promotional tour to drum up publicity for the movie. Vardalos—still an unknown in any territory where people hadn't seen the movie yet—would show up to radio interviews alongside her costar to find they were only interested in talking with John Corbett. Sometimes, she would discover that they had only brought a chair for Corbett until he insisted they bring one for Vardalos as well.

Even as *My Big Fat Greek Wedding* transitioned from tiny indie to word-of-mouth sleeper hit to cultural sensation, Vardalos frequently ended up the target of criticism that veered from passive-aggressive to actively aggressive. "We would do an interview with someone who was, let's say, the local professor in screenwriting. And it would be a lunch, an interview with John and me, for the local paper," says Vardalos. "And when we sat down, that's when they would tell me. It was usually a male. And they would tell me how bad the screenplay was, and how lucky I was, and that John was out of my league. They would say, 'Reviews have said that you don't have the looks to be a leading lady.' And they would say, 'How do you feel when "people" say that?' John and I would walk away, and he would put his arm around me, and say, 'Baby, they hate you. You must be *really* good.'"

Audiences agreed. By the time *My Big Fat Greek Wedding* left theaters, it had earned a whopping $368 million worldwide—enough to make it, in 2002, not just the highest-grossing romantic comedy of all time, but the highest-grossing independent movie of all time. (That record was eclipsed two years later by *The Passion of the Christ*.) The "risky" movie no major studio had gambled on had become the rare movie that seemed to have near-universal appeal. Vardalos, who also earned an Oscar nomination for her screenplay, is deeply proud of the movie's success but dislikes the emphasis frequently placed on the eye-popping numbers attached to it. "I hated the talk of the money, and I still do to this day," says Vardalos. "I hate the final number, the tally, the questions about how much I made, everything. I don't like art being judged with an equation of money attached to it."

Uncomfortable as it may be, success in Hollywood has a professional utility that can be traded on: If your last movie grossed something like sixty-one times what it cost to make, what will your *next* movie do? In an industry that generally accepts that commercial movies will be less artistic, or artistic movies will be less commercial, *My Big Fat Greek Wedding* was a minor miracle: a well-reviewed romantic comedy, eventually nominated for an Oscar for Best Original Screenplay, that also grossed hundreds of millions of dollars.

Here is where it would be tempting to insert yet another happy ending: the moment at which Nia Vardalos, having vastly exceeded the industry's expectations for what she could do, found a line of studio executives begging for her next project. Unfortunately, that was not the case. "The overwhelming thing, that surprised me over and over again, is that my physicality became an issue," says Vardalos. "I was considered not necessarily 'castable.' Doors did not swing open, acting-wise."

If *My Big Fat Greek Wedding* was a lightning strike for Vardalos, it proved harder to make it strike twice. A spin-off sitcom called

My Big Fat Greek Life, which debuted on CBS less than a year after *My Big Fat Greek Wedding* premiered, was the result of a roomful of sitcom writers—sans Vardalos—attempting to figure out how to squeeze the movie's charms into twenty-two minutes with a laugh track. The resulting series reunited much of the movie's cast, including Vardalos, Lainie Kazan, and Constantine, for a sequel focused on Toula and Ian's married life (with Steven Eckholdt replacing John Corbett, who was booked for an FX drama called *Lucky*). Vardalos is credited as a writer only on the premiere episode of *My Big Fat Greek Life*, and her creative role was ultimately limited: "The TV show deal was signed before the movie came out, and then because I was in Europe promoting the film, I couldn't write the TV series," she says. *My Big Fat Greek Life* lasted just seven episodes before the network pulled the plug, and Vardalos does not regret that it didn't run longer.

Though she wrote and starred in other projects over the years—several of which more or less openly attempted to recapture the magic of *My Big Fat Greek Wedding*—nothing had the same success (which is, to be fair, a tall order when your film debut is the biggest rom-com in history). And everywhere she went, Vardalos was asked the same question: When are you going to make a sequel?

Vardalos knew from experience that there were essentially no stories about women over a certain age being produced in Hollywood, and she wanted to do what she could to tell one. "It's maddening for me. If I am looking for scripts, if Gwyneth Paltrow is looking for scripts and Sandra Bullock is looking for scripts, surely Andrea Martin and Lainie Kazan are looking for scripts," she says. "We have to write for each other."

What would the sequel be about? Though Vardalos spent four years kicking around ideas, it quite literally took the passage of time for her to find an answer that satisfied her. On her own daughter's first day of school, as Vardalos grappled with anxiety about her daughter growing up, another mother offered some tough love: "Oh, come on, in thirteen years she's going to go off to *college*." As Vardalos reflected, she knew the story she wanted to tell: one centered largely on three generations of women—Maria, Toula, and Toula's daughter—processing three different phases of life. "I realized it suddenly—boom, that's it: The theme of the second one is we become our parents," says Vardalos.

HOW DO YOU SOLVE A PROBLEM LIKE MARIA

Vardalos had always conceived of *My Big Fat Greek Wedding* as a multigenerational story, and her original script contained an entire B-plot centered on Toula's mother, Maria, who takes inspiration from her daughter and finds her own passions by embracing her community. But the movie's budget wasn't endless, and when Tom Hanks and Gary Goetzman urged Vardalos to "trim the fat" in advance instead of filming scenes that would only be cut later, she made the difficult decision to excise the entire subplot.

Fourteen years later, Vardalos finally got to explore Maria's story in more detail in *My Big Fat Greek Wedding 2*, using the technicality that Maria and Gus were never married as a chance to explore Maria's own frustrations and dreams. "Maybe I could have traveled. I could have cured diseases, wrote poetry, had adventure in my life," she says, before reaching her own epiphany: "Maybe my adventure was to make a family. Marriage is not for everybody, but it worked out okay for me. It's been a good life."

My Big Fat Greek Wedding 2, which finally arrived in 2016, has the warm feeling of a long-awaited family reunion, and fourteen years later, the family has gotten bigger. There's an entire subplot centered on Toula and Ian's daughter Paris (Elena Kampouris), a teenager desperate to go to college far away from her family. This time, the titular wedding is between Toula's mother and father, who discover that their wedding certificate was never actually signed, and have an extremely belated wedding to make it official. "I had a little bit of a subversive idea, to make Lainie Kazan the lead, because of how hard it is to show age on-screen," says Vardalos. "I thought—you know, giving the middle finger to the industry—*I am going to make a seventy-five-year-old woman the lead and put her in a wedding dress.*"

My Big Fat Greek Wedding 2 ends with Toula's family helping Paris move into her dorm at New York University; rather than repeat a version of the cycle that left her so dependent on her family at the start of the original *My Big Fat Greek Wedding*, Toula has managed to love her enough to let her chase her own dreams (with a bottle of Windex left behind just in case). It's a full-circle arc—but it's also, apparently, not the end of the story. In April 2021, Vardalos confirmed long-standing rumors that *My Big Fat Greek Wedding 3* had been in the works since 2020, but that the COVID-19 pandemic had made it difficult to film. At the time of this publication, the details remain vague—and the COVID-19 pandemic has delayed things further due to the difficulties of securing insurance for an independent film—but Vardalos did confirm that the movie will be set in Greece, with the entire cast invited to return. She also made a half-joking request to the franchise's fans: "Although I love your enthusiasm, maybe some of you can stop calling my mom's house and asking if you can be in it."

Jennifer Lopez

THE TRIPLE THREAT

Hollywood didn't know what to do with Jennifer Lopez. Though she had pursued an acting career since she was a teenager, she shot to fame at a time when Hollywood's default "color-blind" approach to casting meant, in practice, that lead roles went to white actresses. It's no accident that her breakout role came in 1997's *Selena*, a biopic of the Latin music icon Selena Quintanilla-Pérez—a role in which Lopez's ethnicity was treated as a necessity and not something that a screenwriter felt the need to justify.

But despite Hollywood's total lack of vision, Jennifer Lopez also had her own plan: starring in a rom-com. "When I first started, one of the things that I wanted to do—because I was Puerto Rican, Latina—was that I wanted to be in romantic comedies," says Lopez. "I felt like all the women in romantic comedies always looked the same way, they were always white. And I was like, if I can do it and just show that I'm every girl—because I am the hopeless romantic, I am that—I am the single working woman, I was those things. And I remember thinking, I need to be the lead in a romantic comedy."

When she finally got the chance, in 2001's *The Wedding Planner*, she first had to overcome the biases of both the studio and the director, who tried and failed to develop versions of *The Wedding Planner* that would have starred Minnie Driver, Jennifer Love Hewitt, and Sarah Michelle Gellar. It was only when none of that panned out that Lopez was finally given a shot (noticing a pattern yet?). "I was honestly resistant to the idea. I didn't perceive her as a romantic comedy person; she seemed too tough to me, frankly," says *The Wedding Planner* director Adam Shankman. (Lopez happened to be coming off a string of thrillers at the time, but it is still difficult not to read this reluctance as coded, unexamined racism.)

The resulting movie is a perfect example of Hollywood's sheer, muddled ham-handedness when it comes to race. In *The Wedding Planner*, Lopez—who is of Puerto Rican descent—was cast as Mary Fiore, an Italian-American woman. Though the movie is packed with Italian caricatures, including Mary's incredibly zealous suitor Massimo, there is no reason the movie couldn't have been rewritten to incorporate Lopez's actual ethnicity. Adam Shankman says he and Lopez mutually agreed not to. "It was a very quick conversation," he says. "We were both like, 'Why can't you be Italian?' There seemed to be no reason; people play different faiths all the time, you know? The thinking is different now. Today, I would say, 'No, we're changing it, and we'll make you what you are.'"

But if *The Wedding Planner* was fuzzy on exactly what Lopez was bringing to the table, Lopez—with characteristic confidence—knew exactly what she was doing. Part of what's fascinating about *The Wedding Planner* is that it catches Lopez just on the peak of superstardom, before even her nickname had become entrenched in popular culture. "I mean, she wasn't J.Lo. She was Jennifer Lopez when I met her," says Judy Greer, who plays her best friend in the movie.

That was about to change. If you need evidence for Lopez's singular brand of superstardom, look no further than the week of January 21, 2001, which kicked off one of the most remarkable full-court presses in modern entertainment history. Tuesday, January 23 saw the release of her album *J.Lo*, which eventually went quadruple-platinum on the back of hits like "Love Don't Cost a Thing" and "I'm Real." On Friday, January 26, Sony released her rom-com debut, *The Wedding Planner*. Within that same time frame, Lopez ensured that the album, the movie, and the entire J.Lo rebranding was inescapable, with promotional appearances everywhere from *The Today Show* to *The Tonight Show* to *The Late Show* to *Saturday Night Live* to the cover of *Rolling Stone.*

By the next year, as her next rom-com arrived in theaters, her profile had dramatically risen. The year 2002 was a time when Jennifer Lopez was still reckoning, both personally and publicly, with what it meant to become J.Lo, the megastar whose relationship with Ben Affleck almost singlehandedly kept a cottage industry of gossip rags in business. This tension was most obvious in "Jenny From the Block," the lead single from her album *This Is Me . . . Then*, which insisted that money and fame wouldn't change her: "No matter where I go, I know where I came from," she sings.

But it's also present in Wayne Wang's *Maid in Manhattan*, released the same year, which casts Lopez as a hotel maid wooed by a senatorial candidate (Ralph Fiennes) who mistakes her for a wealthy fellow guest. Even more so than *Pretty Woman*, *Maid in Manhattan* is blatantly modeled on a fairy tale—the *Cinderella* parallels are so obvious that Charles Perrault probably should've been awarded a screenwriting credit.

Maid in Manhattan was not intended as a commentary on race—both Sandra Bullock and Hilary Swank passed on starring before Lopez was even offered the lead role—but casting a nonwhite actress in the lead makes *Maid in Manhattan* a different kind of movie. In one early scene, a vapid white woman insists, with ample evidence to the contrary, that Marisa (Lopez) "barely speaks English." Another woman can't even be bothered to get Marisa's name right. And in a plot point that *Maid in Manhattan* never really figures out how to reconcile, even Marisa keeps insisting that her love interest (Fiennes, hopelessly miscast) wouldn't even have noticed her if she hadn't borrowed a rich white woman's Dolce & Gabbana coat. "The first time you saw me, I was cleaning your bathroom floor! Only you *didn't* see me," she tells him.

In interviews at the time, Lopez described her role in *Maid in Manhattan* as a uniquely personal one. "Marisa is more like me than any character I've ever played. She's Puerto Rican. She's from the Bronx," she said. But she also bristled at the assumption that *Maid in Manhattan* was semi-autobiographical when she was already famous enough to relate more to Fiennes's character, who is constantly hounded by journalists. "My favorite line in the movie is when I say to Ralph, 'I don't know how you do it, all those cameras in your face all the time!' Did I laugh? Hell yeah!" she said.

Fame and success gave Lopez the clout she needed to make the rom-coms she wanted, and she kept making them. Immediately following *Maid in Manhattan*, Lopez costarred in two rom-coms, *Jersey Girl* and *Gigli*, opposite her then-partner Ben Affleck. Both of those movies bombed (and for good reason), but as a performer with the wattage to do basically anything she wants in music or film, it's striking that her enthusiasm for the genre has never waned. And it's a testament to both her talent and persistence that her pleasantly forgettable rom-coms released over the past decade—looking at you, *The Back-Up Plan* and *Second Act*—haven't made an obvious dent in anyone's appetite for watching Jennifer Lopez fall in love on-screen.

Fittingly enough, the next movie on Lopez's docket seems, at least on paper, like the purest modern distillation of her singular persona. Kat Coiro's *Marry Me* follows a world-famous pop star who impulsively decides to marry a man holding a MARRY ME poster board at one of her concerts. Lopez is, of course, the world-famous pop star.

"True or false: All's fair in love and war."

"True."

"Great answer."

—ANDIE AND BEN, *HOW TO LOSE A GUY IN 10 DAYS*

CHAPTER 9

HOW TO LOSE A GUY IN 10 DAYS

(And the New Generals in the Battle of the Sexes)

IN OCTOBER OF 1998, BANTAM BOOKS PUBLISHED A SLENDER LITTLE PA-
perback titled *How to Lose a Guy in 10 Days: The Universal Don'ts of
Dating*. The book—written and illustrated by coauthors Michele
Alexander and Jeannie Long, who state in their author bios that
their credentials are "having survived approximately 100.5 failed
relationships collectively"—is essentially a self-help book in reverse, pointing out the behaviors that might otherwise turn off the
man of your dreams.

Here is a partial list of the things you will not find in *How to Lose
a Guy in 10 Days: The Universal Don'ts of Dating*: a dog named Krull
the Warrior King, a penis named Princess Sophia, Carly Simon's
"You're So Vain," New York City, characters with names, or
anything even resembling a plot. What you *will* find are a bunch
of crayon stick-figure drawings, which are spread across about
130 pages, telling women "what *not* to say and what *not* to do."
It does not seem like an obvious springboard for a film. Even an
animated short seems like it might stretch the material to the
breaking point.

So how did a little novelty book become a studio rom-com with stars as glittering as Kate Hudson and Matthew McConaughey leaning against each other on its poster? In its earliest form, *How to Lose a Guy in 10 Days* was the passion project of Christine Peters, a protégé of the legendary producer Robert Evans. "There was a little stick-figure book, and it didn't look like much except to me because I saw the vision and everybody else wasn't quite sure what it was," says Peters. She pitched it to several executives, including her then-boyfriend, the billionaire media mogul Sumner Redstone. When he expressed skepticism, she pushed back: "You know, I think this could be something for women, and I believe there's an audience out there that's untapped."

Peters eventually found an audience who understood her vision in Sherry Lansing, the Paramount executive who was—perhaps not coincidentally—the first female head of a Hollywood studio. "Sherry was the only head of a studio that saw what I saw, and together we managed to climb the hurdles of naysayers and produce a hit. I will always be grateful to her," says Peters.

By the time the half-formed *How to Lose a Guy in 10 Days* project finally reached producer Lynda Obst, whose previous rom-coms included *Sleepless in Seattle* and *One Fine Day*, the film was starting to take shape, with Gwyneth Paltrow expressing interest in an early draft of the screenplay by Burr Steers. Directors in the mix included Michael Hoffmann, who had helmed *One Fine Day*, and Mike Newell, whose smash success with *Four Weddings and a Funeral* meant he was frequently a consideration when a rom-com needed a director to put his aesthetic stamp on it. But the hunt for a new director for *How to Lose a Guy in 10 Days* eventually settled on another old hand at the genre: Donald Petrie, who entered rom-com history the moment he cast a young unknown named Julia Roberts in his 1988 romantic dramedy *Mystic Pizza*. In the subsequent years, Petrie had delivered two sizable comedy hits: *Grumpy Old Men* (in which two grumpy old men vie for the same woman) and *Miss Congeniality* (which features an especially charming romantic subplot between Sandra Bullock and Benjamin Bratt). By 2003, he had settled into a groove as one of the first directors you'd call to helm a crowd-pleasing studio comedy. "I knew, when I started in this business, that directors get typecast just as fast or faster than actors," says Petrie. "Nobody's going to go, 'Hmm, we're doing the next *Die Hard*. Let's get that *Miss Congeniality* guy,' right?"

When Donald Petrie joined *How to Lose a Guy in 10 Days*, the script was very different from the version that eventually ended up on-screen. "It was much more about who had money and who didn't," says Petrie. "*Can a rich socialite go out with a beer-drinking guy?* There was a whole subplot where she had this rich mom who would look down on this guy with disdain."

Since no one was entirely happy with the script, *How to Lose a Guy in 10 Days* went through a series of uncredited rewrites that dramatically reshaped it. "Someone who decided not to take credit—but was in my opinion integral to making the movie what it is—was Audrey Wells," says Petrie. Wells—who had already made a splash on the rom-com genre with her own debut script, *The Truth About Cats & Dogs*—spearheaded a back-to-basics approach for *How to Lose a Guy in 10 Days* that, improbably, found a fair amount of inspiration in the original book. Wells simply pulled from the best of the jokes written by Michele Alexander and Jeannie Long—Name His Penis, Bring Him a Plant, Swing by the Animal Shelter and Pick Up a Dog, Call His Mom and Introduce Yourself, Suggest Couples' Therapy—and combined them with actual characters, motivations, and stakes.

If *When Harry Met Sally* had kicked off the modern rom-com era by riffing on the talk-y, New York-y template set by *Annie Hall* and adding a Hollywood ending, it had also retained some of the realism and melancholy of any difficult relationship. But by 2003, the rom-com genre was already trending away from realism, as a series of writers and directors competed to come up with high-concept premises that were even hookier, and grand gestures that were even grander, than whatever audiences had seen in last year's biggest rom-com—which was, among other things, easier to both pitch and market.

How to Lose a Guy in 10 Days makes the decision to unapologetically embrace those age-old tropes, trusting that audiences will be so engaged in this modern-day riff on the Battle of the Sexes that they'll ignore how no one is acting like an actual human being. The contrivances come big and early, when an ambitious magazine writer named Andie pitches an article in which she'll try to get dumped in ten days *just* as an ambitious advertising executive named Ben vows that he can make any woman fall in love with him in ten days. (Technically, Ben is set up to fail by a couple of workplace rivals who know about Andie's side of the story, but the timing is still pretty uncanny.)

In an effort to establish the right tone for *How to Lose a Guy in 10 Days*, Petrie looked to the similarly pitched pleasures of an earlier golden age of rom-com: the slick, fizzy screwball comedies that dominated screens in the 1930s and 1940s. "The pace in those movies was so wonderful. They just *moved*," says Petrie. The movie embeds a few subtle references to signal to audiences that these references are intentional. Listen closely during the diamond party in *How to Lose a Guy in 10 Days* and you'll recognize the background music as "Moon River" and the theme from *Sabrina*—an intentional nod to the romantic comedies of Audrey Hepburn (and especially to *Breakfast at Tiffany's*, which had its own iconic jewelry scene). Even the names of *How to Lose a Guy in 10 Days'* lead characters, Andie Anderson and Benjamin Barry, feel like a direct wink at the screwball comedies of the 1950s, where characters with names like Beauregard Bottomley, Lois Laurel, Oliver Oxley, and Maggie McNulty squared off in the battle of the sexes.

How to Lose a Guy in 10 Days needed an actress *and* an actor who could spar in a way that made sparks fly without either of them permanently burning each other along the way—and then forgive it all and fall in love by the time the credits rolled. Fortunately, the right actress was already attached. Following her Oscar-nominated performance in 2001's *Almost Famous*, Kate Hudson—now pegged as an up-and-comer—was offered a slew of romantic comedies. It seemed like an obvious fit: In addition to being charming and funny in her own right, Hudson, whose mother is Goldie Hawn, was rom-com royalty. Hudson turned all the offers down. "I've seen so many romantic comedy scripts," said Hudson at the time. "They're always the same story you've seen before, and they're cute, but not funny." But *How to Lose a Guy* had a character that appealed to her: magazine writer Andie Anderson, whose ambitions were entirely pitched toward her career, not toward a relationship, and who fell in love unwillingly and entirely by accident over the course of the movie.

Next up was finding the leading man who was attractive and charming enough to make that arc feel plausible. "Finding the guy was difficult, to say the least," says Petrie. "A lot of men who have the same kind of star power—who can be on screen opposite Kate Hudson and hold their own—they *don't* want to play second banana. They don't want to be the guy in the romantic comedy that the girl is the lead in." But to Hudson, *How to Lose a Guy in 10 Days* was a chance to do something different with the modern rom-com: a movie in which the Battle of the Sexes would actually be depicted as a fair fight, splitting the perspective evenly between the two strong-willed protagonists. To pull it off, she'd need a co-star distinctive and charismatic enough not to get buried.

Kate Hudson gave a thumbs-up to Luke Wilson, who she'd end up costarring with that same year in *Alex & Emma*, but Paramount preferred a different leading man. "I'm not going to name names, but the studio was determined to have this other actor," says Petrie. "And we did a screen test with this other actor, and it was very clear—even in that screen test—that you didn't take your eyes off Kate. She just owned the scenes. It wasn't even a contest."

In the end, the casting dispute came down to a meeting with Sherry Lansing, who invited Kate Hudson, Donald Petrie, and producer Lynda Obst to her office with a specific agenda in mind: to get them to sign off on the studio's preferred leading man. "She was going to put Kate's feet to the fire and say, 'This is who *we* want to be in the movie,'" says Petrie. "She basically said, 'Well, Kate . . . if you don't feel this is the right person to be opposite, then maybe we'll just do some other movie sometime'—to which they thought Kate would cave. And I have to hand it to Kate, because she didn't bat an eye. She said, 'Oh, okay then. I'm fine with that. We'll find something else.'" Hudson went on to explain that she was routinely offered "lesser rom-com, *American Pie*–style movies," and turned them all down. "That's not the actress I am, and that's not the kind of movie I want to make," she said.

"Sherry Lansing, to her credit, did a complete about-face right there in the room, and said, 'I get that. Who do *you* think would be right in this?'" says Petrie. "And both Kate and Lynda Obst said, 'What about Matthew McConaughey?'—who was, I'm sure, much more expensive than what the studio had in mind."

Matthew McConaughey had been kicking around Hollywood, looking for the right rom-com role, for the better part of a decade.

As early as 1994, he had been up for the role played by Bill Pull-man in *While You Were Sleeping*. (He was "unbelievably charming and attractive," says director Jon Turteltaub, "but he had a Texas accent and none of us could rewrite this movie to take place in Texas or explain why he was in Chicago at that point.")

A couple of years before *How to Lose a Guy in 10 Days*, McCo-naughey had finally made his rom-com debut in *The Wedding Plan-ner* opposite Jennifer Lopez. McConaughey had only landed the role after Brendan Fraser dropped out just weeks before rehearsals began. He was also the last resort. Director Adam Shankman later confessed that, whatever his other virtues, McConaughey was the only actor on the list who was also available on the day that pro-duction on *The Wedding Planner* needed to start. When the movie finally arrived in January of 2001—opposite Super Bowl XXXV, but with virtually no competition at the box office—it earned dismal reviews, with McConaughey's performance frequently singled out as one of the movie's biggest flaws. "McConaughey is mortally ordinary as a main dish who spends most of his time smiling like a party guest," complained *Entertainment Weekly* in one typical review.

Still, *The Wedding Planner* made money, which meant McCo-naughey was exactly the kind of Hollywood-tested, audience-approved rom-com hunk they needed. There was just one problem: he was absolutely nothing like *How to Lose a Guy in 10 Days*' Benjamin Barry, who was scripted as a slick, fast-talking New York ad executive. When McConaughey was cast, the script was hastily rewritten to include some quick backstory about how Ben moved around a lot as a child because his father was in the Navy. This was added solely to explain McConaughey's drawling Texas accent, but it also changed the character, making him less of a soulless slickster and more of an easygoing charmer—an innate quality that McConaughey would use to great effect in this film and then reuse, over and over again, in rom-coms to come.

Everyone had been focused on chemistry, and Hudson and McConaughey clearly had it in person. But would it translate to the big screen? As soon as *How to Lose a Guy in 10 Days* started

WITH A FRIEND LIKE HAHN

Alongside Carrie Fisher, Joan Cusack, and Judy Greer in the pantheon of best rom-com best friends, you'll find Kathryn Hahn. Unless you count her role as "Woman" in 1997's *Flushed*— "Satisfyingly raunchy!" proclaimed *The Village Voice*—*How to Lose a Guy in 10 Days* marked her film debut.

"She was the first person we had in to read," recalls Petrie. "She was *fantastic*, and she set the bar very high. But nobody casts the first person they read. So we went on, and on, and on, and on. And finally, we went back, and cast the first person we read for the role." (Hahn, for her part, mostly remembers her first meeting with Kate Hudson: "I broke the ice by joking about the horny summers at this theater camp we had both been to when we were kids," she says.)

When *How to Lose a Guy in 10 Days* hit theaters, and Hahn practically stole the movie in a single scene in which she poses as Andie and Ben's couples counselor, it was obvious to every casting director in Hollywood that a new Best Friend had been born. In the years that followed, Hahn turned in similarly memorable performances in a string of rom-coms—including Robert Luketic's *Win a Date with Tad Hamilton!*, Nigel Cole's *A Lot Like Love*, Nancy Meyers's *The Holiday*, and James L. Brooks's *How Do You Know*.

shooting, everyone breathed a sigh of relief: They'd found the balance the movie would require. "From the first dailies, we knew the chemistry between Kate and Matthew was crackling on set, on the monitor, and in the rushes," says Obst. "The energy between them created heat, and that makes a hit."

How to Lose a Guy in 10 Days is a comedy of brinksmanship, with Andie being as obnoxious as possible for the sake of her article, while Ben refuses to dump her for the sake of a bet that might win him a valuable account at his advertising firm. But while the sharp repartee between Hudson and McConaughey makes this feel like a battle of the sexes, it's not quite a fair fight. Even when he's manipulating Andie, Ben is essentially himself: a slick, easygoing ad man. But when Andie drags Ben to a rom-com marathon, crashes his poker game, or drags him to couples therapy, she's riffing on all the qualities she thinks men don't like about women. The *real* Andie loves beer and basketball—the quintessential guy's girl that's frequently held up (and mocked) as a shallow male fantasy. "Where's the sexy, cool, fun, smart, beautiful Andie that I knew?" complains Ben after one particularly bizarre antic. *How to Lose a Guy in 10 Days* belatedly tries to correct for this imbalance when the man who inspired Andie's article shows up and begs for her best friend, Michelle, back despite all of the "dating don'ts" her behavior embodied—but it's clear that the movie prefers the "sexy, cool, fun, smart, beautiful Andie" instead of the one who might suggest vegetarianism or drag her boyfriend to a Celine Dion concert as well.

To root for this couple, you have to believe that their elaborate deceptions are either (1) forgivable or (2) cancel each other out. You *also* have to believe that the real Andie and Ben are not assholes, and that their actual connection is deeper than the game they're playing. The movie does manage to sell that in its best scene, when Ben brings Andie to Staten Island to meet his family. Over a round of the card game Bullshit—a symbolic way to remind the audience that these two can treat lying as a game without anyone getting *too* hurt—Hudson and McConaughey infuse every interaction with the natural-but-charged energy that makes you think these two really belong together.

AND YOUR LITTLE DOG TOO

No discussion of *How to Lose a Guy in 10 Days* would be complete without Krull, the dog Andie buys as part of her plan to drive Ben away, who eventually becomes Ben's comfort at his lowest moment. What would such a dog look like? The screenplay left a lot of room for interpretation: "What was scripted was just 'the ugliest little dog,'" says Donald Petrie.

The production ultimately cast Harry, a Chinese crested hairless dog, who wore his sweater at all times to stay warm. In addition to being functional and adorable, the sweater also provided a handy disguise for the tube that was used to make Harry "pee" on command.

And in the middle of a movie that benefited from improv, even Harry got a turn. As Ben was lamenting his breakup with Andie, holding a ticket to the Knicks playoff game they were supposed to attend, Harry leaned forward and bit down on the ticket—a spontaneous gesture no one had planned for. "It was not scripted. The dog literally just reached out and took the ticket into his mouth," says Petrie.

Fortunately, McConaughey managed to roll with it. "Matthew just went, 'Oh, yeah? You want to go? You want to go to the game?' And he let go of the ticket. Those are the kinds of special things that can happen," says Petrie.

Petrie was aware that the Bullshit scene would be make-or-break for the movie, and he had several key ideas for making it feel authentic. The actors were encouraged to improvise the kind of good-natured banter that comes up at a family game night, and much of what made the final cut was unscripted. To make the dynamic feel even more comfortable, Petrie made a point of casting actors he'd worked with before and was comfortable with: John DiResta, who played Ben's brother-in-law, had played an FBI agent in *Miss Congeniality*, and James Murtaugh, who played Ben's father, Jack, had worked with Petrie in a 1986 episode of the CBS drama *The Equalizer*. And everything about the look of the Barry house needed to be exactly right, which resulted in three different houses being used for this single sequence. "Oddly enough, it was shot in two different countries," says Petrie. "When Kate and Matthew ride up on the motorcycle, that's one house exterior in Toronto. When they actually enter the house and meet Mom, that's a *second* house in Toronto. And all the backyard stuff in Staten Island in New York."

Of course, it's only when these two are falling in love that the movie can pull the rug out from under them, and *How to Lose a Guy in 10 Days* sets the moment at a particularly dramatic setting: a ball being thrown to celebrate the ad agency's big new precious stone account, with a truly insane amount of jewelry draped across everybody for the occasion.

Shooting the scene wasn't easy; the production filmed with real, multimillion-dollar diamonds, which meant the presence of extensive security representing the interests of jeweler Harry Winston on set. The paranoia over the chance of misplacing even a single jewel, while understandable, slowed the production down. "If I shot a take and we were going right away again, it was fine," says Petrie. But if the actors had even a short break while the crew worked to change the camera setup, everyone was required to check all the jewelry back in. "They could not go to the trailer. Could not go to the bathroom. Could not go *anywhere* with those diamonds."

On top of trying to thwart any would-be *Ocean's Eleven*–style jewel heists from the set, the breakdown of Ben and Andie's relationship was proving a nightmare to write. The climax, as originally scripted, was when Andie found out about Ben's bet and excoriated him on stage for it. The problem, Petrie quickly discovered, was that Andie's reaction—given the dishy article she was writing that Ben didn't know about yet—made her look like a hypocrite at best and a villain at worst. The scene was rewritten so Ben found out about the article instead. But that only shifted the onus/burden to his shoulders: Now Ben was the jerk who was calling her out without acknowledging his own deceptions.

DIAMONDS ARE FOREVER

Inspired by *Titanic*'s instantly iconic Heart of the Ocean, Donald Petrie decided that the yellow diamond worn by Kate Hudson at the climactic party needed its own name too.

It was his wife who suggested "the Isadora Diamond." For those who are up on their entertainment history, the name is a morbid little in-joke. It's an homage to the famed dancer Isadora Duncan, who died at age fifty in 1927 when a silk scarf she was wearing got caught in the wheel and rear axle of a moving car, sending her body careening into the pavement (and, according to some accounts, nearly decapitating her in the process).

For a movie in which both protagonists had been lying for the entirety of their relationship, the climax needed to make Andie and Ben both right and wrong at the same time—and, of course, make sure the audience was still laughing while they were doing it. It was frequent Adam Sandler collaborator Tim Herlihy, who also contributed an uncredited rewrite, who found the solution. He rewrote the scene to give it what everyone agreed was the proper balance, inventing an escalating series of twisty contrivances to ensure that Andie and Ben each find out about the other's deception at the exact same time.

In the end, Andie writes her "How to Lose a Guy in 10 Days" article as a mea culpa, revealing that she fell for a man and blew it. Frustrated with her editor, she then quits her job to pursue a career as a political journalist. When Ben reads the article, and learns she's on her way to Washington, D.C., to interview for a job, he hops on his motorcycle to chase her down.

"It was after 9/11. Nobody was going to give anybody a permit to shoot on a bridge," says Petrie—particularly when the closing shot required a helicopter, which was needed for a wide shot of Andie and Ben riding away on a motorcycle together. An off-ramp was offered as a compromise, but after the grandeur of the diamond party, Petrie feared that such an everyday location would make it feel like the movie was ending on an anticlimax.

Veteran location manager Sam Hutchins found a clever workaround. He discovered that the bridge would be shut down on a Sunday for construction and called the construction company directly instead of coordinating with the city. With permission secured, *How to Lose a Guy in 10 Days* had its big Hollywood ending.

Ben races to Andie on his motorcycle and gets the cab to pull over. "Where are you going?" he asks. "I have an interview," she says. "Yeah, in Washington. I know. Where are you going?" he asks. "Ben, it's the only place I can go and write what I want to write," she says. When Ben insists she's just running away, Andie turns to leave; when Ben calls bullshit, she turns back. Ben gives the cabbie some money and tells him to take her luggage back to her Manhattan apartment while they make out on a bridge.

It's here that this battle of the sexes—while theoretically ending in a truce—ends, if you think about it for more than a few seconds, with Ben coming out as the victor. The movie's haste to bring Ben and Andie together leads to the apparently unquestioned assumption that Andie should give up on a promising journalism job in Washington, D.C., the job she's been saying she wants for the entire movie. (And honestly: It's a job *interview*. She'll be back in a few days, man.) Ben may know Andie well enough to call her out in a game of Bullshit. But there's nothing about Andie that makes it seem like she'd tolerate being derailed from what might be the job of her dreams by a guy who rolls up and tells her what to do.

It's a dynamic that *How to Lose a Guy in 10 Days* never quite figures out how to solve: Even what looks like a truce is ultimately tilted toward restoring the status quo represented by our rom-com heroine choosing love above everything else. Even Kate Hudson is skeptical that Andie and Ben would have been a good fit for the long haul. In 2020, when asked where the characters might have ended up, she took a shot: "We probably would have gotten married with kids. We're probably miserable right now!"

Fortunately, audiences didn't actually need to think that far ahead. As the creative team knew from the very beginning, the greatest strength of *How to Lose a Guy in 10 Days*—and the reason audiences saw that ending and left the theater perfectly happy—is the genuine heat between Hudson and McConaughey. *How to Lose a Guy in 10 Days* also arrived at a time when Hollywood desperately

HOW TO LOSE A *HOW TO LOSE A GUY IN 10 DAYS* SEQUEL

As part of what she calls her "never-ending effort to make a career out of *How to Lose a Guy in 10 Days*," Lynda Obst pitched a TV series based on the movie to The CW in 2008, to be written by *Sex and the City* alum Jenny Bicks. "Just as we were about to submit the pilot script to network executives, we got brand-new ideas to add, such as, 'I just heard "I Kissed a Girl" on the radio! Can we come up with a lesbian subplot?'" says Obst. Though they dutifully added "some same-sex overtones," the desperate, last-minute notes were a sign of trouble on the horizon, and the project eventually died a quiet death.

A subsequent idea—titled *How to Get a Guy in 10 Days*, and described by Obst as "not a reboot, not a sequel," but "a movie in that tradition"—was said to be casting in 2013, but never made it into production.

And then there was a brief effort to get a sequel series going at Quibi, a short-form video service that launched in April 2020 and, after failing to garner any kind of meaningful audience, shut down less than a year later. Quibi's take on a *How to Lose a Guy in 10 Days* sequel—described as a "modern take," in an apparent effort to make fans of the original feel really old—was set to follow "a glib young online columnist and an oversexed advertising executive who both need to prove, once and for all, they're capable of being monogamous." The Quibi revival was being written by *The Mindy Project*'s Guy Branum, who announced his involvement in a tweet poking fun at rom-com tropes: "We were all certain you could not make a good romantic comedy anymore because print media is dead and RomCom ladies have to work at magazines."

needed a hot new rom-com couple. It had been four years since Julia Roberts and Richard Gere had sparred in *Runaway Bride*, and five years since Meg Ryan and Tom Hanks had their third cinematic romance in *You've Got Mail*. Maybe Kate Hudson and Matthew McConaughey could fill the gap.

And so, five years after *How to Lose a Guy in 10 Days* hit theaters, Hudson and McConaughey reunited to star in *Fool's Gold*. The movie—directed by Andy Tennant, who had just scored back-to-back romantic comedy hits with 2002's *Sweet Home Alabama* and 2005's *Hitch*—was a blend of rom-com and action-comedy, which were basically the two types of movies McConaughey was interested in making at that time. *Fool's Gold* itself is a needlessly violent and strangely miscalculated movie; even the natural chemistry between Hudson and McConaughey, which feels so potent and charged in *How to Lose a Guy in 10 Days*, feels nonexistent this time around.

Unsurprisingly, it flopped. And when asked about *Fool's Gold* now, both Hudson and McConaughey mostly end up laughing as they describe the disgusting kiss they were forced to perform during a scene in which their characters survive a plane crash and land in the ocean. "He just had snot all over his face," says Hudson.

It's interesting to imagine where the rom-com genre might have gone if Hudson and McConaughey's *How to Lose a Guy in 10 Days* follow-up had been a good movie. As anyone who has directed, starred in, or seen a failed romantic comedy could tell you, chemistry can't be faked. When two actors *really* have it, they should be thrown together in every halfway-decent script you can find, because together they can only improve it.

Instead, both Hudson and McConaughey starred in rom-coms opposite a series of other leads, and never found quite the right chemistry again. McConaughey rebounded from the box-office bomb *Sahara*, which failed to launch a wannabe *Indiana Jones* franchise, by starring in *Failure to Launch*, which paired him with Sarah Jessica Parker, playing a woman hired by parents to date their adult sons until they move out of their parents' houses. The movie was clearly patterned on *How to Lose a Guy in 10 Days*—it even had a poster with Matthew McConaughey leaning on his costar—but by the time the rom-com *Christmas Carol* riff *Ghosts of Girlfriends Past* hit theaters a few years later, it was clear that McConaughey was starting to coast.

"My lifestyle—living on the beach, running with my shirt off, doing romantic comedies—people were throwing that together and going, well that's who McConaughey is," says McConaughey. "On the romantic comedies, I had to say, 'Well, that was fun.' But I'm not feeling as challenged as I want to feel, so I'm going to step in the shadows here, and say no to the things I didn't say no to before. I consciously recalibrated my relationship with my career. I didn't know exactly what I wanted to do, because I wasn't getting those things. But I knew I could say no to the things I'd been doing."

That included a 2010 offer for one unnamed romantic comedy that would have netted him a $14.5 million payday. Even then, McConaughey says it took almost two years before he started getting offers for films that weren't romantic comedies or action comedies. But his patience paid off; just four years after *Ghosts of Girlfriends Past*, he climbed the stage at the Oscars to accept the Best Actor trophy for *Dallas Buyers Club*, in which he starred opposite his *Ghosts of Girlfriends Past* costar Jennifer Garner.

It's hard to define the exact boundaries of the much-heralded "McConaissance" that was widely regarded as a new apex in McConaughey's career, but the transformation was almost universally celebrated. *The New Yorker* said McConaughey's return to stardom after the "prodigal wastefulness" of his rom-com years was "a joy to watch." But it's undeniable that the acclaim came, in large part, from running in the opposite direction from everything that made him a rom-com star. For *Killer Joe*, he played a sociopath; for *True Detective*, he spewed an endless stream of grim nihilism; for *Dallas Buyers Club*, both he and costar Jared Leto lost dozens of pounds. In the grand tradition of extreme body transformation being equated with a great performance, they both won Oscars for it.

Kate Hudson spent the years after *How to Lose a Guy in 10 Days* trying, apparently singlehandedly, to keep the rom-com genre alive, starring in *Alex & Emma*, *Raising Helen*, *My Best Friend's Girl*, *A Little Bit of Heaven*, and *Something Borrowed*. That last one was intended to spawn an entire franchise based around Hudson, literally ending with the words "To Be Continued . . ." as Hudson's character took center stage—though the planned sequel, *Something Blue*, quietly disappeared in the rom-coms slump of the mid-2010s, as studios lost faith in the genre having the kind of cross-gender appeal that had greeted *How to Lose a Guy in 10 Days* in 2003. At the time of this publication, none of Hudson's subsequent roles have met with the critical or popular acclaim that greeted McConaughey—but hope springs eternal for a Hudsonaissance if the industry is savvy enough to harness the unique talents of his rom-com costar. "All I know is this: The movie marketers believe that women go to guys' movies if they're good, but guys won't go to women's movies ever," says Lynda Obst. "I've proved that wrong—as have many others—but they deeply believe that."

Reese Witherspoon

THE PRODIGY

First performances don't come much more acclaimed than Reese Witherspoon's debut in Robert Mulligan's 1991 coming-of-age romance *The Man in the Moon*. "*The Man in the Moon* is like a great short story, one of those masterpieces of language and mood where not one word is wrong, or unnecessary," wrote Roger Ebert at the time, adding that the performances—including the debut of fourteen-year-old Witherspoon— "could not be improved on."

It is always a risk to let your entire movie rest on the shoulders of an untested actor, but director Robert Mulligan was uniquely adept at spotting young talent. A few decades earlier, he was the filmmaker who cast ten-year-old Mary Badham as Scout Finch in his adaptation of Harper Lee's *To Kill a Mockingbird*, a role that eventually made her the then-youngest actress to earn an Oscar nomination. Witherspoon had originally showed up hoping to play an extra, but Mulligan was impressed enough to make her the lead.

In 1991, Witherspoon was obviously a star in the making, but she was also a generation too young to be up for the same roles as rising stars like Meg Ryan, Julia Roberts, and Sandra Bullock, who were at least a decade older. And while the rom-com was as popular as ever, the path to stardom for a young actress was already shifting for the actresses of Witherspoon's generation. Unlike the stars who made romantic comedies on the path to broadening their opportunities in Hollywood, Witherspoon made a diverse array of movies *before* charting a path to romantic comedies.

There is no easy summary for the first decade of Witherspoon's career. Highlights include *Freeway*, a pitch-black modernized riff on "Little Red Riding Hood" with Witherspoon starring opposite Kiefer Sutherland as the Big Bad Wolf; *Pleasantville*, a fantasy-dramedy about a couple of modern teenagers who get sucked into the black-and-white world of a wholesome '50s sitcom; *Election*, a political satire about a hotly contested race to be a high school's student body president; and *Cruel Intentions*, a deliberately trashy and campy riff on Pierre Choderlos de Laclos's 1782 novel *Dangerous Liaisons*, which was (successfully!) pitched squarely at teenagers.

If you don't count *Legally Blonde* as a romantic comedy (and I don't, because the romance with Luke Wilson is just one facet of Elle Woods's character arc), Witherspoon's first step into the genre came more than a decade into her acting career. It also happened to be a throwback: Oliver Parker's 2002 adaptation of the 1895 Oscar Wilde play *The Importance of Being Earnest*. But that same year, Witherspoon anchored in the movie that propelled her, however belatedly, to rom-com superstardom: *Sweet Home Alabama*.

If not for the threat of an actor's strike in 2002 (which, while jumbling plenty of schedules, ultimately never came to pass), *Sweet Home Alabama* would have starred Charlize Theron. After Theron left the project, the creative team behind *Sweet Home Alabama* reworked the script just in time to catch Witherspoon riding the wave of *Legally Blonde*. For the New Orleans–born, Nashville-raised Witherspoon—who once said that "you can learn all you really need to know about acting from repeated viewing of the beauty salon scene in *Steel Magnolias*"—*Sweet Home Alabama* really was a sort of homecoming. As an actress with an eye toward conquering Hollywood, Witherspoon spent the early part of her career trying to shed her Southern accent. Here, she plays a rom-com version of that same arc, forced to choose between life as a New York society woman and a down-home Southern girl.

Sweet Home Alabama never seriously pretends that this is a difficult choice. Melanie Smooter (Witherspoon) may be estranged from her husband, Jake (Josh Lucas)—and engaged to a guy who will probably be the president someday (Patrick Dempsey)—but you can't really argue with the movie's opening scene, in which the ten-year-old Melanie and Jake explain to each other why they should be married. (The answer, for the record, is, "So I can kiss you anytime I want.") Decades later, at her wedding to the other guy, Melanie acknowledges what's been clear all along. "The truth is I gave my heart away a long time ago. My whole heart. And I never really got it back," she says, returning to Jake after all.

Sweet Home Alabama is certainly the most conventional rom-com Reese Witherspoon has ever made. It's also, not coincidentally, the highest-grossing, by a margin of $70 million. And two decades later, it is obviously a movie that remains near and dear to her heart: "I always have the best time working on movies shot in the South that are about Southern people," she said in 2018.

The movie was also, both culturally and financially, the peak of her rom-com stardom. The rom-coms that followed were rangier, higher-concept, and obviously not as close to Witherspoon's own heart. Mark Waters's fantasy rom-com *Just Like Heaven* casts Witherspoon as a comatose woman who manifests as a ghost to haunt and flirt with Mark Ruffalo (who called it "an anti-romantic comedy"). McG's *This Means War* is a lunkheaded and utterly unsuccessful attempt to blend the rom-com with a spy-vs.-spy action-thriller. "I was just kind of floundering career-wise, 'cause I wasn't making things I was passionate about. I was just kind of working, you know?" reflected Witherspoon later. "And it was really clear that audiences weren't responding to anything I was putting out there."

But there is one underappreciated little gem in the mix: James L. Brooks's *How Do You Know*—which was, among several problems, saddled with that title. At the time of its release, much of the buzz around *How Do You Know* focused on how much it cost to make. With $15 million for Witherspoon, $12 million for Jack Nicholson, and $10 million for Owen Wilson, the $120 million budget—still, more than a decade later, the most money ever spent on a rom-com in history—really starts to add up.

It's a shame *How Do You Know*'s production gossip and box-office failure overshadowed the movie itself, because it's also the best romantic comedy Witherspoon has made so far. Unlike *Sweet Home Alabama*, it was written with her in mind: Brooks had decided well in advance that Witherspoon was the only actress who could play the role, and Witherspoon responded by throwing herself into it, committing to three-hour workouts every single day to convincingly portray a softball player gunning for a spot on Team USA (though she barely plays softball in the final cut of the movie).

In the end, Hollywood's primary takeaway from *How Do You Know* was clearly "don't spend blockbuster money on a romantic comedy"—a tough lesson that, when you look at the production costs of the rom-coms that *have* become mega-hits, has some logic to it. And unless you count Hallie Meyers-Shyer's *Home Again* as a romantic comedy (and I don't), it was also Witherspoon's exodus from the genre at the time of this book's publication. But it's also not the end of the story, because Witherspoon's lasting legacy in Hollywood may ultimately come down to the films she produces as well as appears in. After *Legally Blonde* and its sequel, the first movie released by her first production company, Type A Films, was a romantic comedy: 2006's likably offbeat *Penelope*, which casts Christina Ricci as a woman cursed by a witch to have a pig's nose (and featured Witherspoon in a small role).

It wasn't a big hit, but it was a trial run for Witherspoon's now-flourishing career as a producer, with hits like David Fincher's *Gone Girl*, HBO's *Big Little Lies*, and Apple TV+'s *The Morning Show* under her belt. Her stated mission is a practical one, though relatively fresh in Hollywood: "Change the story by changing the storytellers." She and producer Bruna

Papandrea have actively pursued projects featuring strong lead roles for women, with a particular knack for acquiring the rights to promising novels before they've even been published.

And though Witherspoon's biggest successes as a producer to date have been thrillers like *Gone Girl* (which was originally slated to star Witherspoon) and *Big Little Lies* (which does), there are signs that she intends to head back to the romantic comedy. The next two films on her production company Hello Sunshine's slate—both headed for Netflix—are romcoms. The first, titled *Your Place or Mine*, will be written and directed by *27 Dresses* writer Aline Brosh McKenna, with Witherspoon slated to star. The second, *The Cactus*, will be adapted from a novel by Sarah Haywood, which Witherspoon promoted via her book club in June of 2019. Taken together, it's a clever shortcut to fixing a problem that has long derailed the careers of so many talented actresses: If no one is making the movies you want to be in, just make them yourself. "I'm at a point in my life, it's like . . . I can make 20 more movies," says Witherspoon. "But I want to make 20 more movies that matter to me."

"If you look for it, I've got a sneaky feeling you'll find that love actually is all around."

—DAVID, *LOVE ACTUALLY*

CHAPTER 10

LOVE ACTUALLY

(And the Rom-Com That Gave You Ten Love Stories for Christmas)

IF YOU'RE NOT READY, IT CAN STILL FEEL JARRING. BEFORE THE CELE-brated Christmas rom-com *Love Actually* gives you a Christmas song, or a Christmas tree, or the on-screen caption "5 weeks to Christmas," it gives you Hugh Grant monologuing over a montage of people embracing in an airport. And just as his familiar voice is soothing you with warm thoughts about how love is everywhere, *bam*—he drops a reference to 9/11. "When the planes hit the Twin Towers, as far as I know, none of the phone calls from the people on board were messages of hate or revenge. They were all messages of love," he says.

Today, *Love Actually* is so widely recognized as a Christmas movie that the monologue still stuns: Yes, this movie is about 9/11. Arriving in theaters three years before more conventional dramatizations like Oliver Stone's *World Trade Center* and Paul Greengrass's *United 93*, there was *Love Actually*, a romantic comedy whose ten interconnected micro-narratives unfold, sometimes explicitly, within the rapidly changing political landscape that followed the 9/11 terrorist attack.

The decision to invoke 9/11 with no warning, just two years after it happened, would be a bold swing in *any* movie—let alone a romantic comedy aimed at mass audiences that otherwise makes very few claims to realism. *Love Actually* is rooted in a world that was already starting to look alien when the movie hit theaters in 2003. Hugh Grant's gooey opening monologue about the joy of meeting people at the arrivals gate came *just* when increased security made it impossible to meet your loved ones at the arrivals gate. Later, at the movie's climax, a ten-year-old slips past security to chase his crush through the airport—as if that kind of thing wasn't, you know, more likely than not to get you arrested, tased, and/or shot.

To appreciate what *Love Actually* is trying to say about the world in that opening monologue, you have to understand Richard Curtis (yes, that Richard Curtis). Even more than understanding him,

RICHARD & EMMA

Given his career-long penchant for swoony love stories—and, of course, the fact that he made a movie that quite literally contains four weddings, and even packs a few more into the credits—you might be surprised to hear that Richard Curtis and Emma Freud, his partner of thirty years (and with six children), have never been married, and never intend to wed.

"When we were working on *Four Weddings and a Funeral*, we added up the number of weddings we had both been to and it was over 100," says Freud. "Those weddings were the basis of the movie, and also the reason that neither of us could imagine going down an aisle. And I always thought that if we didn't get married, we could never get divorced. He did present me with a ring 27 years ago and ask me if I'd spend the rest of my life not being married to him. He's an excellent boyfriend, and is everything I admire in life."

you have to understand what *Four Weddings and a Funeral* director Mike Newell affectionately calls "Curtisland"—a magical, swooningly romantic place, full of witty repartee, earnest speeches, and dramatic grand gestures, and typically populated by an ensemble that includes one floppy-haired Hugh Grant. Curtis really *does* believe that, if you look for it, love actually is *all around*. "I really do believe that there is a tremendous amount of optimism, goodness and love in the world and that it is under-represented," says Curtis. "But if you do feel it and experience it, then you should write about it."

By the early 2000s, with both *Four Weddings and a Funeral* and *Notting Hill* behind him, Richard Curtis had taken plenty of critical lumps—an experience that had only solidified his belief that his movies were telling their own essential truths. "You write a play about a soldier going AWOL and stabbing a single mother and they say it is a searing indictment of modern British society," he says. "Whereas you write a play about a guy falling in love with a girl, which happens a million times a day in every corner of the world, and it's called blazingly unrealistic sentimental rubbish. People prefer to write about tragedies because they can't get to the bottom of happiness or comedy."

Curtis's romantic comedies may be sentimental, but as he sees it they're also rooted in the real world. For example: *Love Actually*'s opening sequence seems a little less treacly when you learn that the whole idea was pulled from a real-life epiphany Richard Curtis experienced at an airport during the filming of the *Mr. Bean* movie, and cobbled together from real footage that was sneakily shot of actual loved ones reuniting. "I suddenly saw all this extraordinary emotion," says Curtis. "And I thought, *That is the proof that there is so much overflowing love in the world and it's absolutely core to people's lives.* And that was real documentary footage that we shot without anyone knowing we were shooting, and we had to rush up to people and ask for their permission to use it."

It was one of many ideas that eventually made it into the rom-com sampler platter that is *Love Actually*, which sprang out of Curtis's indecision about what his next project should be. Following the success of *Notting Hill*, Curtis kicked around several ideas for his next romantic comedy. One concept centered on a young

HUGH DANCE-Y

A particularly Richard Curtis—ian moment in *Love Actually* comes when the prime minister played by Hugh Grant dances around 10 Downing Street to "Jump (For My Love)," by the Pointer Sisters (though Curtis had originally scripted it as a Jackson 5 song, but couldn't get the rights). It was the last day of shooting, and it was not a scene that Hugh Grant was eager to film. "It was very difficult persuading Hugh to dance around 10 Downing Street," says Richard Curtis. "He kept putting it off. He argued about the song. He was afraid I was going to make his character look un-prime ministerial."

"You know what it's like. To dance at all, you've got to be quite drunk, or by yourself in your pants in front of the mirror," says Grant. "The idea of having to do it stone-cold sober, in front of a film set, was awful. And every time Richard said, 'I think we should rehearse the dance scene,' I found a reason not to do it." He even tried to pick apart the logic of the scene, arguing that the prime minister's dance routine stops making sense as soon as he leaves the room with the radio in it (to which Curtis shrugged, "it's film world"). After much grumbling, Grant filmed the scene. In fact, he got a little *too* into it, singing along in a way that made it much harder for Curtis to piece all the different takes together.

prime minister who fell for one of his staffers. Another followed a heartbroken British novelist and his Portuguese housekeeper, who eventually fall in love despite speaking two different languages.

"*Love Actually* was a kind of joke with myself, trying to write 10 of them at once," says Curtis. "Tonally, I realize, it's a bit uneven, some of the stories don't exist in the same world, but I think that was inherent in what I was doing, and I don't think I could have changed it." Curtis was inspired by films like Robert Altman's *Nashville* and Quentin Tarantino's *Pulp Fiction*, which told numerous stories under a singular connected framework, and was curious to see if the same format could be used for a romantic comedy.

He spent the following months working out quick, romantic sketches that could be used as mini-arcs. "I'd had a back operation and ended up walking around a lot, figuring out each strand. How does it start? What's the complication? How do you end it? It was a joy. It took me back to my sitcom roots, where the plots have quick, simple arcs," he says. His first idea was a man who fantasizes about being at his wife's funeral—"A lot of women in cute black frocks" walking up to him and giving their phone numbers, explaining that they know he won't be capable of a serious relationship anytime soon. "I thought, *Well, there's one bit. What comes second?*" says Curtis.

If you don't think that sounds like a particularly romantic scene on which to open a romantic comedy . . . well, you're not wrong. Though the funeral bit was (blessedly) cut long before the final script for *Love Actually* came together, it's an instructive peek into just how thoroughly Curtis intended to explore the concept of romantic love from some unusual angles.

Curtis's final script for *Love Actually*, while often unabashedly sentimental, is also fairly obsessed with exploring every possible form that love can take via the movie's many characters (who are periodically revealed to be siblings or friends as their stories cross over). In addition to the more conventional rom-com romances between the prime minister and his staffer Natalie, or the novelist Jamie and his housekeeper Aurélia, once you know Curtis's motivations you can experience him ticking less commonly explored types of love off his list. There's the platonic love of aging rocker Billy Mack (Bill Nighy) and his manager Joe (Gregor Fisher), who spend a bittersweet Christmas getting drunk and watching porn.

I FEEL IT IN MY FINGERS . . .

On Richard Curtis's invitation, the band Wet Wet Wet performed a cover of The Troggs' "Love Is All Around" for *Four Weddings and a Funeral.* The song ended up being as big as the movie (and largely *because of* the movie), topping the charts for five straight months. It eventually became so inescapable that a backlash spread across the British music scene; Jarvis Cocker, front man of the rock band Pulp, appeared on the popular British music show *Top of the Pops* and opened his jacket to reveal the words, "I hate Wet Wet Wet." Eventually, even Wet Wet Wet themselves opted to withdraw the single. "It was just time to put the song to bed," says singer Marti Pellow.

When Richard Curtis chose to revisit "Love Is All Around" in *Love Actually,* he cheekily acknowledged the cultural baggage it had accrued, and for which he was largely responsible. In an effort to lock down the all-important Christmas Number One, the singer Billy Mack (Bill Nighy) performs a half-hearted cover of "Love Is All Around" with even cornier Christmas-themed lyrics. He spends the rest of the movie openly roasting the song: "Buy my festering turd of a record," he tells one interviewer.

There's the dutiful, familial love practiced by Sarah (Laura Linney), who breaks off a one-night stand with her crush (Rodrigo Santoro) affair to spend Christmas with her mentally ill brother. There's the warm paternal love of Daniel (Liam Neeson), fending off grief after his wife's death by channeling his energy into raising his young son (Thomas Brodie-Sangster). And—most controversially, for anyone who thinks it's weird to quietly obsess over your best friend's fiancée—there's the love of Mark (Andrew Lincoln), the world's worst Best Man, who shows up on Christmas Eve to confess his feelings for Juliet (Keira Knightley) with a series of poster boards.

The sequence, as immortal as it is squirm-inducing, is probably *Love Actually*'s most famous scene. Curtis came up with a bunch of ideas for how Mark—who, the movie repeatedly emphasizes, has basically never talked to Juliet—could grandly express his feelings for her. From a list that included such swings as filling the entire courtyard outside her house with roses, Curtis selected the poster boards because a straw poll of the women in his office revealed that they found all the other ideas creepier.

In the scene, Mark rings the doorbell while Juliet and her husband, Peter, are cuddling on the couch. When Juliet answers, Mark holds up the first poster, which instructs her to tell Peter carolers are at the door. Over twelve subsequent posters, he spells it all out: TO ME YOU ARE PERFECT, AND MY WASTED HEART WILL LOVE YOU UNTIL YOU LOOK LIKE THIS, he writes, before showing her a picture of a mummy. Somehow, Juliet is charmed enough that she chases him down the street and kisses him. "Enough. Enough now," he mumbles to himself as he walks away—signifying, we're left to assume, that the kiss was enough to satisfy his desire and put his obsession to bed.

It is an instantly unforgettable grand gesture in the John-Cusack-with-a-boom-box vein. It is *also* absolutely bonkers in a way that falls apart when given even the slightest moment of logical analysis. Juliet discovers how Mark really feels when she watches the wedding video he shot, which turns out to be nothing but adoring close-ups of her. But isn't Peter going to watch it someday and realize his best man bungled the job in the creepiest way imaginable? Are we supposed to feel good that Mark turns up on Christmas Eve to covertly confess his love for his best friend's wife? Are we supposed to be satisfied when Juliet responds to the cue-card bit by running after him and kissing him? Since when is Christmas supposed to be the time you tell the truth (*No, Virginia, there is no Santa Claus*)? And if it *is*, shouldn't he drop the posters and confess to Peter that he's been creeping on Juliet all along?

If it's easy to punch holes in the rom-com logic, it's also fair to say that the creative team behind the movie was aware that those holes could be punched. "I think because Andrew was so openhearted and guileless, we knew we'd get away with it," says Richard Curtis (whose script editor and real-life partner Emma Freud also told Lincoln that his character was essentially *Love Actually*'s Richard Curtis analogue). And Lincoln was nothing if not clear on the strangeness of the role. "In one of the most romantic movies of all time, I got to play the only guy who doesn't get the girl," he says. "I got to be this weird stalker guy." Keira Knightley, who was seventeen years old when her scenes were shot, couldn't even remember which man her character ended up with. "I've only seen it once, and it was a really long time ago. So I *don't* go off with Andrew Lincoln?" she asked in 2018.

If *Love Actually* can be said to have a "main" story, it's probably the one featuring Hugh Grant as David, the newly elected prime minister. Like the airport scenes that bookend the movie, it is a fascinating window into the very trenchant cultural and political climate of 2003. David, a bachelor, develops a crush on his staffer Natalie (Martine McCutcheon). When he spots her alone in a room with the visiting president of the United States (Billy Bob Thornton), who enters at the hypothetical midpoint between Bill Clinton and George W. Bush, David is jealous enough to start an international incident over it. At a press conference, he delivers an uncharacteristically forceful speech warning the United States that the United Kingdom won't be bullied any longer.

David's speech was triggered by romantic jealousy instead of, you know, anything actually related to the war. (We're still in Curtisland, after all, so the prime minister doesn't actually need to know or care about politics.) But it also speaks, forcefully, to the actual political landscape of 2003, and the United Kingdom's place in it. At a time when many British citizens were openly skeptical of the "special relationship" that dragged the U.K. into wars being waged by the United States, *Love Actually* let them indulge

POLITICS (ACTUALLY)

Hugh Grant's press conference monologue in *Love Actually* became such a cultural touchstone in the U.K. that it even seeped into *actual* politics. "I know there's a bit of us that would like me to do a Hugh Grant in *Love Actually* and tell America where to get off," said actual prime minister Tony Blair, defending his Iraq War policy at a Labour Party conference in 2005. "But the difference between a good film and real life is that in real life there's the next day, the next year, the next lifetime to contemplate the ruinous consequences of easy applause. I never doubted after September 11th that our place was alongside America and I don't doubt it now."

in the fantasy of a prime minister who dresses down the United States by asserting the U.K.'s cultural contributions to the world. "We may be a small country, but we're a great one, too," he says. "The country of Shakespeare, Churchill, the Beatles, Sean Connery, Harry Potter. David Beckham's right foot. David Beckham's left foot, come to that." If Richard Curtis hadn't been the one writing and directing the scene, *Mr. Bean* or *Four Weddings and a Funeral* could probably have been added to that list.

But this is *Love Actually*, so the audience barely has time to reckon with England's role in the geopolitical landscape before we're zipped along to another love story. Mixed in among the cheesy and clichéd and sometimes off-putting little narratives in *Love Actually*—the less said about Colin, a goofy Brit who flies to Wisconsin to pick up a harem of American women, the better—*Love Actually* also has moments of real emotional power. At one point or another, every single person I've asked about *Love Actually* in the course of writing this book has mentioned Emma Thompson, who delivers a remarkable, wordless performance of shock and grief as she realizes that her husband is having an affair.

Thompson plays Karen in a story that seems, initially, like it might be *Love Actually*'s exploration of love in the context of marital fidelity. Her husband, Harry (Alan Rickman), is contemplating an affair with Mia (Heike Makatsch), an amorous young employee, whose sexual overtures toward him are as overt as she could get without leaping onto him in the office. For Christmas, Harry buys Mia an expensive heart-shaped gold necklace. When Karen finds it—assuming, understandably, that Harry has bought it for her—the stage is set for a tragic round of gift-opening on Christmas. Karen opens the gift, discovers a Joni Mitchell CD instead of the necklace she expected, and realizes that her husband must have bought the necklace for someone else. And then she goes upstairs to reckon with her pain as quickly as possible so Christmas isn't ruined for their children.

Curtis learned to blend his sweetness with a little sour while working on *Four Weddings and a Funeral*, and the most interesting scenes in *Love Actually* approach love from an angle rarely addressed by romantic comedies. The subsequent scene, in which Karen goes upstairs to quietly cry, asks a lot of Emma Thompson. Richard Curtis—a practiced screenwriter but a first-time film director—didn't come armed with the answers. "Emma turns to me and goes, 'Richard, I don't even know my son's name. You haven't given us any information about their Christmas traditions. But I have to act the mother of these children . . .'" says Curtis.

Fortunately, Thompson came ready to deliver anyway. "I just wrote that she goes upstairs, puts on the record, and lets the emotion show. Everything in that scene is just Emma. We did that 12 times in four different sizes. She had to do it again and again. A brutal bit of sorrow," says Curtis. For nearly two minutes, as Joni Mitchell's "Both Sides Now" plays over the soundtrack, the camera stays on Thompson as she cries; wipes her eyes and nose with a tissue; straightens the bedspread, in that way people mindlessly do chores when they don't know what to do with themselves; and finally returns to her family, where she composes herself enough to put on a brave face for the children at Christmas.

In a movie in which, for better or for worse, so many things seem artificial, this particular arc rings true. Years later, Emma Thompson revealed she had drawn on her own experience as her marriage fell apart, when her then-husband, Kenneth Branagh, had an affair with his costar Helena Bonham Carter on the set of *Mary Shelley's Frankenstein*. "That scene where my character is standing by the bed crying is so well known because it's something everyone's been through," says Thompson. "I had my heart very badly broken by Ken. So I knew what it was like to find the necklace that wasn't meant for me."

Here, again, you can imagine a Curtisland moment in which Harry, realizing his horrible mistake, delivers a grand gesture to win his wife's heart back. Maybe he hasn't even had sex with his secretary yet. (The movie is fuzzy on that detail, but for the record, script editor Emma Freud has revealed that—at least in Curtis's mind—Rickman's character *definitely* consummated the affair.) Or maybe Mark could lend him the poster boards that so dazzlingly work for him.

Instead, *Love Actually* gives us Karen confronting Harry directly. "Would you stay, knowing life would always be a little bit worse?" she asks him. When he admits he's been a fool, she breaks: "Yes, but you've also made a fool out of me, and you've made the life I lead foolish too." This is, for all intents and purposes, the end of this very unusual rom-com arc; though we see Harry return to his family near the end of the movie, there's nothing about Karen's reaction that suggests her own anguish is resolved. In a movie full of happy endings, it's a pointedly unresolved note, which is the kind of thing you can get away with when you slip it in among the types of love stories audiences had come to expect. It's also the darkest form of love Curtis explores: the love that someone might have entrusted with the wrong person.

When *Love Actually* was released on November 14, 2003, to mixed reviews, scenes like this one were judged harshly by critics like *The New York Times*'s A. O. Scott, who said *Love Actually* is "most grotesque when it tries for earnest drama." *Love Actually* "is a mess of crossed signals, swerving between cynicism and sincerity without quite knowing the difference between them," he wrote in a review echoed by a number of the movie's detractors.

Curtis has an answer for that criticism in a way that sums up his approach to the romantic comedy, and maybe to life in general. "I believe that cynical people believe that everyone else is cynical," says Curtis. "They regard non-cynical people as simply ultra-cynical. Supposed 'non-cynical people' are merely pretending to be non-cynical in order to make money from other cynical people. So cynics who watch *Love Actually* think it is a cynical

THE CUTTING-ROOM FLOOR

With ten interlocking stories crammed into 136 minutes of film, it's hard to imagine *Love Actually* stuffing much more in—but Richard Curtis originally conceived of fourteen stories, and two of the extra stories were actually filmed before Curtis decided to cut them. The first, which was shot in Kenya, depicted two older African women swapping stories about love, in what Curtis describes as his effort to challenge audiences' preconceptions by showing that love still abounds in "places of the world where life is very hard." The second had a similar goal, turning the audience's sympathies against a stern headmistress at a primary school before revealing that she spends her evenings caring for her dying partner. Both stories were cut to keep the densely interconnected movie from becoming even harder to follow, though Curtis clearly regrets losing them.

Perhaps the biggest cut of all is a twist that would have added an element of the supernatural to *Love Actually*. In a nod to Christmas classics like *A Christmas Carol* and *It's a Wonderful Life*, Curtis originally intended to reveal that Rufus (Rowan Atkinson), the salesman who almost blows up Harry's affair and later distracts the airport staff so Sam can chase after Joanna, was an angel who was trying to help the characters he encountered.

attempt to make money. No amount of evidence could prove to them that it ever had anything to do with good will."

But if critics didn't exactly line up for *Love Actually*, audiences did. Though Curtis admits that, due to the sheer number of interlocking stories, the process of editing *Love Actually* was "murderous," he was committed to delivering his all-encompassing take on love. "Everyone thought it was a big gamble. People said, 'Do we have to do this? Can't we just have Hugh's story?' But I didn't want to do that," he says.

In the end, Curtis's own cinematic grand gesture to express his love for love paid off. *Love Actually* grossed almost $250 million worldwide, topping rom-coms like *How to Lose a Guy in 10 Days* (also that year) and Christmas movies like *Elf*. In effect, Richard Curtis had proven he could direct rom-coms as successfully as he could write them. But having worked so hard to explore so many versions of love in *Love Actually*, he seems to have walked away from the movie feeling he'd said about as much as he needed to say. "The truth of the matter is that by the time I was writing *Love Actually*, I was starting to lose interest in 'boy meets girl for the first time and falls in love'—a film about that, now, I would not be terribly interested in," he says.

In the years immediately after *Love Actually*'s release, he wrote and directed a comedy about pirate radio called *The Boat That Rocked*, wrote a tear-jerking made-for-TV drama about mothers whose sons die of malaria called *Mary and Martha*, and cowrote the screenplay for Steven Spielberg's Oscar-nominated film version of the hit play *War Horse*. When Curtis finally returned to the rom-com genre in the subsequent decade, the movies themselves—like many of the other rom-coms of the era—were extremely high-concept, from the time-travel romance *About Time* to the "What if only one guy remembered the Beatles?" movie *Yesterday*.

LOVE ACTUALLY 2?

A *Love Actually* sequel has never seriously been in the cards—in part because the cast's salaries alone would be enough to break the bank today—but much like *Four Weddings and a Funeral*, fans of the movie *did* get the next best thing in 2017. As part of Red Nose Day, a fundraiser for the U.K. charity Comic Relief, Richard Curtis wrote and co-directed the fifteen-minute short film *Red Nose Day Actually*. The cheeky, somewhat self-aware short film is a sequel that goes out of its way to wrap up some of *Love Actually*'s dangling threads. Among the revelations: Mark (Andrew Lincoln) has married Kate Moss, who was briefly referenced as his crush; Sarah (Laura Linney) has found love with a handsome new suitor (Patrick Dempsey); and Sam (Thomas Brodie-Sangster) and Joanna (Olivia Olson) have reconnected and gotten engaged. Not present, sadly, is Alan Rickman, who died a year before *Red Nose Day Actually* was shot. As a result, Emma Thompson chose not to reprise her role as well, leaving Harry and Karen's troubled marriage unresolved.

Love Actually never got a full sequel, but its success ensured that its formula would be borrowed by other filmmakers. The movie almost instantly sparked legions of imitators, each attempting to add one extra ingredient to Curtis's deliberately simple cocktail. Garry Marshall took the *Love Actually* formula and made its very marketable connection to a holiday even more explicit in a series of movies titled *Valentine's Day*, *New Year's Eve*, and *Mother's Day*. A whole slew of directors were assembled to contribute shorts compiled into singular anthologies that told love stories set in specific cities, starting with 2006's *Paris, Je T'aime* and extending to New York City, Rio, Shanghai, and Berlin. And the people behind

2009's *He's Just Not That Into You* and 2012's *What to Expect When You're Expecting* tried to turn the popular self-help books into narrative films by turning their advice into interconnected love stories featuring as many celebrities as the productions could wrangle.

But even the biggest of those movies never came anywhere near to what *Love Actually* accomplished in box-office earnings or in long-term cultural impact. Curtis may or may not have had

CHRISTMAS IS ALL AROUND

Dating back to the 1940s with movies like Mark Sandrich's *Holiday Inn*, Peter Godfrey's *Christmas in Connecticut*, and Henry Koster's *The Bishop's Wife*, filmmakers have recognized that the natural cheeriness and picturesque snowscapes of Christmas can make an ideal setting for a romantic comedy. But the smash success of *Love Actually*—which happened to come within weeks of Jon Favreau's similarly Christmassy, similarly massive *Elf*—was a harbinger of the spike in Christmas-themed movies that would come out of Hollywood in the years that followed. In addition to children's movies like Robert Zemeckis's *The Polar Express*, ensemble dramedies like Thomas Bezucha's *The Family Stone*, and quip-a-minute action movies like Shane Black's *Kiss Kiss Bang Bang*, audiences were treated to a run of Christmas romcoms that rivaled the number produced around sixty years earlier. Highlights included Nancy Meyers's *The Holiday*, which gave audiences two charming love stories for the price of one. Lowlights included the stunningly unpleasant *Surviving Christmas*, in which Ben Affleck romanced Christina Applegate while bribing her family into spending Christmas with him. (That same cash offer wasn't extended to moviegoers, which might explain why nobody saw it.)

his eye on the movie's long-term future, but he was wise to set his romantic anthology at Christmas, ensuring that fans and detractors alike would have a good reason to revisit it year after year. It's Christmas, more than anything, that accounts for the otherwise curiously long shelf life of *Love Actually*. A 2018 BBC poll led to viewers naming *Love Actually* one of the five greatest Christmas movies of all time, ahead of noted classics like *White Christmas* and *Miracle on 34th Street*.

The close association with the holiday season makes it an annual hit. The movie has been screened with a live orchestra performing the score. It has been screened with an accompanying two-course Christmas dinner. It has been screened as both a sing-along and a quote-along with bottomless alcohol, which could only improve it.

But revisiting it annually also brings the movie's failings into even starker relief. Like all of Richard Curtis's rom-coms, the movie skews largely white, heavily male, and entirely wealthy; Curtis may have intended to explore love in all its forms, but in the end, he decided to cut the lesbian couple and the African women instead of the porno stand-ins or the British guy who's horny for Americans. The love stories, which are almost invariably told from the men's perspectives, end happily—even poor widowed Liam Neeson gets a meet-cute with Claudia Schiffer—while the two most developed female characters, Karen and Sarah, end the movie in an unhappy marriage and single, respectively. And there's a whole hornet's nest about the power dynamics of the prime minister dating a staffer who is exponentially less powerful that *Love Actually* doesn't even seem *aware* of, let alone address.

These retrograde elements have, somewhat paradoxically, earned *Love Actually* a new wave of begrudging fans. The movie may technically exist in the shadow of 9/11, but it already feels like a window into what felt—at least for viewers in *Love Actually*'s target demographic—a simpler, happier time. "Everyone is in a palatial flat, a good-looking neoliberal is in charge, and everyone loves him. The financial crisis is yet to hit, Laura Linney's brother has a care plan, and Colin Firth can easily import a Portuguese wife from France without having to worry about the EU settlement scheme," wrote *Guardian* columnist Rhiannon Lucy Cosslett in 2019.

Still, the *Love Actually* wars restart each holiday season, as devotees and detractors draw lines and argue whether the movie is a modern classic or a crime against cinema itself. For *Love Actually*'s tenth anniversary, *Jezebel*'s Lindy West wrote a takedown so scathing—and so celebrated by the movie's haters—that it eventually led to an entire book on cinema called (what else?) *Shit, Actually*. *The Atlantic*'s Chris Orr called it "the least romantic movie of all time," prompting his colleague Emma Green to rebut his take with an essay titled "I Will Not Be Ashamed of Loving *Love Actually*" a few days later.

The arguments are, at this point, a part of the movie's legacy. In 2013, *The Guardian* attempted to settle the matter once and for all by inviting readers to submit videos attacking or defending *Love Actually*. They failed, of course. Love it or hate it, *Love Actually* isn't going anywhere.

Will Smith

THE ROM-COM HERO WE BARELY GOT

To understand just how big a deal it was when Will Smith starred in a romantic comedy, you need to start with the poster. The poster for 2005's *Hitch* does not feature his love interest, Eva Mendes. It does not feature his costar, Kevin James. It's just Will Smith, grinning straight at the camera as he stands at the center of an off-white void. That is not a lot of information about the movie—but it was more than enough for moviegoers around the world, who drove *Hitch* to a whopping $371 million gross worldwide.

At the time *Hitch* hit theaters, Smith had been on a years-long run of action movies, from the sequels to *Bad Boys* and *Men in Black* to an extremely unfaithful adaptation of Isaac Asimov's *I, Robot*, which doubled as a feature-length commercial for Converse sneakers. It would not have been unreasonable for audiences at the time to assume *Hitch* was an action-comedy starring Smith as a wisecracking hero who saves the world from aliens and/or robots.

Instead, *Hitch* casts Smith as Alex "Hitch" Hitchens, a professional "date doctor" who coaches men on how they can successfully woo the women of their dreams. His opening monologue is about how women who reject men are just lying to themselves. The script wisely includes an entire subplot designed to reassure the audience that Hitch, a true believer in romance, is *not* just making money by helping sleazy guys manipulate women into one-night stands. But in the wrong hands, *Hitch* would not be *that* far removed from the story of a real-life pickup artist like Erik von Markovik, a.k.a. "Mystery," who earned money and fame by teaching men "dating tactics" like insulting women to break down their self-esteem and make them easier to manipulate into sex.

Hitch does not feel like a sleazy paean to pickup artists, and you can lay much of the credit for that on Will Smith. Movie stars like Smith are rarely given the chance to be vulnerable, let alone uncool. The fun of *Hitch* is watching someone with as much natural charisma as Smith become a clumsy, tongue-tied moron whenever Eva Mendes is around.

Audiences around the world loved this version of Smith, and the movie handily outgrossed both *Bad Boys 2* and *I, Robot*. Even in an era where sequels to rom-coms were much less common, *Hitch* must have looked like a possible franchise starter to Sony. And the creative team behind the movie was certainly game for more. There have been no fewer than three failed attempts to adapt *Hitch* into a TV series. As recently as 2020, Eva Mendes was trying to drum up hype for a *Hitch* sequel in which the Date Doctor, put out of business by apps like Tinder and Hinge, has to find a new way to get his mojo back. And director Andy Tennant confirms that ideas for a sequel were kicked around, only for Smith himself to shoot them down: "For whatever reason, it just wasn't something Will needed or wanted to revisit."

So if the question that led to *Hitch* was "Why hasn't Will Smith starred in a rom-com before?" the question it left behind is: Why didn't he ever star in one again?

One possible answer came in a promotional interview Smith did while promoting *Hitch*, in which he revealed that Sony had been opposed to casting a white woman as his love interest—a racist decision that was made, cynically, because the studio wanted to be sure that racism wouldn't dent the film at the box office. "There's sort of an accepted myth that if you have two black actors, a male and a female, in the lead of a romantic comedy, that people around the world don't want to see it," said Smith. "We spend $50-something million making this movie and the studio would think that was tough on their investment. So the idea of a black actor and a white actress comes up—that'll work around the world, but it's a problem in the U.S." In a separate interview, Smith elaborated on the strange paradox of being a Black movie star in an industry and a genre that defaults to whiteness: Casting him opposite a white love interest might be acceptable, à la Sidney Poitier and Katharine Houghton in Stanley Kramer's *Guess Who's Coming to Dinner*—on the condition that the movie's plot was solely focused on the nature of interracial relationships. "Hollywood is happy to do it if the film is *about* racism," says Smith.

It's no knock on Eva Mendes's performance in *Hitch* to note that the studio's "compromise" on the movie's casting—that a Black man could date a Latina woman, but not a white one—is completely insane. It also erected a wall between Smith and the other crossover superstars of the era. Studios wouldn't treat Smith the way they'd treated Mel Gibson with *What Women Want*, or Tom Cruise with *Jerry Maguire*. Even one of the biggest and most bankable movie stars in the world found himself hemmed in by standards that persist, in part, because Hollywood itself won't release the movies that might change them.

If you're going to do the math on what institutional racism in Hollywood has cost us, you can't just factor in the movies that exist; you have to think about the movies we never got to see. It is maddening to imagine what Will Smith's career might have looked like in an industry that wasn't burdened with so much implicit and explicit racism, and it's not just the rom-com genre that has taken the hit. When it was suggested that Bridget Moynahan might play his love interest in *I, Robot*, that was "definitely an issue for the studio," Smith says. In another moment of unusual candor, Smith revealed that he was offered the chance to play Superman in 2006 and turned it down over fear of a backlash. "You can't be messing up white people's heroes in Hollywood!" he said. "You mess up white people's heroes in Hollywood, you'll never work in this town again!"

"Single older women, as a demographic, are about as fucked a group as can ever exist."

—ZOE, *SOMETHING'S GOTTA GIVE*

CHAPTER 11

SOMETHING'S GOTTA GIVE

(And the Rom-Com That Aged Gracefully)

A MONTH AFTER NANCY MEYERS GOT DIVORCED FROM HER LONGTIME partner and collaborator Charles Shyer, she invited her friend Diane Keaton to lunch. The year was 1999, and Meyers was at a professional crossroads. The year before, she had made her directorial debut with a Lindsay Lohan–starring remake of *The Parent Trap*, which she'd cowritten with Shyer. The year after, she was set to direct her first romantic comedy, *What Women Want*—her first movie in which Shyer didn't play some kind of creative role.

But at this particular lunch with Diane Keaton, Meyers's concerns were personal, not professional. "I said, 'So, what's it like being our age and single?'" recalls Meyers. "And she said, 'Forget it. It's over.'"

Long before *Something's Gotta Give* arrived in theaters—and before Meyers herself was either single or in her fifties—she had an idea for a movie. "What if there was this guy that only dated younger women, met the mother of somebody he was dating and fell in love?" says Meyers. "I had it for ten years, and I wasn't drawn to it."

The trick to a Nancy Meyers romantic comedy is that the characters never quite realize that they've stumbled into a romantic comedy until they're too deep to pull out of it. It took the passage of time, as well as another romantic relationship, before Meyers realized the reason she'd been sitting on the idea for so long: She wanted to make a movie about people who fall in love later in their lives than they would ever have expected. "I have spent the last two decades not only being single but writing a couple of movies about divorced women my age—purposely defying the clichés that being older and single meant you were destined to be undesirable, lonely and isolated," Meyers later wrote in *The New York Times*'s "Modern Love" column. "I wrote about women in my films who blossomed post-divorce, much as I had done in some ways. I was driven by a desire not to be put in a box by my age or divorce, and I wanted to project a positive spin for women like me."

But if Meyers was writing for women like her, she was also specifically writing for herself, and working to "straighten out some things in her life" by developing material that was, in part, based on her post-divorce relationship. "You know that scene where she's crying and typing and crying? That was me writing the movie," says Meyers. "That was a lot of Kleenex."

In a process she says was "almost therapeutic," Meyers would start writing the movie at 10 A.M. and work until 7 P.M. every day. When she was finally finished, a full ten months later, she had a 250-page script—which means, according to the old Hollywood rule of thumb that one page is about a minute of screen time, that the original draft of the movie would have stretched to more than four hours.

Looking at the finished work, Meyers "read it, burst into tears, and wanted to throw it out," she says. Instead, she went to bed and woke up the following morning ready to edit. Her first pass lopped out seventy pages. It still wasn't enough, so she went back to work and found even more excess fat to cut. "You just start tearing away at it, and you can't do it all at once. It's impossible to see what it is at first. You just keep taking away and taking away, and it begins to shape up," she says. "Story, you know—you just keep following the story."

The final draft of *Something's Gotta Give*—which, for the record, comes in at a perfectly reasonable 210 pages—has been whittled down so precisely that everything about it feels sharp. Unlike most romantic comedies, *Something's Gotta Give* centers on a love story in which both characters genuinely have no interest in falling in love, with each other or anybody else. Of course, that doesn't stop it from happening anyway. At the outset, Erica Barry is amicably divorced and comfortable alone. Her life is upended when she meets sixty-three-year-old Harry Sanborn, a bachelor who revels in his reputation as a legendary lothario and serial dater, who happens to be having a fling with her twenty-nine-year-old daughter.

WHAT'S IN A NAME?

Throughout development, and even at the beginning of production, *Something's Gotta Give* went under the working title *Untitled Nancy Meyers Project*. The final title was inspired by a 1954 Johnny Mercer song of the same name, which was nominated for an Oscar after it was used in the 1955 musical *Daddy Long Legs*, cowritten by Henry and Phoebe Ephron. (Yes, parents of Nora.) Though "Something's Gotta Give" doesn't appear on the *Something's Gotta Give* soundtrack, Keanu Reeves's character is named Julian Mercer in an homage to Johnny Mercer.

And then Harry has a heart attack. On the advice of a *very* hunky young doctor played by Keanu Reeves, he stays at Erica's home in the Hamptons while he recovers. As Harry spends more time with Erica (and amicably breaks up with her daughter), he falls in love with her, though he's so inexperienced at dating a woman his own age that he's not quite sure what to do about it. Meanwhile, Erica is torn between her attraction to Harry and the advances of the aforementioned hunky young doctor. Erica is "a poster girl for growing old," the script explains. "It's actually hard to imagine 55 looking any better. And not because she looks 35, but because she makes 55 look graceful and right." (It is not for nothing that this descriptor could also be applied to Meyers herself, who turned fifty-four just a few days before *Something's Gotta Give* hit theaters.)

As she pitched *Something's Gotta Give* to room after room full of male studio executives, Meyers could tell that—despite the mammoth success of her rom-com *What Women Want*, which had ended up being the highest-grossing movie ever directed by a woman, just a few years earlier—*Something's Gotta Give* could be a tough movie to sell. At one point, a man she knew advised her to cut a joke about menopause: "Don't mention menopause. Not sexy. Why bring it up?" he warned her. "I could just feel that these people are not making a movie with a fifty-five-year-old woman at the center," says Meyers. "And I went to Sony, and I pitched it to Amy Pascal and John Calley, and it was just a completely different meeting. I felt embraced, and I felt that Amy and John totally got it, and they weren't afraid of it. Amy, being a woman, understood it."

Meyers writes her screenplays with her ideal stars in mind, and she knew exactly who she wanted from the very beginning: Diane Keaton—the closest thing Meyers had to an on-camera muse—and Jack Nicholson, who she felt was "by far the most ir-resistible person I have ever been around." As Meyers worked on the script with a verbal commitment from both actors to star, their faces, voices, and occasionally their active input was her north star: "I had their pictures all over my computer. Always," she says.

The timing of *Something's Gotta Give* was ideal for Keaton, who was coming off a string of box-office failures that included the romantic comedies *The Other Sister* and *Town & Country*. Keaton "was pretty much washed up," she writes in her memoir *Then Again*, when Meyers called for another lunch—this time professional, not personal.

Diane Keaton loved the idea for *Something's Gotta Give* from the very beginning. She was also convinced it would never actually happen. "I'm sorry, but Jack Nicholson is not going to play my boyfriend in a chick flick. That's not his thing," Keaton recalls telling Meyers. "Nancy, you're brilliant, and I'm totally thrilled you want me, but there's no way he's going to accept your offer, which is just another way of saying you'll never get the financing either. So I wouldn't bother getting your hopes up. Don't even try."

As it turned out, Keaton had either underestimated Nicholson, the script, or Nancy Meyers's legendary ability to know—and get—exactly what she wants. Nicholson agreed to star right away. When he later invited Meyers to his house to discuss his personal notes on the screenplay, they had a long, luxurious dinner before Nicholson finally pulled out his copy of the script at about 2 A.M. As he paged through with a little golf pencil, he finally concluded that there was absolutely nothing about the script that needed to be altered—an uncommon concession for a star so powerful that he could essentially demand whatever he wanted. "He was great, he was kind, he was generous, he didn't want to change a word," says Meyers. It didn't hurt that Nicholson would be costarring with Keaton: "I have had a kind of open affection for Diane anyway, ever since I was with her in *Reds*," he says.

But if the two leads fell into place exactly as Meyers had imagined, the supporting cast was harder to come by. Each of Meyers's collaborators—actors, casting directors, production designers—talks at length about her incredible attention to detail, in tones that can vary between admiration and exasperation. "It's like a dog with a bone, babe. If she wants to make it happen, it happens," says Keaton. Meyers knows exactly what she's looking for, but her philosophy isn't always clear to her collaborators; in some cases, the answer is simply that she'll know it when she sees it. "Nancy sees a dozen people and says, 'I don't know. None of them are what I want. Keep looking,'" says Jane Jenkins, the casting director on *Something's Gotta Give*. "Other than Jack and Diane, there was no offering anybody anything. She needed to hear it and see it."

That included Keanu Reeves, who called *Something's Gotta Give* "one of the best scripts that I've ever read, period," and had to actively work to get into the movie at all. Though he was red-hot off his starring role in *The Matrix* trilogy, he was required to attend both a private meeting with Jack Nicholson and a chemistry read with Diane Keaton before Meyers offered him the part of Julian Mercer, the doctor who vies for Erica Barry's heart. Competing with a long list of actresses, Amanda Peet "worked her ass off" to land the part of Erica's daughter Marin, says Jenkins. After six auditions—reading opposite Nicholson, Keaton, and eventually Jenkins in a weekend meeting at Meyers's home as the start of production loomed—Meyers finally decided Peet was right for the role. In some cases, Meyers's search for perfection crashed right up against the hard reality of the filming schedule. Jon Favreau—

who plays Harry's personal assistant, described in the script as "a Gershwin tune of a man"—was cast on a Friday, put through wardrobe over the weekend, and began filming his role on the following Monday. "He's not *exactly* a Gershwin tune . . . but he is in the key, at least," says Jenkins.

At the first *Something's Gotta Give* script read, Meyers sat back and reflected on the point of the movie she was about to make. "I thought, that day, that the movie is about finding out that you don't have to be the person you're convinced you are," says Meyers. "We all do it—*this is who I am, that's it, I'm going to be this forever*—and then something happens, and wow, you *don't* have to be that forever."

Erica Barry certainly thinks she knows who she is at the start of *Something's Gotta Give*. As part of a speech illustrating the differences between the way society treats single men and single women of a certain age, her sister Zoe (Frances McDormand) lays it out pretty succinctly: gorgeous, divorced, over fifty, most successful female playwright since Lillian Hellman, and unable to get a date because guys her age are both intimidated by her success and more interested in dating women in their twenties. Erica is a self-described "turtleneck kind of gal"—which makes it all the more surprising, to herself and to Harry and to the audience, when they finally hook up and she orders him to cut the turtleneck off rather than wait for him to get it unstuck. It's refreshing, and still unusual, for any Hollywood movie—let alone a romantic comedy—to depict an older woman with a sex drive. It certainly catches Erica herself off guard: "I *do* like sex!" she exclaims in her breathless postcoital daze with Harry.

For his part, Harry is undergoing his own later-life crisis, sparked first by a heart attack and then the process of falling in love with Erica. The experience is so unexpected and astonishing to him that it takes him the movie's entire run time to fully process it's happening. "I don't think I've ever had this effect on a woman before," he says, early on. "What effect do you think you're having on me?" Erica replies. "I don't quite recognize it. That's how I know I never had it before," he says.

Over the course of the shoot, which stretched for nearly six months, the cast and creative team—and especially the core trio of Meyers, Keaton, and Nicholson—bonded over their closeness to the material. "You know, the movie was made by three single people our age. So we struggled every day," says Meyers. It was the first time, in his entire career, that Jack Nicholson had been directed by a woman, and Meyers was delighted with the results. "He says lines like you dream," she says. "And then, on the other hand, some of his best moments in the movie, I think, is when he's

LA VIE EN ROSE

One scene that was filmed but ultimately cut from *Something's Gotta Give* featured Harry serenading Erica with "La Vie en rose" at a karaoke bar, complete with an entire verse in French. As Meyers saw it, Nicholson's performance turned out to be *too* romantic for Erica and Harry's relationship at that point in the movie. "He worked really hard on it," says Meyers. "I had to cut the scene out because it just didn't fit the following scene, where he goes out with another woman."

The scene was eventually released as a bonus on the DVD, but Nicholson never got over his disappointment at his big musical number not making the final cut. "He brings it up to me every time I see him," said Meyers in 2012. "Recently I saw him for his birthday and he cornered me and said, 'Now, about that scene . . .'"

saying nothing, because he uses his face like an instrument. And you get a symphony." Nicholson quickly came to respect what Meyers was bringing to the table as well. "She's a tough director, let me tell you that," says Nicholson. "She knows what she wants and she's not afraid to get bloody to get it."

But if plaudits for acting in *Something's Gotta Give* were being doled out, you'd have to put Diane Keaton at the top of the list. Keaton, who earned her fourth Oscar nomination for *Something's Gotta Give*, performed one scene in rehearsal so flawlessly that Jack Nicholson thought she was actually confessing she was in love with him. "He calls me over after one rehearsal. He's all rattled," says Meyers. "I said, 'What's up?' And he goes, 'Diane just told me she loves me.' I couldn't tell if he was horrified or thrilled. So I was like, 'Yes, I know, I wrote that line. It's in the script, Jack.' And he said, 'Oh, okay.' He thought she meant it."

Keaton's best moment in *Something's Gotta Give* is Erica's lengthy breakup with Harry, which takes Meyers's theme about discovering you aren't who you thought you are and makes it explicit, to devastating results. "You know, the life I had before you, I knew how to do that," she says. "I could do that forever. But now look at me. What am I gonna do?" Harry, not yet understanding how he'd even begin to open himself up to an actual relationship, sorrowfully shrugs, "I don't know how to be a boyfriend."

After a feature-length flirtation, this is the big emotional turning point in *Something's Gotta Give*—and while Meyers has never gone into specific detail on the personal relationship that inspired her to write the screenplay in the first place, it's hard to miss the parallels here. In a particularly art-imitates-life flourish, Meyers, writing her own heartbreak into the screenplay, includes a subplot in which Erica writes her own heartbreak over Harry into a stage play. "It's about a divorced woman, a writer. She's this high-strung, over-amped, controlling, know-it-all neurotic . . . who's incredibly cute, and lovable," says Erica. "Clearly, Erica is more Nancy than me," says Keaton.

The Nancy-ness of Erica's character also extends to the production and set design of *Something's Gotta Give*—an often-noted highlight of Meyers's films, though one she wishes critics would spend less time on. "It's never done to male directors who make gorgeous-looking movies, where the leads live in a great house," says Meyers. "It's never brought up."

THOSE WHO LIVE IN FAKE HOUSES SHOULDN'T THROW STONES

It's no fun to spoil a fantasy, but for the record: The interiors of Erica's "Hamptons" house in *Something's Gotta Give* were shot on a soundstage on the Sony Pictures Studios lot in Culver City. The luxurious-looking "swimming pool" was too shallow for anyone to take a dip in it. The kitchen's gorgeous "soapstone" island, which was painted to have a convincingly soapstone-ish sheen, was custom-manufactured and placed on casters so it could be wheeled out of the way by crew members with minimal hassle. This fantasy kitchen, which almost singlehandedly inspired a boom in kitchen renovations, was essentially a special effect.

Still, the illusion was convincing enough that it even worked on the cast and crew, aided by subtle touches like bringing in fresh flowers every day so the set would smell like a well-manicured home in the Hamptons. "It's easy to forget that we're in fact on a set, other than all of the equipment, and looking up to see the soundstage ceiling," says production designer Jon Hutman.

But Meyers's obsessive attention to production design is too often discussed as separate from her filmmaking. In reality, it's an essential part of it. In one interview, Alec Baldwin, who starred in her 2009 rom-com *It's Complicated*, compared Meyers's attention to detail with Martin Scorsese. Meyers herself quotes François Truffaut: "Making movies is an accumulation of details."

And so, while Erica Barry's home in the Hamptons is surely worthy of an *Architectural Digest* spread, it's also an essential window into her character. "Specifically when we talk about *Something's Gotta Give*, people remember the house in that movie because they connect emotionally with the story, period. Houses way more beautiful and perfect than that have been published a gazillion times, and the reason people remember that house in that movie is because they get swept away in the story," says Jon Hutman, Meyers's longtime production designer. Meyers imagined the house as a symbol of Erica's hard-earned success, purchased with the money she earned from her first hit play. It became both her home and her office. "She put the desk in her bedroom, right? Because the bedroom faces the ocean," says Meyers. "And her desk is right in front. She has the view she loves. And also, it continues to tell the story of the fact that she was done with guys."

While the gorgeous houses of her protagonists sometimes draw more ink than they should from critics who fail to engage with the movies themselves, they're also a side effect of Meyers's career-long focus on professional women. Their lengthy, successful careers—Broadway playwright, newspaper columnist, Hollywood producer, business owner—have given them the means to set up their lives exactly as they'd like them to be (even if the plot inevitably brings someone in to be the bull in those carefully crafted china shops). "This is indicative of all Nancy's projects," says Beth Rubino, the set decorator on both *Something's Gotta Give* and *It's Complicated*. "Beautiful. Functional. Heightened, but accessible. She didn't want it to look as if a decorator had come in and done the house. There was luxury, but there was comfort."

"She approves and sees everything and is quite clear about what she likes and doesn't like," says Rubino. "The kitchen was very key for her. That aesthetic is still fairly prevalent. It increased the kitchen renovation industry, as far as contractors and interior designers. Just because of that film."

WHAT NANCY DID NEXT

The Holiday, Nancy Meyers's 2006 follow-up to *Something's Gotta Give*, is a modern rom-com classic (and a Christmas movie!) in its own right. Much like *Something's Gotta Give*, Meyers wrote *The Holiday* with four specific actors firmly in mind for the leads: Kate Winslet, Cameron Diaz, Jack Black, and Hugh Grant. According to Jenkins, who was also Meyers's casting director on the film, all four actors turned it down. After auditioning reams of other actresses for the roles intended for Winslet and Diaz—and concluding that none of them were what she'd had in mind—through sheer persistence, Meyers convinced Winslet and Diaz to star after all.

To Meyers's great frustration, she had less luck with Hugh Grant. "If you read the script, she actually wrote it in his cadence," says Jenkins. "You could hear his voice in the dialogue. And he was not interested. He said, 'I can't do another rom-com.' And then it was very hard to find the guy who could live up to what she wanted from Hugh Grant. And we met a lot of charming British guys, and nobody was hitting it out of the park for her. We went on and on for a long time before she finally said yes to Jude Law."

And if sneering, often sexist critics find Meyers's stories unrealistic . . . well, look at Meyers herself. If Erica Barry's kitchen seems implausibly perfect, click over to Nancy Meyers's own Instagram and take a look at the kitchen in her own home. And if it seems unlikely that every single play Erica Barry writes can turn out to be a hit, look at Meyers's own filmography, in which every movie she's directed, stretching all the way back to 1998, has been a hit.

This is the track record that gets a movie like *Something's Gotta Give*, which was described before its release as a "commercial risk" aimed at "the Viagra set" in *The New York Times*, the $75 million budget Meyers felt she needed to do it the right way. That budget included a trip to Paris to shoot the movie's ending—an indulgence Meyers happily embraced. "When I wrote my first movie, I wrote, 'Exterior: Swamp—night,' and then I was there," says Meyers. "Note to self: Write, 'Exterior: Paris.'"

At this point in the story, Erica is in a relationship with Julian Mercer. But when Harry shows up to see her in Paris, Julian realizes that Erica is still in love with Harry, and—in the grand tradition of Bill Pullman, Patrick Dempsey, and the other members in the Hall of Fame of rom-com runners-up—he gracefully bows out so Eric and Harry can kiss on a bridge in the snow. "Turns out the heart attack was easy to get over," Harry says in his big final monologue. "You . . . were something else. I finally get it. I'm sixty-three years old, and I'm in love for the first time in my life."

It's hard to argue with Paris in the snow, but for a movie that has taken great pains to dig into the genuine joys and pains of failing in love, this ending has always struck me as a little easy. Because the movie elects to zip past it, we're spared the pain of Julian Mercer getting dumped on the night (it is heavily implied) he planned to propose to Erica.

KEANU THE 'SHIPPER

Keanu Reeves has no hard feelings about getting dumped for Jack Nicholson. In fact, he was rooting for Erica and Harry too. "It's a shame that in American cinema, knowledge and life experience aren't really respected," says Reeves. "Older people are either curmudgeons, or overly wise, or dying. It's nice to see the vitality, the love, the search and the union that can still occur."

Erica's decision to leave Julian for Harry, no matter how heartfelt his speech, has been a sticking point for even the movie's most ardent fans that continues today. In a 2020 essay for The Cut, writer Gina Tomaine wrote that Harry "represents everything that's bad about men," and that it's tragic that the movie ends with a brilliant woman like Erica deciding to dump Julian and "spend her precious time emotionally rehabilitating the archetypically lazy, selfish man-child." In his book *Movies (and Other Things)*, Shea Serrano argues that Harry has proven his sincerity enough to be worth the risk: "He goes on this entire journey of self-discovery after they have a falling-out because he knows that he has to be better than what he's been if he wants to be with Keaton."

Personally, I've always felt that ending the movie without Erica and Harry together would be missing the point. From the moment we meet him, Dr. Mercer knows exactly who he is and what he wants—but this is a movie about discovering that the obvious, almost preordained path is the one you should be happy to veer off when something better comes along. Part of what's striking about *Something's Gotta Give* is that it doesn't just indulge the fantasy of winning the heart of Hot Doctor Keanu Reeves; it indulges the fantasy of rejecting him, no matter how dreamy and adoring he may be, for your true love. This, like all things in all Nancy Meyers films, is by design. "She's the only one delivering the fantasy for women over fifty-five," says Diane Keaton. "You're beautiful, charming, and you get two guys instead of one." It's all part of the alchemy of a movie that gains its power, and its unmistakable re-watchability, by creating a world that audiences want to occupy for as long as they possibly can.

Opening in December of 2003, *Something's Gotta Give* was a massive hit, eventually outgrossing two more blatant grabs for the Christmas box-office crown, *Elf* and *Love Actually*. Studios had been skeptical that audiences would turn out for a rom-com about a woman in her mid-fifties; Meyers knew they would, and she was right. "I'm basically the same age as all the women in my movies," says Meyers. "You do go through things your characters go through. It's almost therapeutic." By telling stories about women her age, and with her life experiences, Meyers was reaching a demographic Hollywood had neglected. It was, of course, the same audience who had made romantic comedies one of the most bankable genres of the 1990s; they had aged, and finally there was a rom-com that acknowledged that as a positive, not a negative.

When asked whether it takes a woman to get a movie like *Something's Gotta Give* made in Hollywood, Meyers was characteristically practical: "I don't know. It took a woman."

EARLY RETIREMENT

On the 2015 release of *The Intern*—Nancy Meyers's most recent feature film at the time of this publication—Meyers said she felt she was finished with the rom-com genre: "I didn't want to write another romance. I never wanted to write another scene in a restaurant between a man and a woman. And I felt sort of done with the romantic story. It just wasn't what I was feeling. And I felt I'd covered that subject pretty well: to fall in love, and out of love, and be divorced, be Cameron Diaz's age, or be Meryl Streep's age."

So another Nancy Meyers rom-com is probably out of the question. The real question is whether or not Nancy Meyers is done with filmmaking altogether. Though she released a short, COVID-19-themed *Father of the Bride* "sequel" on Netflix in 2020, Meyers said she was probably retired from more conventional filmmaking. "The length of a movie, I found over time, became exhausting," she says. "Because it's not that I can't work for two years. It's the intensity of it for that amount of time—it never lets up. Making movies used to be much more fun. It was always stressful. There was always a lot of money at stake. It was always a lot of personalities. It was always release dates, and 'get it done,' and 'don't go over budget,' and 'try to stick to the schedule.' There's always those things, but it was just more fun."

There's also the question of whether or not studios are even interested in the kinds of movies Meyers specializes in making. "Once superhero movies really became the only movies studios cared about, the experience of making a movie like mine changed," she says. "I remember when I finished *The Intern*, I thought, *I think this is it.*"

John Cusack

THE RELUCTANT ROMANTIC

When John Cusack was asked in 2020 by *The New York Times* about his "Cusackness"—a.k.a. the boyish charm that made audiences across the world swoon in 1989's *Say Anything*—he was baffled. "It's hard to understand," he answered. "That 'persona' thing might be about me just getting a job in a romantic comedy and trying to put something original in there." Romantic comedies, he added, are "not really my genre or the kind of thing that I like."

But for someone who doesn't like romantic comedies, Cusack certainly did his part to define them. From his breakout role in Rob Reiner's 1985 rom-com *The Sure Thing*, John Cusack has represented a certain kind of romantic ideal: the self-aware, hyper-verbal hero who could be the perfect boyfriend if only he could figure out how to get out of his own damn way.

It's no accident that *Better Off Dead*, the deeply surreal rom-com that Cusack starred in just six months after *The Sure Thing*, has a recurring gag in which his character farcically attempts to commit suicide after being dumped by his girlfriend. The Cusackian hero is forever underscored by his own barely disguised self-loathing. It's his slick self-consciousness about how unworthy he is that makes him, ultimately, *actually* worthy of the woman of his dreams.

No movie has underlined this more succinctly than Cameron Crowe's *Say Anything*, a feature-length romantic dramedy about a lovable, striving underachiever proving that he deserves to be with the overachieving vale-dictorian he loves—to her father, to the world, and to himself. Whether you've seen *Say Anything* or not, you know its famous scene—the one with Cusack holding up a boom box to proclaim his love as Peter Gabri-el's "In Your Eyes" plays with triumphant sentimentality. It's a legitimate contender for the most iconic romantic image in Hollywood history, right next to Ilsa and Rick saying goodbye on the tarmac in *Casablanca*, or Rose and Jack kissing on the prow of the *Titanic*. It turned Lloyd Dobler, and by extension John Cusack, into a fantasy for an entire generation of filmgo-ers—a fact later lamented by the critic and essayist Chuck Klosterman, who grumbled that Dobler set an impossibly high romantic standard for men of his generation to reach. "I once loved a girl who almost loved me, but not as much as she loved John Cusack," he wrote. "I never had a chance."

But there's something funny about that scene in *Say Anything*: As Cameron Crowe sees it, it only works because Cusack himself was *not* fully sold on the swoony romance of the movie to begin with. The scene was shot on the very last day of production, and Crowe had to talk Cusack into filming it at all. "He thought it was too subservient," says Crowe. "The defiance that he has when he's doing the scene is what makes the scene great. He made it work. The way he performs it, it's just blatantly defying you to consider it cheesy. That's why he's so heroic in that moment. He's still doubting whether the boom box scene is going to work at all."

It's not that Cusack himself is unromantic. When asked how much he relates to Lloyd Dobler, he has a quick answer: "On my better days, that's me." The early phase of Cusack's acting career was defined by romances that made him an object of desire for young women (and a relatable avatar for men who fancied themselves as sensitive and soulful as the characters he played), which was altered as he got older: the later phase of his career was largely defined by Cusack's willingness to challenge the romantic archetype that had made him such a bankable star in the first place.

This self-interrogation and transfiguration began in 1997 with *Grosse Pointe Blank*, which was—tellingly—also Cusack's first credit as both a writer and a producer. The movie is a genre-bender, blending the romantic comedy with a shockingly bloody action-thriller. Cusack plays Martin Blank, a professional hitman who decides to attend his ten-year high school reunion while killing somebody in his hometown of Grosse Pointe, Michigan. Martin's homecoming includes an elaborate flirtation with his high school girlfriend, Debi Newberry (Minnie Driver), whom he wordlessly abandoned on prom night so he could join the Army.

In case it's not clear enough from that plot description: Martin Blank is a psychopath. (That's not just me editorializing; both Cusack and director George Armitage say that's exactly what they intended.) But *Grosse Pointe Blank* plays a clever trick. Because we like John Cusack—a product of both his innate star quality and the decade he spent wearing down audiences' collective romantic defenses—we're rooting for him to end up with Debi anyway. And then, just when it looks like Martin has won Debi over, she discovers him covered in blood, crouched over the corpse of a man he just stabbed to death with a pen—which, among other things, gives Lloyd Dobler's heartbroken line "I gave her my heart, she gave me a pen" a whole new resonance whenever you revisit *Say Anything*. Debi's horror at discovering Martin is a killer is so raw and plausible that the ending of *Grosse Pointe Blank* is kind of a mess; when Martin and Debi ride off into the sunset to the strains of the Violent Femmes' "Blister in the Sun," it feels unearned because Cusack has just done such a convincing job demonstrating that Martin never deserved Debi in the first place. Lloyd Dobler belonged on that plane with Diane Court, but Martin Blank belongs alone.

An even more successful rom-com deconstruction came three years later, when Cusack wrote, produced, and starred in an adaptation of Nick Hornby's *High Fidelity*. The novel's London setting was shifted to Chicago, near the suburbs where Cusack had grown up. But the core of the story remains the same. The story opens bitterly, as Rob (Cusack) tries to figure out why and how things went wrong with Laura (Iben Hjejle), the latest in a long string of exes. His solution is to take a nostalgic trip through *all* of his major ex-girlfriends, hoping that revisiting the mistakes of the past will be enough to prevent him from repeating the same mistakes.

What Rob learns, in the end, is that the problem was him—not his exes and certainly not his choice of music (as laid out in the "desert-island" lists he peppers throughout the film). The breakthrough comes when Rob realizes he's been applying an unrealistic standard to his relationships, in what sounds *very* much like someone whose romantic expectations have been filtered through too many romantic comedies. This, too, was not accidental. "If somebody was writing that Rob was a passive-aggressive womanizer, I'd be like, 'All right, somebody got it,'" says Cusack. "I *wanted* to reveal the flaws of the character."

At the climax of *High Fidelity*, Rob tells Laura he's figured out his flaws, and that he's committed to changing them—particularly his unspoken belief that there's always going to be a better relationship around the corner. "That 'other girl,' or other women, whatever—I mean, I was thinking that they're just fantasies, you know?" he tells her. "They always seem really great because there's never any problems. And if there are, they're cute problems like, you know, we bought each other the same Christmas present, or she wants to go see a movie that I've already seen, you know? And then I come home, and you and I have *real* problems." You may think again of Lloyd Dobler, accompanying Diane Court to London with no apparent plan except adoring her, and wonder what real problems they might face.

Even in a revisionist rom-com, there's only so much you can do to color outside the lines. Rob's big speech to Laura in *High Fidelity*, however heartfelt, is another romantic comedy trope—ultimately not *that* different from what you hear from Billy Crystal at the end of *When Harry Met Sally* about realizing you want to spend the rest of your life with someone, and wanting the rest of your life to start as soon as possible. *High Fidelity* ends with Rob, narrating to the audience, explaining that he's only starting to figure out how to do things that will make Laura happy. After two hours of soul-searching, he's still at the beginning of a mature romance, not the apex of one.

High Fidelity also marked the end of Cusack's brief fascination with interrogating the rom-com. It's been twenty years, and at the time of this publication, he's never directed or produced one again, though he starred in several more that played the genre's tropes totally straight. The year 2001 brought *America's Sweethearts*, which Cusack made after a personal appeal from director Joe Roth, and *Serendipity*, which happily traded on his Cusackness to ground its whimsical contrivances with his dreamy charisma. As recently as 2005—in a role Cusack has since conceded was just "the best thing he could get at the time"—he was wooing Diane Lane in *Must Love Dogs*.

Saying he doesn't know what "Cusackness" means is, of course, part of John Cusack's Cusackness (but you know this). Movies like *Grosse Pointe Blank* and *High Fidelity* may have poked and challenged and dismantled both the rom-com genre and Cusack's own persona—but in the end, they came back to the same place, with Cusack's soulful, self-aware heroes undergoing the same arc: By finding happiness with the women they learn how to love, they also find a better version of themselves by the time the credits roll. About this archetype, Cusack is, appropriately enough, both soulful and self-aware. "Perhaps in a way, I had my own brand," he says. "I don't like to think that, but maybe I did. I would have denied it, because that would be pretty unartistic."

"Do you ever wonder how somebody could even like you?"

—PETE, *KNOCKED UP*

CHAPTER 12

KNOCKED UP

(And How Judd Apatow Remade the Rom-Com in His Own Image)

THE YEAR WAS 2002, AND JUDD APATOW HAD JUST ENDURED HIS SECOND crushing cancellation in the span of just two years. First had been *Freaks and Geeks*—a deeply personal, ahead-of-its-time dramedy about the awkward years of a group of teenagers in suburban Detroit, which Apatow had executive-produced. Reviews had been rapturous but ratings hadn't, and NBC killed it before the first season had even finished airing. The experience was so painful to Apatow that he subsequently blamed it for a herniated disc that kept him laid up on painkillers for six months.

What saved him was the chance to make another series, titled *Undeclared*, which Apatow created. Though it aired on Fox this time, it could hardly have been a more obvious successor to *Freaks and Geeks*, chronicling the misadventures of a group of awkward college students navigating their freshman year. Apatow even brought along several *Freaks and Geeks* alums: Seth Rogen, Jason Segel, and Busy Philipps. ("One of the reasons I keep working with them is I feel such responsibility—some of them turned down college to be on my show!" Apatow says.)

Reviews for *Undeclared* were nearly as good as for *Freaks and Geeks*, yet ratings were just as underwhelming, and Fox killed it just months after it premiered. In a bizarre twist of fate, it was cancelled by the same executive who had cancelled *Freaks and Geeks*, who had switched networks in the interim. This time, Judd Apatow sent the executive a framed positive review of *Undeclared*. He also attached a note: "I don't understand how you can fuck me in the ass when your dick is still in me from last time."

Apatow had been kicking around Hollywood as a writer and comedian for more than a decade, but 2002 was a uniquely dispiriting time. Two very personal passion projects—the kind of stories to which he related, and felt uniquely well-suited to tell—had been ripped out of his hands before his intended audience had really had the chance to find them. By his own admission, he never got over it. Two years later, as he prepped his directorial debut, *The 40-Year-Old Virgin*—a time when most filmmakers would be looking forward, not backward—Apatow privately imagined the

JUDD'S ORIGIN STORY

Judd Apatow was thirteen when his parents divorced, and he's quick to cite the difficulty of that experience as the jumping-off point for his love of comedy. "In some way that becomes the original pain that forms your personality, when your parents fight a lot when you're young," says Apatow.

His depression over his parents' divorce also inspired his sympathy for characters that might be written off by other writers as losers. "That was the fuel for my whole journey. On one level, that was really hard," he says. "But on another level, I thank God because it made me work my ass off. It made me connect with people suffering."

movie as the next beat in the story he had wanted to tell all along. "I thought of it as *Freaks and Geeks* 20 years later if one of them never had sex," he says. "That was my secret thought as I made the movie."

The 40-Year-Old Virgin can be traced back to Adam McKay's *Anchorman: The Legend of Ron Burgundy*, on which Judd Apatow was a producer. That movie was loaded with comedy stars who would get even bigger in the years to come, but Steve Carell— then best known as a regular correspondent on *The Daily Show with Jon Stewart*—stole scene after scene as the lovable idiot Brick Tamland. Apatow, the modern filmmaker most adept at spotting and nurturing talent, approached Carell with a standing offer: If you have an idea for something you'd like to star in, let's make it happen.

As it turned out, Carell did have a character in mind—an idea he'd originally come up with for a sketch as part of the improv collective Second City, but had never really had time to explore. "It was about a guy playing poker with his friends and they were all telling really dirty sex stories and slowly you realize that he's a virgin and his stories make no sense," said Carell. It is not hard to imagine what this character might look like in a comedy sketch: an awkward, sniveling, cringe-inducing basement-dweller, riffing on every cultural stereotype about men who can't get laid. Today they might call it *The 40-Year-Old Incel*. (Note to any producers reading: Please don't make that movie.)

But as Apatow and Carell developed the project, both came to the conclusion that they weren't interested in the cheap sketch version of the character; they wanted to explore him as a human being, and in the greater context of American masculinity as a whole. After they'd read a series of blogs from in-the-skin adult virgins, they reached a consensus about Carell's character: He would be "a really normal person" whose anxieties about sex were their own self-fulfilling prophecy, and not a sign that there was anything wrong with him. "We learned from our research when we read a lot of blogs on the internet from virgins that they are all just nice, shy people and they weren't odd. There wasn't any big joke to it," says Apatow.

There were, of course, plenty of jokes in *The 40-Year-Old Virgin*. But the movie's earnestness stood out in 2005, when the previous year's highest-grossing comedy had been *Meet the Fockers*, the *Meet the Parents* sequel in which a cat flushes a dog down the toilet. After the first week of shooting on *The 40-Year-Old Virgin*, Universal

MAN-CHILDREN (AND WORSE)

Judd Apatow's penchant for casting his close friends and family in his movies is a double-edged sword. His affection and generosity for the characters is apparent, giving each of his movies an inherent tenderness—but he's also clearly reluctant to go as hard on them as sometimes might be warranted. When asked about the awful advice passed on by Andy's buddies in *The 40-Year-Old Virgin*—like, to cite one particularly gross example, "tackle drunk bitches"—Apatow was quick to defend them: "Deep down, they are sweet guys with the best of intentions who cover up their own terror with horrible theories on women."

As long as we're on the subject, it's worth noting that there are several beats in *The 40-Year-Old Virgin* that were objectionable then, and remain objectionable now. In particular, it's depressing that Apatow's empathy for his characters doesn't extend to the trans sex worker who has a brief and aborted encounter with Andy, and who is essentially written off in a lazy punch line.

executives took one look at the scenes Apatow had already shot and shut down production, fearing that the protagonist of their big summer comedy looked too much like a serial killer. (Apatow eventually appeased the studio by consenting to defer to an editor of their choosing.) Even the star was starting to have doubts. At one point, Carell asked for a PG-13 version of the script, fearing that the R-rated movie they'd planned might be pushing the envelope too far for mainstream audiences, before Apatow convinced him that their original approach was the right one. "I think he was underestimating his own sweetness and how much that would come across," says Seth Rogen—whom Apatow had cast once again, as an amiable slacker.

No one should have been worried. *The 40-Year-Old Virgin* has some of the anything-for-a-laugh spirit that had driven the success of fellow raunch-com *There's Something About Mary* a few years earlier, including a cringe-inducing hair-waxing sequence in which Steve Carell yells random things—"SWEATY PIE HOLE," "NIPPLE FUCK," "KELLY CLARKSON"—whenever a new strip gets ripped off. But it was also infused with Apatow's bottomless empathy for the misfit, and his distrust of those who seem like they have everything figured out. In the end, the slyest joke in *The 40-Year-Old Virgin* is that Andy, the titular virgin, turns out to be much more well-adjusted than the gaggle of dudes who try to give him advice.

The 40-Year-Old Virgin is also a romantic comedy, though it wasn't sold that way; like that same summer's *Wedding Crashers*, a similarly massive hit, it's obvious that the marketing team behind the movie thought more men would show up if they used gags about foot play and anal sex as a kind of Trojan Horse. Catherine Keener barely appears in the trailer for *The 40-Year-Old Virgin*, but her character's genuinely sweet romance with Andy is the backbone of the movie—a believable adult romance amid all the raunch (and the rare Hollywood rom-com in which a single mother is a love interest, and in which her children are ultimately treated as a net positive for her suitor).

Coming out at the end of the summer, and earning overwhelmingly positive reviews and a $179 million worldwide gross, *The 40-Year-Old Virgin* was a smash success. Even more importantly, it

THE MIND'S TRUE LIBERATION

You can't make a romantic comedy called *The 40-Year-Old Virgin* without the forty-year-old virgin having sex by the time the credits roll. But much like the title character's own dilemma, sex posed a problem for Apatow: After so much buildup (and several mortifying and aborted sex scenes scattered throughout the movie), what kind of sex scene could possibly live up to the audience's expectations for Andy's first time?

It was Apatow's mentor Garry Shandling who texted the suggestion that led to the answer: "You have to make us understand that Andy's sex is better than everybody else's sex in the movie— because he's in love."

How best to depict that feeling without losing the comedy in the final minutes of the movie? First: By having Andy orgasm almost immediately the first time he has sex with Trish. Second: After they have sex again, and Trish asks, "How was that for you?," Andy starts singing The 5th Dimension's "The Age of Aquarius," with the rest of the cast eventually joining in. It's bizarre, completely unexpected, and weirdly moving, because—as "unrealistic" as it is—it achieves a sense of emotional catharsis that no conventional ending would have captured the same way.

was the foundation on which the rest of the Apatow empire was built. The movie proved that there was a sizable mainstream audience for Apatow's precise blend of sweet and raunchy with a heavy dose of improv—and for the actors in his stable, who quickly became bankable comedy stars. "He is a brand," reflected *Freaks and Geeks* creator Paul Feig when asked about Apatow's meteoric rise in 2012. "You go anywhere in the Midwest, you walk into any mall, you say 'Judd Apatow,' and most people know who you're talking about."

How do you follow up a hit like *The 40-Year-Old Virgin?* While Judd Apatow had long since given up on his childhood dream of being a full-time stand-up comedian, he never broke the habit of mining his own life for material, and it's generally pretty easy to take the movies Apatow directs and map them onto his own life. For his follow-up to *The 40-Year-Old Virgin*, Apatow had a vague, amorphous idea for a subject he wanted to tackle: pregnancy. His own daughters with actress Leslie Mann had been born several years earlier, but the memories and stresses of the experience had stayed with him. "Every time my wife and I went through childbirth, terrible things would happen," says Apatow. "I thought, *I've got to write about this because it's so awful that I must get something from it.*"

While working the busy promotional circuit for *The 40-Year-Old Virgin*, Apatow would send himself emails on his BlackBerry with vague, unformed ideas for some kind of movie that would filter his observations and experiences through a comedy lens. "*A couple gets pregnant on the first date*," he wrote in an email with the subject line "Pregnancy" on August 7, 2005. "*The idea of being forced into a relationship for life is the main conflict. A relationship in reverse. A baby, then get to know one another.*"

Not all of Apatow's ideas from his hastily typed BlackBerry emails made the cut—there is no scene in which Ben, the protagonist of *Knocked Up*, is so nervous to meet Alison's family that he accidentally leans in to kiss her brother, or a smash cut that leads to "suddenly huge boobs which squirt milk"—but much of what shows up in the final cut of *Knocked Up* can be traced back to those notes. Apatow even gives his protagonist a name that none-too-subtly revealed his intended star: Seth. (Later drafts changed it to Ben.)

Apatow had believed that Seth Rogen had the talent to be a Hollywood leading man since Rogen had turned up to an open casting call in Vancouver at age sixteen, which was videotaped and mailed to Apatow as he was casting *Freaks and Geeks*. The generic scene Rogen read, which was about a guy who grows weed and disguises it as a cornfield, had nothing to do with the show (though it certainly prefigured the kind of movies Rogen would eventually make, and the lifestyle he has adopted). There was no obvious role for Rogen in the pilot, but Apatow cast him anyway, knowing that the writers would find some clever way to use this weird, funny teenager. He was right; over the course of *Freaks and Geeks'* first season, Rogen's role grows, and his poise as a performer along with it. Why not give him a shot at a starring role?

At the time, Rogen was shopping around an idea for a sci-fi comedy (and meeting studios with little success). "Seth Rogen was pitching me a big, special effects comedy—like a *Ghostbusters* kind of movie," says Apatow. "And I said to him: 'You know . . . I think you're funny just kind of standing there.'" With his ill-defined pregnancy idea still swirling around in his head, Apatow suggested that Rogen just getting someone pregnant would be more than enough material for a comedy. The arc of the movie quickly came into focus for both men. Rogen would play an amiable stoner forced to grow up when a one-night stand results in a pregnancy.

The next challenge was finding the female lead. Leslie Mann, a *Knocked Up* supporting player, once said Apatow wrote the part with *Matchstick Men*'s Alison Lohman in mind (which might be why the character is named Alison). Rogen, eager to prove himself as a leading man, read opposite every actress who came in to audition, which gave him the chance to hone his character, and gave Apatow the chance to look for the chemistry he felt *Knocked Up* would require. Finding the comedy wasn't always easy. "Great actresses would come in, and they would say 'I'm pregnant,' and it made you want to cry," says Apatow. (Rogen, for his part, came up with Ben's incredulous reply to the revelation: "Fuck off." Apatow was delighted. "I never would have thought to write that," he says.)

After a flurry of auditions, Apatow was convinced he had found his star: Anne Hathaway, who had been professionally acting since she was seventeen but had just had her major Hollywood breakthrough in Dave Frankel's *The Devil Wears Prada*. Hathaway was cast, but quickly decided to quit the role, due in part to a

THE MIRACLE OF BIRTH

In his earnest effort to chronicle a live birth in all its glorious, gory detail in *Knocked Up*, Apatow originally intended to hire an actual pregnant woman, wait until she went into labor, and film her vagina for the shot of the baby crowning. Incredibly, he found a woman who was game to do it, but soon ran into an unusual legal snafu: According to the State Labor Board of California, the baby would need a worker's permit to appear on camera—which was also *impossible*, since a worker's permit can't legally be issued to the unborn. In the end, Apatow gave up and simulated the crowning with a prosthetic, and was very relieved when audiences still reacted the way he'd intended: with squirmy, vocal horror.

brief shot during the climactic birth sequence of a baby crowning that—while not depicting Hathaway's own vagina—would have been cut to give audiences the impression it was hers. "She didn't want to allow us to use real footage of a woman giving birth to create the illusion that she is giving birth," explained Apatow at the time. Hathaway later elaborated: "My issue with it was that having not experienced motherhood myself, I didn't know how I was gonna feel on the other side about giving birth. And by the way, I could pop a kid out and think, Oh, well, I really should have done that movie."

Next on the list was Katherine Heigl. She, too, had started her career early—first as a child model, and then as an adolescent performer in '90s junk like *My Father the Hero* and *Under Siege 2: Dark Territory* before she finally landed a lead role in the WB teen sci-fi drama *Roswell*. By 2007, she was emerging as a breakout star in the ABC medical drama *Grey's Anatomy*—a standout in a very crowded ensemble. It was the ideal time for *Knocked Up* to catch such a promising rising star, and they got her at the bargain salary of $300,000.

Heigl plays Alison Scott, an ambitious reporter for *E!* who has a drunken one-night stand with the goofy slacker Ben (Rogen) after they meet at a nightclub. When she realizes she's pregnant, she decides to keep the baby and try to make it work with the guy she barely knows, which gives their love story a handy nine-month time limit as Ben and Alison try to figure out whether or not they might actually work as a couple.

This is as good a time as any to note that *Knocked Up* never seriously grapples with the subject of abortion. The subject comes up early, only obliquely, and only once for each character, and not while they're together. Alison's mom (Joanna Kerns) suggests to Alison that the pregnancy should be "taken care of," and Jo-

BRO-ING OUT

Ben's gaggle of porn-obsessed stoner roommates in *Knocked Up* were played by Rogen's actual friends—fellow Apatow alums Jonah Hill, Jay Baruchel, Martin Starr, and Jason Segel—using their actual names (and in some cases were Rogen's former roommates). The "dirty man competition," in which Martin agrees to an elaborate bet in which he can't cut his hair or shave, was drawn from an actual bet Rogen had with his childhood friend and frequent collaborator Evan Goldberg. "It's basically an excuse to justify why no woman wants to talk to you," says Rogen.

While no one would mistake these guys for the most enlightened men in Los Angeles, their roughness is part of the movie's charm—their banter, drawn from years of real-life friendship, has an authenticity that the movies can't really fake. (And it doesn't hurt that Ben, for all his flaws, looks pretty good by comparison.)

nah (Jonah Hill) coaches Ben to consider something that "rhymes with shmuh-smortion." If Alison and Ben ever seriously discuss it, it happens off-screen. Which means it might not exist at all.

While *Knocked Up* doesn't openly reject a pro-choice perspective, the anti-abortion group Texas Right to Life still declared it a victory in 2007. Apatow says he actually shot five hours of "very, very funny, but really shocking and disturbing" improv in which Ben and his friends debate abortion. "I am pro-choice and I don't think anyone should tell anyone else what to do with their bodies or their points of view. I think those decisions are very personal and no one has the answer, so I am pretty solid in that position," says Apatow. "But I also think it's a very interesting story when you decide not to get an abortion. And I am also kind of surprised that it's shocking to people that they don't get an abortion. Is it so weird in this day and age that people are uncomfortable doing that?"

Knocked Up is theoretically a two-hander in this conversation, but the movie's vague hand-waving of a woman's choice is one of several signals that this is really Ben's movie—the latest example of a shift, traceable from *There's Something About Mary* to *Wedding Crashers* to *The 40-Year-Old Virgin*, that moved men's narratives to the center of the rom-com format and added a bunch of raunch in the process. *Knocked Up* is a benchmark in the growing trend of dude-centric rom-coms that included *Hitch*, *Wedding Crashers*, and Apatow's own *The 40-Year-Old Virgin*, which all came out in 2005, as well as Chris Rock's *I Think I Love My Wife*, Mark Helfrich's *Good Luck Chuck*, and the Farrelly Brothers' *The Heartbreak Kid*, which came out in 2007 alongside *Knocked Up*. With Ben getting the movie's real arc, Alison ends up as a likable but fuzzily drawn figure who spends much of the movie reacting to the other characters in her scenes, from Ben to her bosses at *E!* to her overbearing sister Debbie (Leslie Mann).

The first half of *Knocked Up* is largely centered on Ben and Alison's uneasy but tender romance, as they learn—to her surprise and his delight—that they actually like each other, even as she frets that his laid-back, jobless approach to life will make him a bad partner. The movie also plays up the disparity between Ben and Alison's levels of attractiveness: "You're prettier than I am," he drunkenly mumbles as they strip down before hooking up. But it's Alison who gets repeatedly pressured to lose weight by her employers, and who fears retaliation for her pregnancy. As the stress piles up, Ben's fumbling steps toward maturity, goofy charm, and

THE APATOW WANNABES

The back-to-back successes of *The 40-Year-Old Virgin* and *Knocked Up* led to a mad Hollywood scramble for raunchy dude-bro comedies—but for whatever reason, attempting to replicate the Apatow formula turned out to be less of a money-printing machine than expected. Even casting Apatow regulars didn't seem to help. In 2008, director Kevin Smith released *Zack and Miri Make a Porno*, starring Seth Rogen and Elizabeth Banks in a very Apatow-esque raunchy/sweet rom-com about two friends who shoot a porno and end up falling in love. To Smith's confusion and frustration, the movie underperformed. "That was supposed to be the one that punched us through to the next level," he says. "Everyone thought it would do $60 to $70 million."

A similar fate befell Jim Field Smith's 2010 rom-com *She's Out of My League*, which sought to sell Jay Baruchel, who had a supporting role in *Knocked Up*, as a Rogen-esque leading man. Even the poster for *She's Out of My League* borrows heavily from *Knocked Up*: "How can a 10 go for a 5?" the tagline asks, with a nervous-looking Baruchel staring straight ahead while Alice Eve kisses him on the cheek. This pitch didn't take either; despite decent reviews, the movie topped out at under $50 million worldwide.

unconditional affection for Alison make their relationship, however unlikely, feel plausible.

As funny and sweet as the core relationship can be, the most personal material comes in the last third of the movie. This is, not coincidentally, the part of the story that drove Apatow to make *Knocked Up* in the first place: Apatow says the lengthy birth sequence, which starts with Alison drawing a bath to calm herself down before they get to the hospital, is "almost exactly what happened" when his and Mann's daughter Iris was born. Their doctor really *did* leave town for a bar mitzvah in San Francisco just as Mann went into labor—"He's such a stupid fucking asshole and I hate him," says Mann—and they really *did* get stuck with a doctor who they'd previously rejected, and who was openly rude to them as a kind of petty revenge.

THE DOCTOR IS IN

Knocked Up also marks the film debut of Ken Jeong. A practicing doctor, Jeong says he was doing comedy as a hobby the way other doctors liked to golf when he heard that Apatow was looking to cast an actor with medical experience as Dr. Kuni, the obstetrician who delivers Alison and Ben's baby. "That coincided with me leaving medicine," Jeong says, crediting his wife—also a doctor—with encouraging him to pursue acting full-time, which led to his starring role in *The Hangover* two years later. Even now, Jeong has a backup plan: "Just in case acting ever stalls, I still renew my medical license every year," he says.

From a romantic comedy perspective, what's striking about *The 40-Year-Old Virgin* and *Knocked Up* is that their arcs are essentially the same. A man-child, apparently stuck in a cycle of arrested development, discovers the pleasures of adulthood and breaks his old habits with the help of a woman who has her life together. "Every story I've ever written is someone not trying to grow up," says Apatow. In this case, it's Ben getting his shit together enough to read the baby books, get his own apartment, kick Alison's sister out of the delivery room, and prove himself as a partner Alison can actually count on to do more than "fuck [his] fucking bong." (Her words, not mine.)

There's another key relationship in *Knocked Up* that reveals even more about what was on Apatow's mind at the time. The movie's biggest subplot introduces audiences to the marriage of Debbie (Mann) and Pete (Paul Rudd). Debbie and Pete, who have two daughters, are presented as a kind of cautionary tale for Alison and Ben: If you're not careful, *this* is the kind of passive-aggressive, perpetually frustrated, life-of-quiet-desperation couple you could turn into after your baby is born. "Marriage is like that show *Everybody Loves Raymond*, but it's not funny," Pete warns Ben in one scene. "All the problems are the same, but instead of all the funny, pithy dialogue, everybody is really pissed off and tense." Though Pete eventually acknowledges how much he loves Debbie, it takes tripping on mushrooms in Las Vegas to get there. This is not the kind of couple you normally see in a romantic comedy—the kind whose problems stem not from a Hollywood-ready event like an unexpected pregnancy, but from the million small resentments that can fester and grow if you don't work to weed them out.

Judd Apatow concedes that Pete and Debbie are also barely disguised riffs on himself and Mann, whom he married in 1997, and with whom he has two daughters. The couple's first encounter sounds uncannily like a meet-cute: When Mann came in to audition for the Apatow-produced black comedy *The Cable Guy* in 1995, he said, "There goes the future Mrs. Apatow" when she left the room. "I had a soul connection instantly. I meant it," he says. (Mann admits she had a crush on director Ben Stiller, who was also in the room at the time.) But Apatow and Mann make no secret of their conflicts, either. In 2007, *The New York Times* published a transcript of a recurring fight they had over a Christmas gift, which Apatow purchased and Mann didn't like. It was trivial, sure, but it also rang true: These are the small, irritating little arguments that couples store in their memory banks and revisit whenever some other argument brings them back to the surface.

If you'd like an even clearer picture of the Apatow-Mann marriage, just watch Apatow's movies. "Leslie and I have different ideas about how we want to portray the level of truth involved in our movies," says Apatow. "I probably lean—mostly out of pure

APATOW EXPANDS

The downside to Apatow's instinct to pull from his own life is that his point of view can look narrow. For the first part of his filmmaking career, his main characters were invariably male and relatively well-off. Ben and his roommates may be broke in *Knocked Up*, but they still have all the time in the world to smoke weed and fantasize about the porn site they plan to create that will make them millionaires. *This Is 40*'s Pete and Debbie may be worried about money—but he's still the owner of a record label, she's still the owner of a clothing boutique, and they're raising their daughters in a lavish Los Angeles home.

Yet Apatow's more recent projects have shown a promising impulse to get out of his own head. *Trainwreck*, which came out in 2015 and which Apatow directed from a script by star Amy Schumer, is a clever rom-com that allows its female protagonist to be the one with the arc. And 2020's *The King of Staten Island*, a dramedy based closely on the life of cowriter and star Pete Davidson, still has plenty of bro-y hangout scenes—but it approaches both poverty and grief in a way that feels totally distinct from Apatow's previous work.

laziness—toward talking about it as if it mostly comes from our lives, or at least from an emotionally truthful place. Leslie prefers to say that the majority of what we do has been fabricated. The truth is probably somewhere in the middle." Paul Rudd contributed as well. "Throughout the writing of *Knocked Up*, Judd and I would talk about problems in our own marriages," said Rudd in 2007. "I'd call him and say, 'Here's something that drives me crazy about my wife, and here's something my wife can't stand about me.' I recently had a kid, and one thing my wife took—understandably—as a hostile gesture was the fact that I never read any of those baby books. I said, 'People have been doing this for thousands of years! Cavemen didn't have *What to Expect When You're Expecting!*' That's in the movie."

Maybe the most trenchant piece of writing in the entire Apatow oeuvre comes in *Knocked Up*, when Debbie surprises Pete—and herself—by starting to cry when she learns Pete saw *Spider-Man 3* without her, as part of a broadly self-centered streak in which he insists on his need to be alone. "You just think because you don't yell that you're not mean. But this is mean," she says. This two-line jab is such an accurate observation about a specific kind of man—agreeably low-key, quietly narcissistic, broadly disengaging himself from anything that seems like too much hassle—that it felt like it had to be drawn from real life. Sure enough, that line wasn't written by Apatow; it was spoken off the cuff by his wife, about him, in the middle of an actual fight they were having.

Beyond the raunch and the bromance and all the other buzzwords that greeted Apatow's meteoric rise in the Hollywood comedy scene, these moments are what make him unique: his genuine interest in depicting real, human conflicts without acting like they have straightforward solutions. "I was trying to show real conflict between men and women," says Apatow. "And some of the scenes—which I think are really rough, where people curse each other out and have big fights—are more like fights in real life. It's not like fights in the movies."

Apatow had had a minor crisis as he went through preproduction on *Knocked Up*. "I'm trying to make a movie about two people starting a family while doing something that takes me away from my own family," he said at the time. His solution to the problem was novel, though only really available to the guy on top: bringing his whole family to work with him. He cast his daughters Maude and Iris, then ten and five years old, to play Pete and Debbie's daughters Charlotte and Sadie. As a result, there are pictures from the *Knocked Up* set that look like they could be personal photographs from Apatow and Mann's own home, with the director cuddled up in bed with three of his stars.

"Judd manipulated me, lied to me, and steamrolled me," says Mann, apparently only half-joking, of her husband's decision to cast their daughters. "Three days before shooting he said, 'We had no luck finding kids, so we're using ours.'" But despite her concerns, Apatow was convinced, and eventually felt vindicated, that the movie would work best with his own children in it. "It works because I love my kids and I'm trying to show them that the conflicts you have in relationships are worth it because of them. The film really has been all about trying to send a valentine to my family," he said at the time.

As it turned out, this was not a one-off. Both Maude and Iris, as well as Mann and Rudd, reprised their roles five years later in Apatow's *This Is 40*, which gives the whole enterprise the uncanny feeling of watching an unusually professional home movie, with dad himself behind the camera (and with the somewhat self-aggrandizing choice to cast the twinkly-eyed, eternally youthful

Paul Rudd as his own screen surrogate). If this all strikes you as a little self-absorbed . . . well, that's because it is. Not even Judd Apatow denies that. "I think it's all narcissism," he says. "I don't think anyone makes movies because they are thinking about people."

This Is 40, which arrived in theaters in 2012, fared much worse than *Knocked Up* both critically and commercially, even after a desperate-sounding marketing campaign that described it as "the sort-of sequel to *Knocked Up*." (Neither Heigl nor Rogen actually appear in the movie, though Alison's picture can be seen on the wall in Pete and Debbie's home, and Pete mentions that he scored some weed cookies from Ben.) But *This Is 40*'s failings as a stand-alone comedy make more sense, and become more forgivable, when you look at the movie as another phase of Apatow's career-long interest in exploring what a long-term relationship actually looks like.

More than *Knocked Up*, *This Is 40* is a two-hander, splitting its perspective pretty evenly between Pete and Debbie—something that Apatow is quick to credit to Leslie Mann's own input on the screenplay. "When you're married to an actress you see all the scripts they're offered and you see what's wrong with a lot of them," says Apatow. "So it inspired me to write better parts for women just reading all of the bad parts that are in most of the scripts floating around town."

The rom-com genre has often been criticized for goosing the audience with unrealistic expectations about romantic love. The same cannot be said of *This Is 40*, which features a lengthy list of problems Pete and Debbie need to hash out: money and career woes, conflict with your partner's parent (and the uncomfortable choosing-of-sides that can follow), and being asked to study your partner's asshole to determine whether a bump is a hemorrhoid or something more sinister. *The New York Times* once reported that the original script for *Knocked Up* was "more like Cassavetes than a popcorn flick," in which Alison and Ben were "corrosively incompatible," before it was punched up with a barrage of raunchy jokes and a brighter, more idealized version of the unlikely couple's relationship. *This Is 40* feels like Apatow wrote a first draft in the Cassavetes vein and never got around to the popcorn rewrite. The movie barely has an overarching plot, which is part of what makes it feel a little more like life itself. The tension that exists isn't based on whether or not the characters will get together, but whether they will stay together, and arguably whether they even *should*. There's a reason that romantic comedies typically end when the couple gets together. But Hollywood's relentless push to turn any successful movie into a franchise—which had already become the industry's dream when *This Is 40* arrived in 2012, the same year that *The Avengers* hit theaters—is also a unique opportunity for rom-com filmmakers who are interested in more than courtship. For the first time, industry trends were forcing storytellers to think beyond what happens when a couple finally gets together (as *Bridget Jones's Baby* would ably demonstrate four years later).

But this was also a sign that the rom-com genre itself was aging up—something always seen as ominous in Hollywood, which is always chasing newer and younger. As the next generation of movie stars made their marks in indie dramas or buzzy blockbusters like *The Avengers*—and younger audiences followed them—the audiences that still reliably showed up for rom-coms tended to be older, and so did the people making them. The most successful rom-coms of this era, both critically and commercially, generally center on middle-aged couples navigating the later stages of their love lives. In 2011's *Crazy, Stupid, Love* several love stories are juggled, but the central one is about a man (Steve Carell) who learns his wife (Julianne Moore) is having an affair, dips a toe back into single life, and ultimately realizes that what he wants is his wife back. *Top Five*, which came out in 2014, was a very personal passion project for writer/director/star Chris Rock, playing a comedian also dealing with middle-aged malaise and the sense that his career had careened off in the wrong direction. Even the *American Pie* franchise, which had opened with a bunch of horny high schoolers vowing to lose their virginity, had grown up. Jon Hurwitz and Hayden Schlossberg's *American Reunion*—which picks up nearly a decade after the *American Pie* franchise's previous movie, *American Wedding*—deals with the disappointments that settle in during middle age, long after your pie-humping days are behind you.

This broader shift might be why Apatow's happy endings can feel so unconvincing—because his movies have always seemed infused with the knowledge that a "happy ending" only exists in movies. Painful as it was, the fundamentally unfinished nature of *Freaks and Geeks* and *Undeclared* is likely truer to life than any carefully crafted series finale would have been. "I feel like there are different approaches to making movies and telling stories. I'm probably this weird hybrid of Robert Altman and John Cassavetes," says Apatow. "I'm always attracted to the fact that life is messy, it doesn't fully line up. The slop of it is where I feel truthful."

This is the same reason Apatow says he'll never make a full-blown drama. "I don't think anything is without humor," says Apatow. "Whenever there's a movie that has no jokes in it at all, I always think, *well, that's not even possible*. In any situation somebody is making a heinous joke. At funerals or massacres, someone's making a joke. Someone at a massacre is going, 'Can you believe this is happening to us right now?'"

Still, there's always the promise of what's next; if real love stories never have endings, none of Apatow's romantic comedies are permanently resolved either. In 2020, I asked Apatow if there was any chance Pete and Debbie could become his version of Jesse and Celine in Richard Linklater's *Before* series—a couple whose ups and downs he would revisit, in real time, over the rest of his career. "I do have some ideas," he says. "I don't know if anyone in my family is interested. That's the first mystery. But I have a rough outline. We'll see if I can come up with something that's strong enough to bother everybody with."

Katherine Heigl

THE APOLOGIST

In a 2008 *Vanity Fair* cover story that, in retrospect, managed to capture Katherine Heigl at what turned out to be the apex of her A-list film career, *27 Dresses* director Anne Fletcher gave a lengthy, glowing quote that pitched Heigl as America's newest Sweetheart. "She is a superstar, without question," said Fletcher. "She has the 'It' factor. You can't buy it; you can't learn it; you can't create it; it just is. We haven't had one of her in many years. Julia Roberts, Sandra Bullock, Meg Ryan—those have been our go-to girls for romantic comedy for a very long time, but we haven't had a new one. Katie has beauty, vulnerability, identifiability. She's funny, charming, lovely to watch. Her slightest eye movement is captivating; you know instantly what's going on. The screen eats her up. She's a brilliant comic actor and an unbelievable dramatic actor as well, and she's going to have whatever she wants."

But Fletcher's glowing appraisal of Katherine Heigl's future is not what anyone talked when the profile actually ran, and it's certainly not what anyone remembers about it now. Because this happens to be the same *Vanity Fair* profile in which Heigl's tossed-off criticism of *Knocked Up* ended up reorienting, and then defining, and then haunting the rest of her career.

Heigl's comments on *Knocked Up* have often been quoted out of context, so it's worth examining what she said in full. *Knocked Up* is "a little sexist," Heigl said to *Vanity Fair*'s Leslie Bennetts, about six months after the movie arrived in theaters. "It paints the women as shrews, as humorless and uptight, and it paints the men as lovable, goofy, fun-loving guys. It exaggerated the characters, and I had a hard time with it, on some days. I'm playing such a bitch; why is she being such a killjoy? Why is this how you're portraying women? 98 percent of the time it was an amazing experience, but it was hard for me to love the movie."

If you've seen *Knocked Up*, you might note that everything Heigl says here is basically true (and that having an amazing experience "98 percent of the time" is a pretty incredible ratio). Seth Rogen's character, Ben, gets a whole gaggle of friends to smoke weed and goof around with, as well as charming new buddy Paul Rudd, who takes him on a mushroom-fueled trip to Las Vegas. Katherine Heigl's character, Alison, gets her tightly wound sister and her awful mother. There's a scene in which Ben makes the distinction that Alison's *hormones*, and not Alison herself, are the ones acting like a "crazy bitch"—but either way, Alison is the one who ends up apologizing for breaking up with him at the climax of the movie.

But let's move on from the substance of Heigl's observation, whatever you think of it, and look at the incredibly disproportionate reaction to it. In a public-facing industry in which so much of the griping happens behind closed doors, her comment was regarded as a major breach of decorum, and when she made a truly ill-advised (but broadly accurate) knock on the writing for her character in season four of *Grey's Anatomy* later that summer, the narrative was set: Katherine Heigl is an ungrateful diva.

If you look at Heigl's comments *after* 2008, what you see are apologies. Over and over and over again, Heigl attempts to clarify that her comments about *Knocked Up* were a criticism of her own performance, and maybe of the rom-com genre itself, but not a specific attack on the film or Apatow or Rogen. "I allowed myself to be perceived [as ungrateful] because I was being whiny and I was griping and because I made these snarky comments," she said to *Entertainment Weekly* in 2010. "So much about living life, to me, is about humility and gratitude. And I've tried very hard to have those qualities and be that person and I'm just so disappointed in myself that I allowed it to slip." Six years later, she was still answering the same question. "This was an incredible experience for me and they were incredibly good to me on this movie, so I did not mean to shit on them at all," she said on *The Howard Stern Show* in 2016. "I absolutely owe anyone an apology I unwittingly offended or disrespected. I get it. It was an immature dumbass moment." When asked about Seth Rogen in an interview later that year, Heigl could hardly have ladled on more kindness: "I just feel nothing but love and respect," she said.

This was a trap. There was no apology Heigl could make that would satisfy her critics. By 2021, Heigl had issued so many justifications and apologies for something she said thirteen full years earlier that she was able to recognize, with characteristic clarity, that there was always going to be a bottomless and inexhaustible demand for more of them. "The more I said I was sorry, the more they wanted it," says Heigl. "The more terrified and scared I was of doing something wrong, the more I came across like I had really done something horribly wrong."

It didn't help matters that Apatow and Rogen clearly reveled in snarking about Heigl's interview whenever the subject came up. On a 2009 appearance on *The Howard Stern Show*, Seth Rogen and Judd Apatow sniped at Heigl's then-upcoming romantic comedy *The Ugly Truth*. "That looks like it really puts women on a pedestal in a beautiful way," said Rogen. "I hear there's a scene where she's wearing underwear with a vibrator in it, so I'd have to see if that was uplifting for women," said Apatow. In 2014, Apatow groused to Louis C.K. about Heigl's interview yet again, prompting C.K. to retort that it was "amazing" that Heigl was unhappy because *Knocked Up* was "the best thing she ever did." By 2016, Rogen at least acknowledged that, "as an egomaniac," he was cold to Heigl because she hurt his feelings.

Following *Knocked Up* (and the bad press that followed), Heigl kept making rom-coms. In 2008, she starred opposite James Marsden in Anne

Fletcher's *27 Dresses*, a delightful rom-com that drew strong numbers at the box office. In 2009, she starred opposite Gerard Butler in Robert Luketic's *The Ugly Truth*, a hateful rom-com that, nevertheless, also drew strong numbers.

But owing to a general downturn in the rom-com genre—more on that soon—and, unfortunately, the quality of the movies themselves, the string of rom-coms that came after didn't fare nearly as well. Her second collaboration with Luketic, starring opposite Ashton Kutcher in the 2010 action-comedy *Killers*, was met with a collective shrug (though to be fair, it also wasn't the only spy-themed action rom-com to flop *that month*). In the years that followed, as studio and audience taste for romantic comedies seemed to wane, Heigl kept making them: *Life as We Know It*, *One for the Money*, *The Big Wedding*, *Jenny's Wedding*.

Unlike many rom-com stars—who generally have some ambivalence about being too associated with a genre that is routinely dismissed by critics and snubbed by awards voters—Katherine Heigl always wanted to star in romantic comedies. As a rising star, she openly idolized actresses like Meg Ryan and Julia Roberts, and sought to emulate their career arcs.

"I love romantic comedies. I was so stoked to be doing them. But maybe I hit it a little too hard," she says. "I couldn't say no. There's nothing wrong with them, but maybe I overloaded my audience. I should have done a superhero movie or a psychological thriller."

None of the movies Heigl made in this particular sprint is a lost classic, but it's hard to blame her for it; she was pegged as the next rom-com star at a time when a good rom-com script was incredibly hard to come by in Hollywood, and you can't make bricks without straw. Heigl—still, after all these years, unusually honest in interviews—says she thinks all of her candid "transgressions" in interviews would have been overlooked if those post–*Knocked Up* rom-coms had made more money. She's probably right; plenty of actors have gotten away with much worse behavior as long as they kept churning out hits. (Of course, most of those actors were also men.)

At the time of this writing, as the demand for rom-coms bounces back, Heigl has settled into a new niche as the star of the Netflix series *Firefly Lane.* Maybe she'll even do another rom-com; there have been rumblings about a possible *27 Dresses* sequel for years. But if that happens, and she ends up on the cover of a glossy magazine again, don't expect her to apologize anymore. "I may have said a couple of things you didn't like, but then that escalated to 'she's ungrateful,' then that escalated to 'she's difficult,' and that escalated to 'she's unprofessional,'" says Heigl. "What is your definition of 'difficult'? Somebody with an opinion that you don't like? Now, I'm 42, and that shit pisses me off."

"I really have to stop buying into this bullshit Hollywood cliché of true love. Shut up, Katherine Heigl, you stupid liar!"

—JAMIE, *FRIENDS WITH BENEFITS*

CHAPTER 13

FRIENDS WITH BENEFITS

(And Hollywood's Increasingly Desperate Attempts to Capture Modern Love)

THE STARS WERE ALIGNING FOR WILL GLUCK. IN 2010, HE HAD SCORED A massive hit with his second feature—a teen rom-com called *Easy A* that had, in the grand tradition of movies like *Clueless* and *10 Things I Hate About You*, drawn a sizable audience by drawing inspiration from a literary classic and moving the action into a high school. (In the case of *Easy A*, the base text was *The Scarlet Letter*.) Just a year later, he had his next rom-com lined up: a sexy, self-aware take on hookup culture called *Friends with Benefits*, starring Mila Kunis and Justin Timberlake as friends who start having sex long before they actually fall in love. It was snappy, it was modern, and it felt like an inversion of the rom-com formula in a way that might actually attract filmgoers, particularly younger ones, who were increasingly put off by the genre's contrivances and clichés.

There was just one problem: *Friends with Benefits* had been beaten to the punch by another snappy, modern rom-com titled—what else?—*Friends with Benefits*. That movie, starring Natalie

Portman and Ashton Kutcher, was written and sold by Elizabeth Meriwether under the attention-grabbing title *Fuckbuddies*, which was deemed, understandably, unworkable for marketing purposes. The movie, which was eventually retitled *No Strings Attached*, hit theaters about six months before *Friends with Benefits*.

MORE FRIENDS, MORE BENEFITS

Incredibly, a *third* project called *Friends with Benefits* also arrived in 2011. An unrelated sitcom, also titled *Friends with Benefits*, premiered on NBC less than a month after the movie *Friends with Benefits* arrived in theaters. The series, co-created by *(500) Days of Summer* writers Scott Neustadter and Michael H. Weber, followed five friends enjoying casual hookups while figuring out their lives in Chicago. Don't feel too bad if you don't remember it: *The New York Times* called the series "an attempt at a wised-up 21st-century *Friends* with all the emotion and most of the laughs scoured out," and the series was quietly cancelled even before the full first season had aired.

How did two movies with near-identical premises and the exact same title go into production, independently, at two different studios? The answer to that question—beyond the weird, competitive kismet that previously led to bitter Hollywood synergies like *Volcano* vs. *Dante's Peak*, *Deep Impact* vs. *Armageddon*, and *A Bug's Life* vs. *Antz*—is the same premise that drove much of Hollywood's flailing efforts at romantic comedies over the past decade: What does modern love look like, anyway?

Will Gluck, who did a full rewrite of Keith Merryman and David A. Newman's original script for *Friends with Benefits* with Kunis and Timberlake's voices in mind, was nothing if not self-aware about the tropes of the rom-com genre. "I mean, listen, every romantic comedy over the last twenty years is about the same thing, right?" says Gluck. "The two characters in this movie played by Justin and Mila are in this generation where they've grown up on romantic comedies. They comment about these romantic comedies throughout the movie, and as they go through their storyline, they realize that they're in a romantic comedy story—as two regular people who *aren't* in a movie would comment on. They're very cognizant that they're in this story, and they're like, 'Oh, we know how this is gonna end,' and they think they're gonna be different, but they end up embracing the fact that they're going through a romantic comedy moment."

Friends with Benefits centers on Jamie (Kunis), a corporate headhunter, and Dylan (Timberlake), an up-and-coming art director whose head she hunts for a job at *GQ*. As the movie opens, both of them get dumped by partners who succinctly break down their flaws. Dylan is emotionally unavailable; Jamie seems composed but is emotionally damaged. These are two people who are in no place to leap into another relationship. So they decide not to. They just have sex instead.

Much like *How to Lose a Guy in 10 Days* had done almost a decade earlier, Will Gluck decided to treat his modern love story as a riff on the classic Battle of the Sexes comedies, but centered on two characters who had actually seen enough of those movies to feel weird about it. "It's basically like a '50s movie. A big Hepburn and Tracy movie, a two-hander, big, big comedy, big huge budget in New York and L.A.," he says. "I really wanted to do a big movie of two people kind of falling in love, but conscious of the fact that they're falling in love the whole time."

Gluck realized he needed to show on-screen the kind of old-fashioned romantic comedy Jamie and Dylan think they're too smart to stumble into. Jamie is fixated on a movie-within-a-movie

DISAVOWING THE ROM-COM

In the long saga of Hollywood marketing teams clumsily trying to convince men that they should watch romantic comedies—a problem that, for the record, more or less takes care of itself if the movie is good—a 2009 promotional video for *He's Just Not That Into You* deserves its own special place in the history books. The video, which features *He's Just Not That Into You* stars Bradley Cooper, Justin Long, and Kevin Connolly, is titled "*He's Just Not That Into You*: Ten Chick Flick clichés that are NOT in this movie."

The introduction to the video is a master class in trying too hard. "Hold the phone. I know what you *guys* out there are thinking," says Long. "You're all thinking to yourselves, 'Oh, great, fantastic. Another *chick* flick. This is just what I need. I just started dating this girl, and she's going to drag me to go see it. This *sucks!*'"

As rough as that intro turns out to be, the list that follows is a reasonably accurate summary of the clichés that had settled into the genre by 2010, including An Elderly Person Who Says Something Inappropriate, A Shot Where Heads Fall Into Frame and Land on Pillows, and A Scene Where Someone Shows Up to Work the Next Day and Finds Out That They Actually Slept with Their New Boss. Still, the gambit didn't work; though *He's Just Not That Into You* overperformed Warner Bros.' expectations, the audience for its opening weekend was a whopping 80 percent female.

that's only a marginally exaggerated version of the rom-coms that topped the box office two decades before *Friends with Benefits* arrived. We even get a shot of Jason Segel delivering his big *When Harry Met Sally*–style "here's what I love about you" speech to Rashida Jones: "I love that sunsets make you cry. And I don't care that you failed your real-estate exam. And I'm glad that you have a five-date rule," he says, before throwing down his bouquet of flowers and embracing her. Jamie swoons, wishing her life was more like the movie; Dylan mocks the closing credits, which are set to "Hey Soul Sister."

That joke doesn't fully pay off until the closing scene, when Dylan and Jamie—having spent the movie hooking up, catching feelings, getting mad at each other, and realizing they're in love after all—go on their "first date" to the strains of "Hey Soul Sister." The too-cool-for-cheesy-romantic-comedies duo has ended up in a cheesy romantic comedy after all. So has the audience, which might have been fooled by a PR sweep in which much of the film's creative team disavowed romantic comedies, in what felt like a preemptive strike against rom-com detractors. "I never wanted to do a romantic comedy. But I don't look at this film as a romantic comedy. I'm not a huge fan of romantic comedies," said Timberlake in one interview at the time. "We were all very conscious of making it funny for guys when we made this movie," promised Gluck in another.

But for a movie with so much reflective self-awareness, and a premise that passes for provocative on paper, *Friends with Benefits* ultimately ends up being conservative in its approach to relationships. The movie gradually unfolds backstories that explain both Jamie and Dylan's commitment-phobia. She has been influenced and damaged by her own mother's free-spirited promiscuity. He

314 FROM HOLLYWOOD WITH LOVE

I KNOW WHO I WANT TO TAKE ME HOME

For all its self-aware flexing, *Friends with Benefits* is a romantic comedy, and its climax is the perfect example of the rom-com genre at war with itself. In an effort to get Jamie back, Dylan has organized, I don't know, four hundred people to form a flash mob and perform an elaborate choreographed dance routine to Semisonic's "Closing Time." "You said you wanted your life to be like a movie!" says Dylan. But the movie also can't resist another self-aware gag, as Dylan realizes that Jamie can't actually hear anything he's saying; in the movies, they dub the music in later so the heroine can actually hear the hero deliver the big speech.

was abandoned by his mother in the past, leaving him alone to care for his father, who has Alzheimer's, in the present. The impulse that leads Jamie and Dylan to seek their low-stakes relationship is a flaw to be fixed, and eventually they find the solution in committing to each other. The movie never seriously grapples with the idea that being comfortable in a casual relationship might be an active choice, not a character flaw.

It's a quality the movie shares with its box-office rival *No Strings Attached*, which makes even less of an effort not to put Natalie Portman and Ashton Kutcher through the standard rom-com beats. That film ends with the couple forgoing sex and sitting down for breakfast together, hashing out the pet names they'll use and the amount of snuggling and hand-holding they'll indulge in. The closing shot is Kutcher spooning Portman, domestic normalcy restored.

The basic concept for *No Strings Attached*—remember, then titled *Fuckbuddies*—originated with sixty-four-year-old director Ivan Reitman and producing partner Tom Pollock, who pitched the concept to screenwriter Elizabeth Meriwether. "We always liked this idea of people in their twenties at a time of Facebook and texting, who have romantic relationships where they don't even see each other for half their conversations. It seemed like an opportunity to do a good comedy," says Reitman.

You can see the generation gap between the contemporary material and director Ivan Reitman—married for thirty-five years—who openly spoke about how he was trying to wrap his head around the difference between the way he had dated and the way modern singles were dating. "I noticed from my own kids that with this generation in particular, young people find it easier to have a sexual relationship than an emotional one," said Reitman at the time. *No Strings Attached* is, in the end, a romantic comedy about a type of relationship the director doesn't actually believe in. "I think it's possible to have a no-strings-attached relationship,

STRINGS VERY MUCH ATTACHED

In a story that's cute enough that someone should really make a rom-com about it, Ashton Kutcher and Mila Kunis—who had previously costarred on *That '70s Show*—hooked up for real shortly after their rival romantic comedies were released. They agreed that they would keep the fling fun and casual. "Three months later, we're living together, six months later, we're married and have a kid," says Kunis. "We clearly didn't watch the end of either one of our movies."

but it's probably going to be a short one," he says. "The simplicity of 'no strings' soon starts to dissolve."

In the end, neither *No Strings Attached* nor *Friends with Benefits* is about why a generation of young people—overworked, underpaid, and facing financial and cultural barriers to traditional measures of adulthood like getting married, buying a house, or having children—might choose to have casual flings with a hot friend instead. They are about why those characters are *wrong* to be having casual flings with their hot friends, and why they should be in a committed, long-term relationship instead. Neither *Friends with Benefits* nor *No Strings Attached* ever takes seriously the idea that these characters might benefit from a no-strings-attached relationship with a friend—a fact that miffed critics who felt it was time for the rom-com genre to evolve. *Friends with Benefits* is "a rom-com that wants to have its cake and eat it too, drawing attention to and making fun of the clichés of the genre even as it indulges in them,"

A FRIENDLY RIVALRY

For the record: The filmmaking teams behind *Friends with Benefits* and *No Strings Attached* were very aware of their cinematic doppelgängers. "I have seen it. I liked it. I have no ill will towards them. To me, it's not that I shake my fist at *No Strings Attached*," says Gluck. "I shake my fist at people who think it's the same movie. When you walk past a steak restaurant you don't go, 'Awww another steak restaurant? How could they have another steak restaurant here? It's absurd!' You might go there and the steak might be different."

said Leah Rozen in *The Wrap*. *No Strings Attached* "continues the long tradition of Hollywood rom-coms, from *When Harry Met Sally* to *Knocked Up*, that bait with amusing, naughty sex and then switch to reassuring romantic commitment," complained Lisa Schwarzbaum in *Entertainment Weekly*.

Maybe this level of deviation from happy monogamy is too much to expect from a mainstream Hollywood romantic comedy, which—*My Best Friend's Wedding* excepted—have rarely drawn a Hollywood-sized box office without letting the audience indulge in a happily-ever-after. Rom-coms have ended in happy monogamous unions since at least the days of Shakespeare, and it's hard to argue with a formula that has worked for the past four hundred years.

But this reflex was also increasingly at odds with the way young people were conducting themselves in romantic relationships. In 1969, 21 percent of Americans said there was nothing wrong with premarital sex; by 2009, that number had risen to 60 percent. A 2011 study by the Pew Research Institute found that 44 percent of Millennials thought that marriage was becoming obsolete. The same study found that a significant majority of Millennials believed being single made absolutely no difference for a person's ability to achieve financial security, social status, a fulfilling sex life, or happiness in general. These are, in theory, the types of people at the center of the relationships in *Friends with Benefits* and *No Strings Attached*—but in the end, both filmmakers settled for the same solution that rom-coms have been offering for centuries.

I've been picking on *Friends with Benefits* and *No Strings Attached*, but it's not just casual relationships that Hollywood couldn't quite embrace. In movie after movie released around the same time, filmmakers took authentic, interesting modern relationship problems and gave them the same one-size-fits-all rom-com solutions. Take 2010's *Going the Distance*, starring Drew Barrymore and Justin Long, which tackles the very modern problem of two ambitious young professionals trying to maintain a long-distance relationship. Screenwriter Geoff LaTulippe, wary of a possible stigma against the rom-com genre, decided he'd sell his movie as a "comedy about a romance" instead, with the emphasis on the "comedy" part. He also worked to consciously subvert what he saw as the tired clichés of the genre: "I hate—I *hate*—romantic comedies that end with somebody running through an airport." There was just one problem: It is very hard to write a romantic comedy about a long-distance relationship without at least one dramatic scene in an airport. So LaTulippe scripted what he thought was a clever subversion: a scene in which Justin Long impulsively chases Drew Barrymore into an airport for a grand romantic gesture, only to return and discover the police had towed his car away because he left it in a no-parking zone. Eventually, the studio delivered its verdict: Audiences *like* running-through-an-airport scenes. And so the final cut of the movie includes the scene as LaTulippe wrote it, but lops out that final gag. With one cut, *Going the Distance* morphed from a winkingly self-aware riff on the rom-com chase into yet another rom-com with a desperate, romantic airport chase.

Countless versions of this conflict played out in miniature across Hollywood, as studios scrambled to figure out what modern audiences now wanted from their romantic comedies. Mark Mylod's *What's Your Number?*, starring Anna Faris and Chris Evans, is about a woman who frets that she's slept with too many men to find "The One." Don't worry; she finds him, and it was her neighbor all along. Tom Gormican's *That Awkward Moment*— originally (and more accurately) called *Are We Officially Dating?*, but

THE ROM-COM GOES META

The winking self-awareness of *Friends with Benefits* was a precursor to the *extremely* self-aware rom-coms on the horizon. David Wain's *They Came Together*—starring Amy Poehler and Paul Rudd, who play up the classic rom-com tropes so hard that their characters just seem deranged—is a searing spoof of the rom-com genre that openly references *When Harry Met Sally* and *You've Got Mail*. A few years later, the meta-rom-com trend reached its self-referential apex in Todd Strauss-Schulson's *Isn't It Romantic*, which stars Rebel Wilson as a rom-com hater who wakes up in a world governed by rom-com rules. To make sure he was getting the genre right, Strauss-Schulson says he watched somewhere between eighty and one hundred rom-coms over the span of about two weeks before production began. "It made my heart so tender and my brain turn to mush," he says.

retitled to capitalize on an already dated internet meme—follows a group of bros who, having grown tired of women pressing them to put specific labels onto their relationships, make a pact to stay single. None of them pull it off. That same year, the truly dreadful *Playing It Cool* goes full meta, opening with a voice-over monologue that reveals its lead character—known only as "Me"—is struggling to write a rom-com screenplay because he's never been in love. Would you believe he finds true love by the time the credits roll?

I could go on, listing more early-aughts rom-coms you might not even remember if you've seen them. In every case, the question was clearly the same: "How do we make a romantic comedy that actually captures how people are dating and falling in love today?"

BREAKING UP ISN'T (THAT) HARD TO DO

As young rom-com screenwriters and filmmakers tried to come up with ideas that would both subvert the expected tropes and more accurately reflect how people date, a different trend began to settle in: romantic comedies in which the protagonist ends up single at the end. What had been a novelty in *My Best Friend's Wedding* became a mini-trope of its own. Mark Webb's *(500) Days of Summer*, an indie smash that was inspired by co-screenwriter Scott Neustadter's own awful breakup, pointedly ends with Summer married to another man, and Tom apparently headed toward a promising new romance with a woman named—*groan*—Autumn. Dan Mazer's *I Give It a Year* is a deliberate inversion of the typical rom-com formula, with protagonists Nat and Josh getting married at the beginning of the movie and amicably divorcing at the end. Alice, the protagonist of Christian Ditter's *How to Be Single*, spends much of the movie grappling with the title after a breakup, but ultimately ends up alone—happily looking toward the future on a Grand Canyon hike on New Year's Day.

In almost every case, the answer turned out to be: by doing the same thing we were doing before, but with more casual sex.

This, in itself, is not a bad answer; as *Knocked Up*, and later *No Strings Attached* and *Friends with Benefits*, showed, it's interesting to watch a rom-com that makes sex the inciting incident instead of— pun not intended, I swear—the climax. *Sleeping with Other People*, Leslye Headland's satisfyingly adult riff on the *When Harry Met Sally* formula, features a pair of protagonists (Alison Brie and Jason Sudeikis) who become friends only after they've lost their virginity to each other in college, and only circle back to each other as possible soul mates many years (and many partners) later. The same year also saw the release of *Man Up*, a winning, modernized screwball riff about a woman (Lake Bell) who impulsively pretends to be a man's (Simon Pegg) blind date, resulting in an elaborate comedy of errors that's only resolved when both of them drop the lies and admit who they really are and what they really want.

If you had easy access to a time machine, it is not hard to imagine a world in which you could take either of those scripts and—after a now-standard round of Hollywood script-doctoring—end up with a massive studio hit starring Julia Roberts and Richard Gere, or Meg Ryan and Tom Hanks, or any other America's Sweethearts of your choice. But this was 2015—a particularly low ebb for the rom-com genre, which at this point the Hollywood studios had largely abandoned—which meant that both *Sleeping with Other People* and *Man Up* screened not in two thousand theaters across the country, but at the Tribeca Film Festival, garnering largely appreciative reviews from critics but no meaningful cultural footprint. After an exceedingly modest theatrical release that capped out at a box-office gross of under $1 million for *Sleeping with Other People*, and no domestic theatrical release whatsoever for *Man Up*, both movies shifted straight to video-on-demand, to live forever as reliable entries in the "great rom-coms you probably haven't seen" listicles that pop up on the internet every Valentine's Day.

What happened? Before this chapter gets too bleak about where the rom-com genre went wrong, it's worth pausing to highlight the greater forces and trends at work in the cultural landscape. The studios weren't exactly *wrong* when they zeroed in on casual hookups as a growing trend in the way young people were dating, but they were also missing the bigger picture. The 2010s were a time when American culture was undergoing a much deeper shift in its approach to love. The campaign for marriage equality was already escalating. The battles for racial equality and feminism, while far from finished today, were entering mainstream cultural discourse with a renewed vigor. Young people really *were* engaged in a reimagining of modern love that was more diverse and inclusive than anything that came before. Hollywood, by and large, just either didn't want to, or didn't know how to, tell stories that could capture it.

But to say no one pulled it off is painting with much too broad a brush. To that end, it's worth highlighting one more movie that tells a classic rom-com story in a modern context: Gillian Robespierre's *Obvious Child*. An inattentive reader could mistake a description of *Obvious Child* for *Knocked Up*: After a drunken one-night stand, a woman discovers that she's pregnant and has to figure out what she's going to do next. The hook, in this case, is that her answer is "get an abortion."

Obvious Child doesn't spend any time interrogating its protagonist Donna's decision; it simply accepts that it's hers to make. "We just wanted to tell a story about a woman who is actually funny, and looks and sounds like us, and has all the best jokes in the movie, and also has a face and has a positive experience with a shame-free abortion," says Robespierre. "We knew the conflict wasn't going to be 'Will she or won't she?' I've already seen the movie where somebody's torturing themselves over the decision." But pivotally, *Obvious Child* situates the abortion in the context of Donna's stop-and-start romance with the guy who got her pregnant. When he finally finds out, he brings her flowers, goes with her to Planned Parenthood for the procedure, and accompanies her back home after, where they make tea and settle in for a viewing of *Gone with the Wind*. It's one uncommonly tender idea of what a truly twenty-first-century rom-com, rooted in feminist expectations and values, might look like—a series of small gestures that, in their unwavering support and affection, become grand.

Ryan Reynolds and Dane Cook

TWO ROADS DIVERGED

In the brief, magical window when the DVD market was robust enough that a movie could become a word-of-mouth success—and launch the careers of a whole roster of young actors in the process—came Rob Mc-Kittrick's *Waiting*, an indie comedy about how much it sucks to work at a chain restaurant. (Think Kevin Smith's *Clerks*, but with more bodily fluids being served to the customers, and you'll be in the ballpark.) *Waiting* was a modest hit at the box office in 2005, but in the years that followed, it blew up on DVD, forming a kind of Unholy Trinity for frat boys alongside a dog-eared copy of Tucker Max's sleazy memoir *I Hope They Serve Beer in Hell* and a battered CD of Dane Cook's stand-up album *Retaliation*.

It is no coincidence that Dane Cook himself appears, opposite star Ryan Reynolds, in *Waiting*. At the time, the two actors, born just a few years apart, were also on similar career tracks. Reynolds's first big film role, as a smirky party animal doing his best to avoid graduating college in 2002's *National Lampoon's Van Wilder*, could easily have been played by

Cook, whose rapidly developing comic persona was basically Van Wilder off-campus.

By 2002, Cook was a rising comedy star who was also forward-thinking enough to use the internet as a personal megaphone. He spent $25,000 of his own money to get DaneCook.com up and running, and set up a Myspace page at a time when social media wasn't even on most performers' radar. It is undoubtedly part of what helped him sell out all 20,789 seats at New York City's Madison Square Garden in 2006—no small feat for any performer, let alone a comedian. And with a direct pipeline to those 1.2 million Myspace friends as he figured out what to do next, Cook certainly had the potential, on paper, to be a box-office draw. The challenge was figuring out how to package him. If the 1990s had taught Hollywood anything, it's that the easiest way to make audiences fall in love with a red-hot but otherwise untested talent was to put that actor in a romantic comedy. And if the genre was already starting to flag a little at the box office . . . well, wasn't the plan for Cook to bring something new and vital to the table? Why *couldn't* he save the romantic comedy?

Cook was very aware that a window had opened up—and he knew exactly the kinds of romantic comedies he wanted to star in: the ones that would essentially allow him to play himself. "After *Wedding Crashers* and *40-Year-Old Virgin*, for me, I put my fist in the air because I don't like being restricted. When those movies were successes, I looked at it as my window of opportunity," he said. "I've seen *Knocked Up*, I've seen *Superbad*, and I know we hang with those guys."

And so, in the span of just three years, Cook starred in three romantic comedies. Greg Coolidge's *Employee of the Month* casts Cook as a fast-talking, foul-mouthed slacker with a heart of gold. Mark Helfrich's *Good Luck Chuck* casts Cook as a fast-talking, foul-mouthed slacker with a heart of gold. Howard Deutch's *My Best Friend's Girl* casts Cook as . . . you get it.

It's no accident that Cook played virtually the same character in the same kinds of romantic comedies over and over again; in interview after interview, he makes it clear, with apparent sincerity, that these rom-coms are passion projects for him. "I really wanted to make a sex romp, a raunchy sex romp with a sweet center," says Cook of *Good Luck Chuck*. For what it's worth, costar Jessica Alba remembers the film differently: "It's porn! It wasn't supposed to be like that," she said, complaining that the film's creative team, encouraged by Cook, rewarded themselves at the end of each shooting day by filming a couple of sex scenes. "There were all these actresses who got conned into being completely naked," she says. "Some were strippers, probably. But every day when I was done, I ran away." ("We all read the script. We did what we read," said Cook in reply. "Not a day went by that we weren't in communication with each other and having a blast.")

By the time his third consecutive rom-com disappointed at the box office, it was clear that Dane Cook was not the next big thing in the genre. At the time of this publication, it's been well over a decade since Cook has appeared in a romantic comedy, much less starred in one. More than a decade later, history has not been kind to Dane Cook's brief, aborted career as a leading man—nor, frankly, to his brand of comedy in general, which tended toward rambling stories peppered with fratty quips about painful shits and dirty vaginas. The best rom-coms work because of the chemistry between two people, but Cook's ego-driven approach didn't really leave room for anyone besides Dane Cook. When *My Best Friend's Girl* bombed, despite a costarring role for reliably bankable rom-com star Kate Hudson, Cook took to his Myspace to blame the (admittedly awful) Photoshop on the poster. He had grandiose, probably impossible visions for the future of his career—at one point he went all in on the "SuFi," a double-middle-finger he envisioned as "a Bat signal, my Nike swoosh"—but all of them centered on ensuring that Dane Cook, both the person and the brand, always remained in the spotlight.

Was there another way forward? You don't have to look far for a test case. In the same year he appeared in *Waiting*, Ryan Reynolds starred in the romantic comedy *Just Friends*. The movie, directed by *The Sweetest Thing*'s Roger Kumble, is a mixed bag that starts on the wrong foot by putting Reynolds in a surreally unconvincing fat suit. But *Just Friends* wasn't a custom-built Ryan Reynolds vehicle. It's a romantic comedy in the classic sense, and it only ended up starring Ryan Reynolds after names like Adam Sandler, Jimmy Fallon, and Bradley Cooper didn't work out. Even more importantly, it surrounds Reynolds with real characters instead of thin, dusty stereotypes written solely to prop up his arc in the movie.

In the years that followed, Reynolds—while showcasing an internet savvy that wasn't too far removed from what Dane Cook pulled off in the Myspace era—also demonstrated an uncanny knack for being likable in romantic comedies that *didn't* make him the center of attention. Adam Brooks's *Definitely, Maybe* gives Reynolds three distinct love interests *and* an adorable adolescent daughter who happily steals scenes from him. Greg Mottola's coming-of-age romantic dramedy *Adventureland* makes Reynolds a tragicomic figure whose good looks and charisma disguise the fact that he's an absolute loser, cheating on his wife and alluding to glory days as a musician that never actually existed. Anne Fletcher's terrific *The Proposal* thrives on the chemistry of its leads—but it's ultimately Sandra Bullock's movie, and Reynolds was cast two full months after she was locked in. Every great comedian needs a straight man, and by then, Reynolds had proved himself uniquely qualified to add plenty of flair to a rom-com without taking over the movie entirely. "To be honest, I think my attitude is what's prevented me from becoming a colossal asshole," he says. "You meet some young actors now who think that any less than superstardom is failure. And that's wrong."

CHAPTER 14

UNTITLED ROYAL WEDDING COMEDY

(And the End of the Affair)

IT WAS APRIL 27, 2011—JUST TWO DAYS BEFORE PRINCE WILLIAM AND Kate Middleton tied the knot in a royal wedding that was viewed by tens of millions of people all over the world—when *(500) Days of Summer* screenwriters Scott Neustadter and Michael H. Weber successfully sold their pitch for what was known then, and will now always be known, as *Untitled Royal Wedding Comedy*.

"Everyone was going crazy, and I was like, 'They would *not* be going crazy if she was not Kate,'" says Neustadter. "'What if she was American? What if she came from a background they didn't like?' All the things that later happened with Harry and Meghan."

Inspired by the timeliness of their idea, the pair sat down and worked out a plot, complete with a meet-cute where the prince—a secret movie buff—would sneak incognito into a cinema playing Jean-Luc Godard's *Band of Outsiders* and meet the American heroine, who was the only other person in the theater. A whirlwind courtship later, a bunch of royal hijinks would lead to a royal wedding.

Neustadter and Weber could hardly have been savvier in their timing. At the end of a dramatic bidding war, Sony beat out several studio rivals—paying what was described in the Hollywood trades as a "seven-figure sum"—to write a romantic comedy that was pitched as *Notting Hill* meets *Meet the Royal Parents*.

With an undeniably hooky concept and two highly-in-demand writers, *Untitled Royal Wedding Comedy* was off to a strong start. But it got dramatically better in May of 2012, when no less a rom-com luminary than Nancy Meyers signed on to polish the script. Before long, the trades reported that Meyers was going to direct the movie as well.

Nothing is a sure thing—but even if it had never been given a real title, it is hard to imagine how *Untitled Royal Wedding Movie* could have failed. The stars seemed aligned: a buzzy screenwriting duo, a director with a stronger rom-com track record than literally any filmmaker still working today, a timely hook, and at least two roles—a lovable American woman and a dashing British prince—that practically seemed engineered to turn the heads of the hottest young actors in Hollywood. Imagine this movie opening in 2011 with, say, Robert Pattinson and Jennifer Lawrence. Tom Hiddleston and Anne Hathaway. Eddie Redmayne and Emma Stone. Picture a scene where, I don't know, he says he needs to get a crown, and she assumes he's talking about dental work. How could it fail?

By September of 2013, *Untitled Royal Wedding Comedy* was dead. The Hollywood trades reported that Sony was concerned that the movie's budget would be too high with Meyers at the helm. (I'll pause here to note that this was the same year Sony shelled out $130 million for M. Night Shyamalan's Jaden Smith vehicle *After Earth*.) Meyers, for her part, says the problem came down to casting: "I didn't really find a girl that I thought was right for it," she says.

What happened in those two years? How does a movie like *Untitled Royal Wedding Comedy*—which seemed so obviously destined for success that Sony paid seven figures just for the *pitch*—end up as nothing more than a hypothetical footnote in a book about romantic comedies?

Nancy Meyers, as usual, has an answer. "I felt between *It's Complicated* in 2009 and *The Intern* in 2015, the business took a huge turn," says Meyers. "The kind of movies I was making—I don't know what they're called. Some of them are romantic comedies; some of them are comedies. I don't know, whatever the genre is—movies about people, let's call them, that are funny—they weren't anybody's pride and joy anymore."

WE ARE GATHERED HERE TODAY . . .

Any funeral should come with a few eulogies, which is probably why seemingly every publication that covers movies ran a "death of the rom-com" feature at some point in the mid-2000s. "After a decade of essentially printing money, the genre abruptly ran out of box-office steam in 2012," wrote *The Atlantic*'s Christopher Orr in 2013, lamenting "the long decline from Katharine Hepburn to Katherine Heigl" at the box office. "The rom-com is dead. Good," wrote Emily Yahr in *The Washington Post* in 2016, citing "the current generation's cynical view of romantic comedies." And at *Vox* in 2018, Emily VanDerWerff dissected the reasons for Hollywood's broad retreat from the genre, citing factors ranging from "Hollywood's general antipathy toward stories about women" to "Rachel McAdams and Anne Hathaway" (and, more specifically, their decisions to throw their creative weight behind blockbusters instead).

Here, in brief, is the argument critics typically make about what happened to the romantic comedy. Once-bankable stars, like Julia Roberts, Sandra Bullock, Hugh Grant, and Matthew McConaughey, either aged out or lost interest in the genre. Younger stars, like Jennifer Lawrence, Emma Stone, Chris Hemsworth, and Robert Pattinson, generally opted to make blockbusters (more often than not featuring superheroes) instead. Filmgoers were too familiar with the tropes, and too jaded about love in general, to indulge in the fantasy rom-coms offered. And the rom-coms that *did* get made sometimes underperformed, scaring the studios and creating a feedback loop in which writers and directors realized that trying to sell a rom-com, now that the genre was no longer in vogue, was a career risk that it might not be worth taking. At the same time, a broader sea change (and the increasing importance of the international box office) led Hollywood to aim for massive, four-quadrant blockbusters at the expense of mid-range movies aimed at a narrower slice of the audience.

There's some truth in all of this; if there wasn't, you'd probably have seen Nancy Meyers's *Royal Wedding Comedy*—now with an actual title—on a basic cable network a dozen times by now. But a closer analysis reveals that the rom-com, despite what a plethora of headlines would have had you believe, never died at all. It was more like going into a cocoon to reemerge, in a few years, as something both familiar and different.

Let's take this point by point. It's no coincidence that a dip in the genre happened as the once-reliable rom-com stars of the 1990s and 2000s pivoted to other genres (and were rewarded with critical acclaim and/or gold trophies for doing it). As we've established, Hollywood always skews toward newer and younger, and a genre aging up is not typically a sign of a genre in good health. But pinning it on the exodus of the old stars doesn't quite work either—because when the older rom-com stars did show up, audiences didn't. There was a time when a movie like 2011's *Larry Crowne* might have been regarded as the *King Kong vs. Godzilla* of the romantic comedy, taking the genre's two biggest titans of the '90s—Tom Hanks and Julia Roberts—and, at long last, letting them smooch on-screen. And yet, when *Larry Crowne* hit theaters in the summer of 2011—sandwiched cleverly as a bit of adult-friendly counter-programming between *Transformers: Dark of the Moon* and *Harry Potter and the Deathly Hallows Part 2*—the adults just . . . didn't show up. The movie (which is good!) opened at #4 with a tepid $13 million, earned reviews that were generally either indifferent or dismissive, and left essentially no cultural footprint behind.

What about the young stars? While it's true that there were no young actors you could easily pigeonhole as rom-com stars, that's

YOU WANTED A HIT

Hollywood may have slowed down on producing romantic comedies, but in some international markets demand was hotter than ever. In 2016, Stephen Chow's rom-com *Mei ren yu*, which was released internationally as *The Mermaid*, told the story of a wealthy investor who falls in love with a mermaid who has been sent to kill him. (Think *Splash* meets *Pretty Woman* meets *Avatar* meets *Aquaman* meets a Three Stooges short and . . . well, you still won't quite have *The Mermaid*, but you'll at least be in the ballpark.)

Though *The Mermaid* received only a small limited release via Sony in the United States, it was massive in China, opening to $120 million over the Lunar New Year holiday frame and eventually grossing $526 million, making it one of the highest-grossing rom-coms of all time.

not because they weren't starring in rom-coms; it's because they weren't *only* starring in rom-coms. Throughout this "death of the rom-com era," there were a number of rom-coms featuring young stars that did just fine at the box office (including both of the aforementioned friends-with-benefits movies). While white-hot young stars like Jennifer Lawrence and Emma Stone had their superhero franchises and Oscar-friendly dramas, they were making the occasional hit rom-com too. *Silver Linings Playbook* and *Crazy, Stupid, Love* could easily have starred Julia Roberts or Sandra Bullock if they'd been made a couple of decades earlier. Both Lawrence and Stone could, and did, jump from dramas to rom-coms to superhero blockbusters without anyone batting an eye. If you had to pin the death of the rom-com on somebody, you couldn't really blame actors for failing to do their part to keep it alive.

In reality, romantic comedies were disproportionately impacted by a trend that had overwhelmed all of Hollywood. As studios and audiences alike became obsessed with blockbusters—especially those centered on superheroes—*all* mid-range movies struggled to find traction. An increasing fixation on franchises, best exemplified by the endless permutations of the Marvel Cinematic Universe, meant that even a hit looked less appealing if it couldn't also spawn a series of sequels that might also be hits. *Silver Linings Playbook* was huge, but it didn't leave much room for *Silver Linings Playbook 2: Rewriting the Rules.* "Chick flicks don't tend to be sequel-izable," said Lynda Obst in 2013. It didn't help that rom-coms, which tend to be more culturally specific, character-driven, and aimed at a smaller slice of the overall moviegoing audience, have a harder time selling to worldwide audiences than blockbusters. (Explosions, of course, are the same in every language.) The comedies that *did* hit with international audiences tended to be bigger and brasher. "There are cultural nuances that don't travel.

Broad comedies play because falling on a banana peel is funny in every culture, but nuance—cultural nuance, or wit—are peculiarities. They don't travel," says Obst.

Though the market grew less friendly to non-blockbusters, there was still interest in bringing home critical acclaim and Academy Awards, so adult-skewing dramas still made it into production. But by and large, romantic comedies were uniquely

SMALL-SCREEN LOVE STORIES

If audiences were disappointed in the downturn in rom-coms at the box office, they could always turn on the TV, where comedic love stories were thriving. NBC's Americanized remake of *The Office*—which remains, nearly a decade after it went off the air, the most popular TV show across the streaming landscape—gave audiences a will-they/won't-they for the ages in Jim (John Krasinski) and Pam (Jenna Fischer). *How I Met Your Mother*, which ran for nine seasons on CBS, was explicitly sold as a romantic comedy in which the starry-eyed romantic would be the man, not the woman. The CW's brilliant musical dramedy *Crazy Ex-Girlfriend* is both a rom-com and a critique of rom-coms, with romance-obsessed protagonist Rebecca Bunch (Rachel Bloom) filtering her experiences through a personal lens that has been heavily and unhealthily skewed by musicals and romantic comedies.

Most of all, there's the absurdly massive ABC reality series *The Bachelor*, which builds the arc of romantic comedies into its very structure: starting with a meet-cute (as contestants pile out of limos and attempt to do something sweet or quirky or sexy enough to make a real impression), and ending with the incredible pressure to give audiences a happy ending by proposing marriage to the winner at the end of a season.

disadvantaged in this model. No matter how successful, a romantic comedy would never reach the billion-dollar international grosses of a modern Disney blockbuster. (Never mind that you could, quite literally, fund seventy-one *My Big Fat Greek Wedding*s for the cost of one *Avengers: Endgame*.) And no matter how well-crafted or acclaimed, a romantic comedy would struggle to gain the same kind of traction that Academy voters have historically doled out to movies they deem "serious" enough for the awards circuit. (Though at this same time, *Midnight in Paris* and *Silver Linings Playbook*—two rom-coms that overcame the typical stigma by dealing with literary history and mental illness, respectively, and by centering their love stories on a man—got glowing reviews, hefty box-office grosses, and Best Picture nominations.)

All of these factors contributed, to one degree or another, to a general downturn in both the quality and the quantity of rom-coms getting produced. But after a thorough review of the evidence, if you had to pin the "death of the rom-com" on one thing, it would have to be critics who kept insisting that rom-coms were dead.

In reality, the "death of the romantic comedy"—while a catchy headline—was greatly exaggerated. Like any genre, the rom-com has waxed and waned in popularity over the years without ever fully going away. In 2013—the same year *The Atlantic* declared that the rom-com was over—audiences could still head to multiplexes to see Domhnall Gleason and Rachel McAdams in Richard Curtis's *About Time*, Nicholas Hoult and Teresa Palmer in Jonathan Levine's *Warm Bodies*, Tina Fey and Paul Rudd in Paul Weitz's *Admission*, Amy Acker and Alexis Denisof in Joss Whedon's *Much Ado About Nothing*, or Joseph Gordon-Levitt and Scarlett Johansson in Gordon-Levitt's directorial debut, *Don Jon*. Some of those movies were hits, some of those movies were flops, and some of

LOVE LETTERS

In the midst of what was largely viewed as a fallow time for the rom-com genre, Fox scored both a commercial hit and a cultural watershed moment with Greg Berlanti's *Love, Simon*, which was the rare Hollywood romantic comedy to focus on a gay protagonist (and the first to center on a gay teenager).

Nick Robinson plays Simon, a closeted teenager who pours out his true feelings in emails with an anonymous fellow student. The emails are eventually leaked to the school, and Simon shares his true feelings with his pen pal. The boys get their happy ending—something that was important to Berlanti, who was frustrated with the industry's focus on telling tragic stories about gay couples, and who had successfully convinced the studio that audiences would turn up for a movie about a gay couple if it was "marketed and sold as a mainstream romantic comedy." *Love, Simon* went on to gross at least four times its production budget, won the GLAAD Media Award for Outstanding Film, and led to a similarly successful and acclaimed TV spin-off, *Love, Victor*, which premiered on Hulu in June of 2020.

those movies were unconventional enough that they weren't even really recognized as romantic comedies by the audiences that did see them. But even if they occupied a smaller place at the box office than they had in the preceding decades, they did exist, keeping the genre relevant for anyone who cared enough to seek them out.

Still, one thing was undeniably true: After an incredible boom period in the 1990s that routinely saw romantic comedies near the top of the yearly box office—*and* launching the careers of an entire generation of actors—the genre had become one of the lowest priorities among studios in Hollywood. In an era where every major Hollywood studio was putting its resources toward trying to turn out $1 billion grossing blockbuster smashes calibrated for maximum worldwide appeal, there would always be room for an indie rom-com to slip through the cracks and find an appreciative audience. But could a big, splashy romantic comedy ever break through with mainstream audiences? And if it was possible, what would a movie like that even look like?

Mindy Kaling

THE SCHOLAR

In a 2011 article for *The New Yorker*, Mindy Kaling made a confession. "What I'd really like to write is a romantic comedy. This is my favorite kind of movie," she wrote. "I feel almost embarrassed revealing this, because the genre has been so degraded in the past twenty years that saying you like romantic comedies is essentially an admission of mild stupidity."

In the essay that follows, Kaling dissects the genre, breaking down every trope and archetype with unwavering precision, from the Klutz ("a hundred-percent-perfect-looking female who is perfect in every way except that she constantly bonks her head on things") to the Woman Who Works in an Art Gallery ("How many freakin' art galleries are out there?") to the Ethereal Weirdo ("essential to the male fantasy that even if a guy is boring he deserves a woman who will find him fascinating and perk up his dreary life by forcing him to go skinny-dipping in a stranger's pool").

On the surface, Kaling's analysis aligned with much of the criticism that has been leveled at rom-coms by skeptics for years. The key difference is that Kaling recognized the artifice of the romantic comedy and, instead of sneering at it, embraced it wholeheartedly anyway. "I regard romantic comedies as a subgenre of sci-fi, in which the world operates according to different rules than my regular human world," she wrote. "For me, there is no difference between Ripley from *Alien* and any Katherine Heigl character. They are equally implausible."

Kaling's affection for the rom-com genre stretches all the way back to her adolescence. "I was a real wallflower and late bloomer and I think that because I had no access to any legitimate romance as an 11, 12, 13-year-old, I really fantasized a lot about romance," she says. "I really just love the genre and I've always felt that it is an undervalued genre. I feel like people talk about romantic comedies they love, and they say that they're their guilty pleasures. But I truly don't believe in guilty pleasures, I only believe in pleasures."

Early in her career, Kaling blogged under the name Mindy Ephron, amused at the idea that she might have been a long-lost Ephron sister. She released a list of her personal favorite romantic comedies, which spanned everything from *The Princess Bride* ("page for page the best written romantic comedy script") to *The Apartment* ("structurally perfecto") to *The Holiday* ("I love a story built around temporary subletting"). When she broke into film, she took on supporting roles in rom-coms over and over again—in Judd Apatow's *The 40-Year-Old Virgin*, in Ken Kwapis's *License to Wed*, in Ivan Reitman's *No Strings Attached*, in Nicholas Stoller's *The Five-Year Engagement*, in Doug Liman's *Locked Down*.

Yet Mindy Kaling has never, at the time of this publication, actually starred in her own Hollywood rom-com. Instead, she channeled all her knowledge and affection for the genre into *The Mindy Project*, which aired three seasons on Fox before moving over to Hulu for three more. *The Mindy Project* wove its protagonist's deep affection for romantic comedies squarely into the plot (and even modeled episodes on modern rom-com classics like *When Harry Met Sally*, *Sleepless in Seattle*, and *You've Got Mail*).

Kaling's PhD-level knowledge of romantic comedies is also the thing that makes her so interested, as a creator, in figuring out how to modernize the genre. In the years since *The Mindy Project* concluded, Kaling has remained a tireless advocate for romantic comedies even as Hollywood largely abandoned them. In 2019, Kaling co-created a modernized miniseries adaptation of *Four Weddings and a Funeral* for Hulu, which tries to honor the genre's past while charting a different course for its future. There are still four weddings and one funeral, and Hulu's *Four Weddings* tips the hat to the old days by casting Dermot Mulroney and Andie MacDowell—as well as Alex Jennings, who nearly beat out Hugh Grant for the lead in the original movie—in supporting roles. But it also lines up an ensemble cast that's vastly more diverse than the lily-white original, with Nathalie Emmanuel and Nikesh Patel slotted into the Hugh Grant and Andie MacDowell roles. "It just goes to show that when you have people of color and women in the writers' room, what a difference that makes in casting," says Emmanuel. "The whole cast is very, very inclusive. That instantly makes it modern."

Of course, diversity isn't exactly modernity; it's the long-overdue correction for a long-standing imbalance in the stories the Hollywood studios often *did* default to telling. And while representation is only the first step in a more equitable film industry, it's still an important one.

After shepherding several small-screen rom-coms over the past decade, it looks like Kaling will finally star in a big-screen rom-com of her own. At the time of this publication, Kaling is cowriting a script for a "buddy comedy with romantic comedy elements" set at a wedding. She intends to play the lead role, as an Indian-American woman who travels to India for the first time; Priyanka Chopra, who originally approached Kaling with the suggestion that they should make a comedy together, will costar.

For a writer and actress who has loved rom-coms from the very beginning, this is a hopeful and thrilling time, both in the specifics of her career and for the genre in general. Unsurprisingly, Kaling has already surveyed the field and done the analysis. "Romantic comedies used to be through the lens of a certain type of couple—usually a white couple falling in love, then out of love, and finding each other again. What's been really great about the past couple of years is we're seeing couples that we don't normally see," says Kaling. "It's now considered bankable and exciting to have people in the leads who are unconventional—and I hope *that* becomes conventional."

"I just wanted you to know that one day—when he marries another lucky girl who is enough for you, and you're playing with your grandkids while the Tan Huas are blooming, and the birds are chirping—that it was because of me: a poor, raised-by-a-single-mother, low-class, immigrant nobody."

—RACHEL CHU,
CRAZY RICH ASIANS

CHAPTER 15

CRAZY RICH ASIANS

(And the Triumphant Return of the Hollywood Rom-Com)

IF YOU HAPPENED TO BE IN DOWNTOWN LOS ANGELES ON APRIL 23, 2018, the hottest ticket you could get was for a movie that wouldn't even be released for another four months. At the Ace Hotel, director Jon M. Chu and much of the sprawling ensemble cast of *Crazy Rich Asians* took the stage in front of 1,200 artists and influencers from the Asian American community. It was the earliest screening of its kind that Warner Bros. had ever scheduled, and the mood was rapturous as Chu took the microphone. "It's not a movie, it's a movement," he promised shortly before the movie began. Reporting immediately after the screening, *The Hollywood Reporter*'s Rebecca Sun described a theater full of joyful weeping: "A generation of Westernized Asians has gone 25 years never seeing something like this."

But before any of that, it was a buzzy, fizzy novel that sprang out of the mind and experiences of novelist Kevin Kwan. *Crazy Rich Asians* can technically be traced to a poem Kwan wrote for a creative writing class in college, though it took him another twenty years to revisit the material in what eventually morphed into his first novel. Though Kwan's family immigrated to Texas when he was twelve, he was inspired by his childhood memories of the unfathomably wealthy friends they had in Singapore. One house had a tennis court and a private jet. Another had a neat row of at least fifteen expensive cars. "As a child, you're cloistered in this world," he says. "You don't know how other people live until you leave that world and realize not everyone has an airplane in their garage."

Kwan's novel is a classic fish-out-of-water story, with protagonist Rachel Chu—a professor of economics at New York University—traveling to Singapore to meet the family of her boyfriend, Nick Young, and belatedly discovering that he's the scion

CRAZY BEYOND BELIEF

After he turned in his first draft of *Crazy Rich Asians*, Kevin Kwan's editor asked him to tone down some of the more ostentatious details about the uber-rich characters that populate the book—not because they were inaccurate, but because they were so extravagant that she feared audiences would get annoyed at Kwan because they thought he was exaggerating too much. "I did a lot more simplifying and cutting out of the decadence and the excess than I did of adding it on, if you can believe that," he says. "Sometimes I had to actually take details out, because my editor was like, 'No one will believe this.' And I would say, 'But this really happened,' and she'd reply, 'It doesn't matter. You're going to lose readers because it's going to seem so unreal that people would spend this much money, or do something this excessive.' So those parts were changed."

of one of the wealthiest families in Asia. Though the core of the novel is the culture clash between Rachel and Nick's family, the narrative invites readers to vicariously experience an entire world built around unimaginable wealth, with an elaborate social structure and (often unspoken) code of conduct governing who rises and falls in it.

Upon its publication in 2013, *Crazy Rich Asians* was an instant hit, but Kwan didn't even need to wait that long; the buzz on the novel was already hot enough that Hollywood producers came knocking *before* the book actually hit shelves. But if instant success was exciting, it was also an infuriating glimpse into Hollywood's wariness over any narrative that didn't center on a white person. One producer approached Kwan to pitch the idea that a film adaptation should turn Rachel, his Chinese-American protagonist, into a white woman. "It's a pity you don't have a white character," said another.

Kwan had heard enough. In the end, he wanted someone who wanted to make *Crazy Rich Asians* without diluting the "Asians" part. So he sold the rights to producers Nina Jacobson and Brad Simpson—for the very non-crazy-rich price of one dollar, with more money kicking in at key points in the movie's creative development, production, and release—on the condition that he could remain creatively involved.

From the first time he goofed around with a clunky old VHS camcorder in elementary school, Jon M. Chu knew he wanted to be a director. His parents—who immigrated to the United States from Taiwan and Hong Kong and opened a successful restaurant in Los Altos, California—did what they could to nurture his dream. His mother bought him books about filmmaking, insisting that he needed study and hard work if he was going to make it; his father talked to customers in the tech industry about his son's film-making aspirations, and they would pass along excess computers, video cards, and editing software for him to practice on.

Chu, who graduated from USC film school in 2003, almost instantly drew attention with his senior film project: a twenty-minute short called "When the Kids Are Away: A Musical Celebration of Mothers," which delivers a fanciful, candy-colored musical depicting stay-at-home moms singing and dancing after their children go to school. Pegged as a hot up-and-comer, Chu lined up a series of projects, including a feature-length musical called *Moxie*, a romantic comedy called *The Prom*, and a buzzy new version of the Tony Award–winning musical *Bye Bye Birdie*.

If you don't remember any of those films, it's because none of them ever entered production. As Chu waited for his big break, he watched everything to which he'd attached himself languishing in various stages of development hell. Five years later, and desperate for a chance to prove himself, Chu managed to upsell what was conceived as a $7 million direct-to-DVD sequel to the teen dance movie *Step Up* and turn it into a $22 million sequel with a wide theatrical release. When it arrived in theaters in February of 2008, *Step Up 2: The Streets* grossed more than $35 million more than the original, and Jon M. Chu had a filmmaking career.

In the years that followed, Chu became one of the go-to names for music films, directing another *Step Up* sequel and the concert films *Justin Bieber: Never Say Never* and *Justin Bieber's Believe*, as well as sequels to substandard blockbusters like *Now You See Me* and *G.I. Joe: The Rise of Cobra*.

"I never thought of myself—and of course I know that I'm an Asian American filmmaker—but I never categorize myself as that," says Chu. "I had just wanted to be compared to the top directors in the world, like Steven Spielberg and Tim Burton. I didn't want to be seen as this 'other' thing." But Chu started asking himself questions about the kinds of movies he might be uniquely well-positioned to make after seeing the viral Twitter hashtag #StarringJonCho, which was kicked off by digital strategist William Yu in May of 2016 and motivated by the previous year's #OscarsSoWhite hashtag, which decried the lack of diversity in that year's Academy Award nominees. In a series of Photoshopped posters, images of the actor Jon Cho were placed over the white actors typically cast to star in big Hollywood movies, creating a glimpse into a hypothetical world where an actor like Cho could be James Bond or Captain America without anyone

TRUTH IS STRANGER THAN FICTION

Long before Jon M. Chu had signed on to direct *Crazy Rich Asians*, he made a brief cameo in Kevin Kwan's novel. When Chu met Kwan to discuss the project, he noted a quick reference in the book about Rachel Chu's filmmaking cousin who lives in California, saying what a strange coincidence it was that a California Chu might end up directing the movie after all. Kwan stopped him: "No, I *am* talking about you," he said.

Kwan went on to explain that Jon M. Chu's cousin Vivian was one of his closest friends, and that she frequently told him anecdotes about her extended family in California, including Jon. "Her stories inspired me when I created the character of Rachel Chu and her family," says Kwan. "I never dreamed that he would one day direct the film based on my book, a film with a heroine who is inspired by the women in his own family."

batting an eye. It made Chu contemplate his own responsibility, and his own opportunity, to push for more Asian representation in Hollywood. "I'm one of the few people who actually are on the ground, makes movies," says Chu. "I can literally say 'I want to cast this person' and go to battle for whatever that is."

As he contemplated what project might be worth battling for, his sister called with a suggestion: Kwan's *Crazy Rich Asians*, which was already being developed by producers Nina Jacobson and Brad Simpson. Curious, Chu called his agent and asked if there was already a director attached. His agent, startled, asked how Chu already knew about it; Jacobson and Simpson had already sent the script for *Crazy Rich Asians* two days earlier, asking if Chu might be interested. "It was a serendipitous moment that I was meant to do this movie," he says.

When Chu signed on, an adaptation had already been written by Peter Chiarelli, who had proven his rom-com bona fides with 2009's *The Proposal*. Chiarelli's draft gave Kwan's sprawling novel a three-act structure and a cleaner conflict, casting the main drama as a battle between Rachel and Nick's intimidating mother, Eleanor, with Nick caught in the middle. Everyone liked the draft, but Chu knew a writer who he thought could add a new dimension to the material: Adele Lim.

Lim, who was born and raised in Malaysia, moved to the United States at nineteen. After graduating college, she replied to an ad she saw in a trade magazine and landed a job as a writer's assistant on *Xena: Warrior Princess*, which led to a steady string of gigs on shows like *One Tree Hill* and *Private Practice*. At one point, she and Jon M. Chu had worked together on a pilot about dancers for Fox, which the network ultimately passed on. "It's the thing that happens in TV pilots year after year. They would say, 'Well, we're ready for a different show, more diverse cast, more interesting stories,'" says Lim. "But it was an unsaid rule that you couldn't really sell a dramatic pilot with an Asian lead. And so a lot of us didn't even try."

Crazy Rich Asians was a welcome chance to work with Chu again, and a welcome chance to tell a story that centered on Asian characters. As a bonus, Lim found plenty she could relate to in the material itself. "My family isn't crazy *rich*, but they're fucking crazy," says Lim. Her draft, written in close conversation with Chu, would focus on strengthening the emotional arcs—particularly for the female leads—and adding the specific details that would make *Crazy Rich Asians* an accurate look at a culture that had almost always been hand-waved and generalized by Hollywood, in the rare cases that it was depicted at all.

The goal was to approach the material with the specificity that was frequently lacking in Hollywood movies that weren't about white people. To help, Chu and Lim enlisted the expertise of Singaporean-born associate producer Janice Chua, who could speak with authority about the proper way to represent her home country on-screen. "One thing that was argued about a lot was using Singlish. It's a mixture of English, Bahasa Melayu, and Tamil dialects," Chua says. "We didn't really translate it, and we didn't really want to explain it. But I think sometimes filmmakers underestimated the audience ability to catch things within context. But I feel like people who are immigrants, or people from southern Asia, will appreciate it."

The fact that—to name one example—an actress like Michelle Yeoh could ad-lib in Cantonese when necessary gives you some sense of what *Crazy Rich Asians* needed from its sprawling cast. The novel contains dozens of named characters—many of whom are related by either blood or marriage—and their complicated web of relationships is part of what gives the story its unique frisson. Adding a tricky wrinkle to consider was that some relatively minor supporting characters in *Crazy Rich Asians* would have much more to do in the sequels, if they were produced. "As you can imagine, there's no IMDb for Asian actors. We're really underrepresented," says Janice Chua. To cast as wide a net as possible, Jon M. Chu dispatched casting directors all around the world: to Vancouver, Hong Kong, the United Kingdom, Australia, Malaysia, Singapore, and Beijing. Chu even put out a YouTube video

FINDING THE SOUND

Jon M. Chu's open YouTube casting call didn't turn up the right actor to play Nick Young, but it *did* lead to one major addition to the movie. Singer Cheryl Koh, who goes by Cheryl K, impressed the film's creative team by singing an a capella version of Jessie J's "Mamma Knows Best," which eventually led to an offer to sing a cover of The Beatles' "Money (That's What I Want)" for the *Crazy Rich Asians* opening credits. "When I got the news that Jon wanted me to do it, I couldn't stop screaming," says Koh.

If you like the rest of the music in *Crazy Rich Asians*, you can thank Janice Chua, who personally compiled two Spotify playlists of Chinese songs for Jon Chu—a number of which ended up making the final cut. "One playlist consists of all the modern Chinese pop songs and hip-hop. And the other was Chinese jazz, mostly swing jazz, from the '40s to the '80s," she says. "Jon shared it with his mom, and she said, 'This is the music that I grew up and danced to.'"

that acted as an open casting call, inviting "aspiring actors!" and "cool personalities with hidden talents!" to submit a two-minute video. "This is not a contest. You don't get a prize. You could actually get a *job*," he says.

In the end, the lead role of Rachel Chu went to a relatively established actress: Constance Wu, who had broken out in the ABC sitcom *Fresh Off the Boat* a few years earlier. When she found out that the movie's schedule conflicted with her shooting dates for the TV show, she wrote Jon M. Chu a personal letter asking him to consider shifting the production dates: "Dates are dates, and if those are immovable, I understand. But I would put all of my heart, hope, humor and courage into the role. What this could do means so much to me. It's why I advocate so much for young Asian-American girls so they might not spend their life feeling small or being commanded to feel grateful to even be at the table." It was exactly the passion *Crazy Rich Asians* needed, and production was shifted four months to accommodate her.

Now that *Crazy Rich Asians* had its Rachel Chu, it needed its Nick Young. And for all the time and effort Chu had put into his deep-dive casting hunt, discovering Henry Golding—who was eventually cast to play Nick—was the unlikeliest break of all. After a long and fruitless search in which none of the contenders felt quite right, Henry Golding was suggested by an accountant working on the movie, who recalled swooning when she saw him present at an awards show years earlier. Chu checked out Golding's Instagram account, not expecting to be wowed, and found himself utterly entranced by Golding's self-shot videos about food and cats.

Maybe it was his delivery. He certainly had the practice: Though he'd never acted, Golding had spent the previous decade hosting travel shows set in places like Malaysia, Japan, and Kuala Lumpur. When Chu reached out about *Crazy Rich Asians*, Golding had just wrapped a particularly intense shoot for a Discovery Channel series called *Surviving Borneo* and gotten married to longtime partner Liv Lo. With the lead role in *Crazy Rich Asians* in the balance, he cut his honeymoon short to shoot a screen test, and landed the role.

Even more than most romantic comedies, which tend to come with a heavy dose of built-in escapism, part of the joy of *Crazy Rich Asians* comes from the sheer lifestyle porn it offers. The movie is loaded with gilded mansions, high fashion, and about $2.5 million in jewelry. One of Adele Lim's jobs as a screenwriter was to signal to the audience that there was a deeper cultural meaning behind the seemingly gauche displays of wealth. "There is a rationale, and love, underneath all those gestures that are seemingly silly and materialistic," says Lim. "For so much of Asian culture, money is love. It's not a materialistic thing. It's an indication of how you take care of each other, of how you show affection and love. You don't *say* 'I love you,' because talk is cheap. You show your family you love them by working hard and providing for them."

This philosophy came to a head in the character that most changed (and benefited) from Lim's rewrite: Nick's mother, Eleanor (Michelle Yeoh). In the first draft of *Crazy Rich Asians*, Eleanor had been a snobbish villain blocking her son's happiness. Lim was tasked with finding a way to make Eleanor's dislike of Rachel comprehensible, and maybe even oddly sympathetic, by discovering ways to explicate the cultural differences that lead to conflict between the two women. "That is a very easy character to demonize. The Asian 'Dragon Lady,' and the evil mother-in-law, is an easy go-to. It's easy to have a character like Eleanor and see her as the unreasonable, hysterical, xenophobic Chinese mom who's just materialistic, and wants him to marry within the class, and stay close to home," says Lim. "But I really wanted to make sure that the role did justice to her, and also to the moms—to our Chinese moms. At the end of the day, it's not a story about Asians with money. At the end of the day, it's a story of a woman afraid to lose her son."

Throughout the movie, Rachel is judged by Eleanor in ways that might not always be legible to Western audiences—who are used to being regarded as the default—because her behaviors are specifically tactless to Eleanor, whose perspective is naturally rooted in Eastern culture. Rachel is a prototypical rom-com heroine: lovable, confident, and headstrong. When she meets Eleanor for the first time, she describes, with great pride, how much work it took to become an economics professor at a prestigious university. Rachel fails to notice, until it's too late, that Eleanor is utterly unimpressed by this bootstrap narrative. And while audiences' sympathies might naturally align with the heroine when Eleanor responds with icy passive-aggression, it's also important to understand how Rachel has misstepped. "In Asian culture, you always put your family first. But when we look at someone who is born [in the U.S.], you go, 'Well, because society dictates that you're more American, you put yourself first.' You have to learn to be independent and do your thing," says Michelle Yeoh. "It wasn't about Rachel not being smart enough, clever enough, or being not rich enough. It's because I think Eleanor recognizes the fact that [Rachel] would not be able to sacrifice and put Nick first, before her own needs."

The conflict between Rachel and Eleanor finally climaxes in the movie's best scene, which actually isn't in the book: a mahjong game in which Rachel asserts her own quiet power by choosing to let Eleanor win. It is a very unconventional victory, and it took Chu and Lim a while to find it. "There were versions of the mahjong scene where Rachel was pushing back in a much more traditional way—getting up and throwing tiles and storming off," says Lim. "Because that's the American comedy arc. You say, 'To hell with the world, to hell with everyone else, fuck you,' and you ride your love into the sunset. And it felt very wrong to me."

Lim and Chu sat down and conceived a version of the scene that would symbolize the central conflict between Rachel and Eleanor, and highlight Rachel's Western roots and her newfound understanding of Eastern culture. Much of this is unspoken—made clear simply by the steely confidence with which Rachel shuffles her mahjong tiles. "Mahjong is not one of those games that you can learn and act like you've been doing it your whole life, because there's a physical aspect to it," says Lim. "How you build your stacks, how you move . . . there's a very specific order to everything. It's like this symphony of sound and of movement. Nobody says, 'Oh, it's your turn.' There's a muscle memory to it. Eleanor has been accusing Rachel of not understanding the culture, or being a part of it. And what Rachel is showing Eleanor in that moment—without saying it—is, 'I am more of the culture than you even understand, and this is how I'm showing it.' She was taught that game by her mother, too."

In the final flourish of the mahjong scene, Rachel plays the tile that allows Eleanor to win, while making it clear that she's always been several steps ahead in the game. "There's no winning. You made sure of that," Rachel says—drawing on the collegiate expertise game-theory training that Eleanor so clearly disdained when they first met.

This turns out to be enough to impress Eleanor, who gives her blessing. Nick proposes—this time on an airplane!—Rachel accepts, and *Crazy Rich Asians* has its crowd-pleasing ending. Better yet, for an industry that never tires of a sure thing, there are still two sequel novels ripe for adaptation.

By the time *Crazy Rich Asians* was primed for distribution, everyone knew they had a big winner on their hands. Netflix, which was just beginning to recognize the value of a full slate of original romantic comedies for its subscribers, made an aggressive bid for the rights to *Crazy Rich Asians*. Their pitch included massive paydays, artistic freedom, and a guarantee that an entire trilogy based on Kwan's novels would be green-lit upfront. Warner Bros., which had made the highest bid among the traditional studios, was also offering something more traditional, though no less meaningful: a full-blown international theatrical release, with a marketing campaign to match.

After a quick debate (because Warner Bros. had given them only fifteen minutes to decide), Chu and Kwan went with the traditional studio. In the end, the payday couldn't compete with the idea of making *Crazy Rich Asians* an event—something that would make people around the world call a babysitter, pay for parking, shuffle up to a box office, and spend their time and money to see a cast of Asian actors in a big-screen romantic comedy. "I was in complete agreement with him. It was a passion project. I wasn't doing it for the money at that point. I did it because I'd never gotten to write for my people, ever," says Lim.

There were dicey moments when the creative team behind *Crazy Rich Asians* wondered whether they should have taken that guaranteed Netflix money. "When we were testing it, we couldn't get people to come see a free screening," says Chu. "Asian people, if they didn't know the book, thought the title was offensive. If they did know the book, they thought Hollywood would ruin it. Other ethnicities thought it wasn't for them."

Then came that fabled, cathartic April screening in front of 1,200 Asian American influencers at the Ace Hotel, and a host of other similar events leading up to the movie's August release. The buzz was promising, but the team was worried. "There's a pressure we all felt as Asian filmmakers," says Lim. "If we shat the bed on this, it would be another twenty-five, thirty years before Hollywood would agree to another contemporary movie with an all-Asian cast."

So everyone breathed a sigh of relief when *Crazy Rich Asians* opened to almost universally glowing reviews and a solid $26 million opening weekend at the box office. By the end of its run, it had earned $238 million worldwide, proving to any doubters in Hollywood that a movie with an Asian cast could still have plenty of crossover appeal. "Some of the best reactions I got were from people from Puerto Rican families, or people from Mexican families saying, 'Oh, my God, those are the exact dynamics in our culture that we don't see in any movies,'" says Lim (a lesson that somehow hadn't been learned sixteen years earlier when the same thing happened with *My Big Fat Greek Wedding*). Fortunately, Warner Bros. trusted the *Crazy Rich Asians* team enough to let them tell the story as they imagined. "To the studio's credit, they never once asked for anything to be whitewashed, or dumbed down, or diluted for the mass audience—because I think they understood the more specific we got, the more universal it would feel," says Lim.

There is always a temptation to treat a movie like *Crazy Rich Asians* as a stand-alone win instead of a stepping-stone. The real

DIVERSITY

Though *Crazy Rich Asians* was frequently celebrated as a new landmark in Hollywood diversity, it was also slammed for not being diverse enough. In addition to complaints about casting the half-white, half-Asian Henry Golding as Nick Young—replied Golding: "How Asian do you have to be to be considered Asian?"— *Crazy Rich Asians* was criticized for filling its main roles with Chinese, Japanese, and Korean actors while relegating South and Southeast Asians to background roles as guards and servants. "If the film puts Asian America in the spotlight, it does so for a very slim portion of that demographic," wrote Mark Tseng-Putterman in *The Atlantic*. "It is diverse when you look at it in the scope and context of Hollywood, which is predominantly white. But in terms of representing all Asians and Asian Americans, it doesn't hit that mark. It is a very specific story to a specific enclave, and even within that enclave, a specific class of that enclave," said Biola University sociology chair Nancy Wang Yuen in an interview with *The Washington Post*.

In an interview when the movie was released, Jon M. Chu expressed skepticism that one movie could make up for Hollywood's severe lack of representation. "It's unfair for one movie to represent all these people. One movie that represents [all] Asians—that's just ridiculous," he told *Deadline*. But in a subsequent 2021 interview with *Insider*, he acknowledged the criticism as valid and said he wished he could go back to the film and address it. "That's a lesson that I did not understand until it happened," he says, vowing to "pay more attention" to similar concerns in his future films.

challenge will be seeing if any Hollywood studio, other than the people making the sequels, picks up the gauntlet thrown down by *Crazy Rich Asians* and runs with it. If there is a lesson in *Crazy Rich Asians* beyond "people still want rom-coms"—and yes, the studios *absolutely* leave money on the table if they avoid making rom-coms—it's that letting filmmakers tell a story as authentically as possible isn't just a good creative decision; it's a good business decision. Before *Crazy Rich Asians* was a $238 million international smash, it needed to go through a number of people who understood and believed in the material enough to do it authentically, and without any compromises. Whether the studios will take that lesson to heart remains an open question. "We've been at this point before. When *The Joy Luck Club* came out a few decades ago, we thought, *Well, this is going to be a whole new world for all those actresses and for those filmmakers*, and that didn't happen," says Lim. "I think *Crazy Rich Asians* helped to put a hairline fracture in the dam, put it this way, but I don't think the dam is in any way broken," says Kevin Kwan.

For now, all eyes are on the sequel, *China Rich Girlfriend*, which remains unreleased at the time of this publication. Unfortunately, this last part of the story also comes with a note of discord. When offered $110,000 to return for *China Rich Girlfriend*, Adele Lim discovered co-screenwriter Peter Chiarelli would make as much as $1 million for the sequel. Though Warner Bros. described the disparity as "industry standard" based on their respective experience levels, Adele Lim quit the sequel in September of 2018, and declined another offer to return in the following February, when Chiarelli offered to split his salary with her. By then, the damage had long since been done. "Pete has been nothing but incredibly gracious, but what I make shouldn't

CRAZY RICH SEQUELS

A mid-credits scene in *Crazy Rich Asians* teases a spark between Astrid (Gemma Chan)—who has just left her cheating husband, Michael (Pierre Png)—and a handsome, mysterious man at a party (Harry Shum Jr.). Fans of the original novel and its sequels, *China Rich Girlfriend* and *Rich People Problems*, will recognize this man as (minor spoiler alert!) Astrid's hunky ex-boyfriend Charlie Wu, whose relationship with Astrid is a major arc in the following two books.

Jon M. Chu reveals that a lengthier dance scene between Astrid and Charlie was shot, but ultimately cut to keep the focus on Astrid's journey toward independence in *Crazy Rich Asians*. That hasn't stopped *Crazy Rich Asians* fans from clipping a few frames of Astrid and Charlie dancing, briefly glimpsed in the movie's first teaser, and turning them into GIFs to throw heart-eye emojis at.

be dependent on the generosity of the white-guy writer," she said in 2019.

When asked about this disappointing coda to the success of *Crazy Rich Asians*, Lim chooses her words carefully. "I didn't want to detract from the movie, and the goodwill, love, and warmth. How much it really built, and brought a lot of the Asian community together," she says. "But I was shocked when my agent first told me what the number was. I literally burst out laughing. I thought he was fucking with me. Because, honestly . . . what they were offering, I would have made more money being a mid-level TV writer on a CW show."

A rom-com as successful and enjoyable as *Crazy Rich Asians* is, undeniably, a major and important step forward. But it's also just *one* step, and many more will need to be taken before the film industry can fully take credit for finding, championing, and fairly compensating the creators who are going to push the romantic comedy—and the rest of Hollywood—to new and more interesting places.

Henry Golding

When he was looking for an actor to star as the romantic lead in *Crazy Rich Asians*, director Jon M. Chu issued his casting directors a warning: "You're not going to find them at an agency. Agencies won't rep them because there's no roles for them."

This is, of course, a self-fulfilling prophecy. Nobody writes movies centered on Asian leads because, people are warned, there are no bankable Asian actors to play them. And then, because they've been told there are no bankable Asian actors, no one writes leading roles for them.

It's not very often that a star truly comes out of nowhere. "Breakout" rom-coms stars, like Tom Hanks and Hugh Grant, had been working for years before the movies that propelled them to superstardom arrived. Chu was right, of course. In a version of an arc that will likely become more common as YouTube, TikTok, and other forms of social media end up surfacing the next generation of stars, Henry Golding ended up in *Crazy Rich Asians* because an accountant happened to remember seeing him being charming years before *Crazy Rich Asians* even existed.

No one could have predicted it, but Golding's personal background happened to dovetail perfectly with the charming, worldly rom-com hero novelist Kevin Kwan had originally conceived. "It was serendipitous because Henry's and Nick's backgrounds are so similar. Henry was born and grew up in Malaysia before being sent away to school in England, where he became very British," says Kwan. "We found the perfect combination of an actor who is comfortable with both Eastern and Western cultures, while remaining deeply rooted in his family obligations."

Golding, prone to following his whims wherever they take him, had dropped out of school at age sixteen to work as a hairdresser in London. When he tired of that, he moved to Kuala Lumpur, put together his own demo reel, and broke into a career as TV host. It wasn't *exactly* the arc of Nick Young, a dashing and cosmopolitan figure who split his time between three different continents—but Golding's curiosity and vague, amiable sense of restlessness were just what the character needed to come to life on the big screen.

Superstardom came fairly easily to Golding as well; just months after making his film debut in *Crazy Rich Asians*, *GQ* put him on the cover as a Man of the Year. "When I finished filming it, but before the movie was out, I went to a lot of these general Hollywood meetings," says Golding. "They'd have to look at the paper that had my face on it and a little bit of a bio. And they're like, '*Crazy Rich Asians*. What the hell is that? Is this, like, a television show? Is it a web series?' I'd be like, 'No, no. It's a movie. I think it's gonna be pretty big.'"

Owing, in part, to the fact that no one had seen him in anything else, Golding makes a strong impression from the first moment he walks onto the screen in *Crazy Rich Asians*. Handsome, charming, and entirely self-possessed, it's the kind of performance that should lead to a fast-track to stardom—as long as Hollywood is wise enough to open its doors this time around. Too often, a script written for a generic everyman is read, by un-thinking default, as a white guy, and plenty of would-be leading men who aren't white have been sidelined because of it.

But in his maneuvers since *Crazy Rich Asians* arrived, it's clear that Golding has a plan, and it seems to be working. In an interview with the *Los Angeles Times* leading up to the release of *Crazy Rich Asians*, Golding laid out his acting role models. "I want to bring back that old Hollywood charm. I want to be a leading man who is suave and sophisticated. I want to bring a little bit of intelligence back into leading men—the days of Gregory Peck, the days of Cary Grant, Paul Newman."

It's worth noting that all three of the men listed by Golding were also known for their versatility. Over the course of his career, Gregory Peck played heroes as novel as *To Kill a Mockingbird*'s Atticus Finch and villains as evil as the Nazi Josef Mengele. Cary Grant leapt from rom-coms like *His Girl Friday* and *The Philadelphia Story* to thrillers like *Suspicion* and *Notorious*. And Paul Newman frequently veered from charismatic to tortured within the same movie, and sometimes the same scene, before capping off his career by cheerfully voicing a talking car.

It's easy for actors to get pigeonholed—but if Golding's goal is a similar kind of versatility, he's off to a strong start. Having broken out in *Crazy Rich Asians*, Golding capitalized on his success with an eclectic slate. In addition to the upcoming *Crazy Rich Asians* sequels, and a second (and underrated!) holiday rom-com called *Last Christmas*, there was Paul Feig's campy thriller *A Simple Favor*, which weaponized Golding's charisma by making him a possible villain in his wife's disappearance; *Monsoon*, an intimate drama about a man returning to his native country to spread his parents' ashes; *The Gentlemen*, a Guy Ritchie action-comedy about British gangsters doing British gangster stuff; and *Snake Eyes*, a blockbuster about a G.I. Joe character you might remember if you were collecting action figures in the 1980s.

Maybe the most hopeful sign of Golding's career as an actor is his next project: appearing opposite Dakota Johnson in a new version of Jane Austen's *Persuasion*. Though he'd be an obvious fit for the romantic hero, Frederick Wentworth—described by Austen as "a remarkably fine young man, with a great deal of intelligence, spirit, and brilliancy"—Golding will instead play the sketchy Mr. Elliot, in what the Hollywood trades describe as a deliberate effort to play against type. It's the left-field kind of choice an actor makes when he's just starting to figure out what he can really do.

"This is our story, and we're still at the beginning."

—LARA JEAN, *TO ALL THE BOYS: P.S. I STILL LOVE YOU*

CHAPTER 16

TO ALL THE BOYS I'VE LOVED BEFORE

(And What Happens After Happily-Ever-After)

IN 2017, SCREENWRITER TIFFANY PAULSEN HEADED TO TEXAS TO MODER-
ate a panel at the Austin Film Festival. The panelists were a
who's-who of modern writers who specialize in rom-coms, from
Tess Morris—writer of *Man Up*, owner of a cat named after Nora
Ephron—to *(500) Days of Summer*'s Scott Neustadter and Michael H.
Weber.

The subject of the panel was romantic comedies, and since the
year was 2017, the conversation quickly shifted to the question of
whether the romantic comedy was dead. "It was funny," reflects
Paulsen. "The panel was literally held in this big church. Like,
'We are gathered here today' . . ."

Viewed today, the panel offers a fascinating snapshot of the
rom-com in transition. In 2017, the stigma at the studios was still
very real; Neustadter and Weber admit that anytime they sensed
that their pitch for a rom-com was making a producer wary, they
would start describing it as a "relationship movie" instead. "Even
then, sometimes they're like, 'Are there superheroes?'" said Neustadter. Meanwhile, in defiance of what seemed like the way the

wind was blowing, Tess Morris counseled the screenwriters in the audience to persevere. "If you love the genre, write the genre," she said. Her agent might have offered different advice.

Cut to a year later. It was November of 2018, and Tiffany Paulsen had been working on a movie called *Holidate* for the better part of a decade. It was a classic will-they/won't-they setup with a simple hook: A man and a woman, hoping to spare themselves the awkwardness of a string of nights alone, agree to be each other's platonic date to every holiday party over the course of a year, inevitably falling in love along the way. "I can't even tell you how long I had that idea," Paulsen says. "I wrote it, and I loved it. And it just became one of those things: 'Oh, this is really cute, Tiffany. Nobody's making romantic comedies anymore.'"

Until—quite suddenly, they were. McG, the director who had kicked off his Hollywood filmmaking career with movies like *Charlie's Angels* and *Terminator: Salvation*, had quietly carved out a side career producing romantic comedies for Netflix, including Ari Sandel's *When We First Met* and Nzingha Stewart's *Tall Girl*. When the *Holidate* script was sent his way, he knew he wanted it, and he wanted to make sure no one else would beat him to the punch. "He said, 'Give us twenty-four hours and let us see, give us an exclusive window,'" Paulsen says. It was a short window, but McG was true to his word. "I got the phone call the next day: 'Netflix loves it and we're going to make your movie.'" Netflix signed off on *Holidate* in November of 2018. By January of 2019, Emma Roberts was set to star. By May of 2019, the movie was in production.

Netflix is a maddeningly impenetrable company. They don't release official viewership numbers, and their internal metric for what counts as a "hit" is dubious at best. If you're going to judge

CRUNCHING THE DATA

Netflix's notoriously guarded approach to its viewership data even extends to the people behind its own movies. "What you get from them is top secret, and it's almost nothing. You're in those very, very confidential meetings, and you have to sign away your first three children," says Tiffany Paulsen. "They know exactly who's watching it, exactly when, exactly how many times. That had never been possible, really, before. I was getting these reports: '645,000 minutes of *Holidate* have been streamed.' I'm like . . . Is that good? I don't know if that's good."

what's working for the company on a real, tangible level, your best bet is to queue up the Netflix app, take a long scroll, and say, "Why are they producing so much of *this* right now?" And by that metric, the real story of Netflix's success over the past few years is romantic comedies.

A rare moment of genuine candor from Netflix came in 2018, when co-heads of indie film Matt Brodlie and Ian Bricke sat down with *The Hollywood Reporter* to explain why the streaming service had suddenly gone all-in on romantic comedies. As is typical for a tech start-up, it began with recognition that there was a gap in the marketplace. "We knew romantic comedies used to be a key piece of the studio slate, but the business has moved away from that model," says Bricke. "Where's *My Best Friend's Wedding* now? Where is *The Holiday*? Where are these films now? We asked our colleagues who keep track of what everyone is watching, and they said people are heavily watching our rom-coms from various studios. Our hunch was that people would like to see newer versions of them," says Brodlie.

As they reached out to agents and producers to see if they had any rom-com scripts, the Netflix team discovered, to their delight, that they were essentially alone in the market—able to pick and choose the best scripts available without fear of getting outbid by a studio or a rival streaming service. The first big acquisition was *The Kissing Booth,* which characteristically fell into a very specific target audience Netflix thought they could reach: teenagers who were growing out of movies aimed at kids, but not quite satisfied by rom-coms aimed at adults. "It felt like it was in this interesting spot in that it was a little bit more adult in sensibility than a Disney Channel movie but lighter than a lot of the teen/YA romance films we were seeing in the marketplace. We thought maybe there was a lane there," says Bricke.

The Kissing Booth is a singularly great example of how circuitous and unexpected the path to success can be in the streaming era. The story on which the movie was based was originally posted by fifteen-year-old British author Beth Reekles onto Wattpad, an online community where writers can post their stories for an audience of eager readers. As Reekles added a new chapter every few days, the story quickly caught on with the site's audience, eventually winning the Wattpad Award for Best Original Teen Fiction, which—in true, Netflix-style algorithmic fashion—got the story in front of even more eyeballs. It also drew the attention of an editor from Penguin Random House, who slipped into Reekles's DMs and offered her a three-book deal.

The novel was adapted and helmed by a little-known writer/director named Vince Marcello, who specialized in made-for-TV stuff for kids with titles like *Teen Beach Movie* and *Liar, Liar Vampire.* Netflix snagged the rights in 2016. When *The Kissing Booth* finally premiered in 2018, it was with very little fanfare, and it was shredded by the few critics who even bothered to review it. In one typical review, *IndieWire*'s Kate Erbland called it "a sexist and regressive look at relationships that highlights the worst impulses of the genre." Netflix didn't care, and by their account, its subscribers didn't either. Shortly after *The Kissing Booth*'s release, Netflix CEO Ted Sarandos claimed it was "one of the most-watched movies in the country, and maybe in the world." Later, Netflix asserted that *The Kissing Booth* had achieved a metric that no one ever had the ability to track before, until Netflix's innate ability to harvest data could be exploited: One in three viewers who watched *The Kissing Booth* later ended up watching it *again*.

This ratio might sound astounding in an era of unprecedented choice, where anyone who is looking for something new to watch has dozens of options—premiering across at least a dozen different services—every single week. But it will not sound astounding to anyone who loves romantic comedies, which have always benefited from the innate, comforting rewatchability of seeing lovely people fall in love. For a key subset of Netflix subscribers, rewatching *The Kissing Booth* was just the modern equivalent of rewinding and putting a worn-out copy of *Pretty Woman* back into your VCR. "There's a really intense level of engagement from a big part of this audience," says Bricke. "It's usually that sense of ownership—I found this, I want to share it with my friend, I want to watch it again and again."

As disruptive as they've been, Netflix's model is a simple one: Figure out what its subscribers want, and then figure out how to give them more of it. On a macro level, the success of Netflix rom-coms means more Netflix rom-coms. But on a micro level, the breakout success of an individual rom-com leads to a different series of questions: Can this individual rom-com generate one sequel? Two sequels? A full-blown fictional universe? In the case of *The Kissing Booth*, the answer was obvious: as many sequels as quickly as possible.

And so—thanks largely to Netflix (though a general shift toward franchises in the entertainment landscape certainly didn't hurt)—we've officially entered the age of the rom-com franchise. On a service like Netflix, the lines between film and TV are blurrier; it's all content for subscribers to stream, and there's every incentive in the world to follow up a hit movie with more of the same. *The Kissing Booth* premiered in the summer of 2018, as part of a full-court rom-com press that Netflix called the Summer of Love. When *The Kissing Booth* broke out more than fellow Summer of Love movies like *Ibiza* and *Alex Strangelove*, they were ready

IT'S BEGINNING TO LOOK A LOT LIKE CHRISTMAS

If you need more evidence of Netflix's far-reaching plans for its rom-coms, look no further than the strangely interconnected universe laid out in its cheesy Christmas rom-coms, which are clearly designed to compete with the similarly pitched movies that air every December on Lifetime and Hallmark. Netflix's *The Princess Switch: Switched Again*, which is set in the fictional country of Belgravia, ends with a royal wedding attended by Queen Amber and King Richard of Aldovia—who happen to be the couple at the center of Netflix's *Christmas Prince* trilogy. Maybe it's just an Easter egg for loyal viewers, but come on, you know *somebody* is out there trying to figure out how to make the *Avengers* of Christmas rom-coms.

to pounce; by the summer of 2021, two *Kissing Booth* sequels were available to stream on demand.

Unlike traditional Hollywood studios, Netflix doesn't build options for sequels into its deals with talent. Decisions are made only after a movie premieres on the service, when Netflix can gauge how the movie has performed, as well as which slice of its audience might be interested in watching more, and negotiate for future installments accordingly.

What makes a hit Netflix rom-com? There's no formula, but there are some similarities—most notably, a full pivot from the vaguely desperate-feeling sense of irony that has characterized the rom-coms being released before the mid-2000s crash. "I feel like the rom-com genre had moved in an edgier direction, and I think the audience is really responding to that sincerity and earnestness, that emotional directness that isn't trying to be too clever," says Ian Bricke. "I think that really connects."

If you want to look at the ideal test case for the Netflix model, your best bet is one of the streamer's most unambiguous crossover hits: the rom-com trilogy *To All the Boys I've Loved Before*.

Like *The Kissing Booth*, *To All the Boys* had a following long before it had a Netflix adaptation: author Jenny Han had released it as a YA novel in 2014. Like Kevin Kwan with *Crazy Rich Asians*, Jenny Han was approached by producers before her book was even published. And like Kevin Kwan with *Crazy Rich Asians*, Jenny Han turned down producers who wanted to make her Asian American protagonist white for the film. "I ended up deciding to work with the only production company that agreed the main character would be played by an Asian actress. No one else was willing to do it," says Han. "Still, I was holding my breath all the way up until shooting began because I was scared they would change their minds."

In the end, *To All the Boys* ended up being adapted by screen-writer Sofia Alvarez, who was committed to sticking to the book as closely as possible—an ideal draw for fans of the novels, who have largely come to prefer adaptations that are as literal to a 1:1 translation of the source material as possible. "With these kinds of adaptations, you have to have a really soft hand," says Alvarez. "For a book like this, that has such a loyal fanbase—you don't want to make too many changes, because you don't want them to not get what they paid for."

Like so many great rom-coms, *To All the Boys* has an irresist-ible hook. Whenever Lara Jean (Lana Condor), our high school heroine, has a crush, she writes a gushing letter to the object of her affection to get all the feelings out, knowing she'll never send it. When her younger sister actually mails all the letters, the morti-fied Lara Jean is forced to deal with the awkwardness while figur-ing out which guy she actually likes.

To All the Boys was directed by Susan Johnson, who had made her debut with the teen dramedy *Carrie Pilby* in 2016. Johnson shared Alvarez's vision of an extremely faithful adaptation that would please fans of the novel—even enlisting an assistant to keep tabs on what the online fan communities were saying so she could integrate their thoughts into her film. "All the way down to colors of shirts," she says.

More than anything, the fans were obviously most interested in the actors who would be cast to play Lara Jean; her neighbor and crush Josh, who receives one of her letters; and Peter Kavin-sky, the charming, popular jock who receives another letter and eventually becomes her primary love interest across the trilogy. As Johnson recalls, she had narrowed it down to roughly five ac-tors for each role, including eventual stars Lana Condor, Noah Centineo, and Israel Broussard. "Lana was quite the exciting find.

Once she walked in the room, I was like, 'Oh, we have our movie now. It's going to happen,'" she says. Casting Cetineo and Broussard was slightly more complicated—not because she doubted that they were right for the film, but because she couldn't decide which was better for Peter Kavinsky and which was better for Josh. "They were almost interchangeable to me. I was like, 'What if Israel plays Peter, and Noah plays Josh?' It could have worked, but I'm sure glad that we went a different way," she says. The decision finally came down to a chemistry read between Condor and Centineo. "They just clicked really quickly," says Johnson. "They were so close on set. It was never romantic, but they could flip into that really quickly."

Like so many classic romantic comedies, that chemistry is apparent on-screen, and it manifested on set in some telling ways. (The lock screen on Lara Jean's phone—a picture of Lara Jean and Peter cuddling on a couch—was a candid snap taken by the set photographer of Condor and Centineo resting during a night shoot, which inevitably sent the fan base into a breathless tizzy.) It's a dynamic that charges the entire movie, which delves into

CASTING CORBETT

According to Susan Johnson, casting John Corbett as Lara Jean's doting dad was an intentional nod to his own memorable place in rom-com history. "Those guys were too young to know what that means," she says. "I was excited to hire someone my own age for that role. I was a big *Sex and the City* fan, and a big *My Big Fat Greek Wedding* fan. He was at the top of my list. He never even read for us. And we were so happy when he said yes."

teen-soap plotting—a fake relationship, an embarrassing cell phone video, a stolen scrunchie—but is always compelling when the focus is on Lara Jean and Peter Kavinsky. By the end of the movie, it's impossible not to be rooting for these kids—and even more importantly for Netflix, to want to see more of them.

When Netflix acquired *To All the Boys*, it was already completed, and they requested no changes. Instead, they came in with a team of marketing wizards who sat down and explained exactly how they would get the movie in front of as many eyeballs as possible across the entire globe. "You sit down at a table with like eighteen different people, and they all have completely different jobs, and it's very intensive," says Johnson. "They show you colors, and pictures, and thoughts on where they're going to release it, and how, and what it's going to look like in other countries. To say they 'got' the film is an understatement. I'm convinced that

HOW NETFLIX GETS IN YOUR HEAD

One of Netflix's most pragmatic methods for figuring out how to get subscribers to click on their content is A/B testing, in which the "Recommended" window that pops up after you finish streaming one movie or TV series can be used to promote another movie or TV series using artwork specifically tailored to each subscriber's previous viewing habits. Unlike traditional movie posters—which are necessarily static, since they're, uh, printed on paper—Netflix can generate many different pieces of art for a single movie, and micro-target each image to the type of subscribers they think would be most likely to click on it. "Hypothetically, you watch *Riverdale* and a shot of shirtless Jacob Elordi shows up for you for *The Kissing Booth* and you're like, 'Oh, I'll watch that,'" says Ian Bricke.

at 6:00 P.M., that office building at 6:00 P.M. goes down into the ground. Like magic. I mean, clearly they're running the world at this point."

Netflix's plan worked. More importantly, it was proof that a rom-com could amass a staggering amount of buzz, and launch an entire franchise, on Netflix. Just two days after *Crazy Rich Asians* hit theaters, the service had its own charming summer rom-com—ready to stream for anyone who didn't feel like trekking to a movie theater, or whose appetite had been whetted for more rom-coms after doing it. "I'm a tried-and-true film person. I try to see everything in the theater. But *To All the Boys* really was a turning point for me," says Johnson. "Seeing it come out in so many countries at the same moment was a really amazing experience, because you started to see it blossom online within the first twenty-four hours. And then the first forty-eight hours. And then the week. And people were sharing stories, and talking about how much it meant to them *immediately*. You don't get that experience from a traditional release."

It's hard not to think of a streaming-only movie like *To All the Boys* as existing in the shadow of a splashy theatrical release like *Crazy Rich Asians*, but while Netflix still refuses to release its numbers, there's a very real chance more people ended up seeing *To All the Boys* across the globe. "*To All the Boys* was a hit everywhere for us—everywhere in the world," says Ian Bricke. "At one point we were all sitting down and they said, 'This is the most rewatched movie in the history of Netflix, and here are the numbers'—which were *enormous*," says Johnson. "And your brain goes, 'Oh, gee, if I got ten cents of every ticket, I would be buying countries at this point.'"

Which meant, of course, that *To All the Boys* was no longer a stand-alone romantic comedy; it was the first installment in a

SOCIAL STARS

In the absence of traditional ratings, one of Netflix's most unconventional metrics for success is pegged directly to the social-media clout of its stars. Shortly after *The Kissing Booth* premiered, Netflix CEO Ted Sarandos attempted to prove its success by citing the IMDb Star-o-Meter, which ranks actors based on search popularity. Following *The Kissing Booth*, Joey King had jumped from somewhere in the 17,000s to number six, and Jacob Elordi had jumped from somewhere in the 25,000s to number one. In a similar vein, after *To All the Boys I've Loved Before* premiered, Netflix bragged about its popularity by citing the Instagram account of star Noah Centineo, which had gained 13.4 million new followers since the movie premiered.

promising new Netflix franchise. And fortunately, Jenny Han's two sequel novels made it quick and easy for Netflix to rush two more Lara Jean stories for eager fans to stream. "I look at all three books and all three films as one story. So, each film is just an act within that larger, Lara Jean journey," says Michael Fimognari, the director of the second and third installments in the franchise. And that's more or less what he released. The subsequent two movies—which followed Lara Jean as she was courted by a rival suitor, then ended as she and Peter Kavinsky embarked on a long-distance relationship at two different colleges by writing each other letters—wrapped up their love story in a clever, circular fashion. Better still, it guaranteed that Netflix would have an acclaimed and bingeable or (re-bingeable) rom-com trilogy for present or future subscribers to enjoy anytime they like—the same way a previous generation of teenagers might have returned to a treasured VHS copy of *Pretty Woman*.

Incredibly—though, given the hit-hungry climate in Hollywood, not surprisingly—that's still not the end of the story. Netflix may have run out of *To All the Boys* sequels to adapt, but that's not going to stop them from building out the *To All the Boys* universe. The streaming service is in the process of developing a series centered on Lara Jean's younger sister Kitty and chronicling her own "quest to find to true love," as part of a broader scheme to turn its biggest hits into interconnected franchises that will flow seamlessly between film and TV installments—at least as long as the data shows that subscribers still want more. And when they move on, there will be reams of data and algorithms to point them toward the next rom-com they're likeliest to love.

DON'T COUNT HULU OUT

Netflix may be leading the charge in the streaming rom-com revival, but don't count Hulu out of the race. In 2020, Hulu put out statements announcing that two of its biggest movies that year were rom-coms: the acclaimed time-loop rom-com *Palm Springs*, which the service bought for a record amount at the Sundance Film Festival, and Clea DuVall's semi-autobiographical rom-com *Happiest Season*, which was snapped up by Hulu after Sony cancelled a planned theatrical release due to the COVID-19 pandemic. The streamer also made an effort to reimagine classic rom-coms as TV shows, with series based on both *High Fidelity* and *Four Weddings and a Funeral*—though neither made it past a single season.

Conclusion

IF YOU READ THIS BOOK'S SUBTITLE CAREFULLY, YOU'LL KNOW THAT THIS story is almost over: We've covered the rise, the fall, and the rise again of the romantic comedy. There's only one question left to answer: Where are rom-coms going next?

It starts, in an increasingly nostalgia-focused industry, with replaying the old hits, which are finding new life with new audiences. There are already stage musicals based on *Pretty Woman, Sleepless in Seattle, My Best Friend's Wedding,* and *The Wedding Singer,* with *There's Something About Mary* close behind. Others have received belated reimaginings on television, including the recent BET sequel series to 1992's *Boomerang* and the upcoming small-screen riffs on *Waiting to Exhale* and *How to Lose a Guy in 10 Days.*

But this book is about movies—and like pretty much every other genre, everything is trending toward franchises, with any hit being evaluated for whether it might be able to spawn more hits. From *To All the Boys* to *The Kissing Booth* to *The Christmas Prince,* Netflix has never had a win it wasn't happy to double down on. At the traditional studios, there may be a fourth *Bridget Jones,* and there will surely be a third *Big Fat Greek Wedding.* Those blockbusting *Crazy Rich Asians* sequels are still coming. And you know it's only a matter of time before someone sells their pitch for a full-blown Rom-Com Cinematic Universe, set in an adorable town full of star-crossed lovers who can cross paths in any number of combinations—a *Love Actually* that unfolds its tangled web of love stories over a half-dozen movies instead of one.

The rise of the rom-com is not just hypothetical. The smash success of *Crazy Rich Asians* has encouraged both Hollywood studios and Hollywood stars to return to the genre, and at the time of this publication there are a number of rom-coms bound for actual movie theaters. The year 2022 will feature Jennifer Lopez's triumphant rom-com return in two different movies: *Marry Me* (from Universal) and *Shotgun Wedding* (from Lionsgate). Even Sandra Bullock, who had previously indicated her reluctance about the genre, is set to star opposite Channing Tatum in *The Lost City of D*, an action rom-com in the vein of the genre classic *Romancing the Stone*. Soon after will come Universal's *Bros*, a passion project for cowriter and star Billy Eichner, who has long lamented a lack of romantic comedies centered on gay men.

It's always wise to maintain some healthy skepticism about Hollywood, which has repeatedly failed to evolve when it was obviously needed on both moral and business grounds. But there really *are* promising signs that talented writers, filmmakers, and performers are finding never-before-available opportunities to tell rom-com stories that reflect the full spectrum of love—which has the welcome bonus of ensuring that the genre is more relevant, to a wider and more diverse audience, than it ever was before.

There will surely be ups and downs for the rom-com genre in the decades to come—but for now, it's enough to appreciate that the genre seems to have an unusually bright future on the horizon.

The "death" of the rom-com was always greatly exaggerated, be-cause there will always be filmmakers who want to tell love stories, actors who want to be in them, and—most of all—moviegoers who are always ready to laugh and swoon at them. It's like they've always said: Real love stories never have endings.

Acknowledgments

THIS BOOK WOULDN'T EXIST WITHOUT THE CONTRIBUTIONS, HARD WORK, and support of many, many people. I'd like to express my personal gratitude to:

The dozens of people who agreed to be interviewed for this book. I'm deeply appreciative of your time and candor and am humbled that you trusted me with your stories.

Noah Ballard, who understood and believed in this idea since our first conversation about it.

Matthew Daddona and Rosy Tahan, my tireless, attentive, and endlessly thoughtful editors, whose notes sharpened my thinking and improved every page.

The team at HarperCollins who played key roles in bringing this book to life: Joel Holland, Michelle Crowe, Melanie Bedor, Jeanie Lee, Andrew DeWerd, and Christina Joell.

Alex Kittle, an artist whose talent is matched only by what a joy it is to collaborate with her.

Barb Eggerth, who transcribes so quickly and accurately that it must qualify as a superpower.

Brian and Marcia Freeman, who are invariably quick and generous with their wisdom and perspective.

Mom and Dad, who nurtured and encouraged my fascination

with film from the very beginning (and who once celebrated their anniversary with a custom WHEN DOUG MET JENNY poster).

Jen, whose role in this process (and in my life) can't possibly be summarized here.

Cora, who teaches me something new about love every day.

Notes

INTRODUCTION

3 the premature eulogy: https://www.nytimes.com/2008/02/03/movies/03scot
.html.

CHAPTER 1: WHEN HARRY MET SALLY . . .

5 "almost like a romantic comedy meeting": https://www.youtube.com/watch?v
=eox8bdJDT_Q.

6 "It didn't interest me at all": *When Harry Met Sally . . .* screenplay (New York:
Knopf, 1990), introduction.

7 fought for script approval: https://www.newyorker.com/magazine/2009/07/06
/nora-knows-what-to-do.

7 "She interviewed us like a journalist": https://www.thedailybeast.com/rob
-reiner-remembers-nora-ephron-the-sally-to-his-harry.

8 Ephron had originally imagined: Rachel Abramowitz, *Is That a Gun in Your
Pocket? The Truth About Female Power in Hollywood* (New York: Random House,
2002), 381.

8 who called the writing sessions: Abramowitz, 382.

8 Ephron originally called: https://www.thedailybeast.com/when-harry-met
-sally-turns-25-director-rob-reiner-reveals-the-secrets-of-the-romcom-classic?
ref=scroll.

8 "essentially Woody's *Scenes from a Marriage*": https://timesmachine.nytimes
.com/timesmachine/1977/04/21/issue.html?auth=login-email.

10 "Rob always said it's the kind of movie": https://archive.seattletimes.com/ar
chive/?date=20010216&slug=harry16.

10 Reiner's *actual* best friend: https://www.thedailybeast.com/when-harry-met-sally-turns-25-director-rob-reiner-reveals-the-secrets-of-the-romcom-classic?ref=scroll.

10 As Crystal recalls it: Billy Crystal, *Still Foolin' 'Em: Where I've Been, Where I'm Going, and Where the Hell Are My Keys?* (New York: Henry Holt & Co., 2013), 133.

11 names like Debra Winger and Molly Ringwald were kicked around: https://www.thedailybeast.com/when-harry-met-sally-turns-25-director-rob-reiner-reveals-the-secrets-of-the-romcom-classic?ref=scroll.

12 as "another director": https://www.youtube.com/watch?v=XcQ3Tg0wTAA.

12 "The movie was so personal to him": Crystal, 134.

13 "After most of our shooting days": Crystal, 135.

13 "People would ask me: 'I don't understand.'": https://www.youtube.com/watch?v=XcQ3Tg0wTAA.

14 "something that women know but men don't know": https://www.usatoday.com/story/life/movies/2019/04/12/when-harry-met-sally-meg-ryan-multiple-fake-orgasm-scenes/3444171002/.

14 "That day was a very odd day for Meg": https://www.youtube.com/watch?v=XcQ3Tg0wTAA.

15 as Rob Reiner later recalled: https://www.cheatsheet.com/entertainment/princess-diana-when-harry-met-sally.html/.

15 "You've got a whole restaurant": https://www.youtube.com/watch?v=XcQ3Tg0wTAA.

15 "Well, there's a whole world of that, too": https://www.youtube.com/watch?v=XcQ3Tg0wTAA.

16 recalled Reiner: https://film.avclub.com/rob-reiner-on-his-favorite-films-and-why-he-changed-th-1798251871.

16 "I was bemoaning my lack-of-woman fate": https://www.nytimes.com/1989/07/09/movies/film-can-men-and-women-be-friends.html

16 "People ask me all the time": https://www.youtube.com/watch?v=XcQ3Tg0wTAA.

17 "We had nothing to do with his movie": Delia Ephron, *Sister Mother Husband Dog* (London: Penguin, 2013).

17 She had already taken a lesson: Abramowitz, 381.

18 "When I wrote *When Harry Met Sally*": Abramowitz, 442–443.

19 "The studio was going to release it wide": Ephron, 198.

19 "couldn't do it": https://abcnews.go.com/Entertainment/julia-roberts-passed-sleepless-seattle/story?id=24934295.

19 Meg Ryan and Kevin Costner in mind: https://www.pennlive.com/life-and-culture/erry-2018/11/71b2bd34041075/sleepless-in-seattle-screenwri.html.

20 "Romantic comedy, as a genre": https://www.nytimes.com/1998/12/13/movies/film-she-s-a-director-with-an-edge-she-s-a-writer.html.

21 "Tom Hanks had a lot of input": Ephron, 202.

22 "Our dream was to make a movie": Liz Dance, *Nora Ephron: Everything Is Copy* (Jefferson, NC: McFarland & Co., 2015).

22 for that matter: Lynda Obst, *Hello He Lied: And Other Truths from the Hollywood Trenches* (New York: Crown, 1996), 18.

ESSAY: MEG RYAN: AMERICA'S SWEETHEART (UNTIL SHE WASN'T)

24 a whopping 20 million viewers: https://www.inquirer.com/philly/entertain ment/20100914_As_the_world_stops_turning__we_honor_its_super-couples .html.

25 "and been funny": https://www.vanityfair.com/hollywood/1995/05/meg-ryan -cover-story.

25 "The girl next door to what?": https://www.today.com/popculture/meg-ryan -says-dennis-quaid-cheated-her-wbna26859077.

25 "couldn't find a false note in": https://www.rogerebert.com/reviews/when-a -man-loves-a-woman-1994.

25 *Forget Paris*: https://ew.com/article/1995/07/14/paris-match-became-french -kiss/.

26 Quaid himself had been unfaithful: https://www.today.com/popculture/meg -ryan-says-dennis-quaid-cheated-her-wbna26859077.

26 a friend of Ryan's at the time: https://people.com/archive/cover-story-meg-on -her-own-vol-56-no-2/.

26 "rude and stupid": https://www.irishtimes.com/life-and-style/people/meg -ryan-graham-norton-cancer-and-me-michael-parkinson-at-80-1.2557222.

26 played out in the British press for months: https://www.theguardian.com /film/2003/dec/15/2003inreview.

27 "I felt done when they felt done, probably": https://www.nytimes.com/interac tive/2019/02/15/magazine/meg-ryan-romantic-comedy.html.

27 "they're not things I want to do": https://www.nytimes.com/interactive /2019/02/15/magazine/meg-ryan-romantic-comedy.html.

27 a "scarlet woman": https://www.today.com/popculture/meg-ryan-says-dennis -quaid-cheated-her-wbna26859077.

27 "with the intention to delight": https://www.nytimes.com/interactive/2019 /02/15/magazine/meg-ryan-romantic-comedy.html.

27 "It's actually pretty enriching and great": https://www.latimes.com/entertain ment/movies/la-et-mn-meg-ryan-ithaca-profile-20160915-snap-story.html.

CHAPTER 2: PRETTY WOMAN

32 The Vivians That Weren't: Meir Doron and Joseph Gelman, *Confidential: The Life of Secret Agent Turned Hollywood Icon Arnon Milchan* (Jerusalem: Gefen, 2011), 205.

32 "the whole of womankind": https://www.marieclaire.co.uk/entertainment/tv
-and-film/julia-roberts-pretty-woman-650054.

32 "Really exciting": https://nymag.com/nymetro/arts/theater/15247/.

33 "I didn't have a job": https://variety.com/2019/tv/features/patricia-arquette
-julia-roberts-escape-at-dannemora-the-act-homecoming-1203231800/.

34 "'Are they going to animate it?'": https://variety.com/2019/tv/features
/patricia-arquette-julia-roberts-escape-at-dannemora-the-act-homecoming
-1203231800/.

34 "and everyone else": https://www.latimes.com/archives/la-xpm-1991–06–09
-ca-675-story.html.

35 "other half were saying the opposite": https://ew.com/article/1991/11/22
/julia-roberts-price-fame/.

35 on the last possible day: https://www.latimes.com/archives/la-xpm-1991–06–09
-ca-675-story.html.

36 "rooted for no one": https://screenwritingfromiowa.wordpress.com/2012/10
/03/writing-rewriting-pretty-woman-part-2/.

39 "school of happy endings": https://www.biography.com/news/julia-roberts
-pretty-woman-dark-ending.

41 yes, *that* Sting: https://www.latimes.com/archives/la-xpm-1991–06–09-ca-675
-story.html.

42 "a Donald Trump–style executive with a vulnerable side": https://screenwrit
ingfromiowa.wordpress.com/2012/10/03/writing-rewriting-pretty-woman
-part-2/.

42 "I still hadn't decided": https://ew.com/article/2012/08/31/richard-gere-gere/.

43 "I had to find a way of playing this guy": https://abcnews.go.com/Entertain
ment/video/3221990-richard-gere-talks-pretty-woman-29844280.

43 "complained every day on the movie": https://www.hollywoodreporter.com
/news/julia-roberts-honors-garry-marshall-at-pretty-woman-musical-1132051.

43 he never even read: https://www.youtube.com/watch?v=YBjBW_smZTA.

45 his vision of *Pretty Woman* as a fairy tale: https://www.biography.com/news
/julia-roberts-pretty-woman-dark-ending.

46 "when we got there": James Spada, *Julia: Her Life* (New York: St. Martin's Press,
2004), 134.

47 There were three contenders: Spada, 156.

48 "but put a glass slipper on": https://www.nytimes.com/1993/12/12/movies
/film-julia-roberts-after-the-layoff-and-with-lyle.html.

49 a whole parade of stars joined: https://www.latimes.com/archives/la-xpm
-1999-aug-03-ca-62033-story.html.

50 "we didn't find anything we liked": https://people.com/movies/garry-marshall
-death-behind-the-scenes-of-pretty-woman/.

ESSAY: SANDRA BULLOCK: MISS CONGENIALITY

52 conceived as a riff on *Sleeping Beauty*: https://www.washingtonpost.com/life style/style/while-you-were-sleeping-sandra-bullock-oral-history/2020/04/20 /13f37222-7e8b-11ea-9040-68981f488eed_story.html.

52 "You just wouldn't believe that": https://www.washingtonpost.com/lifestyle /style/while-you-were-sleeping-sandra-bullock-oral-history/2020/04/20/13f 37222-7e8b-11ea-9040-68981f488eed_story.html.

53 "The press started this whole rivalry": https://www.oprah.com/omagazine /oprah-interviews-julia-roberts/3.

53 "I think Julia and I should": https://www.eonline.com/news/868935/the-ever -adorable-sandra-bullock-how-her-private-life-has-kept-her-grounded-through -20-years-of-being-america-s-reluctant-sweetheart.

53 $12 million asking price: https://ew.com/article/1995/12/15/demi-moore -julia-roberts-and-sandra-bullock-find-greener-pastures/.

54 "let's get back to being funny!": https://www.theguardian.com/film/2010 /mar/21/sandra-bullock-the-blind-side.

54 "happens to be amongst friends": https://metro.co.uk/2013/07/21/sandra -bullock-the-heat-is-a-love-story-between-me-and-melissa-mccarthy-3892071/.

54 2015's *Our Brand Is Crisis*: https://ew.com/article/2015/10/30/sandra-bullock -our-brand-crisis/.

55 both of those roles, too: https://www.latimes.com/archives/la-xpm-2009-dec-16 -la-et-globesfilm16-2009dec16-story.html.

CHAPTER 3: FOUR WEDDINGS AND A FUNERAL

58 French softcore pornos called *Emmanuelle:* https://www.telegraph.co.uk/culture /film/10292266/Richard-Curtiss-muse-exposed-as-mother-of-four-who-broke -his-heart.html.

58 "I owe her my movie career": https://www.telegraph.co.uk/culture/film/10292 266/Richard-Curtiss-muse-exposed-as-mother-of-four-who-broke-his-heart.html.

58 "put life right": https://cherwell.org/2009/11/19/interview-richard-curtis/.

59 "with a bit of love in it": https://cherwell.org/2009/11/19/interview-richard -curtis/.

60 inconsistent on the exact number: https://www.mentalfloss.com/article/735 09/15-splendid-facts-about-four-weddings-and-funeral#:~:text=SCREEN WRITER%20RICHARD%20CURTIS%20HAD%20PLENTY,upped%20 the%20number%20to%2072.

60 "failed to follow up on it": https://deadline.com/2019/03/four-weddings -funeral-richard-curtis-working-title-mike-newell-british-industry-1202575370/.

60 "every minute they spent together": https://www.irishtimes.com/news/richard -the-uncrowned-king-of-britfilm-1.187923.

61 the movie needed a funeral: https://www.theguardian.com/film/2009/mar /22/richard-curtis-the-boat-that-rocked.

61 "got some profundity in my work": https://www.irishtimes.com/news/richard -the-uncrowned-king-of-britfilm-1.187923.

61 "shamelessly nicked incidents": *Four Weddings and a Funeral* published screenplay.

61 "watching with a notebook": https://www.standard.co.uk/news/londoners -diary/londoner-s-diary-bernard-jenkin-bites-back-at-his-old-love-rival-richard -curtis-10427480.html.

61 He says he "lived in terror": *Four Weddings* published screenplay (p. 9).

61 an outright disaster: https://www.theguardian.com/film/2003/nov/13/british identity.

62 who read *Four Weddings and a Funeral* was Duncan Kenworthy: https://www .screendaily.com/features/stars-of-tomorrow-one-to-one-duncan-kenworthy -and-loran-dunn/5122818.article.

63 "acting would last about a year": https://www.latimes.com/entertainment-arts /tv/story/2020–11–27/the-undoing-hbo-hugh-grant.

63 multiple takes of the same scene: https://www.youtube.com/watch?v=QFF H2YWuxE0.

64 "managed to sell out": https://www.npr.org/transcripts/940175187.

64 audiences in the United States: https://archive.vanityfair.com/article/2003/5 /runaway-bachelor.

64 "and bad accents": http://www.bbc.co.uk/films/2002/04/17/hugh_grant_ about_a_boy_interview.shtml.

64 "'you sent me a good script'": https://www.cheatsheet.com/entertainment /hugh-grant-said-his-early-acting-choices-almost-killed-his-career-1-movie -changed-everything.html/.

64 "it slightly sickened them": https://www.digitalspy.com/movies/a600650 /hugh-grant-nobody-wanted-me-in-four-weddings-and-a-funeral/.

65 "you may never be asked to write another one": *Four Weddings* published screen- play (p. 10).

66 "starting thesis of the film": https://www.radiotimes.com/tv/comedy/richard -curtis-hugh-grant-was-too-good-looking-not-too-posh-for-four-weddings/.

66 "would get the girl": https://www.npr.org/transcripts/940175187.

66 "the world's worst haircut": https://www.npr.org/transcripts/940175187.

67 "'You didn't need the extra money'": https://www.theguardian.com/film/2014 /apr/27/four-weddings-and-a-funeral-20-years-richard-curtis-remembers.

68 while he was on a personal vacation: https://www.independent.co.uk/arts -entertainment/films/features/gosh-crikey-has-it-been-20-years-four-wed dings-and-funeral-9160162.html.

68 "one of the best I've ever come across": https://www.theguardian.com/film /2019/nov/19/how-we-made-four-weddings-and-a-funeral-andie-macdowell -mike-newell.

68 "40 years earlier": https://ew.com/article/1994/05/06/four-weddings-and -funeral-surprise-hit/.

69 "Excessive Thrusting": https://www.theguardian.com/film/2014/apr/27/four -weddings-and-a-funeral-20-years-richard-curtis-remembers.

70 "or what she'd done": https://www.theguardian.com/film/2020/dec/03 /richard-curtis-on-four-weddings-i-dont-know-how-fully-i-thought-through -andie-macdowells-character.

70 "playing the truths rather than the gags": https://ew.com/article/1994/05/06 /four-weddings-and-funeral-surprise-hit/.

70 "not just three funny lines": https://ew.com/article/1994/05/06/four-weddings -and-funeral-surprise-hit/.

71 "And then you make them cry": https://www.youtube.com/watch?v=Feyn I7hpkJA.

71 "if there's proper pain somewhere": http://www.style.com/w/feat_story /032102/full_page.html.

71 it sold 275,000 copies: https://www.bl.uk/20th-century-literature/articles/an -introduction-to-stop-all-the-clocks#.

74 $245 million worldwide: https://www.the-numbers.com/movie/Four-Wed dings-and-a-Funeral#tab=box-office.

75 "pretty people in pretty clothes": https://ew.com/article/1994/05/06/four -weddings-and-funeral-surprise-hit/.

76 published by *Entertainment Weekly*: https://ew.com/article/1994/05/06/four -weddings-and-funeral-surprise-hit/.

77 A 2012 investigation: https://www.latimes.com/entertainment/la-et-unmask ing-oscar-academy-project-20120219-story.html.

77 the numbers had only shifted: https://www.goodmorningamerica.com/cul ture/story/oscars-2019-makes-academy-voting-body-voting-process-6083 0793.

ESSAY: HUGH GRANT: THE HARDEST-WORKING CAD IN HOLLYWOOD

80 "kissing Sandra Bullock": https://www.nytimes.com/2002/05/17/movies/at -the-movies.html.

80 "make me better": https://www.latimes.com/entertainment-arts/tv/story/2020 -11-27/the-undoing-hbo-hugh-grant.

80 "He took Hugh with him": https://www.theguardian.com/film/2020/dec/03 /richard-curtis-on-four-weddings-i-dont-know-how-fully-i-thought-through -andie-macdowells-character.

81 "It's really kind of Richard": https://www.latimes.com/entertainment-arts/tv /story/2020-11-27/the-undoing-hbo-hugh-grant.

81 "any particular interest in that genre": https://www.youtube.com/watch?v =QFFH2YWuxE0.

81 "must provide some service": https://www.latimes.com/entertainment-arts/tv /story/2020-11-27/the-undoing-hbo-hugh-grant.

81 "which has been a great blessing": https://www.smh.com.au/culture/tv-and -radio/hugh-grant-is-old-ugly-and-not-appropriate-for-romantic-comedies -and-he-s-loving-it-20201019-p566bl.html.

82 "felt like she had been shot": https://www.theguardian.com/film/from-the -archive-blog/2015/jun/26/hugh-grant-arrest-prostitute-divine-brown-20 -1995.

83 "the greatest PR save of all time": https://www.independent.co.uk/news /people/news/divine-redemption-hugh-grant-look-greatest-pr-save-all-time -almost-20-years-after-he-was-arrested-prostitute-9073158.html.

CHAPTER 4: WAITING TO EXHALE

85 personally sent out thousands of letters: https://www.nytimes.com/1992/08/09 /magazine/mcmillan-s-millions.html.

85 $4.75 million lawsuit: https://www.latimes.com/archives/la-xpm-1990-10-29 -vw-2633-story.html.

85 "record orders of her books": https://www.nytimes.com/1992/08/09/maga zine/mcmillan-s-millions.html.

87 "I've had 1,500 people show up": https://www.nytimes.com/1992/08/09/mag azine/mcmillan-s-millions.html.

91 "always wanted" Angela Bassett for Bernadine: https://www.newyorker.com /magazine/1996/04/29/a-crossover-star.

92 first year of its release: https://www.cheatsheet.com/entertainment/the-wait ing-to-exhale-movie-soundtrack-was-released-24-years-ago-and-was-the-first -to-include-this.html/.

92 "shoops started to make sense to me": https://www.billboard.com/articles /columns/the-juice/6762502/babyface-waiting-to-exhale-soundtrack-20-year -anniversary.

93 "We thought this movie would start a chain of films": https://www.blackfilm .com/read/2012/07/director-reginald-hudlin-talks-boomerang-20-years-later -black-panther-django-unchained/.

93 she had resolved to quit acting: https://www.latimes.com/archives/la-xpm -1996-03-30-ca-52846-story.html.

93 Rochon called in favors: https://www.dailymotion.com/video/x7wbjsi.

93 had booked the role: https://www.dailymotion.com/video/x7wbjsi.

94 "small roles in good films": https://www.orlandosentinel.com/news/os-xpm -1996-08-16-9608150790-story.html.

94 "by strangers in public": https://zora.medium.com/angela-bassett-and-her -waiting-to-exhale-co-stars-on-that-scene-967263cc58e2.

93 "hard and long": http://www.classicwhitney.com/interview/ebony_may1995.htm.

94 "I loved that": https://zora.medium.com/angela-bassett-and-her-waiting-to-exhale-co-stars-on-that-scene-967263cc58e2.

95 "That is a bunch of bull": https://www.latimes.com/archives/la-xpm-1996–01–14-op-24329-story.html.

98 "response to this movie": https://www.latimes.com/archives/la-xpm-1996–01–09-ca-22497-story.html.

98 "the story of four black girls did well": https://www.newyorker.com/magazine/1996/04/29/a-crossover-star.

98 "You guys need to pay attention": https://www.latimes.com/archives/la-xpm-1996–01–14-op-24329-story.html.

99 "That's it": https://www.latimes.com/archives/la-xpm-1996–01–14-op-24329-story.html.

100 *The Best Man*'s Malcolm D. Lee: https://thegeekiary.com/malcolm-d-lee-continues-his-beloved-franchise-with-hollywood-homecomings-the-best-man/94322.

100 *Brown Sugar*'s Rick Famuyiwa: https://www.latimes.com/archives/la-xpm-1997-nov-30-ca-58989-story.html.

100 "you really can only fail once": https://www.nytimes.com/2019/07/03/movies/black-directors-1990s.html.

101 "complicated lives of their daughters": https://deadline.com/2020/11/waiting-to-exhale-drama-series-reboot-sequel-followup-lee-daniels-abc-1234618077/.

102 the movie would only be delayed: https://www.vulture.com/2012/02/fox-will-press-on-with-waiting-to-exhale-after-whitney-houstons-passing.html.

ESSAY: BILL PULLMAN, PATRICK DEMPSEY, ET AL.: THE OTHER GUYS

103 "the one you really love": http://www.thebaxtermovie.com/.

105 "to take the first male lead": https://www.avclub.com/bill-pullman-on-how-to-play-the-president-and-being-the-1798235663.

CHAPTER 5: MY BEST FRIEND'S WEDDING

111 "Everyone knows that": https://www.usmagazine.com/entertainment/pictures/biggest-costar-feuds-and-fights-ever-w207187/charlies-angels-bill-murray-vs-lucy-liu-w207197/.

111 slated to star: https://people.com/archive/cover-story-hidden-star-vol-39-no-5/.

111 "first person they offered it to": https://variety.com/2019/film/features/gwyneth-paltrow-shakespeare-in-love-20th-anniversary-oscars-1203141616/.

111 the story was false: https://www.huffpost.com/entry/gwyneth-paltrow-interview-howard-stern_n_6472500.

112 no matter how banal: https://www.vanityfair.com/news/1999/06/canoodling-with-julia.

113   "Charles Grodin's character in 1984's *The Woman in Red*": https://www.ad vocate.com/media/2020/11/20/history-gay-best-friend-film-and-tv#media -gallery-media-2.

113   "to death like that": https://www.vulture.com/2018/10/rupert-everett-inter view-oscar-wilde-and-the-happy-prince.html.

119   "'Rupert *is* this part'": Rupert Everett, *Red Carpets and Other Banana Skins* (New York: Grand Central Publishing, 2007), 250.

120   "a vivid relationship effortlessly materializes": Everett, 252.

120   couldn't relax around Cameron: https://www.dailymail.co.uk/tvshowbiz/arti cle-403481/Rupert-Everett-My-life-divas-1.html.

ESSAY: JUDY GREER: THE BEST BEST FRIEND

129   "'Kate Hudson running around'": https://www.hollywoodreporter.com/news /kathryn-hahn-was-definitely-a-best-friend-chapter-my-career-i-love-dick -comedy-actress-roundtable-1013475.

CHAPTER 6: THERE'S SOMETHING ABOUT MARY

136   "quit thinking about it": https://www.nytimes.com/2013/11/03/movies /letting-a-milquetoast-live-large.html?_r=1&.

137   "the funnier it was": https://www.youtube.com/watch?v=FeynI7hpkJA.

141   "the audience walks away happy": https://www.youtube.com/watch?v=Feyn I7hpkJA.

142   "I wouldn't feel good about that": https://www.cbssports.com/nfl/news/brett -favre-was-third-something-about-mary-choice-behind-bledsoe/.

142   "I would have never done it": https://www.cbssports.com/nfl/news/brett-favre -was-third-something-about-mary-choice-behind-bledsoe/.

151   "space for my personal life": https://www.buzzfeed.com/marissamuller /cameron-diaz-on-retiring-from-acting.

152   "It never excited me": https://www.newyorker.com/magazine/2012/06/25 /funny-is-money.

ESSAY: ADAM SANDLER: THE UNLIKELY LEADING MAN

154   "cinematic soulmate": https://www.huffpost.com/entry/drew-barrymore -blended_n_5366545.

156   collaboration with Drew Barrymore: https://www.huffpost.com/entry/drew -barrymore-blended_n_5366545.

156   sent him a script: http://www.bbc.co.uk/films/2004/03/12/peter_segal_50 _first_dates_interview.shtml.

156   turning men away: https://ew.com/movies/2019/02/18/50-first-dates-untold -stories/.

CHAPTER 7: BRIDGET JONES'S DIARY

159 "for being too silly": bridgetarchive.altervista.org/index1995.htm.

160 "almost by accident and out of desperation": http://bridgetarchive.altervista .org/bjd_emotional.htm.

163 her tight deadline: http://bridgetarchive.altervista.org/bjd_emotional.htm.

163 in real time: https://www.independent.co.uk/life-style/bridget-jones-s-diary -1237174.html.

163 in that week's diary entry: bridgetarchive.altervista.org/index1996.htm.

164 "vapid, consumerist, and self-obsessed": https://www.theguardian.com/com mentisfree/2013/sep/30/why-i-hate-bridget-jones.

164 "strident feminist": https://www.theguardian.com/books/2013/dec/20/brid get-jones-effect-life-thirtysomething-single-woman.

165 "defeatist view of womanhood": https://www.theguardian.com/books/2020 /jul/05/i-cant-believe-the-sexism-in-bridget-joness-world-says-helen-fielding.

165 "wasn't thinking about how it would be received": https://www.theguardian .com/books/2020/jul/05/i-cant-believe-the-sexism-in-bridget-joness-world -says-helen-fielding.

167 "He nicknamed me Stalker Maguire": https://ew.com/article/2001/04/24 /meet-inner-circle-made-bridget-joness-diary/.

167 "I signed on the dotted line": http://bridgetarchive.altervista.org/bjd_hugh _grant.htm.

168 "as he is often called": http://bridgetarchive.altervista.org/bjd_articles.htm.

168 "free for the next five years": https://ew.com/article/2001/04/24/meet-inner -circle-made-bridget-joness-diary/.

168 "it's more amusing for me as well": http://bridgetarchive.altervista.org/bjd _articles.htm.

169 "Either it's themselves or it's their friend": http://bridgetarchive.altervista.org /bjd_articles.htm.

169 500 pounds for the privilege: http://bridgetarchive.altervista.org/bjd_lewis .htm.

170 "Who Will Play Scarlett O'Hara?": https://www.washingtonpost.com/ar chive/lifestyle/1998/05/18/bridget-joness-lonely-hearts-club-fans/fda3484a -e554-49ae-a12c-6643de493d9e/.

170 "'any more of your stupid ideas'": http://bridgetarchive.altervista.org/bjd_ar ticles.htm.

170 "'Oh fuck, she's a Texan'": http://bridgetarchive.altervista.org/bjd_articles .htm.

170 "clunking, Hollywood idiocy": https://archive.vanityfair.com/article/2000/7 /the-girl-of-summer.

171 "haven't got very far on the equality front, have they?": https://archive.vanity fair.com/article/2000/7/the-girl-of-summer.

171   "because I have to eat so much of it": https://archive.vanityfair.com/article
       /2000/7/the-girl-of-summer.

171   "if he did the same thing for a role": https://www.yahoo.com/lifestyle/renee
       -zellweger-has-never-understood-why-bridget-205252095.html.

171   "when her name was brought up": http://bridgetarchive.altervista.org/bjd
       _hugh_grant.htm.

172   for her three-week stint: https://www.theguardian.com/film/2001/apr/04/fic
       tion.features.

174   "one of the most organic things ever committed to film": https://www.yahoo
       .com/entertainment/colin-firth-revisits-bridget-joness-diary-and-his-cowardly
       -fight-with-hugh-grant-145744441.html.

176   a "modern *Pride and Prejudice*": https://www.theguardian.com/film/2001
       /apr/18/janeausten.

178   "I think they are going to make one anyway, without me": https://www.you
       tube.com/watch?v=oia3lufC8WA&t=107s.

178   "There's some very funny stuff in it": https://www.bustle.com/articles/177894
       -why-isnt-hugh-grant-in-bridget-joness-baby-the-reason-might-surprise-you.

180   "who are relatable throughout my life": https://www.hollywoodreporter
       .com/features/jennifer-lopez-scarlett-johansson-lupita-nyong-o-drama-actress
       -roundtable-1254056.

180   "one of the best characters ever created": https://collider.com/colin-firth-brid
       get-joness-baby-kingsman-2-interview/.

ESSAY: DREW BARRYMORE: THE SELF-MADE SUPERSTAR

182   Thomas and Louisa Lane on the other: https://www.biography.com/news
       /drew-barrymore-family.

183   Drew's own cowritten memoir: Drew Barrymore and Todd Gold, *Little Girl Lost*
       (New York: Simon & Schuster, 1990), 29–30.

183   "going on a mature 29": https://www.latimes.com/archives/la-xpm-1989–01
       –12-vw-48-story.html.

183   staked out various rehab centers: https://www.latimes.com/archives/la-xpm
       -1989–01–12-vw-48-story.html.

184   "then to nothing": https://www.theguardian.com/culture/2015/oct/25/drew
       -barrymore-mother-locked-up-in-institution-interview.

184   "I was convinced of us doing something together": https://soundcloud.com/how
       ardstern/drewbarrymore_sandler?in=howardstern/sets/sternshow_10–27–15.

185   "it just kind of got romantic": https://www.eonline.com/news/913415/how-the
       -wedding-singer-changed-everything-for-drew-barrymore-and-adam-sandler.

185   while promoting *Blended* in 2014: https://www.eonline.com/news/913415
       /how-the-wedding-singer-changed-everything-for-drew-barrymore-and
       -adam-sandler.

186 "what is important and what isn't": https://www.instagram.com/p/BwE5so
GnCzl/.

186 "What's going to get us out of bed in the morning?": https://www.theguardian
.com/film/2010/mar/27/drew-barrymore-interview.

186 One representative clip: https://www.facebook.com/watch/?v=33227973145
3055.

187 "That might be the coolest thing you ever do in your life": https://www.the
guardian.com/culture/2015/oct/25/drew-barrymore-mother-locked-up-in
-institution-interview.

CHAPTER 8: MY BIG FAT GREEK WEDDING

190 the problem as she saw it: Nia Vardalos, *Instant Mom* (New York: HarperCollins,
2013), 36.

190 "send you out as a Hispanic": Vardalos, 56.

191 "'classic' classical actor": Vardalos, 25.

194 "'but she's Italian'": http://www.screenmancer.tv/screentalk/vardalos.htm.

194 to a Hispanic family: Vardalos, 41.

194 "like inner sonar homing devices": https://www.huffpost.com/entry/nora
-ephron-rita-wilson_b_1631064.

199 "I wasn't embarrassed": https://abcnews.go.com/Entertainment/things-knew
-big-fat-greek-wedding/story?id=52938441.

199 "'Oh, they're having an affair'": https://abcnews.go.com/Entertainment
/things-knew-big-fat-greek-wedding/story?id=52938441.

200 "a Valentine to immigrant America": http://palmbeachartspaper.com/film
-feature-joel-zwicks-big-fat-greek-killing/.

200 "that we're at war": Vardalos, 260.

202 "We were basically a pariah": http://palmbeachartspaper.com/film-feature
-joel-zwicks-big-fat-greek-killing/.

202 to cover all marketing costs: https://www.latimes.com/archives/la-xpm-2003
-jan-14-et-gold14-story.html.

203 giving the movie three stars: https://www.rogerebert.com/reviews/my-big-fat
-greek-wedding-2002.

207 had been in the works: https://www.today.com/popculture/nia-vardalos
-responds-my-big-fat-greek-wedding-3-rumors-t214401.

ESSAY: JENNIFER LOPEZ: THE TRIPLE THREAT

208 "I need to be the lead in a romantic comedy": https://www.hollywoodreporter
.com/features/jennifer-lopez-scarlett-johansson-lupita-nyong-o-drama-actress
-roundtable-1254056.

208 who tried and failed: https://www.yahoo.com/entertainment/the-wedding

-planner-jennifer-lopez-matthew-mcconaughey-adam-shankman-interview-22 0823688.html.

209 *The Wedding Planner* director Adam Shankman: https://www.yahoo.com/en tertainment/the-wedding-planner-jennifer-lopez-matthew-mcconaughey -adam-shankman-interview-220823688.html?ncid=twitter_yahooenter_qb2 vkwfmnkw.

209 "'we'll make you what you are'": https://www.yahoo.com/entertainment /the-wedding-planner-jennifer-lopez-matthew-mcconaughey-adam-shank man-interview-220823688.html?ncid=twitter_yahooenter_qb2vkwfmnkw.

210 promotional appearances everywhere: https://ew.com/article/2001/01/23 /jennifer-lopez-aims-hit-album-and-movie/.

210 was even offered the lead role: https://ew.com/article/2002/11/08/maid-man hattan/.

211 "She's from the Bronx": http://www.bbc.co.uk/films/2003/02/13/jennifer _lopez_maid_in_manhattan_interview.shtml.

211 "Hell yeah!": https://craftychica.com/2002/12/interview-with-jennifer-lopez -maid-in-manhattan/.

CHAPTER 9: HOW TO LOSE A GUY IN 10 DAYS

213 "having survived approximately 100.5 relationships collectively": https://www .amazon.com/How-Lose-Guy-Days-Universal/dp/0553380079.

214 "everybody else wasn't quite sure what it was": https://www.hollywoodreporter .com/news/christine-peters-my-18-year-relationship-with-sumner-redstone -guest-column.

214 "there's an audience out there that's untapped": https://www.hollywoodre porter.com/news/christine-peters-my-18-year-relationship-with-sumner-red stone-guest-column.

214 "I will always be grateful to her": https://medium.com/authority-magazine /words-of-wisdom-from-one-of-hollywoods-king-and-queen-makers-christine -peters-2b56ba7a54f1.

217 "so many romantic comedy scripts": https://ew.com/article/2003/02/06/just -how-adorable-kate-hudson-anyway/.

219 "unbelievably charming and attractive": https://www.washingtonpost.com /lifestyle/style/while-you-were-sleeping-sandra-bullock-oral-history/2020 /04/20/13f37222-7e8b-11ea-9040-68981f488eed_story.html.

219 needed to start: https://www.dailymail.co.uk/tvshowbiz/article-9191699 /The-Wedding-Planner-director-Adam-Shankman-says-starred-Minnie -Driver-Brendan-Fraser.html.

219 in one typical review: https://ew.com/article/2001/02/09/movie-review -wedding-planner-2/.

220 "when we were kids": https://ew.com/movies/2018/02/07/kathryn-hahn-how
-to-lose-a-guy-in-10-days-anniversary/.

221 "that makes a hit": Lynda Obst, *Sleepless in Hollywood: Tales from the New Abnormal in the Movie Business* (New York: Simon & Shuster, 2013), 127.

222 "pee" on command: https://humanehollywood.org/production/how-to-lose-a
-guy-in-10-days/.

226 "We're probably miserable right now!": https://www.elle.com/beauty/a3379
7653/kate-hudson-inbloom-interview/.

227 "'Can we come up with a lesbian subplot?'": Obst, *Sleepless in Hollywood*, 210.

227 was said to be casting in 2013: https://www.huffpost.com/entry/hot-in-holly
wood-producer_b_3457326.

227 "they're capable of being monogamous": https://www.latimes.com/enter
tainment-arts/story/2019-07-31/can-quibi-reinvent-mobile-storytelling.

227 "RomCom ladies have to work at magazines": https://twitter.com/guybranum
/status/1156985087327494144?s=20.

228 "He just had snot all over his face": https://www.yahoo.com/lifestyle/matthew
-mcconaughey-responds-kate-hudson-kissing-scenes-criticism-222544178.html.

229 "well that's who McConaughey is": https://deadline.com/2014/06/emmys
-matthew-mcconaughey-qa-on-following-oscar-with-the-game-changing-hbo
-series-true-detective-740222/.

229 "say no to the things I'd been doing": https://deadline.com/2014/06/emmys
-matthew-mcconaughey-qa-on-following-oscar-with-the-game-changing-hbo
-series-true-detective-740222/.

230 "a joy to watch": https://www.newyorker.com/culture/culture-desk/the-mc
conaissance.

230 "but they deeply believe that": https://www.vulture.com/2013/06/george
-lucas-steven-spielberg-on-hollywood-blockbusters.html.

ESSAY: REESE WITHERSPOON: THE PRODIGY

231 "not one word is wrong, or unnecessary": https://www.rogerebert.com/re
views/the-man-in-the-moon-1991.

232 would have starred Charlize Theron: https://ew.com/article/2002/08/16
/sweet-home-alabama/.

232 beauty salon scene in *Steel Magnolias*: Reese Witherspoon, *Whiskey in a Teacup* (New York: Simon & Schuster, 2018), 86.

233 "that are about Southern people": Witherspoon, 293.

233 an anti-romantic comedy: https://www.campuscircle.com/review.cfm?r=1436
&h=Reese-Witherspoon-Couples-With-Mark-Ruffalo-for-i-Just-Like-Heaven-i.

233 "I was just kind of working, you know?": https://www.cbsnews.com/news
/reese-witherspoon-ready-for-a-change/.

234 the most money ever spent on a rom-com in history: https://www.hollywoodre porter.com/news/price-tag-120-million-50-58410.

234 three-hour workouts every single day: https://www.nytimes.com/2010/03/23 /movies/23brooks.html.

234 Her stated mission: Witherspoon, 14.

235 "20 more movies that matter to me": https://www.cbsnews.com/news/reese -witherspoon-ready-for-a-change/.

CHAPTER 10: LOVE ACTUALLY

238 "everything I admire in life": https://www.stylist.co.uk/happy-place/emma -freud-explains-why-shell-never-marry-richard-curtis/197948.

239 "then you should write about it": https://newhumanist.org.uk/articles/1407 /charity-balls-laurie-taylor-interviews-richard-curtis.

239 "happiness or comedy": https://newhumanist.org.uk/articles/1407/charity -balls-laurie-taylor-interviews-richard-curtis.

240 "ask for their permission to use it": https://www.vulture.com/2013/10/rom -com-king-richard-curtis-is-a-fool-for-love.html.

240 for his next romantic comedy: https://www.vulture.com/2013/10/rom-com -king-richard-curtis-is-a-fool-for-love.html.

240 as a Jackson 5 song: https://www.thedailybeast.com/love-actuallys-10th -anniversary-the-cast-and-crew-reminisce-about-the-christmas-classic.

240 "look un-prime ministerial": https://www.youtube.com/watch?v=FeynI7hp kJA.

240 "I found a reason not to do it": https://www.youtube.com/watch?v=FeynI7hp kJA.

240 "it's a film world": https://www.cheatsheet.com/entertainment/love-actually -hugh-grant-pointed-out-the-iconic-dancing-scene-actually-makes-no-sense .html/.

241 "I don't think I could have changed it": https://cherwell.org/2009/11/19 /interview-richard-curtis/.

241 "quick, simple arcs": https://www.empireonline.com/movies/features/paul -feig-richard-curtis-discuss-love-actually/.

244 "we knew we'd get away with it": https://people.com/movies/andrew-lincoln -looks-back-at-his-weird-stalker-guy-role-in-love-actually/.

244 Richard Curtis analogue: https://people.com/movies/andrew-lincoln-looks -back-at-his-weird-stalker-guy-role-in-love-actually/

244 "I got to be this weird stalker guy": https://ew.com/movies/2017/04/03 /andrew-lincoln-love-actually-character-stalker/.

244 "So I *don't* go off with Andrew Lincoln?": https://www.indiewire.com/2018/10 /keira-knightley-has-only-seen-love-actually-once-1202016824/.

245   "and I don't doubt it now": http://news.bbc.co.uk/2/hi/uk_news/politics /4287906.stm.

247   "the mother of these children . . .": https://www.empireonline.com/movies/fea tures/paul-feig-richard-curtis-discuss-love-actually/.

247   "A brutal bit of sorrow": https://www.elle.com/culture/movies-tv/news /a14967/love-actually-10-year-anniversary/

248   "the necklace that wasn't meant for me": https://www.vogue.co.uk/article /emma-thompson-on-how-kenneth-branagh-split-inspired-love-actually?utm _medium=Social&utm_source=Facebook#Echobox=1544142527.

248   Rickman's character *definitely* consummated the affair: https://ew.com/arti cle/2015/12/15/love-actually-karen-harry-emma-thompson-alan-rickman -outcome/.

249   in what Curtis describes as his effort: https://www.youtube.com/watch?v= oD21hpLrvxM.

250   "anything to do with good will": https://newhumanist.org.uk/articles/1407 /charity-balls-laurie-taylor-interviews-richard-curtis.

250   editing *Love Actually* was "murderous": https://www.slashfilm.com/richard -curtis-interview-yesterday/.

250   "But I didn't want to do that": https://www.empireonline.com/movies/fea tures/paul-feig-richard-curtis-discuss-love-actually/.

253   with a live orchestra performing the score: https://www.marieclaire.co.uk/en tertainment/tv-and-film/love-actually-screening-live-orchestra-673657.

253   two-course Christmas dinner: https://theexhibit.co.uk/film-screening-love -actually/.

253   quote-along with bottomless alcohol: https://secretmanchester.com/love -actually-screening/.

254   wrote *Guardian* columnist Rhiannon Lucy Cosslett in 2019: https://www.the guardian.com/commentisfree/2019/dec/08/love-actually-christmas-fantasy -sexism-stalking.

254   "the least romantic movie of all time": https://www.theatlantic.com/entertain ment/archive/2013/12/-em-love-actually-em-is-the-least-romantic-film-of-all -time/282091/.

254   "I Will Not Be Ashamed of Loving *Love Actually*": https://www.theatlantic .com/entertainment/archive/2013/12/i-will-not-be-ashamed-of-loving-love -actually-i/282160/.

ESSAY: WILL SMITH: THE ROM-COM HERO WE BARELY GOT

256   to adapt *Hitch* into a TV series: https://deadline.com/2014/10/hitch-series-fox -will-smith-857697/.

256   As recently as 2020: https://ew.com/movies/2020/02/26/eva-mendes-hitch-2/.

256 "wanted to revisit": https://ew.com/movies/2019/02/11/hitch-five-things-did -not-know/.

257 "but it's a problem in the U.S.": https://www.today.com/popculture/was-race -issue-hitch-casting-wbna7019342.

257 "if the film is *about* racism": https://www.femalefirst.co.uk/celebrity/Will +Smith-2966.html.

257 "definitely an issue for the studio": http://www.bbc.co.uk/films/2005/03/01 /will_smith_hitch_interview.shtml.

257 "you'll never work in this town again!": https://www.cheatsheet.com/entertain ment/will-smith-racism-superheroes.html/.

CHAPTER 11: SOMETHING'S GOTTA GIVE

259 "what's it like being our age and single?": https://charlierose.com/videos/10190.

259 "What if there was this guy": https://charlierose.com/videos/10190.

260 "to be undesirable, lonely and isolated": https://www.nytimes.com/2020/02/28 /style/modern-love-nancy-meyers-rom-com.html.

260 "That was me writing the movie": https://www.vulture.com/2015/09/nancy -meyers-amy-larocca-in-conversation.html.

260 "almost therapeutic": https://www.vulture.com/2015/09/nancy-meyers-amy -larocca-in-conversation.html.

260 "wanted to throw it out": https://nofilmschool.com/nancy-meyers-interview -process.

261 "begins to shape up": https://gointothestory.blcklst.com/how-they-write-a -script-nancy-meyers-7c8787d682ce.

261 "inspired by a 1954 Johnny Mercer song": https://www.chicagotribune.com /news/ct-xpm-2003-12-12-0312120304-story.html.

262 "Why bring it up?": https://www.nytimes.com/2003/12/14/movies/film -diane-keaton-meets-both-her-matches.html.

262 "fifty-five-year-old woman at the center": https://www.vulture.com/2015/09 /nancy-meyers-amy-larocca-in-conversation.html.

263 "by far the most irresistible person": https://www.vulture.com/2015/09/nancy -meyers-amy-larocca-in-conversation.html.

263 "I had their pictures all over my computer. Always": https://charlierose.com /videos/10190.

263 "pretty much washed up": Diane Keaton, *Then Again* (New York: Harper-Collins, 2011), 228.

263 "That's not his thing": Keaton, 228.

263 "didn't want to change a word": https://charlierose.com/videos/10190.

264 "I have had a kind of open affection": *Playboy* (fiftieth anniversary issue), 2003.

264 "If she wants to make it happen, it happens": http://madeinatlantis.com /movies_central/2003/somethings_production_details.htm.

264 "one of the best scripts that I've ever read, period": https://moviehole.net /interview-keanu-reeves-somethings-gotta-give/.

265 "the person you're convinced you are": https://charlierose.com/videos /10190.

266 "So we struggled every day": https://charlierose.com/videos/10190.

266 "He says lines like you dream": https://charlierose.com/videos/10190.

266 "every time I see him": https://www.wmagazine.com/story/diane-keaton-jack -nicholson-love-trick-somethings-gotta-give.

267 "A tough director, let me tell you that": https://www.nytimes.com/2003/12/14 /movies/film-diane-keaton-meets-both-her-matches.html.

267 "He's all rattled": https://www.wmagazine.com/story/diane-keaton-jack-nichol son-love-trick-somethings-gotta-give.

268 "Clearly, Erica is more Nancy than me": https://www.nytimes.com/2003/12/14 /movies/film-diane-keaton-meets-both-her-matches.html.

268 "where the leads live in a great house": https://www.hollywoodreporter.com /news/nancy-meyers-critical-fixation-her-kitchen-scenes-films-1216750.

268 "looking up to see the soundstage ceiling": http://madeinatlantis.com/movies _central/2003/somethings_production_details.htm.

269 compared Meyers's attention to detail with Martin Scorsese: https://www.ny times.com/2009/12/20/magazine/20Meyers-t.html.

269 "Making movies is an accumulation of details": https://www.nytimes .com/2009/12/20/magazine/20Meyers-t.html.

269 "get swept away in the story": https://www.vulture.com/article/whats-it-like -to-be-directed-by-nancy-meyers.html.

269 "the bedroom faces the ocean": https://www.vulture.com/2015/09/nancy -meyers-amy-larocca-in-conversation.html.

271 "commercial risk": https://www.nytimes.com/2009/12/20/magazine/20Meyers -t.html.

271 "and then I was there": https://gointothestory.blcklst.com/how-they-write-a -script-nancy-meyers-7c8787d682ce.

272 "knowledge and life experience aren't really respected": http://madeinatlantis .com/movies_central/2003/somethings_production_details.htm.

272 In a 2020 essay for The Cut: https://www.thecut.com/2020/02/i-think-about -this-a-lot-keanu-in-somethings-gotta-give.html.

272 Shea Serrano argues: https://www.vulture.com/2019/10/shea-serrano-book -excerpt-diane-keaton-essay.html.

273 "delivering the fantasy for women over fifty-five": https://www.nytimes .com/2009/12/20/magazine/20Meyers-t.html.

273 "the same age as all the women in my movies": https://www.vulture.com/2015 /09/nancy-meyers-amy-larocca-in-conversation.html.

273 "I don't know. It took a woman": https://gointothestory.blcklst.com/how-they -write-a-script-nancy-meyers-7c8787d682ce.

274 "I didn't want to write another romance": https://www.vulture.com/2015/09 /nancy-meyers-amy-larocca-in-conversation.html.

274 "The length of a movie": https://www.vulture.com/2020/12/nancy-meyers -interview-on-retirement-hygge-and-her-career.html.

274 "the experience of making a movie like mine changed": https://www.vulture .com/2020/12/nancy-meyers-interview-on-retirement-hygge-and-her-career .html.

ESSAY: JOHN CUSACK: THE RELUCTANT ROMANTIC

275 "or the kind of thing that I like": https://www.nytimes.com/interactive/2020 /09/14/magazine/john-cusack-interview.html.

276 "whether the boom box scene is going to work at all": https://www.usatoday .com/story/life/movies/2019/04/14/say-anything-anniversary-boombox -scene-immortal/3454645002/.

276 "On my better days, that's me": https://www.usatoday.com/story/life/movies /2019/04/14/say-anything-anniversary-boombox-scene-immortal/345464 5002/.

277 both Cusack: https://www.nytimes.com/interactive/2020/09/14/magazine /john-cusack-interview.html.

277 and director George Armitage: https://www.filmcomment.com/blog/interview -george-armitage/.

278 "I *wanted* to reveal the flaws of the character": https://www.nytimes.com/inter active/2020/09/14/magazine/john-cusack-interview.html.

279 "the best thing he could get at the time": https://www.nytimes.com/interac tive/2020/09/14/magazine/john-cusack-interview.html.

279 "that would be pretty unartistic": https://www.nytimes.com/interactive/2020 /09/14/magazine/john-cusack-interview.html.

CHAPTER 12: KNOCKED UP

281 on painkillers for six months: https://www.hollywoodreporter.com/news /general-news/judd-apatow-this-is-40–400607/.

281 "some of them turned down college to be on my show": https://www.theguard ian.com/film/2009/aug/27/interview-judd-apatow.

282 He also attached a note: https://www.theguardian.com/film/2009/aug/27 /interview-judd-apatow.

282 "when you're young": https://www.hollywoodreporter.com/news/general -news/judd-apatow-reveals-his-penis-689436/.

282 "It made me connect with people suffering": https://www.hollywoodreporter .com/news/general-news/judd-apatow-this-is-40–400607/.

283   "my secret thought as I made the movie": https://www.ign.com/articles /2005/08/18/interview-judd-apatow-romany-malco-and-seth-rogan.

283   "his stories make no sense": Judd Apatow, *Sick in the Head: Conversations About Life and Comedy* (London: Bloomsbury, 2015), 550.

283   they reached a consensus about Carell's character: Apatow, 550.

284   "There wasn't any big joke to it": https://www.ign.com/articles/2005/08/18 /interview-judd-apatow-romany-malco-and-seth-rogan.

284   "horrible theories on women": http://madeinatlantis.com/movies_central /2005/virgin.htm.

285   too much like a serial killer: https://ew.com/article/2015/12/17/steve-carell -40-year-old-virgin-serial-killer/.

285   an editor of their choosing: https://ew.com/article/2015/12/17/steve-carell-40 -year-old-virgin-serial-killer/.

285   a PG-13 version of the script: Apatow, 551.

285   as an amiable slacker: Apatow, 551.

286   "because he's in love": https://www.nytimes.com/2007/05/27/magazine/27 apatow-t.html.

287   when asked about Apatow's meteoric rise in 2012: https://www.gq.com/story /judd-apatow-profile-gq-january-2013.

287   "*I must get something from it*": Apatow, 552.

287   subject line "Pregnancy" on August 7, 2005: https://gointothestory.blcklst .com/how-judd-apatow-wrote-a-screenplay-using-his-email-8a079360fea.

288   traced back to those notes: https://gointothestory.blcklst.com/how-judd -apatow-wrote-a-screenplay-using-his-email-8a079360fea.

288   The generic scene Rogen read: https://www.hollywoodreporter.com/news /general-news/judd-apatow-reveals-his-penis-689436/.

288   "'just kind of standing there'": https://www.youtube.com/watch?v=AFnA0 W4jgFE.

289   Alison Lohman in mind: https://film.avclub.com/leslie-mann-1798212403.

289   "it made you want to cry": http://madeinatlantis.com/movies_central/2007 /knocked_up.htm.

289   "I never would have thought to write that": https://www.hollywoodreporter .com/news/general-news/judd-apatow-reveals-his-penis-689436/.

289   an unusual legal snafu: https://filmschoolrejects.com/35-things-we-learned -from-the-knocked-up-commentary-f2a65c8e511c/#.b9f6a3716.

290   explained Apatow at the time: https://www.nytimes.com/2007/05/27 /magazine/27apatow-t.html.

290   "I really should have done that movie": https://www.allure.com/gallery/anne -hathaway#slide=6.

290   bargain salary of $300,000: https://www.vanityfair.com/news/2008/01/heigl 200801.

291 declared it a victory in 2007: https://www.politico.com/story/2007/06/rhymes-with-shmashmortion-004367.

292 "uncomfortable doing that?": https://collider.com/judd-apatow-interview-knocked-up/.

294 Iris was born: Apatow, 375.

294 "He's such a stupid fucking asshole and I hate him": Apatow, 375.

294 "That coincided with me leaving medicine": https://www.npr.org/2015/03/08/391708149/ken-jeong-doctor-by-day-comedian-by-night.

294 "I still renew my medical license every year": https://www.hollywoodreporter.com/news/ken-jeong-how-ditch-medicine-817478.

294 "someone not trying to grow up": https://www.hollywoodreporter.com/news/general-news/judd-apatow-reveals-his-penis-689436/.

295 "I meant it": https://www.usmagazine.com/celebrity-news/news/judd-apatow-fell-in-love-with-leslie-mann-the-moment-he-saw-her-20121710/.

296 *The New York Times* published a transcript: https://www.nytimes.com/2007/12/23/fashion/23mann.html?_r=3&ref=fashion&oref=slogin&oref=slogin&oref=slogin.

297 "probably somewhere in the middle": Apatow, 367.

297 "problems in our own marriages": https://www.wired.com/2007/05/ff-apatow/.

297 an actual fight they were having: Apatow, 555.

298 "It's not like fights in the movies": Apatow, 40.

298 decision to cast their daughters: Apatow, 368.

298 "a valentine to my family": https://www.nytimes.com/2007/05/27/magazine/27apatow-t.html.

299 "because they are thinking about people": https://www.hollywoodreporter.com/news/general-news/judd-apatow-reveals-his-penis-689436/.

299 "most of the scripts floating around town": https://www.hollywoodreporter.com/news/general-news/judd-apatow-reveals-his-penis-689436/.

300 "more like Cassavetes than a popcorn flick": https://www.nytimes.com/2007/05/27/magazine/27apatow-t.html.

301 "The slop of it is where I feel truthful": https://www.theguardian.com/film/2017/jul/08/judd-apatow-freaks-and-geeks-big-sick-lena-dunham.

301 "'Can you believe this is happening to us right now?'": https://www.hollywoodreporter.com/news/general-news/judd-apatow-reveals-his-penis-689436/.

ESSAY: KATHERINE HEIGL: THE APOLOGIST

304 "it was hard for me to love the movie": https://www.vanityfair.com/news/2008/01/heigl200801.

305 "I allowed it to slip": https://ew.com/article/2010/04/07/greys-anatomy-katherine-heigl-cover-story/.

305 "It was an immature dumbass moment": https://www.usmagazine.com

/celebrity-news/news/katherine-heigl-i-was-a-dumbass-for-criticizing-knocked
-up-w203438/.

305   "I just feel nothing but love and respect": https://abcnews.go.com/Entertain
ment/katherine-heigl-love-respect-seth-rogen-knocked/story?id=41299111.

305   "something horribly wrong": https://www.washingtonpost.com/arts-entertain
ment/2021/01/28/katherine-heigl-firefly-lane-profile/?arc404=true.

305   "on a pedestal in a beautiful way": https://www.vulture.com/2009/07/even
_seth_rogen_now_hating_on.html.

305   "if that was uplifting for women": https://www.vulture.com/2009/07/even
_seth_rogen_now_hating_on.html.

305   Apatow groused to Louis C.K.: Apatow, 398.

305   because she hurt his feelings: https://abcnews.go.com/Entertainment
/katherine-heigl-love-respect-seth-rogen-knocked/story?id=41299111.

306   "or a psychological thriller": https://www.marieclaire.co.uk/news/celebrity
-news/katherine-heigl-is-marie-claire-s-august-cover-star-63265#index=.

306   rom-coms had made more money: https://www.washingtonpost.com/arts
-entertainment/2021/01/28/katherine-heigl-firefly-lane-profile/?arc404=true.

307   "that shit pisses me off": https://www.washingtonpost.com/arts-entertainment
/2021/01/28/katherine-heigl-firefly-lane-profile/?arc404=true.

CHAPTER 13: FRIENDS WITH BENEFITS

310   "most of the laughs scoured out": https://www.nytimes.com/2011/08/08/arts
/television/friends-with-benefits-fridays-on-nbc-review.html.

311   "going through a romantic comedy moment": http://movieline.com/2010/08
/19/will-gluck-interview-easy-a/2/.

312   "they're falling in love the whole time": http://screencrave.com/2010-09-14
/interview-director-will-gluck-for-easy-a/.

312   a 2009 promotional video: https://www.youtube.com/watch?v=FeynI7hpkJA.

312   whopping 80 percent female: https://ew.com/article/2009/02/08/borept-hjntiy/.

313   "not a huge fan of romantic comedies": https://www.advocate.com/arts
-entertainment/film/2011/07/25/justin-and-mila-more-just-friends.

313   "when we made this movie": https://www.bbc.com/news/entertainment-arts
-14787785.

315   "either one of our movies": https://www.cheatsheet.com/entertainment/friends
-with-benefits-mila-kunis-fell-asleep-during-her-sex-scene-with-justin-timber
lake.html/.

315   "an opportunity to do a good comedy": http://filmfestivaltraveler.com/film
-arts/film-arts-interviews/1140-no-strings-attached-roundtable.

315   "a sexual relationship than an emotional one": https://usatoday30.usatoday
.com/life/movies/news/2010-11-04-nostrings04_ST_N.htm.

316   "starts to dissolve": https://flickdirect.com/flickvision/411/watch-movie/director

-ivan-reitman-discusses-no-strings-attached/no-strings-attached/streaming -video.ashx.

316 "the steak might be different": https://www.indiewire.com/2011/07/will-gluck -says-the-lack-of-skin-in-friends-with-benefits-was-a-conscious-choice-117228/.

317 "even as it indulges in them": https://www.thewrap.com/friends-benefits -standard-rom-com-new-product-placements-29308/.

317 "switch to reassuring romantic commitment": https://ew.com/article/2011/01 /28/no-strings-attached-4/.

317 In 1969, 21 percent of Americans: https://www.pewresearch.org/social-trends /2010/11/18/ii-overview/.

317 A 2011 study by the Pew Research Institute: https://www.pewresearch.org /social-trends/2011/03/09/iii-millennials-attitudes-about-marriage/.

318 "somebody running through an airport": https://www.youtube.com/watch?v =9H9Y2YwLpI8.

319 "my brain turn to mush": https://www.slashfilm.com/isnt-it-romantic-inter view-director-todd-strauss-schulson/.

322 "a shame-free abortion": https://archive.sltrib.com/article.php?id=58113593& itype=CMSID.

322 "torturing themselves over the decision": http://www.nytimes.com/2014/06/01 /movies/jenny-slate-in-gillian-robespierres-obvious-child.html.

ESSAY: RYAN REYNOLDS AND DANE COOK: TWO ROADS DIVERGED

325 1.2 million Myspace friends: https://www.forbes.com/forbes/2006/0703/156 .html?sh=3caa41c32fa5.

325 "I know we hang with those guys": https://www.comingsoon.net/movies /features/37346-dane-cook-is-good-luck-chuck.

326 says Cook of *Good Luck Chuck*: http://www.mtv.com/news/1579717/dane-cook -on-jessica-alba-knocking-good-luck-chuck-we-all-read-the-script/.

326 "I ran away": https://www.elle.com/culture/celebrities/a9149/dont-mess-jess -19115/.

326 "having a blast": http://www.mtv.com/news/1579717/dane-cook-on-jessica -alba-knocking-good-luck-chuck-we-all-read-the-script/.

326 Photoshop on the poster: https://www.firstshowing.net/2008/my-best-friends -girl-poster-lead-dane-cook-hates-it/.

326 "a Bat signal, my Nike Swoosh": https://www.forbes.com/forbes/2006/0703 /156.html?sh=66ad37362fa5.

327 didn't work out: https://film.avclub.com/the-filmmakers-behind-just-friends -tell-the-story-of-th-1845898799.

327 after she was locked in: https://www.hollywoodreporter.com/news/reynolds -wed-proposal-145595.

327 "And that's wrong": https://www.theguardian.com/global/2016/jan/31/ryan
-reynolds-deadpool-actor-interview.

CHAPTER 14: UNTITLED ROYAL WEDDING COMEDY

330 "seven-figure sum": https://www.thewrap.com/500-days-summer-writers-sell
-sony-pitch-seven-figures-26857/.

330 *Notting Hill* meets *Meet the Royal Parents*: https://deadline.com/2011/04/sony
-pictures-acquires-royal-wedding-pitch-126266/.

330 Nancy Meyers signed on to polish the script: https://www.hollywoodreporter
.com/news/royal-wedding-movie-nancy-meyers-326877.

330 *Untitled Royal Wedding Comedy* was dead: https://www.hollywoodreporter.com
/news/rip-romantic-comedies-why-harry-634776.

330 "that I thought was right for it": https://www.vulture.com/2020/12/nancy
-meyers-interview-on-retirement-hygge-and-her-career.html.

331 "they weren't anybody's pride and joy anymore": https://www.vulture.com
/2020/12/nancy-meyers-interview-on-retirement-hygge-and-her-career.html.

331 "ran out of box-office steam in 2012": https://www.theatlantic.com/magazine/ar
chive/2013/03/why-are-romantic-comedies-so-bad/309236/?single_page=true.

331 "the current generation's cynical view of romantic comedies": https://www
.washingtonpost.com/lifestyle/style/the-rom-com-is-dead-good/2016
/10/06/6d82a934–859c-11e6-ac72-a29979381495_story.html.

331 Emily VanDerWerff dissected the reasons: https://www.vox.com/culture
/2017/2/14/14604300/romantic-comedy-dead-netflix-crazy-rich-asians.

332 the argument critics typically make: https://www.laweekly.com/who-killed
-the-romantic-comedy/.

334 "Chick flicks don't tend to be sequel-izable": https://www.vulture.com/2013/06
/george-lucas-steven-spielberg-on-hollywood-blockbusters.html.

335 "They don't travel": https://www.huffpost.com/entry/hot-in-hollywood-pro
ducer_b_3457326.

337 "marketed and sold as a mainstream romantic comedy": https://ew.com
/movies/2017/10/31/love-simon-first-look/.

ESSAY: MINDY KALING: THE SCHOLAR

339 "an admission of mild stupidity": https://www.newyorker.com/magazine
/2011/10/03/flick-chicks.

340 "They are equally implausible": https://www.newyorker.com/magazine/2011
/10/03/flick-chicks.

340 "I only believe in pleasures": https://www.audible.com/blog/arts-culture
/mindy-kaling-romantic-comedy-love.

340   a list of her personal favorite romantic comedies: https://www.vulture.com
      /2016/01/mindy-kalings-favorite-romantic-comedies.html.

341   "That instantly makes it modern": https://www.latimes.com/entertainment
      -arts/tv/story/2019–07–29/mindy-kaling-four-weddings-and-a-funeral-hulu.

341   "buddy comedy with romantic comedy elements": https://www.marieclaire
      .com/culture/a30228163/mindy-kaling-priyanka-chopra-rom-com/.

341   "I hope *that* becomes conventional": https://www.marieclaire.com/culture
      /a30228163/mindy-kaling-priyanka-chopra-rom-com/.

CHAPTER 15: CRAZY RICH ASIANS

343   Reporting immediately after the screening: https://nextshark.com/lucky-vips
      -saw-crazy-rich-asians-last-night-heres-verdict/.

343   a poem Kwan wrote: http://kinokuniya.com.sg/wp-content/uploads/2018/08
      /CRA-Kevin-Kwan-QA_19-June-2018.pdf.

344   "not everyone has an airplane in their garage": https://www.straitstimes.com
      /lifestyle/arts/im-no-crazy-rich-asian-says-author-kevin-kwan.

345   into a white woman: https://ew.com/movies/2017/11/03/hollywood-wanted
      -to-whitewash-crazy-rich-asians/.

345   non-crazy-rich price of one dollar: https://www.vulture.com/2018/08/the
      -long-crazy-road-to-crazy-rich-asians.html.

346   editing software for him to practice on: https://caamedia.org/blog/2016/12/09
      /this-is-the-time-director-jon-m-chu-on-the-making-of-crazy-rich-asians/.

346   Chu lined up a series of projects: https://www.nytimes.com/2008/02/18
      /movies/18chu.html.

346   "but I never categorize myself as that": https://caamedia.org/blog/2016/12/09
      /this-is-the-time-director-jon-m-chu-on-the-making-of-crazy-rich-asians/.

347   "I didn't want to be seen as this 'other' thing": https://www.huffpost.com
      /entry/crazy-rich-asians-director-jon-m-chu_n_5b688fc5e4b0b15abaa5c133.

347   that year's Academy Award nominees: https://www.nytimes.com/2016/05/11
      /movies/john-cho-starring-in-every-movie-ever-made-a-diversity-hashtag-is
      -born.html.

347   "No, I *am* talking about you": https://www.hollywoodreporter.com/movies
      /movie-news/crazy-rich-asians-cast-reveal-secrets-set-1134294/.

347   "the women of his own family": https://www.instagram.com/p/BlvxCs9FcRZ
      /?utm_source=ig_embed.

348   "go to battle for whatever that is": https://www.huffpost.com/entry/jon-m-chu
      -starring-john-cho-movement_n_5c6daa07e4b0e37a1ed4445a.

348   "I was meant to do this movie": https://caamedia.org/blog/2016/12/09/this-is
      -the-time-director-jon-m-chu-on-the-making-of-crazy-rich-asians/.

350   dispatched casting directors all around the world: https://caamedia.org/blog

/2018/08/09/director-jon-m-chu-on-crazy-rich-asians-you-feel-the-confidence
-coming-off-of-the-screen/.

350 acted as an open casting call: https://www.youtube.com/watch?v=kSg2lIls
WA0.

350 "I couldn't stop screaming": https://www.nytimes.com/2018/08/08/movies
/crazy-rich-asians-cast.html.

351 she wrote Jon M. Chu a personal letter: https://www.vulture.com/2018/08
/the-long-crazy-road-to-crazy-rich-asians.html.

351 Chu checked out Golding's Instagram account: https://www.vulture.com
/2018/08/henry-golding-crazy-rich-asians-casting.html.

352 about $2.5 million in jewelry: https://www.hollywoodreporter.com/news
/general-news/crazy-rich-asians-inside-fabulous-amazing-costumes-sets-113
0966/.

353 "before her own needs": https://www.harpersbazaar.com/culture/film-tv/a22
794930/michelle-yeoh-crazy-rich-asians-interview/.

355 made an aggressive bid: https://www.hollywoodreporter.com/movies/movie
-features/crazy-rich-asians-how-asian-rom-happened-netflix-1130965/.

355 had only given them fifteen minutes to decide: https://www.hollywoodreporter
.com/movies/movie-features/crazy-rich-asians-how-asian-rom-happened
-netflix-1130965/.

356 "Other ethnicities thought it wasn't for them": https://www.hollywoodreporter
.com/news/jon-m-chu-his-crazy-rich-year-industrys-new-wave-1186986.

357 "a very slim portion of that demographic": https://www.theatlantic.com/enter
tainment/archive/2018/08/asian-americas-great-gatsby-moment/568213/.

357 "that's just ridiculous": https://deadline.com/2018/08/jon-m-chu-interview
-crazy-rich-asians-warner-bros-diversity-inclusion-1202444128/.

357 in his future films: https://www.insider.com/jon-chu-crazy-rich-asians-white
washing-stereotypes-tropes-2021-6.

358 "I don't think the dam is in any way broken": https://www.hollywoodreporter
.com/news/kevin-kwan-talks-new-summer-rom-book-sex-vanity-1300296.

358 Adele Lim discovered co-screenwriter Peter Chiarelli: https://www.hollywood
reporter.com/news/general-news/crazy-rich-asians-screenwriter-adele-lim
-exits-sequel-pay-disparity-dispute-1236431/.

359 "dependent on the generosity of the white-guy writer": https://www.hollywood
reporter.com/news/crazy-rich-asians-screenwriter-adele-lim-exits-sequel-pay
-disparity-dispute-1236431/.

359 Astrid's journey toward independence in *Crazy Rich Asians*: https://ew.com
/movies/2018/08/15/crazy-rich-asians-mid-credits-scene-harry-shum-jr
-gemma-chan/.

ESSAY: HENRY GOLDING: NEW STAR IN TOWN

361 "because there's no roles for them": https://variety.com/2021/film/news/lin -manuel-miranda-john-m-chu-in-the-heights-1234945239/.

362 "deeply rooted in his family obligations": http://kinokuniya.com.sg/wp -content/uploads/2018/08/CRA-Kevin-Kwan-QA_19-June-2018.pdf.

362 broke into a career as TV host: https://www.gq.com/story/henry-golding-men -of-the-year-2018.

362 "'I think it's gonna be pretty big'": https://www.gq.com/story/henry-golding -men-of-the-year-2018.

362 "I want to bring back that old Hollywood charm": https://www.latimes.com /entertainment/movies/la-et-mn-crazy-rich-asians-henry-golding-20180810 -story.html.

363 a new version of Jane Austen's *Persuasion*: https://deadline.com/2021/05/henry -golding-netflix-persuasion-movie-dakota-johnson-1234750259/amp/?__twitter _impression=true.

363 a deliberate effort to play against type: https://deadline.com/2021/05/henry -golding-netflix-persuasion-movie-dakota-johnson-1234750259/amp/?__twit ter_impression=true.

CHAPTER 16: TO ALL THE BOYS I'VE LOVED BEFORE

365 "'Are there superheroes?'": https://scriptmag.com/features/romcom-not-dead -seriously.

366 "If you love the genre, write the genre": https://scriptmag.com/features/rom com-not-dead-seriously.

367 "the business has moved away from that model": https://www.hollywoodre porter.com/news/general-news/how-netflix-revived-rom-genre-1169776/.

368 "We thought maybe there was a lane there": https://www.hollywoodreporter .com/news/how-netflix-revived-rom-genre-1169776.

368 *The Kissing Booth* is a singularly great example: https://techcrunch.com/2018 /06/14/netflixs-latest-hit-the-kissing-booth-is-a-wattpad-success-story/.

369 "the worst impulses of the genre": https://www.indiewire.com/2018/05/the -kissing-booth-netflix-teen-romantic-comedy-sexist-1201969234/.

369 "and maybe in the world": https://www.vulture.com/2018/06/how-netflix -swallowed-tv-industry.html.

369 *The Kissing Booth* had achieved a metric: https://www.hollywoodreporter.com /news/set-it-up-rise-studio-rom-1121694.

369 "I want to watch it again and again": https://www.washingtonpost.com/en tertainment/books/how-the-kissing-booth-went-from-a-teenagers-passion -project-to-a-netflix-sensation/2018/07/13/712c0072–84fe-11e8–9e80–403a22 1946a7_story.html.

371 into its deals with talent: https://www.hollywoodreporter.com/news/teenage
     -dream-young-adult-hits-become-netflixs-first-franchises.

371 "I think that really connects": https://www.hollywoodreporter.com/news
     /how-netflix-revived-rom-genre-1169776.

371 "I was scared they would change their minds": https://www.nytimes.com
     /2018/08/17/opinion/sunday/crazy-rich-asians-movie-idol.html.

372 "to not get what they paid for": https://www.youtube.com/watch?v=rYMv
     UQ0x4mU.

374 "'Oh, I'll watch that'": https://www.hollywoodreporter.com/news/how-netflix
     -revived-rom-genre-1169776.

375 "everywhere in the world": https://www.hollywoodreporter.com/news/how
     -netflix-revived-rom-genre-1169776.

376 the IMDb Star-O-Meter: https://www.vulture.com/2018/06/how-netflix
     -swallowed-tv-industry.html.

376 by citing the Instagram account of star Noah Centineo: https://www.holly
     woodreporter.com/movies/movie-news/teenage-dream-young-adult-hits
     -become-netflixs-first-franchises-4133564/.

376 second and third installments of the genre: https://observer.com/2021/02
     /michael-fimognari-to-all-the-boys-always-and-forever-interview/.

377 in the process of developing a series: https://deadline.com/2021/03/to-all-the
     -boys-ive-loved-before-spinoff-series-anna-cathcarts-kitty-covey-netflix-jenny
     -han-1234725581/.

377 bought for a record amount: https://apnews.com/article/groundhog-day-us
     -news-ut-state-wire-film-festivals-movies-0517642df1f39105cf67958478252b7a.